When evangelicals confuse an improper passion for novelty with a proper pursuit of academic and pastoral relevance, the results can be distressing. I cannot express how grateful I am for the well-formed wisdom with which this book points to the abiding and decisive relevance for future route-finding of the old theological paths.
　　　—J. I. PACKER, *Professor, Regent College*

These insightful essays explore issues of extreme importance for evangelical thought. For those evangelicals who—like myself—are increasingly troubled by extravagant claims made by various evangelical scholars about the nature of the "postmodern" challenge, as well as by earnest calls to develop new epistemological and theological perspectives in response to this challenge, the writers of these essays shed much light. This book is must-reading for everyone who wants to promote a clear-thinking evangelicalism for our contemporary context.
　　　—RICHARD J. MOUW, *President and Professor of*
　　　Christian Philosophy, Fuller Seminary

Here is a collection of intelligent, provocative, gutsy essays that dare to fly into the eye of the scholarly storm over evangelical identity. Though different perspectives are present even here, the underlying thesis is clear and worth heeding: the eager, and sometimes uncritical, embrace of postmodernist paradigms may be as premature as it has proven to be unproductive for the well-being of the evangelical church. One of the most important books of the new century!
　　　—TIMOTHY GEORGE, *Dean,*
　　　Beeson Divinity School, Samford University

Provocative, timely, and controversial!
　　　—DONALD G. BLOESCH, *Professor of Theology Emeritus,*
　　　Dubuque Theological Seminary

Evangelicalism is in big trouble, and the root problem is theological accommodation. Compromise and confusion stand at the center of evangelicalism's theological crisis, and a clear-headed and convictional analysis of the problem has been desperately needed. Thankfully, *Reclaiming the* ... s Erickson, Helseth, and Taylor have assemble ... each chapter is must reading for all concernec ... *Reclaiming the Center* will open evangelical e ... waken this generation to the peril of accomm ...
　　　—R. ALBERT MOHLER, JR.,
　　　The Southern Baptist Theological Seminary

D1502485

Reclaiming the Center offers a coherent and challenging engagement with recent attempts to redefine the center of evangelicalism. The authors of this well-designed volume provide a bold and well-argued response to what is sometimes called "post-conservative evangelicalism." This important conversation regarding the essence, center, and boundaries of evangelicalism is here explored, interpreted, and assessed from a well-informed theological, philosophical, and historical perspective.

Though readers will quibble over some aspects of the essays, I am confident that this valuable and impressive collection will help advance this important conversation in a constructive way. I heartily commend this volume and trust it will find a large readership.

    —DAVID S. DOCKERY, *President, Union University*

RECLAIMING THE CENTER

RECLAIMING THE CENTER

CONFRONTING
EVANGELICAL ACCOMMODATION
IN POSTMODERN TIMES

EDITED BY

MILLARD J. ERICKSON,
PAUL KJOSS HELSETH, JUSTIN TAYLOR

CROSSWAY BOOKS

A PUBLISHING MINISTRY OF
GOOD NEWS PUBLISHERS
WHEATON, ILLINOIS

Library of Congress Cataloging-in-Publication Data
Reclaiming the center : confronting evangelical accommodation in
postmodern times / edited by Millard J. Erickson, Paul Kjoss Helseth,
Justin Taylor.
    p. cm.
   Includes bibliographical references and indexes.
   ISBN 13: 978-1-58134-568-1 (tpb)
   ISBN 10: 1-58134-568-2
   1. Evangelicalism—United States. 2. Postconservative theology—
United States. 3. Postmodernism—Religious aspects—Christianity.
I. Erickson, Millard J. II.Helseth, Paul Kjoss, 1962- . III. Taylor,
Justin, 1976- .
BR1642.U5R44   2004
230'.04624—dc22   2004015254

MLY		17	16	15	14	13	12	11	10	09	08	07
15	14	13	12	11	10	9	8	7	6	5	4	3	2

In memory of three theologians
who were instrumental in the resurgence of evangelical theology
in the twentieth century:

Edward John Carnell
(1919–1967)

Carl F. H. Henry
(1913–2003)

Bernard L. Ramm
(1916–1992)

CONTENTS

CONTRIBUTORS

Chad Owen Brand. Associate Professor of Christian Theology, The Southern Baptist Theological Seminary and Boyce College.

A. B. Caneday. Professor of New Testament Studies and Biblical Theology, Northwestern College, St. Paul, Minnesota.

D. A. Carson. Research Professor of New Testament, Trinity Evangelical Divinity School.

Garrett DeWeese. Associate Professor of Philosophy and Philosophical Theology, Talbot School of Theology, Biola University.

Kwabena Donkor. Associate Director at the Biblical Research Institute, Washington, D.C. (on appointment).

Millard J. Erickson. Distinguished Professor of Theology, Western Seminary, Portland.

Paul Kjoss Helseth. Associate Professor of Christian Thought, Northwestern College, St. Paul, Minnesota.

Douglas R. Groothuis. Professor of Philosophy of Religion and Ethics, Denver Seminary.

J. P. Moreland. Distinguished Professor of Philosophy, Talbot School of Theology, Biola University.

James Parker III. Professor of Worldview and Culture, The Southern Baptist Theological Seminary.

R. Scott Smith. Associate Professor of Ethics and Christian Apologetics, Talbot School of Theology, Biola University.

Justin Taylor. Director of Theology and Executive Editor, Desiring God.

William G. Travis. Professor of Church History Emeritus, Bethel Seminary, St. Paul, Minnesota.

Stephen J. Wellum. Associate Professor of Christian Theology, The Southern Baptist Theological Seminary.

ACKNOWLEDGMENTS

THE EDITORS WOULD LIKE to extend their appreciation to a number of individuals whose outstanding work helped make this volume possible. We would like to thank our contributors for their timely, thoughtful, and substantive essays. Our gratitude goes to the folks at Crossway Books—especially Lane Dennis, Marvin Padgett, and Bill Deckard—for enthusiastically embracing and supporting this project. A special word of thanks to Marshall Wall for his fine work assembling the indexes. Finally, we thank the Lord for his mercy and grace in our lives, and for giving us wives—Virginia Erickson, Marla Helseth, and Lea Taylor—who fear God and love his Word.

PART ONE
INTRODUCTION

1

AN INTRODUCTION TO POSTCONSERVATIVE EVANGELICALISM AND THE REST OF THIS BOOK

Justin Taylor

IN THIS INTRODUCTORY CHAPTER, my aim is not only to introduce the rest of this book, but also to sketch the broad contours of postconservative evangelical theology. I will first provide an overview of postconservatism and its proponents. I will then provide an overview of and a justification for our response.

POSTCONSERVATISM

Deciding whether postconservatism is a "movement" or simply a "mood" is rather unimportant for our purposes.[1] What is important—and what is by and large no longer questioned—is that a significant shift is taking place in some segments of evangelicalism. The proponents of this perspective have assumed various labels with varying connotations—postconservatives,[2] reformists, the emerging church, younger evangelicals, postfundamentalists,

---

[1] Roger Olson referred to postconservatism in 1995 as a "small and diverse movement," a "movement in its infancy," and in 2002 as a "mood (not movement!)." In 2003, he clarified that it is "a movement of mood; a paradigm shift without organization" (Roger E. Olson, "Postconservative Evangelicals Greet the Postmodern Age," *Christian Century* 112 [May 3, 1995]: 480; idem, "Reforming Evangelical Theology," in *Evangelical Futures: A Conversation on Theological Method,* ed. John G. Stackhouse, Jr. [Grand Rapids, Mich.: Baker, 2000], 201; idem, "Postconservative Evangelical Theology and the Theological Pilgrimage of Clark Pinnock," in *Semper Reformandum: Studies in Honour of Clark H. Pinnock,* ed. Stanley E. Porter and Anthony R. Cross [Carlisle, England: Paternoster, 2003], 20 n. 11).

[2] This is the term we adopt throughout this book, though its use by some has been rather elastic. For example, Roger Olson seems to claim that even J. I. Packer's essay in *Evangelical Futures* is "postconservative" ("Reforming Evangelical Theology," 201-202). The editor of *Evangelical Futures,* John Stackhouse, disagrees, saying that Packer is "surely no one's idea of a 'postconservative'" ("Preface," in *Evangelical Futures,* 10). And although Kevin Vanhoozer uses the term to identify his own position ("The Voice and the Actor: A Dramatic Proposal About the Ministry and Minstrelsy of Theology," in *Evangelical Futures,* 76-77ff.), a number of our contributors strongly advocate Vanhoozer's methodology over and against that of someone like Stanley Grenz.

postfoundationalists, postpropositionalists, postevangelicals[3]—but they all bear a family resemblance and can be grouped together as having a number of common characteristics. They are self-professed evangelicals seeking to revision the theology, renew the center, and transform the worshiping community of evangelicalism, cognizant of the postmodern global context within which we live. They desire a "generous orthodoxy"[4] that would steer a faithful course between the Scylla of conservative-traditionalism and the Charybdis of liberal-progressivism. At the risk of oversimplification and for the purposes of this introduction, I will refer to Stanley Grenz as postconservatism's Professor, Brian McLaren its Pastor, and Roger Olson and Robert Webber its Publicists,[5] summarizing in what follows their basic perspectives and contributions. My purpose at this point is primarily description, not analysis.

The Publicists: Olson and Webber

Postconservatism—in its broad conception—involves not only methodological proposals for the discipline of theology, but also historiographical and sociological analyses of the evangelical movement. Roger Olson and Robert Webber have been significantly involved as advocates and promoters of postconservatism. The term *postconservatism* itself is most often associated with Olson, who claims to have coined the term in a 1995 article entitled "Postconservatives Greet the Postmodern Age."[6] He identified two loose and often warring coalitions within North American evangelical theology: the *traditionalists* and the *reformists*. The traditionalists, he argued, have a mindset that "values traditional interpretations and formulations as binding

---

[3] Those who use this label are quick to insist that the term does not mean non- or anti-evangelical. For example, Dallas Willard writes that *"post*-evangelicalism is by no means *ex*-evangelicalism. There are, of course ex-evangelicals, and even anti-evangelicals, but post-evangelicals *are* evangelicals, perhaps tenaciously so. However, post-evangelicals have also been driven to the margins by some aspects of evangelical church culture with which they cannot honestly identify" (Dallas Willard, "Smothering Jesus in a Heap of Trivialities," foreword to Dave Tomlinson, *The Post-Evangelical*, rev. North American ed. [Grand Rapids, Mich.: Zondervan, 2003], 11).

[4] The phrase, coined by Hans Frei, is often used by Stanley J. Grenz, *Renewing the Center: Evangelical Theology in a Post-Theological Era* (Grand Rapids, Mich.: Baker, 2000), passim. *A Generous Orthodoxy* is also the title of a new book by Brian McLaren (Grand Rapids, Mich.: Zondervan, 2004).

[5] Stanley Grenz is Pioneer McDonald Professor of Baptist Heritage, Theology, and Ethics at Carey Theological College (Vancouver, B.C.). Brian McLaren is the founding pastor of Cedar Ridge Community Church (Spencerville, Maryland). Roger Olson is Professor of Theology at Truett Theological Seminary, Baylor University (Waco, Texas). And Robert Webber is the William R. and Geraldyn B. Myers Professor of Ministry at Northern Seminary (Lombard, Illinois).

[6] Olson writes, "In a *Christian Century* essay [May 3, 1995], I coined the label 'postconservative' to describe a new mood arising within North American evangelical theological circles" ("Reforming Evangelical Theology," 201). It should be pointed out, however, that Clark Pinnock was using the term and making virtually all of the same sociological-theological identifications five years earlier. See his *Tracking the Maze: Finding Our Way Through Modern Theology from an Evangelical Perspective* (San Francisco: Harper & Row, 1990), 63-76.

and normative and looks with suspicion upon doctrinal revisions and new proposals arising out of theological reflection." The reformists, on the other hand, have "a mindset that values the continuing process of constructive theology seeking new light breaking forth from God's Word."[7] Whereas traditionalists view the church as a bounded set, with strong boundary identification as a sign of authentic evangelical faith, reformists see the church as a centered set: the boundaries are open and undefined, so we should focus upon the center—usually identified as the oft-cited Bebbington quadrilateral: *"conversionism,* the belief that lives need to be changed; *activism,* the expression of the gospel in effort; *biblicism,* a particular regard for the Bible; and . . . *crucicentrism,* a stress on the sacrifice of Christ on the cross."[8]

Postconservatism is to conservatism what postliberalism[9] is to liberalism: both desire to move beyond their forebears while retaining some of their positive qualities. Postconservatives and conservatives hold in common the Bebbington center, but the "old guard" of evangelical scholars is obsessed with battles over inerrancy, higher criticism, and liberal theology. In this way conservatives and liberals are unlikely bedfellows in their obsession with the modern mind. Conservatives are sliding headlong toward fundamentalism, unaware of the promises and possibilities of postmodernity's unexplored terrain.

The postconservatives, on the other hand, have seized the opportunity to reform, reshape, and revision theology. They are eager to engage and learn from nonevangelical theologians, healing the divisions caused by modernity. They see the essence of Christianity not in doctrine but in a narrative-shaped experience. Sources for theology include not only the Bible, but also Christian tradition, culture, and the contemporary experience of God's community. Postconservatives are open to open theism, have a hope of near-universal salvation, and place a renewed emphasis on synergy in the divine-human rela-

---

[7] Roger E. Olson, "The Future of Evangelical Theology," *Christianity Today* 42 (February 9, 1998): 41.

[8] D. W. Bebbington, *Evangelicalism in Modern Britain: A History from the 1730s to the 1980s* (London: Unwin Hyman Ltd, 1989), 3.

[9] Postliberalism is usually associated with Yale University and theologians George Lindbeck, Hans Frei, Paul Holmer, and David Kelsey. Lindbeck's *The Nature of Doctrine: Religion and Theology in a Postliberal Age* (Philadelphia: Westminster, 1984) seeks to move beyond the modernistic, totalizing foundations of conservatism (cognitive-propositional) and liberalism (experiential-expressionists). Over against these, Lindbeck proposes a *cultural-linguistic* turn, wherein doctrine is to theology what grammar is to language. The function of doctrine is not to correspond to objective reality or to express universal experience, but to serve as the communal rules of discourse, attitude, and action. For a symposium of postliberals and evangelicals, see Timothy R. Phillips and Dennis Okholm, eds., *The Nature of Confession: Evangelicals and Liberals in Conversation* (Downers Grove, Ill.: InterVarsity Press, 1996). For a critique, see Michael S. Horton, "Yale Postliberalism: Back to the Bible?" in *A Confessing Theology for Postmodern Times,* ed. Michael S. Horton (Wheaton, Ill.: Crossway, 2000), 183-216. And for a recent, clarifying exchange between Lindbeck and Avery Cardinal Dulles, see the October 2003 and January 2004 issues of *First Things* (57-61; 13-15). Olson has also used the analogy that postconservatism is comparable to progressive Roman Catholic theology after Vatican II ("Postconservative Evangelical Theology and the Theological Pilgrimage of Clark Pinnock," 20).

tionship. They are willing to rethink the language and concepts of Chalcedonian Christology, viewing Jesus' divinity in relational terms. They are impatient with triumphalism, epistemological certainty, and theological systems, judging that traditional evangelicalism is "suffering from a kind of hubris with regard to truth-claims."[10]

In a recent article, Olson identifies the following characteristics of post-conservative evangelical theology and its theologians: they (1) are thoroughly and authentically evangelical; (2) embrace a vision of critical and generous orthodoxy; (3) believe in experience rather than doctrine as the enduring essence of evangelical Christianity; (4) express discomfort with foundationalism and embrace critical realism; (5) have a strong interest in dialogue between diverse groups of theologians; (6) have a broad and relatively inclusive vision of evangelicalism; (7) have a relational view of reality, including a relational vision of God's being; and (8) have an inclusivist attitude toward salvation. Postconservatism's one major unifying motif—its one universal interest—is a *commitment to ongoing reform of evangelical life, worship and belief in the light of God's word.*"[11]

This is all set over against Olson's understanding of "traditionalism" or "conservatism." He cautions that just because someone adopts a particular label does not mean that the person fits all of the characteristics he is identifying. He is "dealing with ideal types and not individual persons or institutions."[12] Nevertheless, some general characteristics can be described:

> A conservative evangelical places such value on the *status quo* that he or she is closed-minded with regard to theological creativity and innovation even when they are fueled by faithful exegesis and believing reflection on God's word. . . . 'Fundamentalism' is being replaced with the label 'conservative evangelicalism' while retaining fundamentalistic habits of heart and mind. When a person proclaims himself or herself a 'conservative evangelical', more often than not it indicates commitment to strict biblical inerrancy, a fairly literalistic hermeneutic, a passionate commitment to a perceived 'golden age' of Protestant orthodoxy to be rediscovered and preserved, and a suspicion of all new proposals in theology, biblical interpretation, spirituality, mission and worship.[13]

For Olson, the differences between the two pictures he has painted are

---

[10] Olson, "Postconservative Evangelicals Greet the Postmodern Age," 482.
[11] Olson, "Postconservative Evangelical Theology and the Theological Pilgrimage of Clark Pinnock," 36, emphasis his.
[12] Ibid., 18.
[13] Ibid.

rather stark. The postconservatives and their proposals are "liberated," "bold," "vibrant," "interesting," "new," "relevant," "committed," "faithful," "fresh," and "fascinating." The traditionalists are "old guard," "obsessive," "reactionary," "highly rationalistic," "rigid" "naysayers" with a "scholastic spirit" who love nothing more than "gatekeeping," "control[ling] the switches," and "patrol[ling] the boundaries."[14]

Robert Webber joins Olson—though certainly framing his discussion in a more charitable and irenic fashion—by distinguishing between twentieth-century evangelicals and twenty-first-century evangelicals.[15] However, he divides twentieth-century evangelicals into two camps: the *traditional evangelicals* (1950–1975, led by Billy Graham) and the *pragmatic evangelicals* (1975–2000, led by Bill Hybels). The emerging set of leaders is termed the *younger evangelicals* (2000 and beyond, led by Brian McLaren).

Webber works through a series of perspectives (e.g., on history and tradition, theology, apologetics, ecclesiology, etc.), and shows how the traditionalists, the pragmatists, and the younger evangelicals approach them. Traditionalist evangelicals tend to have the characteristics of rationalism, denominationalism, and separatism. They want to retain Reformation distinctives, focus on church-centered programs, and use mass evangelism and printed materials for outreach. Pragmatic evangelicals focus more on therapeutic models and success-oriented apologetics, high-energy leaders, and interdenominationalism. They are interested in the innovative, focusing on outreach programs and using seeker services and broadcast tools for outreach. The younger evangelicals, on the other hand, practice an embodied or incarnational apologetic, see the church as a community of faith, and are intentionally ecumenical. They take an "ancient-future" approach to tradition, whereby the future runs through the past. For outreach they look to "process evangelism" and interactive communication on the Internet.

"Younger" designates not only those "young in age," but also those "young in spirit." "The younger evangelical is anyone, older or younger, who deals thoughtfully with the shift from twentieth- to twenty-first-century culture. He or she is committed to construct a biblically rooted, historically informed, and culturally aware new evangelical witness in the twenty-first century."[16] According to Webber, the younger evangelicals value tradition

---

[14] And this is from just one article! See Olson, "Reforming Evangelical Theology," passim. For some thoughts on the phenomena of pejorative labels under the ostensible category of analysis, see Millard Erickson's chapter at the end of this volume.

[15] Robert E. Webber, *The Younger Evangelicals: Facing the Challenges of the New World* (Grand Rapids, Mich.: Baker, 2002).

[16] Ibid., 16.

over ahistoricism; stories over propositions; a communally embodied apologetic over rational argumentation; and the visible over the invisible church.

The Pastor: McLaren

The primary focus of our book is on the academic aspect of the postconservative movement. In this introductory chapter, however, my aim is to give a broad overview of this mood and its movement. Therefore, it is important to look at Brian McLaren, an increasingly influential pastor/writer/speaker in the Emergent Church Movement. McLaren's developing perspective is impossible to separate from his own story or narrative. "Raised among the tiny Plymouth Brethren, shaped by the Jesus Movement, trained in the secular academy, impassioned by art, music, philosophy and nature—McLaren doesn't fit neatly into any evangelical stereotype."[17] After teaching English at the University of Maryland and Montgomery College, he entered pastoral ministry full-time in 1986 as the founding pastor of what would eventually become Cedar Ridge Community Church in the Washington-Baltimore area.

As McLaren interacted with unchurched postmodern seekers and studied church history, he began to reexamine not only his changeable methods but also his "so-called unchanging message." He realized that his fairly standard "method-message system" was relatively new in comparison with the varied tradition of Christendom. As he searched for an unchanging message, an irreducible doctrinal core of "mere Christianity" held in common by all Christians at all times, he began to despair at the diversity of interpretations and proposals. His doubts about both his methods and his message continued to grow.

In 1994, at the age of 38, he faced a crisis of faith and a seemingly insurmountable dilemma: (1) continue practicing and promoting a version of Christianity that he had deepening reservations about, or (2) leave Christian ministry, and perhaps the Christian path, altogether.[18] A process of wrestling and rethinking led to an alternative between hypocrisy and apostasy: learn to be a Christian in a new way.[19] In the mouth of one of his fictional characters, McLaren summarizes his discovery:

---

[17] Greg Warner, "Brian McLaren Unlikely Leader of 'Emerging Church' Movement," *Associated Baptist Press* (May 13, 2003). See http://www.abpnews.com/abpnews/story.cfm?newsId=3587.

[18] The story is recounted in Brian L. McLaren, "The True Story Behind This Story," in *A New Kind of Christian: A Tale of Two Friends on a Spiritual Journey* (San Francisco: Jossey-Bass, 2001), ix-xviii.

[19] To facilitate this end, he also helped to found Emergent (www.emergentvillage.com)—a "growing generative friendship among missional Christian leaders." McLaren is a senior fellow of this international theological network.

What a relief to have a third alternative—to read the Bible as a pre-modern text, emerging from a people who believed that truth is best embodied in story and art and human flesh, rather than abstraction or outline or moralism. . . . According to the Bible, humans shall not live by systems and abstractions and principles alone, but also by stories and poetry and proverbs of mystery.[20]

McLaren's *A New Kind of Christian,* the first installment of his theological trilogy, was published in 2001. It is written in a narrative format as a philosophical dialogue between two fictional characters: Dan, a frustrated evangelical pastor, and Neo, a pastor-turned-high school teacher, who serves as McLaren's prototype for this new kind of Christian. The sequel, *The Story We Find Ourselves In,* was released in 2003, and another volume is forthcoming (at the time of this writing). *A New Kind of Christian* proved both popular and controversial.[21] At the crux of his proposal is a call for us to break free from the bondage of modern categories. As an "emergent postmodernist," he advocates dialogue over debate, community over individualism, experience over proof. McLaren argues that evangelicals tend to think that the gospel is about how individual souls get into heaven when they die; emergent postmoderns point instead to Jesus' message about the kingdom of God, which concerns *the here-and-now,* not just heaven; *community,* not just individuality; *all of creation,* not just the individual soul.

Through McLaren's struggle over his dissatisfaction with the old kind of Christianity came four seminal ideas about the gospel across time and cultures that led him to believe that "our message (like our methods) must change from time to time and place to place in order to remain truly the gospel of Jesus and the gospel about Jesus."[22] (1) *The gospel is story.* We need to be "depropositionalized" and realize that the gospel is narrative and story, not propositions, mechanisms, abstractions, or universal concepts. (2) *The gospel is many-versioned, many-faceted, many-layered, and Christ-centered.* The story of the gospel lies embedded beneath multiple stories, versions,

---

[20] McLaren, *New Kind of Christian,* 159

[21] *Christianity Today* granted the book an "Award of Merit" in their best books edition of 2002. And *Books and Culture* commissioned three essays on the book, along with a response by McLaren. See Andy Crouch, "Let's Get Personal," *Books and Culture* 8 (January/February 2002): 12; Mark Dever, "Reformed or Deformed?" *Books and Culture* 8 (March/April 2002): 26; Tony Jones, "Post-Evangelicalism," *Books and Culture* 8 (May/June 2002): 32; Brian D. McLaren, "Faithfully Dangerous," *Books and Culture* 8 (May/June 2002): 33.

[22] The following summary is drawn from Brian D. McLaren, "The Method, the Message, and the Ongoing Story," in *The Church in Emerging Culture: Five Perspectives,* ed. Leonard Sweet (Grand Rapids, Mich.: Zondervan, 2003), 191-230. This book has an intriguing format whereby the other contributors' comments—both critiques and agreements—are embedded within the individual essays, not unlike an extended email exchange. Michael Horton's critique of McLaren is, in my opinion, extremely insightful. Horton thinks that much of popular postmodernism is in fact "most-modern."

facets, and layers—all of which center not in a theory about Christ or an idea of Christ, but in Christ himself. (3) *The gospel is cumulative*. It did not arrive in a vacuum. It includes and continues the Jewish prequel, as well as the continued acts of Jesus by the Spirit throughout history. Jesus continues to work, the story continues to unfold, and the unchanging story continues to change and grow richer and deeper. (4) *The gospel is performative and catalytic*. The gospel is not just told, heard, and affirmed; it performs, catalyzes, and saves. The gospel, empowered by God's Spirit, brings about transformation among the community of faith in order that God's will might be done on earth, inaugurating the kingdom of God.

Knowing the gospel means knowing the times. We live in a postmodern era—but what does that mean? McLaren distinguishes and defines three forms of postmodernism: (1) *absurd postmodernism*—which denies truth, reality, and morality—is virtually nonexistent and is used by modernists to scare people; (2) *adolescent postmodernism*—associated with relativist pluralism, consumerism, alienated European intellectuals, and political correctness—is dying; and (3) *emerging postmodernism*—the approach advocated by McLaren—is an attempt to move beyond both the reductionistic rationalism of modernism and the relativist pluralism of adolescent postmodernism. It is not fully definable, and may still be decades away from mature definition. McLaren argues that the people of faith will not only be instrumental in defining the term, but in shaping the era. This postmodern transition will likely be a 75-year or 100-year process.

McLaren certainly doesn't claim to have all the answers for how best to define, or how best to live, in this transitional age. He has emerged, however, as an influential voice among younger evangelicals.

The Professor: Grenz

Stanley Grenz has been at the forefront of scholarly work from a post-conservative perspective. His theoretical commitments and theological methodology are dealt with in some detail in the pages that follow, so I will provide here a broad overview by focusing on his *Revisioning Evangelical Theology* (1983), an early programmatic work on evangelical method. Nearly a decade later he collaborated with John Franke to produce *Beyond Foundationalism*,[23] a full-scale work on theological method in the postmodern context that seeks to flesh out what was sketched and suggested in

---

[23] Stanley J. Grenz and John R. Franke, *Beyond Foundationalism: Shaping Theology in a Postmodern Context* (Louisville: Westminster John Knox, 2001).

Revisioning. His recent appraisal of evangelicalism, *Renewing the Center,* is summarized in some detail in chapter 2 of our book.

Grenz's proposal involves revisioning evangelical identity and spirituality, and revisioning the task of and sources for theology, biblical authority, theology's integrative motif, and the church. He argues that our transitional age, with the death of modernism and the advent of postmodernity, "demands nothing less than a rebirth of theological reflection among evangelicals. . . ."[24] In Grenz's view, "to be 'evangelical' means to participate in a community characterized by a shared narrative concerning a personal encounter with God told in terms of shared theological categories derived from the Bible" (chapter 1).[25] This means that evangelicals have now shifted from a creed-based to a spirituality-based identity. Spiritually rooted theology is the essence and ethos of the evangelical movement (chapter 2). What is the foundation for this new theological vision? Traditional evangelical theologians have seen propositional revelation as foundational material for the theological enterprise. But Grenz rejects this as the product of an outdated modernist mindset that ignores the social nature of theological discourse. Building upon but going beyond Lindbeck, Grenz argues that "theology systematizes, explores and orders the community symbols and concepts into a unified whole—that is, into a systematic conceptual framework."[26] In other words, theology is the intellectual reflection on faith we share as the believing community in a particular context (chapter 3). Whereas traditional evangelicals tend to see Scripture as the only source of theology, Grenz argues that we must also draw upon the theological heritage of the church and the thought-forms and issues of our historical-cultural context (chapter 4). All evangelicals acknowledge the authority of the Bible, but they differ on *why* it is authoritative. Traditional evangelicals have stressed the divine to the neglect of the human side of the Bible, and Grenz argues that therefore the Spirit-Scripture link must be revisioned. The Bible is the product of and the vehicle for the working of the Holy Spirit. In other words, its authority lies not in the text itself, but rather in the Spirit speaking through the Scriptures (chapter 5). Grenz next turns to the issue of theology's integrative motif. The kingdom of God is an appropriate but insufficient candidate, for the *content* of the kingdom is left undefined. Its proper content, Grenz argues, is the community of God. With a view toward the already and not yet, the kingdom of

---

[24] Stanley J. Grenz, *Revisioning Evangelical Theology: A Fresh Agenda for the Twenty-first Century* (Downers Grove, Ill.: InterVarsity Press, 1993), 17.
[25] Ibid.
[26] Ibid., 78.

God and the community of God function together as the proper integrating concept for theology (chapter 6). Finally, since the church is the proper context for theology, Grenz applies his conclusions on theological methodology to the doctrine of the church. He advocates an eschatological-process model of ecclesiology: the church is the eschatological community of love constituted by its destiny as the company of the kingdom that reflects its King.

The response in academia to Grenz's work has been varied. All recognize its ambition and creativity. Some have judged it remarkable and revolutionary as a methodology that takes seriously the postmodern situation; others have seen it as a dangerous and damaging accommodation to the spirit of this age. Due to the serious, extensive literature Grenz has produced in this area, we believe his work merits our sustained engagement.

OUR RESPONSE

This book is an interdisciplinary work that critically engages this proposal for evangelical methodology and identity. Our desire is not merely to debate, but to enter into dialogue; not only to denounce, but to accurately and charitably describe; not only to critique, but to learn. No doubt we have not done so perfectly, but that is the spirit in which these chapters are presented.

As alluded to above, the next chapter in this book is a review by *D. A. Carson* of *Renewing the Center,* summarizing and critiquing the broad outlines of Grenz's vision for evangelicalism. Carson argues that Grenz's historical conclusions are either tendentious or highly questionable and that his theoretical commitments are in danger of domesticating the gospel to postmodernism, with the result that his program could be largely irrelevant to the world and devoid of power. Grenz warns against evangelical accommodation to modernism, but Carson fears that it is Grenz who is in danger of being held captive to an unbiblical, postmodern epistemology.

In the opening chapter of the section on philosophy, *Doug Groothuis* observes that something philosophically significant is afoot among purported evangelicals, for the received concept of truth is being jettisoned in favor of postmodern models. He examines the coherence, pragmatic, and postmodern theories of truth against the standard of the correspondence theory of truth, showing that only the latter is sufficient and acceptable for evangelicals.

Whereas postconservatives routinely celebrate the "demise of foundationalism," epistemologists *J. P. Moreland and Garry DeWeese* suggest that the obituary has been written prematurely. While denouncements and assertions regarding foundationalism are rampant, specific arguments have been rather rare. Moreland and DeWeese, however, identify three theoretical com-

mitments that are key to the postconservative package: (1) the rejection of the
correspondence theory of truth in favor of an epistemic or deflationary theory
of truth; (2) a rejection of metaphysical realism in favor of a theory of socially
or linguistically constructed reality; and (3) a rejection of the referential theory of language in favor of a semiotic theory. Moreland and DeWeese provide
rebuttals and offer a positive case for modest foundationalism as the correct
general epistemological theory of justification, and modal reliabilism about
evidence as the best form of modest foundationalism. They then proceed to
show that modal reliabilism about evidence comports with biblical inerrancy.

Scott Smith, who has written extensively on the language-world relationship, argues that the core of the postconservative view is that we are inside language and have no epistemic access to the world as it is in itself. In other words,
they believe that we live in a linguistic world of our own making. Our discourse is simply an expression of the way in which our localized communities
talk. But which community? And if their claims are nothing more than this,
then who cares? The way in which postconservatives actually argue their case
demonstrates that they are inconsistently presupposing what they purport to
deny, namely, epistemic access to the real world. Smith goes on to apply this
linguistic constructionism to some central doctrines of the Christian faith.

The next section turns to theological method. *Ardel Caneday* shows that
Grenz and Franke view Scripture as functional over against propositional. In
so doing, the postconservatives have bought into a false disjunction. The
locus of God's revelation and authority is not to be found in the text of
Scripture, they argue, but rather in the Spirit's appropriation of Scripture for
the contemporary community of believers. Over against Grenz and Franke's
adaptation of Lindbeck's cultural-linguistic method of theology, Caneday
proposes that we look instead to Kevin Vanhoozer's canonical-linguistic
approach,[27] with its recovery of a robust biblical theology that draws upon
the categories and structure of Scripture.

Steve Wellum continues this examination of the Grenz-Franke model,
explaining how they understand postmodernism and its importance for
doing theology, what their alternative proposal is, and the role that Scripture
plays within it. After delineating some of its positive features, Wellum offers
a number of criticisms. Their interpretation of postmodernism is overly optimistic, and their linking of Scripture as an inerrant foundation with
Enlightenment foundationalism is grossly unfair. Employing coherentism,
pragmatism, and epistemological and metaphysical nonrealism as resources

---

[27] See Kevin J. Vanhoozer, *The Drama of Doctrine: A Canonical-Linguistic Approach* (Louisville:
Westminster John Knox, forthcoming).

for their theological method, they have obvious difficulties stating and defending the truth question. Finally, their doctrine of Scripture is incompatible with the Bible's own claims for itself and weakens the possibility of doing theology in a normative fashion. It is this surrender of biblical authority that Wellum ultimately finds most disconcerting. He closes by offering summary reflections on what is necessary for the doing of theology that honors Scripture as fully authoritative, seeks to be faithfully biblical, and is applicatory for all of life.

In the final chapter of this section, African theologian *Kwabena Donkor* describes and evaluates postconservative methodology by focusing mainly upon Grenz's proposal. An attractive feature of postconservative theology is that it welcomes the perspective of the Third World and seeks to make sense of our global context. But Donkor sees a dilemma between the necessity of missiology and a consistent postmodern methodology. In his view, the postconservative incredulity to metanarratives undermines the very legitimacy of apologetics and evangelism. With respect to the question of how we can maintain the finality of the Christian vision when all religions claim to foster community, Donkor detects conceptual difficulties at every turn. He then applies this to the African context in particular, arguing that the proper way forward runs contrary to the postconservative ethos and is inconsistent with postconservative principles.

In the next section we turn to the historiographical discipline. One of our concerns about postconservative epistemology has been well-expressed by Richard Mouw:

> I worry . . . about an iconoclastic spirit that often manifests itself in evangelical calls for new constructive theological initiatives. If we cannot be fair to our past in spelling out our heritage, I am not confident that we will accomplish much that is good in our efforts to clear the way for new theological paths.[28]

Historiography of evangelicalism is essential to the postconservative program. "If they can convince enough people that evangelicalism has *always* been primarily a movement defined not by beliefs and doctrines, but by other concerns, then it becomes easier to stretch the label 'evangelical' to include more and more people today who ignore these doctrinal distinctions."[29]

---

[28] Richard J. Mouw, "Comments on Grenz Paper and 'The Word Made Fresh,'" unpublished paper read at the annual meeting of the American Academy of Religion, Toronto, November 2002.

[29] D. A. Carson, *The Gagging of God: Christianity Confronts Pluralism* (Grand Rapids, Mich.: Zondervan, 1996), 458.

Paul Helseth begins this section by explaining that the postconservatives see Old Princeton's theology of Scripture as owing more to Scottish Common Sense Realism and Enlightenment-foundationalist rationalism than it does to the Word of God. While this historiography certainly fits into the postconservative perspective, Helseth argues that recent scholarship suggests this is a superficial, caricatured reading. The Princetonians viewed reason in a moral, not merely rational, fashion—advocating what Warfield termed "right reason." Helseth then turns the tables on the postconservatives, arguing that since they can offer no justifiable reason for validating Christianity's truth-claims, it is the *postconservatives* who are therefore necessarily imperialistic, triumphalistic, and elitist. In other words, the postconservatives have become a new incarnation of the fundamentalism they so despise.

Postconservatives pan the Princetonians, but they praise the Pietists. According to Grenz's historiography, the material principle or essence of evangelicalism is "convertive piety"—a personal experience of God through new birth coupled with a transformed life. In the mid-twentieth century, however, the neo-evangelicals added a formal principle of "correct doctrine," with the result that the formal has now subsumed the material. Postconservatives, by championing convertive piety, are calling evangelicalism to return to its roots. Historian *Bill Travis* examines this revisionist historiography through a detailed analysis of Pietism in the seventeenth and eighteenth centuries, along with studies of Methodists, Lutherans, and others in the United States. Travis shows that Philipp Jakob Spener, August Hermann Francke, and those influenced by them were very much concerned with orthodox doctrine, seeing the relationship between doctrine and experience as one of both/and, not either/or.

Despite an array of theological and sociological perspectives on the state of contemporary evangelicalism, many seem to agree on one thing: evangelicalism has become an "essentially disputed concept"[30] trapped in a "definitional quandary"[31] and "descriptively anemic."[32] Whereas Helseth and Travis examined specialized aspects within the story of evangelicalism (the Princetonians and the Pietists, respectively), *Chad Brand* steps back to examine the nature of evangelicalism in general. He is convinced that despite the difficulties of definition, it is still possible to use the term "evangelical" in a meaningful sense to describe the broad coalition of conservative Christians

---

[30] Kevin J. Vanhoozer, "Foreword," in Bernard L. Ramm, *The Evangelical Heritage: A Study in Historical Theology* (Grand Rapids, Mich.: Baker, 2000), xiii.

[31] Jon R. Stone, *On the Boundaries of American Evangelicalism: The Postwar Evangelical Coalition* (New York: St. Martin's, 1997), 7.

[32] David F. Wells, *No Place for Truth, or, Whatever Happened to Evangelical Theology?* (Grand Rapids, Mich.: Eerdmans, 1993), 134.

today. Early on in his essay he offers a minimalist working definition: "a movement within generally North American and British circles that empha- sizes the classic Protestant doctrines of the authority and reliability of Scripture (especially over against a rising liberal reconstruction of the doctrine of Scripture), the triune God, and the historical second coming of Christ, and which promotes the need for fervent evangelism, a conversion experience, and a life of discipleship before God." Before refining and expanding upon this, he first explores the roots of evangelicalism by providing a look at three major periods: the eighteenth-century Awakenings, the conservative response to liberalism, and the transition from fundamentalism to evangelicalism. Evangelicalism is certainly a variegated movement, and yet the "evangelicals" were united around certain core beliefs until the mid-twentieth century. These commitments included the sole sufficiency of Scripture as the source of our theological knowledge, the complete and utter reliability of God's Word, and the nature of theology as a study of what God has said to us. In the next major section Brand asks whether the postconservatives have been faithful to this tradition. His conclusion is that the postconservatives are mobilizing against these core beliefs in the interest of defending relational theology, defeating foundationalism, contextualizing Scripture, and emphasizing tradition.

In the final section, we explore postmodernism's future. *Jim Parker* sug- gests that postmodernism's demise is now all but certain, and asks, "Whither shall we go?" Following Paul Vitz, he argues that a significant cultural shift is on the horizon: a coming *transmodern* period is emerging that avoids the extremes of both modernism and postmodernism, while drawing upon the strengths of each. This transmodern vision is elucidated through a brief exam- ination of new trends within the diverse disciplines of music, the visual arts, architecture, poetry, cinema, ethics, and social-political philosophy.

In the final chapter of this book, *Millard Erickson* attempts to clear away some of the fog by drawing together the insights of the previous chapters and sketching the contours of the type of theology we need in order to navigate our way into the post-postmodern period. The future evangelical theology will be *global,* broadening itself to include the voices of Third World and female theologians. It will seek to be *objective*—not in the naïve modernist sense, but as a careful return to the correspondence theory of truth and metaphysical realism presupposed by Scripture, an adoption of neo-foundationalism, and a rejection of the new historicism. This new conservative theology will be *prac- tical and accessible,* with contributions by and application toward those in practical areas of ministry, not just the small and isolated ivory tower. It will be *postcommunal,* recognizing not just the value of community but also the liabilities therein, including the tendency of groups to gravitate toward that which is new and creative. Instead, it will bring critical thinking and healthy skepticism to bear, asking of every new proposal, "Yes, but is it true?" This new theology will be *metanarratival,* insisting that the exclusivity and universality of the biblical message not merely be dogmatically asserted, but be substantiated with support. It will be *dialogical,* not in the sense of being improperly polemical, but in interacting with differing claims, considering those claims, and advancing cogent argumentation. Finally, this new evangelical theology will be *futuristic,* anticipating and preparing for the future and the forthcoming need to contextualize our message.

DEBATE, THE ACADEMY, AND THE CHURCH

If good theology, faithful philosophy, and accurate historiography didn't matter—or if we all agreed—books like this wouldn't need to be written and debates wouldn't need to be undertaken. But it does matter, and we don't all agree. Although the notion that "bounding lines must exist"[33] is inherently offensive to some and elicits caricatures and pejorative labeling, we feel obligated nonetheless to engage our friends across the aisle.

Nothing could be clearer from the New Testament, it seems to me, than the idea that God has given us universally true doctrinal revelation that can be understood, shared, defended, and contextualized. "The faith" has been once for all delivered to the saints (Jude 3). We are to guard "the good deposit" entrusted to us (1 Tim. 6:20; 2 Tim. 1:14), instructing in "sound doctrine" and rebuking contrary doctrine (Titus 1:9; 2:1). False doctrine is associated with conceit and ignorance (1 Tim. 6:3-4), and we are commanded not to be tossed to and fro by its winds (Eph. 4:14).

These commands and warnings are set forth in the context of purifying and protecting the *church*. Why, then, have we labored to assemble a largely *academic* tome? The reason is that as goes the academy, so goes the church. Sociologist James Davison Hunter, writing at the height of the culture wars in the 1980s, observes:

> The struggle over the ivory tower is significant for the contemporary culture war for the simple reason that its outcome will ultimately shape the ideals and values as well as the categories of analysis and understanding that will guide the next generation of American leaders.[34]

---

[33] The expression is from C. S. Lewis, "Christian Apologetics," in *Essay Collection and Other Short Pieces,* ed. Lesley Walmsley (London: HarperCollins, 2000), 147-148. The entire essay is worth a careful read.
[34] James Davison Hunter, *Culture Wars: The Struggle to Define America* (New York: Basic Books, 1991), 211.

If this is true of the culture wars, how much more so is it true within the church? For good or ill, the postconservative project is already influencing the church. Postconservatives have raised extensive questions regarding the nature of theology and the nature of evangelicalism itself. And we judge it a worthwhile investment—ultimately for the health of the church—to engage the postconservative proposal with seriousness and candor.

AVOIDING TWO ERRORS AND RECLAIMING THE CENTER

It is possible to turn both the past and the present into idols and objects of functional worship. Some confess with their lips that the church is *semper reformanda,* but their hearts are far from it. Others tend to operate on the notion that "the newer is the truer, only what is recent is decent, every shift of ground is a step forward, and every latest word must be hailed as the last word on its subject."[35] Needless to say, both attitudes must be avoided.

Postconservatives complain of a "conflictual polarity" between the categories of liberalism and conservatism.[36] But one of the arguments throughout this book is that the postconservatives have set forth their own set of debilitating dichotomies: focus on the center versus preoccupation with boundaries; convertive piety versus correct doctrine; appropriation of postmodernism versus stagnant traditionalism. In this book, we want to argue that these polarities are misguided. The path forward is to reclaim the historic center of evangelical theology, which is centered on the glorious gospel of Jesus Christ—both in its doctrinal assertions of objective and accessible truth and its experiential effects of transforming our lives.

Al Mohler has expressed our conviction well, and with this I conclude our introduction:

> A word that can mean anything means nothing. If "evangelical identity" means drawing no boundaries, then we really have no center, no matter what we may claim. The fundamental issue is truth, and though the modernist may call us wrong and the postmodernist may call us naive, there is nowhere else for us to stand. . . .[37]

Soli Deo gloria.

---

[35] J. I. Packer, "Is Systematic Theology a Mirage? An Introductory Discussion," in *Doing Theology in Today's World: Essays in Honor of Kenneth S. Kantzer,* ed. John D. Woodbridge and Thomas Edward McComiskey (Grand Rapids, Mich.: Zondervan, 1991), 21.

[36] Grenz, *Renewing the Center,* 331.

[37] R. Albert Mohler, Jr., "Reformist Evangelicalism: A Center Without a Circumference," in *A Confessing Theology for Postmodern Times,* 146.

2

DOMESTICATING THE GOSPEL:
A REVIEW OF GRENZ'S
RENEWING THE CENTER[1]

D. A. Carson

RESPONSIBLE THEOLOGICAL REFLECTION must simultaneously embrace the best of the heritage from the past, and address the present. If theologians restrict themselves to the former task, they may become mere purveyors of antiquarian artifacts, however valuable those artifacts may be; if they focus primarily on the latter task, it is not long before they squander their heritage and become, as far as the gospel is concerned, largely irrelevant to the world they seek to reform, because wittingly or unwittingly they domesticate the gospel to the contemporary worldview, thereby robbing it of its power. Stan Grenz, I fear, is drifting toward the latter error.

CONTENT

As usual in his writings, Grenz in this book is free of malice, and, provided one is familiar with the jargon of postmodern discussion, reasonably lucid. The book's ten chapters can be divided into two parts. Grenz begins by citing a representative sample of voices that find contemporary evangelical theology in disarray—though admittedly these analyses do not all agree. So in

---

[1] Stanley J. Grenz, *Renewing the Center: Evangelical Theology in a Post-Theological Era* (Grand Rapids, Mich.: Baker, 2000). A slightly different form of this review was published in 2001 on the Internet at www.modernreformation.org. Dr. Grenz asked for space to respond, and his response was posted on the same website. About the same time, my review article was published in hardcopy in *Southern Baptist Journal of Theology* 6, no. 1 (Spring 2002): 82-97. For his part, Dr. Grenz published his response as an article, "Toward an Undomesticated Gospel: A Response to D. A. Carson," *Perspectives in Religious Studies* 30 (2003): 455-461. In this form of my review article, I have introduced only the most minor changes in the text itself, but I have introduced footnotes in which I have briefly responded to Dr. Grenz's riposte. Because I refer to the Internet form of his response, I have not included page references, but his words are easy enough to find.

the first four chapters, and part of the fifth, Grenz treats evangelicalism historically "as a theological phenomenon," trying to "draw from the particularly theological character of the movement's historical trajectory" (15). Accepting William J. Abraham's analysis—that the term "evangelical" embraces at least three constellations of thought, viz. the magisterial Reformation, the evangelical awakenings of the eighteenth century, and modern conservative evangelicalism—Grenz devotes the first two chapters, respectively, to the material principle and the formal principle of evangelical thought. In both cases he is attempting to tease out a "trajectory" of historical development. With respect to the material principle: Luther's commitment to justification by faith, modified by Calvin's quest for sanctification, augmented by Puritan and Pietist concern for personal conversion, sanctified living, and assurance of one's elect status, decline into comfortable conformity to outward forms, until the awakenings in Britain and the American colonies charged them with new life. The effect was a focus on "convertive piety" (*passim*) and concern for transformed living, rather than adherence to creeds. Evangelical theology focused on personal salvation.

As for the formal principle (chapter 2), contemporary conservative views of the Bible have not been shaped exclusively by Luther or Calvin, but also by Protestant scholastics who "transformed the doctrine of Scripture from an article of faith into the foundation for systematic theology" (17). At the end of the nineteenth century the Princeton theologians turned the doctrine of the inspiration of Scripture into "the primary fundamental" (17). This was passed on to neo-evangelical theologians, the thinkers who from the middle of the twentieth century tried to lead evangelicalism out of its introspection and exclusion, and into engagement with the broader culture.

Chapters 3, 4, and 5 carry on Grenz's analysis of contemporary evangelicalism by studying three pairs of men. The first generation of neo-evangelical theologians can be represented by Carl F. H. Henry and Bernard Ramm, the former setting a rationalistic and culturally critical cast to neo-evangelical theology, and the latter trying to lead evangelical theology out of "the self-assured rationalism he found in fundamentalism. Consequently, he became the standard-bearer for a more irenic and culturally engaging evangelicalism" (18). In the next generation, the polarity is Millard Erickson and Clark Pinnock, the former an establishment theologian who systematized neo-evangelical theology, the latter reflecting a theological odyssey that wanted to fulfill the evangelical apologetic ideal by engaging in dialogues with alternative views. He thereby carries on the irenic tradition of Ramm. The fifth chapter proposes that the polarities in the third generation can be aligned with Wayne Grudem and John Sanders.

Is this polarity so great that David Wells is correct in thinking that we are on the verge of evangelicalism's demise? Or does Dave Tomlinson's announcement of a post-evangelical era point the way ahead? In the second half of chapter 5, Grenz opts for neither stance, but suggests that the emerging task of evangelical theology is coming to grips with postmodernity. Recognizing the ambiguities in this term, Grenz identifies the heart of postmodernism in the epistemological arena. It adopts a chastened rationality (his expression), and marks a move from realism to the social construction of reality, from meta-narrative to local stories. The rest of the book teases out Grenz's proposal.

The next three chapters constitute the heart of the book. Chapter 6, "Evangelical Theological Method After the Demise of Foundationalism," is a summary of the book Grenz jointly wrote with John R. Franke entitled *Beyond Foundationalism*.[2] Grenz provides his take on "the rise and demise of foundationalism in philosophy" (185) before offering his own alternative. Here, he says, he has been influenced especially by Wolfhart Pannenberg and George Lindbeck. The former's appeal to the eschatological nature of truth, i.e., to the eschaton as the "time" when truth is established, responds to the reality that "God remains an open question in the contemporary world, and human knowledge is never complete or absolutely certain" (197). Lindbeck's rejection of the "cognitive-propositionalist" and the "experiential-expressive" approaches in favor of a "cultural-linguistic" approach supports Pannenberg's emphasis on coherence (the view that affirms that a structure of thought is believable because its components *cohere*—they hang together). In the shadow of Wittgenstein, Lindbeck in effect insists that doctrines are "the rules of discourse of the believing community. Doctrines act as norms that instruct adherents how to think about and live in the world" (198). Like rules of grammar, they exercise a certain regulative function in the believing community, but they "are not intended to say anything true about a reality external to the language they regulate. Hence, each rule [doctrine] is only 'true' in the context of the body of rules that govern the language to which the rules belong" (198). Lindbeck calls for an "intratextual theology" that aims at "imaginatively incorporating all being into a Christ-centered world" (199).[3] Within evangelicalism, Grenz

---

[2] Stanley J. Grenz and John R. Franke, *Beyond Foundationalism: Shaping Theology in a Postmodern Context* (Louisville: Westminster John Knox, 2000).

[3] Quoting from George A. Lindbeck, *The Nature of Doctrine: Religion and Theology in a Postliberal Age* (Philadelphia: Westminster, 1984), 16. In other words, an *intratextual* theology is concerned to show that all the parts of the (biblical) text cohere to present an ordered structure—but it is not necessarily claiming that what the text ostensibly says about realities *outside* the text is necessarily true.

finds most hope in the work of Alvin Plantinga and Nicholas Wolterstorff, espe-cially in their claim that Christian theology "is an activity of the community that gathers around Jesus the Christ" (201). This constitutes a "communitar-ian turn" in evangelical theology: "we have come to see the story of God's action in Christ as the paradigm for our stories. We share an identity-consti-tuting narrative" (202). This is not the same as old-fashioned liberalism, Grenz asserts, because (1) liberalism was itself dependent on foundationalism, which Grenz rejects; and (2) older liberalism tended to give primacy to experience such that theological statements were mere expressions of religious experience, while in the model that Lindbeck and Grenz are propounding "experiences are always filtered by an interpretive framework that facilitates their occurrence. . . . [R]eligions produce religious experience rather than merely being the expres-sions of it" (202-203). Grenz wants to go a step farther, a step beyond Lindbeck: the task of theology, he argues, "is not purely *descriptive* . . . but *prescriptive*" (203, emphasis his), i.e., it "*ought* to be the interpretive framework of the Christian community" (203). Taking a leaf out of Plantinga's insistence that belief in God may be properly "basic," Grenz writes, "In this sense, the specif-ically Christian experience-facilitating interpretative framework, arising as it does out of the biblical gospel narrative, is 'basic' for Christian theology" (203). This is not a return to foundationalism by another name, Grenz insists, because the "cognitive framework" that is "basic" for theology does not precede the-ology; it is "inseparably intertwined" with it (203-204). The appropriate test becomes coherence, not the disparate and often unintegrated data of founda-tionalism (exemplified, Grenz asserts, in a Grudem).

In all this, Grenz does not want to lose sight of the Bible, which must be the "primary voice in theological conversation" (206). But he wants to dis-tance himself from the modern era's misunderstanding of Luther's *sola Scriptura*. The theologians of the modern era, Grenz says, traded the "ongo-ing reading of the text" for their own grasp of the doctrinal deposit that they found in its pages and which was "supposedly encoded in its pages centuries ago" (206). It is far wiser to incorporate speech-act theory, and be sensitive to what the text *does,* how it *functions,* what it *performs.* "The Bible is the instrumentality of the Spirit in that the Spirit appropriates the biblical text so as to speak to us today" (207). The reading of text, in this light, is "a com-munity event." Grenz agrees with Walter Klaassen: "The text can be prop-erly understood only when disciples are gathered together to discover what the Word has to say to their needs and concerns" (208). Thus if the Bible is the "primary voice," that voice must never be thought of as independent of the culturally bound situation of the community of readers. "The ultimate authority in the church is the Spirit speaking through Scripture. The Spirit's speaking through Scripture, however, is always a contextual speaking: it always comes to its hearers within a specific historical-cultural context. This has been the case throughout church history, for the Spirit's ongoing provision of guidance has always come, and now continues to come, to the community of Christ as a specific people in a specific setting hears the Spirit's voice speaking in the particularity of its historical-cultural context" (209). Thus tradition may play a secondary role, a kind of reference point, as the members of a community of faith recognize that they belong to a community that spans centuries. Moreover, evangelical theologians must not look only to the voice of the Spirit through the Scripture. They must also "listen intently for the voice of the Spirit, who is present in all life and therefore precedes us into the world, bubbling to the surface through the artifacts and symbols humans construct" (210), even though that voice "does not come as a speaking against the text" (210). In short, "We listen for the voice of the Spirit who speaks the Word through the word within the particularity of the hearer's context, and who thereby can speak in all things, albeit always according to the Word who is Christ" (211). This approach is what opens the way, in the wake of foundationalism's demise, "for an evangelical method that views constructive theology as an ongoing conversation involving the interplay of Scripture, tradition, and culture" (211).

Because the "one God, Christians assert, is triune" (212), communitarian focus is mandated. Following "the lead of Reformed epistemologists," then, Grenz declares that the church, the community of believers, is "basic" in theology (214). This in turn "opens the way for introducing *community* as theology's integrative motif. That is, community—or more fully stated, persons-in-relationship—is the central organizing concept of theological construction, the theme around which a systematic theology is structured. Community provides the integrative thematic perspective in light of which the various theological foci can be understood and significant theological issues explored" (214-215, emphasis his). Christian theology is not the theology of the individual, but of the community. "Christian theology must be communitarian, because it is linked to a particular community, namely, the community of the disciples of Jesus" (215).

This leads to chapter 7, whose title ("Theology and Science After the Demise of Realism") does not immediately disclose where Grenz is going. He begins by asking the question, "Exactly *how* are theologians scientists?" (220, emphasis his), and sketches "three paradigmatic Christian theological answers to the question" (220). (1) According to the modern paradigm, theology is like science, emphasizing data, controlled thought-experiments complete with hypotheses to be tested and which are themselves "members of a larger network held together by a [sic] overarching program that consists of certain methodological rules that guide the research process" (227). Grenz argues that this model is no longer tenable, since scientists "are no longer agreed as to what 'the scientific method' in fact entails" (228). (2) According to the medieval paradigm, theology is the queen of the sciences. Perhaps this model reached its apogee with Thomas Aquinas: theology presides over a hierarchy of *scientias speciales*. Although that model is now behind us, a form of it is being given new life today: in this view, "theology brings the sciences together into a unified whole" (232), a stance expounded in detail by Pannenberg. Grenz thinks that although this approach correctly reflects the fact that "the scientific portrayal of the universe is also fundamentally religious in tone" (235), it retains "a potentially problematic objectivist orientation" (235). (3) Under the postmodern paradigm, science is theology. Here Grenz sides with the postmodern writers who insist that scientific method is not as objective and neutral as it thinks it is. Kuhn has taught us to recognize shifting paradigms, and a host of others have insisted on the constructionist elements of science. Science and theology alike are social constructions. So-called "critical realists" may demur and maintain that "scientific theories seek to approximate a natural world that actually exists apart from scientific descriptions of it" (242), but Grenz insists that we do not inhabit the "world-in-itself": social construction is unavoidable. So Grenz concludes that "both theologians and scientists are involved in the process of constructing 'world'" (244).

That raises the question, of course, whether Christian theology can continue to talk about an actual world at all, this side of "the postmodern condition characterized by the demise of realism and the advent of social constructionism" (244). To put it slightly differently, "can Christian theology make any claim to speak 'objective truth' in a context in which various communities offer diverse paradigms, each of which is ultimately theological? . . . Does the move to nonfoundationalism entail a final and total break with metaphysical realism?" (245). Grenz judges that the question is "both improper and ultimately unhelpful" (245). It would be better to ask, "How can a postfoundationalist theological method lead to statements about a world beyond our formulations?" (245). Christians, after all, like critical realists, do maintain "a certain undeniable givenness to the universe" (245). But this "givenness" is not the putative objectivity of what some think of as "the world as it is," but, "seen through the lenses of the gospel, the objectivity in the biblical narrative is the objectivity of the world as God wills it," and which is suggested in the petition, "Your will be done on earth as it is in heaven" (246). And this universe that God wills "is primarily a future, rather than a present, reality" (246); it is the eschatological world, the ultimate new creation. It is the order that cannot be shaken (Heb. 12:26-28), which is "far more real, and hence more objective, than the present world, which is even now passing away (1 Cor. 7:31)" (246). Christians therefore adopt an "eschatological realism," which "gives shape to a social constructionist understanding of our shared human task" (246). "This divine eschatological world is the realm in which all creation finds its connectedness in Jesus Christ (Col. 1:17) who is the *logos* or the Word (John 1:1), that is, the ordering principle of the cosmos as God intends it to be. The centrality of Christ in the eschatological world of God's making suggests that the grammar that constructs the 'real' world focuses on the narrative of Jesus given in Scripture. . . . In short, in contrast to the driving vision of much of modern science, the Christian faith refuses to posit a universe without recourse to the biblical God who is 'the Creator of the heavens and the earth.' And the only ultimate perspective from which that universe can be viewed is the vantage point of the eschatological completion of God's creative activity" (247).

Grenz concludes:

> In the task of viewing the universe from a theocentric perspective, both theology and science play important roles. Through the use of linguistic models that they devise, explore, and test, practitioners of both disciplines construct a particular world for human habitation. For its part, theology sets forth and explores the world-constructing, knowledge-producing, identity-forming "language" of the Christian community. The goal of this enterprise is to show how the Christian belief-mosaic offers a transcendent vision of the glorious eschatological community God wills for creation, and how this vision provides a coherent foundation for life-in-relationship in this penultimate age. In so doing, theology assists the community of Christ in its mission to be the sign in the present, anticipatory era of the glorious age to come, and to anticipate that glorious future in the present (247).

Chapter 8 turns to other religions. In a postmodern world, the question of the "truth" of Christianity must be posed not only with regard to science but also in conversation with other religions. Initially, Grenz works through the traditional categories used to evaluate whether or not salvation is available in other religions, viz. the categories of exclusivism, inclusivism, and pluralism. Grenz is most sympathetic to inclusivist models. He concludes that the "evangelical heart" deeply desires "to hold out hope that the eternal community will include persons who have been found by the God of the Bible even though they appeared to live beyond the reach of Christian evangelists" (268), while "evangelical zeal" rightly maintains the urgency of evangelism. As for the place of other religions, Grenz's light survey of the biblical material leads him to conclude "that the Bible allows no . . . unequivocal rejection of the possibility of either faith or true worship beyond the central salvation-historical trajectory of Israel and the church. This, in turn, leads to the suggestion that human religious traditions may indeed participate in some meaningful manner in the divine program for creation, even if only in the present penultimate age" (275)—which, I think, means that even if such religions cannot save in the ultimate sense, they may participate, at the present time, in the divine plan to build community: "the providential place of human religious traditions may lie with their role in fostering community in the present" (276).

What, then, of traditional Christian claims regarding the finality of Christ in a pluralist world? Most evangelicals want to privilege the Christian claims by insisting that their theological vision is in fact true. But this, Grenz insists, is to retreat to a foundationalist epistemology. The way forward (with Mark Heim) is not to ask "Which religion is true?" but to ask "What end is most ultimate, even if many are real?" (280-281). Hence Grenz argues:

> The communitarian reminder that the goal of all social traditions is to con-struct a well-ordered society (although the various communities might well differ from each other as to what that society entails) suggests that the truth question is better formulated: Which theologizing community articulates an interpretive framework that is able to provide the transcendent vision for the construction of the kind of world that the particular community itself is in fact seeking? Hence, rather than settling for the promotion of some vague concept of community, the communitarian insight leads to the question, Which religious vision carries within itself the foundation for the community-building role of a transcendent religious vision? Which vision provides the basis for community in the truest [sic!] sense? (281).

As with other community-based visions, "a central goal of the Christian message of salvation is the advancement of social cohesion, which it terms 'community' or 'fellowship'" (281). The goal of life is community, i.e., fellowship with God, with others, with creation, "and in this manner with oneself" (281). All human religions do this to some extent. That, Grenz asserts, is what the Melchizedek story affirms: "wherever people are drawn to worship the Most High God, there the true God is known. And wherever God is truly known, the God who is known is none other than the one who is revealed through Jesus Christ" (281).

Evangelicals go farther. We firmly believe, Grenz says, that the Christian vision sets forth the nature of true community life more completely than any other religious vision. "Viewed from this perspective, the Christian principle of the finality of Christ means that Jesus is the vehicle through whom we come to the fullest understanding of who God is and what God is like. Through the incarnate life of Jesus we discover the truest vision of the nature of God" (283). And if this entire approach may seem to some to undercut any claim to universality, Grenz thinks he can avoid the problem by affirming "the universality of the divine intent," since "God's eschatological goal is not designed for only a select few but for all humans" (283), and God's "eschatological new creation is present in embryonic form in creation, and the seed that will blossom into the renewed inhabitant of the eternal community lies within our human nature as created by God 'in the beginning.' And this is a design or purpose that all humans share. This universal divine purpose for humankind means that insofar as it arises from an understanding of God's intent for us, the Christian vision is for all" (284).

The central line of argument in chapters 6–8 leads to chapter 9, "Evangelical Theology and the Ecclesiological Center." Like many others, Grenz holds that evangelicalism has lacked a strong ecclesiology. Its reliance on parachurch organizations has led to its emphasis on the invisible church, which emphasis has resulted in an impoverished understanding of the empirical church, and therefore a depreciation of true community. Moreover, pressure from ecumenists has led evangelicals to insist that biblical fellowship and biblical unity take place among individual true believers—and this sidesteps the obligation to pursue organizational unity. This leads Grenz to argue for a "renewed missional evangelical ecumenism" (*passim*), characterized by four marks of the church: (1) the church in active mission is apostolic, i.e., it stands in continuity with the apostles' doctrine proclaimed in word and sacrament; (2) the church in mission "is truly catholic, insofar as it is a reconciling community" (320); (3) the church in mission is holy, i.e., it is set apart for God's use and attempts "to pattern life after the example of God" (321); and (4) the church in mission "is intended to exert a unifying effect" (321).

The final chapter, somewhat briefer and more diffuse than the others, calls for the church of Jesus Christ to be characterized by a "generous orthodoxy" (*passim*). Grenz wants us to abandon what he calls the two-party paradigm of people who are "in" and people who are "out": the dichotomy, he says, cannot be sustained in a postmodern age, and so is *"dangerously* anachronistic" (330, emphasis his). He quotes with approval the comment of Gerald T. Sheppard regarding the older paradigm: "A common historical, referential grammar supported their conflict on political, ethical, and doctrinal matters. One side or the other could thus be deemed right or wrong. Conflict over 'truth' made sense" (330). Grenz concludes:

> The postmodern condition calls Christians to move beyond the fixation with a conflictual polarity that knows only the categories of "liberal" and "conservative," and thus pits so-called conservatives against loosely defined liberals. Instead, the situation in which the church is increasingly ministering requires a "generous orthodoxy" characteristic of a renewed "center" that lies beyond the polarizations of the past, produced as they were by modernist assumptions—a generous orthodoxy, that is, that takes seriously the postmodern problematic. Therefore, the way forward is for evangelicals to take the lead in renewing a theological "center" that can meet the challenges of the postmodern, and in some sense post-theological, situation in which the church now finds itself (331).

This "center" to which Grenz is calling us is not the "center" of political power, of being at the heart of the nation's life, but is "a *theological* center, and the quest to renew the center involves restoring a particular *theological* spirit to the center of the church" (333). Because of his emphasis on "convertive piety" as one of the core values of evangelicalism, Grenz argues that even the great turning points in evangelical history—the magisterial Reformation, Puritanism, the rise of Pietism—were not "greatly concerned about full-scale doctrinal renewal" (339-340). "These were not doctrinally oriented reform movements in the strict sense. The concern of the Reformation was to return the gospel of justification by faith alone to the church; the intent of Puritanism was to restore a duly constituted church; and the burden of the Pietists was to place regeneration or the new birth at the heart of the church. Apart from these emphases, the precursors of evangelicalism were content to accept the orthodox doctrines hammered out in earlier centuries of church history" (340). What finally "gave impetus to the introduction of a concern for doctrinal renewal into the fellowship of purveyors of convertive piety was the modernist-fundamentalist controversy" (340). The emergence of the postmodern situation calls us to rethink such priorities and return to our roots as a people of convertive piety, "calling the whole church to a generous orthodoxy that is truly orthodox" (340). "Understood as the constellation of beliefs that forms the Christian interpretive framework, sound doctrine plays a crucial role in the life of faith" (344).

"Doctrine, then, is the set of propositions that together comprise the Christian belief-mosaic. But the task of formulating, explicating, and understanding doctrine must always be vitally connected to the Bible, or more particularly, to the biblical narrative" (345)—but we must recognize that "every telling of the narrative always takes the form of an *interpreted* story" (345).

As for catholicity, "the language of a renewal of the center that is catholic in vision can no longer limit itself to self-consciously evangelical or even Protestant denominations" (347). The postmodern, global reality in which we live calls us to be a renewal movement that transcends such limitations (350).

CRITIQUE

If the success of a book is measured by the extent to which readers want to argue with it, then this reader at least must judge *Renewing the Center* to be a highly successful book. At the very least, Grenz has helped me to sharpen my thinking by forcing me to analyze where and why I agree or disagree with him.

To engage him fully would require a book as long as his. But perhaps some progress will be made if I focus on the following points.

(1) Almost every time Grenz offers historical judgments, they are deeply tendentious, in need of serious qualification, or simply mistaken. One might ask if the delineation of "trajectories" is the best approach. One might appeal to other models, e.g., expanding concentric circles, or shifting centers in overlapping fields. But even if one prefers trajectories, one must ask if the trajectories that Grenz develops accurately reflect evangelicalism. Is it true, for instance, that Puritanism, which gave us the Westminster Confession, was relatively uninterested in doctrine, but was primarily characterized by "convertive piety"? How deep are the changes from Calvin to Calvinist scholastics? The answers are disputed, of course, but in the light of serious works of scholarship that discern more continuity (e.g., Joel Beeke), we have a right to expect more than reductionistic labeling.

The problem is deeper. One must ask how "evangelical" and "evangelicalism" should be defined. Today there are several schools of thought. Without arguing the case, Grenz adopts a sociological/historical approach, following William Abraham. The result is that "evangelicalism" is a word that applies to various groups that think of themselves as evangelicals—and this means that Grenz is able to smuggle into the rubric various contemporary scholars and movements whom *no* evangelical thinker would have admitted as "evangelical" a mere half-century ago. I have long argued that "evangelicalism" must be defined first and foremost theologically, or else it will not be long before the term will become fundamentally unusable to its core adherents.

I must mention two more examples where Grenz's historical analysis controls his discussion and yet is highly questionable. Grenz argues that in the nineteenth century the Princetonians transformed the doctrine of Scripture from an article of faith into the foundation for the faith, into the "primary fundamental."[4] A decade and a half ago, a small group of scholars, well exemplified by Jack Rogers and Donald McKim, tried to convince the world that the Princetonians had transformed the historic doctrine of Scripture into an indefensible precisionism, an indefensible inerrancy. Their own historical errors were nicely put to rest by John Woodbridge and others, whose close knowledge of the primary sources dealt this revisionist historiography a deathblow. The result is that no one of stature makes the same mistake today. But now Grenz is attempting his own wrinkle. The Princetonians may not have changed the doctrine, but they elevated it from one article of faith to the foundation for faith. I very much doubt that this sweeping claim can be sustained. The Princetonians had more to say about Scripture than some of their forebears, precisely because that was one of the most common points of attack from the rising liberalism of the (especially European) university world. Beyond this, I suspect that even-handed reading of the evidence would not find Hodge or Warfield adopting a stance on Scripture greatly different from that of Augustine or Calvin, so far as its role in the structure of Christian theology is concerned.

More importantly for his book, Grenz sets up the polarities Henry/Ramm, Erickson/Pinnock, and Grudem/Sanders. Grenz does not ask which member of each pair represents the greater bulk of evangelical thought.

---

[4] This is the first place where Grenz responds. He points out, rightly, that what he actually wrote was that "the character of the Scripture focus among many evangelicals today is also the product of the approach to bibliology devised by the Protestant scholastics, which transformed the doctrine of Scripture from an article of faith into the foundation for systematic theology. The nineteenth-century Princeton theologians appropriated the scholastic program in their struggle against the emerging secular culture and a nascent theological liberalism. Drawing from this legacy, turn-of-the-twentieth-century fundamentalism elevated doctrine as the mark of authentic Christianity, transformed the Princeton doctrine of biblical inspiration into the primary fundamental, and then bequeathed the entire program to the neo-evangelical movement." He objects, fairly enough, that he actually used the expression "the primary fundamental" *not* of the Princetonians but of the fundamentalists who followed them. But my criticism is far deeper than this response recognizes. He insists that the Protestant scholastics "transformed" the doctrine of Scripture, that the Princetonians "appropriated the scholastic program," and that the fundamentalists then "transformed the Princeton doctrine . . . into the primary fundamental." That is a lot of transformation. Since in this reconstruction the Protestant scholastics had already "transformed the doctrine of Scripture from an article of faith into the foundation for systematic theology," I am not entirely clear what it means to say that the fundamentalists then turned Scripture into "the primary fundamental"—and that, plus reasons of space, is why I truncated the argument. I am entirely happy to expand it—but the thrust of my criticism remains unchanged. There is a competent and detailed literature that shows that a "high" view of Scripture is paradigm-independent, or, more accurately, that it keeps recurring in every century of the Christian church.

In the last case (Grudem/Sanders), I'm not sure that either is highly representative, and, in historical terms, I'm not even sure that Sanders should be called "evangelical" at all. To assert that Ramm and Pinnock represent a more "irenic" tradition than Henry and Erickson is wrongheaded: their writings are not more "irenic" than those of their respective opposites, but are open to more stances not historically central, or in some cases even admissible, to traditional evangelicalism. It is tendentious to say that theologian X is more "culturally engaging" and "irenic" than theologian Y, if both engage the culture a great deal and with respect but X absorbs more of it into his or her system than Y. That may simply prove that X is more compromised than Y—but in any case, the point must be evaluated and argued, not simply blessed with positive adjectives or cursed with negative ones.[5]

These and other historical misjudgments would be merely irritating if they were not being used to determine the direction of Grenz's argument.

(2) Grenz is right to see that at the heart of postmodernism lies a profound shift in epistemology. But postmodern epistemology has been shaped by several streams, including the hermeneutical analysis of the Germans and the linguistic/deconstruction priorities of the French. Interestingly enough, these trends are now being trimmed in their own countries. Grenz focuses almost exclusively on analyses of postmodern epistemology that think of all "knowledge" in terms of social construction (a predominantly American approach).

But there is a more fundamental flaw in Grenz's approach to postmodernism. He is utterly unable to detect any weakness in postmodern epistemology, and therefore all of his prescriptions for the future assume the essential rightness of postmodernism. Postmodernism has displaced modernism: the latter was so wrong Grenz can say almost nothing good about it, and the former is so right Grenz can say almost nothing bad about it. The approach is like a 1950s western: there are light hats and dark hats, and everywhere the reader knows in advance which side is going to win.[6]

---

[5] It is true, of course, as Grenz points out, that he can later in his book use the term "irenic" of Grudem, and this sort of detail prompts him to insist that I have misunderstood or misrepresented his polarities. It seems to me this usage simply shows he can use the word in different contexts. Nevertheless, I happily encourage readers to reread chapter 3 of *Renewing the Center* to determine if my summary of the polarities that Grenz proposes is in the slightest unfair or misleading.

[6] In his riposte, Grenz insists he nowhere vilifies modernism, but merely wants to create "an apologetic theology that brings classic orthodoxy into conversation with the contemporary situation" (to use the language that he himself cites from his book [183]). I heartily agree that that is Grenz's *motive*. But it is not his motive with which I disagree. I have no doubt he thinks that what he is doing is in line with what theologians have long done. My criticism is that by dismissing modernist epistemology as out-of-date and no longer tenable, and buying into postmodernism, he is in danger of repeating the errors of the modernists he criticizes—constructing a form of Christianity that is so deeply indebted to a reigning

In particular, wittingly or otherwise Grenz has bought into one of the fundamental antitheses embraced by postmodernism: either we can know something absolutely and omnisciently, or our "knowledge" of that thing is nothing more than a social construction that has the most doubtful connection with reality, i.e., with the thing-in-itself. If you think that this antithesis is a convincing analysis of the alternatives, then you will be driven to a pretty radical postmodernism, because one can always show that human beings know nothing omnisciently— so if the antithesis is reasonable, there is only one alternative left. Postmodernism is entirely right to remind us that all human knowing is necessarily the knowledge of finite beings, and is therefore in some ways partial, non-final, conditional, dependent on a specific culture (after all, language itself is a cultural artifact). But nuanced alternatives abound to the absolute antithesis so beloved of postmoderns and everywhere assumed by Grenz. Various scholars have developed the hermeneutical spiral, the pairing of "distanciation" and "fusing of horizons," asymptotic approaches to knowledge.[7] All of these have argued, convincingly and in detail, that notwithstanding the genuine gains in humility brought about by postmodernism, finite human beings may be said to know some things truly even if nothing absolutely/omnisciently.

Quite frankly, it is shocking that Grenz does not engage this very substantial literature. He has bought into a simplistic antithesis, and he never questions it. This leads him to a merely faddish treatment of science. For instance, why does he not engage with Kuhn's critics, who appreciate his contribution but carefully surround the insights into paradigmatic shifts with convincing qualifications?[8] To cite Polkinghorne to the effect that scientific method cannot be reduced to some mere formulation is not the same as saying that no knowledge of the objective world has been gained, even if that

---

epistemology that it sells something of its birthright. That is clearly what Grenz thinks has happened within modernism (hence his discussion, for instance, on how later groups of modernists "transformed" the doctrine of Scripture). That some modernist Christians *did* err in this way cannot be gainsaid; my fear is that some postmodern Christians are repeating the error within postmodernism. True, Grenz says he wants a critical appropriation of postmodernism. What is it within postmodernist epistemology, then, that he will happily criticize and reject? And does he espouse a similarly critical appropriation of modernism? I think a fair reading of him is that he constantly gives reasons why we must abandon modernism and any theology he thinks is too tightly tied to it, and constantly espouses what he judges to be the entailments of postmodern epistemology, without a whiff of rigorous critique of postmodernism itself. Why should we think that *any* epistemological "ism" this side of the new heaven and the new earth, still in a broken and noetically flawed world, should be embraced so warmly? Surely thoughtful Christians, though they may see some strengths in both modernism and postmodernism, will want to embrace neither as wholeheartedly as some earlier theologians embraced modernism and as Grenz embraces postmodernism.

[7] For systematic treatment of these and other approaches, see my *The Gagging of God: Christianity Confronts Pluralism* (Grand Rapids, Mich.: Zondervan, 1996).

[8] See, for instance, Gary Gutting, ed., *Paradigms and Revolutions: Applications and Appraisals of Thomas Kuhn's Philosophy of Science* (Notre Dame, Ind.: University of Notre Dame Press, 1980); Frederick Suppe, ed., *The Structure of Scientific Revolutions,* 2nd ed. (Urbana: University of Illinois Press, 1977).

knowledge is not the knowledge of omniscience. The fundamental data of the periodic table, for example, are beyond cavil. Even the big paradigm shifts, such as the move from Newtonian physics to relativity, do not, interestingly enough, overthrow everything in the earlier paradigm. Thus Newton's equations continue to hold good for many bodies in limiting conditions. "Critical realism" receives short shrift; the nature of empirical testing of hypotheses is not adequately explored; the differences between a "hard" science and historical disciplines are not probed. The different branches of knowledge are merely social constructions, and that is all there is to it. The element of truth in this postmodern assertion, of course, is that human beings are finite, and therefore their knowledge is never absolute/final/omniscient. Moreover, all human articulation is necessarily within the bounds of some culture or other, and can thus truly be said to be a social construct. But to run from this fair observation to the insistence that it is improper to talk about objective truth, or about human knowledge of truth, is merely a reflection of being hoodwinked by that one untenable antithesis. We may not know truth with the knowledge of omniscience, and insofar as postmodernism has reminded us of this, it has debunked some of the idolatry of modernism. But that is not the same thing as saying that we can know some things truly, even if nothing omnisciently. We can know that the water molecule is made up of two atoms of hydrogen and one of oxygen, that Jesus Christ died on the cross and rose from the dead, that God is love, and countless more things. We cannot know any of them omnisciently, but we can know them truly. Think of the many things the Bible says that believers do know, know to be the truth, and are obligated to pass on to others *as the truth*. Grenz does not discuss such texts, or use them to temper the postmodern antithesis that has snookered him.[9]

(3) Grenz tries to avoid the postmodern antithesis by having recourse to Pannenberg. "In this world human knowledge is never complete or absolutely certain," he writes, and opts for the certainty of the eschatological world, the ultimate world, the world that is not passing away, and argues that this eschatological reality can ground our epistemology.

But there is a triple problem. *First,* one might reasonably ask how one *knows* that the eschatological reality will put everything to rights. One knows this only because of the specific revelation that has been given us in Scripture. But the same Scripture gives us revelation about the past and present, too, and about atemporal truths. If we can know enough about the

---

[9] Although I have read his riposte several times, and the relevant parts of his book many times, there is nothing in the foregoing paragraphs I would want to change. I think that my analysis of Grenz's approach is right—and the fact remains that Grenz does *not* treat the countless texts that speak of truth (even propositional truth), of knowing true things, etc., and then integrate them into his discussion.

future, through Scripture, to let its promise ground our epistemology (even though our knowledge of that future is not omniscient), why not say something similar about other things that are revealed in Scripture?

Second, Grenz introduces a category mistake. The fact that this world is passing away while the eschatological world is final and eternal does not mean that the latter is more "real" than the former, and is therefore something better known. That is to confuse the category of temporality with the category of reality. Something that is temporary, while it (temporarily) exists, is just as "real" as something that is eternal.[10]

Third and most important, even when we arrive in the eschaton, we will never be more than finite beings. Omniscience is an incommunicable attribute of God. True, we will no longer be blinded by sin, and we will be living in a transformed order of perfection. But we will *never* enjoy absolute/omniscient knowledge. (Incidentally, the closing verses of 1 Corinthians 13 do not challenge this point. Paul insists that the eschaton brings unmediated knowledge, not omniscient knowledge.) If finiteness is the grounding for the epistemological limitations so beloved by postmodernists, the new heaven and the new earth will not enable us to escape them. So why does Grenz think they will?[11]

(4) Grenz's reliance on Lindbeck is even more troubling. Doctrines are rules of discourse "not intended to say anything true." They are the rules of discourse that constitute the "belief mosaic" of the believing community. But this is a mistake of the first water. The Bible does not encourage us to think

---

[10] "Despite this objection," responds Grenz, "I stand by the perspective set forth in *Renewing the Center*, for I believe that it reflects the outlook of Scripture. Moreover, giving priority to the eternal, understood in the sense of what will abide forever, places me squarely within a long tradition of Christian thought from Augustine to C. S. Lewis." It certainly does, and I stand within that tradition as well, emphatically so. But "giving priority" to the eternal does not make it better known. This is merely to confuse priority with epistemology.

[11] Grenz's response to me on these matters is especially thin, I fear: "This leads to what may in fact be the fundamental point at which Carson and I disagree. Much of what I write in *Renewing the Center* is driven by the desire to call us to elevate God's eternal purposes, God's *telos* for creation, as the ultimate perspective from which the world ought to be viewed. As a consequence, I want to deny any final autonomy to the human knowing project outside of Christ. Carson's review suggests to me that in the end he is critical of my stance regarding what is 'real' not so much because he thinks that it is unbiblical, but because he does not share my perspective regarding the centrality of theology and he is not sympathetic to my rejection of the autonomy of the human sciences. It [*sic*] can only surmise that at least here he retains many of the epistemological and ontological assumptions of modernity, despite the disclaimer that comes near the end of his review." For the life of me I cannot fathom how anything I have said suggests I am not committed to "the centrality of theology" or that I myself uphold "the autonomy of human sciences." Meanwhile, Grenz has not responded to the central points. To say that God's eternal purposes constitute the ultimate perspective from which everything must be viewed is true, indeed for the Christian a truism. But how do we know what those purposes are? Indeed, how do we know that we *ought* to view things from that perspective? Christians appeal to what God has revealed about such matters in Scripture—the same Scripture that also tells us true things, *from God's perspective*, of our past, our present, of facts in history (like the death and resurrection of Jesus). Grenz weaves together his response as if, because I have disagreed with him, it can only mean that I want to affirm the "final autonomy to the human knowing project outside of Christ." Astonishing. Meanwhile, the points I have raised remain entirely unanswered.

that we are saved by ideas that have no extratextual referentiality, i.e., that do not refer to realities beyond the text. We are not saved by ideas (doctrines) that are merely the discourse rules of a believing community. We are saved by the realities to which those ideas refer. Anything else is a merely intellectualist game, and is not the gospel.

For some time I have been wondering if I should write an essay with the title, "The Bibliolatry of George Lindbeck." The point is that even the most right-wing fundamentalist thinks that the Bible refers to realities beyond the ideas themselves that are found on the Bible's pages. In that sense, no fundamentalist can rightly be charged with bibliolatry, since the Bible is not the ultimate object of veneration, but rather the realities to which the Bible refers (God, Christ, Christ's death and resurrection, etc.). But if Lindbeck denies that biblical extratextual referentiality is crucial and utterly essential to faithful Christian existence, he uses the Bible as no fundamentalist ever does: he goes back to the Bible, and stops. That is bibliolatry. (It may be that in some of his very recent essays, Lindbeck is beginning to change his mind; I'm not sure. But this is irrelevant in a review of Grenz, since Grenz does not attempt to trace the development of Lindbeck's thought.)

This should have warned Grenz that there is something wrong with postmodernism, at least that form of postmodernism that buys into the crucial antithesis I have already discussed. But it doesn't. So eager is Grenz to avoid saying that what the Bible says at any point is *true* or *authoritative* or *binding* that the most he can affirm is that the Bible is our "primary communication partner." Contrast the ways in which, say, Jesus and Paul can speak of the truth and the binding authority of antecedent Scripture. Appeal to speech-act theory will not free Grenz from the dilemma. For speech-act theory, however useful it is at helping us to understand the diverse ways in which language actually functions, certainly does not deny that one of the things that language does is tell us true things. Nor does it help to tell us that the ultimate authority is the Spirit speaking through Scripture—at least not when we are promptly told, first, that the Spirit speaks through everything in the creation, and second, that all of the Spirit's speaking is a contextual speaking. There are vague senses, of course, in which these claims are correct, but they actually misdirect the argument and hide the fundamental issues.[12] In one sense,

---

[12] It is precisely the context of such discussions that is troubling because it is so vague. In his rebuttal, Grenz says that by linking Word and Spirit he is doing no more than what the Westminster Divines do. "My proposal, therefore, is an attempt to return to the Reformation, with its close linking of Word and Spirit." Just about everyone "links" Word and Spirit; the burning question is the nature of the link. Reread from the Westminster Confession of Faith chapter 1, "Of the Holy Scripture," with its final reference to "the Holy Spirit speaking in Scripture," and ask whether or not the link that the Westminster Divines were trying to forge is the same link that Grenz says he is trying to forge.

for instance, it would be entirely correct to say that God himself holds the ultimate authority. But that does not sort out for us what role Scripture must play in our knowledge-formation. It is correct to say that all interpretations of Scripture are shaped by the context of the interpreter: postmodernism is right to remind us of our finitude, our dependence on specific languages, and so forth. But unless one buys into that one unconscionable antithesis which I have already dismissed, it does not follow that we cannot know some true things from Scripture, or that we cannot be shaped by it both in our beliefs and in our conduct, or that Scripture itself, precisely because there is an omniscient Mind behind it, cannot be objectively authoritative. Certainly that is the way Scripture views Scripture. Grenz's reformulation of the doctrine of Scripture is so domesticated by postmodern relativism that it stands well and truly outside the evangelical camp (whether "evangelical" is here understood theologically or socially/historically).[13]

By chapters 9 and 10, Grenz eventually recalls enough of his evangelical roots that he says encouraging things about the incarnate Jesus being the truest vision of God, and the new creation being embryonic in the old creation, and the importance of adhering to the apostles' doctrine, and even the importance of holding to "sound doctrine." Still, it is difficult to avoid the impression that what the right hand giveth, the left hand taketh away. For instance, the reference to "sound doctrine" is lodged in a crucial sentence:

---

[13] Grenz responds to these criticisms by saying that my engagement with his book is marred by a misunderstanding of the *reason* (emphasis his) why he introduced Lindbeck and Pannenberg into the discussion. He charges me with thinking that he has bought into Lindbeck uncritically. "By assuming that I must be saying what Lindbeck is saying," Grenz writes, "Carson fails to see that one key purpose of my book is to move beyond, or to correct, Lindbeck by offering a proposal for understanding the extra-linguistic referential character of Christian doctrine." Dr. Grenz, please show me where, in your book, you correct Lindbeck by offering a proposal for understanding "the extra-linguistic referential character of Christian doctrine." That is *exactly* what I have said is needed, and *exactly* what you did not propose. When you go "beyond" Lindbeck, it is never to insist on the extratextual referentiality of Scripture, but to insist on the prescriptive nature of the Christian tradition for Christians. In other words, those who live within this tradition must abide by it; there is an implicit "ought" to living within this tradition. But Scripture keeps saying that we "ought" to believe certain things, and act on them, because they are *true*. When it comes to the resurrection of Jesus, for instance, Paul in 1 Corinthians 15 does not encourage us simply to live within the tradition of the resurrection, but to recognize that the resurrection of Jesus objectively *happened*—so much so that if we could imagine that it didn't happen, we would have to conclude (a) the apostles are liars, talking about something as if it were true when it isn't; (b) we are still in our trespasses and sins; (c) our faith is vain (no matter how intense or public a tradition it is!); and (d) we are of all people most to be pitied, because we are believing something that isn't *true*. In other words, Paul does not simply say that we must live within the "tradition" (i.e., what has been handed down)—though he can say that—but insists that our faith is properly grounded only if its object is *true*. Now if either Lindbeck or Grenz had asserted that sort of thing, I would feel much happier. But the only way in which Grenz has gone "beyond" Lindbeck, as far as I can see, is by insisting, "There is no generic religious experience, only experiences endemic to specific religious traditions, i.e., experiences that are facilitated by an interpretive framework that is specific to that religious tradition" (203). Within that tradition, "The task of theology is not purely *descriptive* . . . but *prescriptive*" (203). He adds, "The theologian seeks to articulate what *ought* to be the interpretive framework *of the Christian community* [emphasis added]. In this sense, the specifically Christian experience-facilitating interpretive framework, arising as it does out of the biblical gospel narrative, is 'basic' for Christian theology" (203). And still not a word about extratextual referentiality.

"Understood as the constellation of beliefs that forms the Christian interpretive framework, sound doctrine plays a crucial role in the life of faith." But does "sound" mean "true"? What makes the doctrine "sound"? Is it simply the fact that it is part of the belief-mosaic of a peculiar Christian community? *Any* doctrine held by finite human beings is necessarily "interpreted" doctrine, but (apart from that nasty antithesis again) it does not follow that it is unintelligible to assert that the interpretation is true. Moreover, in the light of his earlier reliance on Lindbeck, I wonder how Grenz reaches the conclusion that the incarnate Jesus is the truest vision of God. And precisely *why* should we hold (with both Lindbeck and Grenz) that the Christian interpretative framework is not merely descriptive but prescriptive? Do we hold that simply because we belong to a Christian community where the doctrines in question are part of the essential "grammar" of discourse? Or do we hold those doctrines because they are true, or at very least we claim that they are true? How do we *know* that the one God is triune? On what basis do we assert it? Merely because the "belief mosaic" of one community asserts it? In that case, the lessons that Grenz draws about the importance of being-in-relationship is grounded not on God as he is but on the grammar of discourse of the community. How can the grammar of discourse of the community properly ground the grammar of discourse of the community?

(5) Grenz places enormous emphasis on the Christian community. In part, this is tied to his view that all human "knowledge" is a *social* construct rather than a reflection of reality. But I fear that every major turning point in his argument is weak. Apart from that wretched antithesis, which rises again here (i.e., because human "knowledge" is a social construct, it cannot be claimed to be true), the crucial weaknesses are as follows:

First, Grenz makes a fascinating jump from "is" to "ought." Because postmodernism has taught us that all human knowledge is a social construct, therefore in this postmodern age we ought to emphasize the community. But that misunderstands postmodernism's point. If all human knowledge is a social construct, then the ostensible knowledge gathered by modernism was also a social construct. Postmodernism is arguing that the social construct model is inevitable, not that we should opt for it. If postmodernism is right on this point, then despite what it might have thought it was doing, modernism was as socially constructed as postmodernism. No "ought" is required; the "is" is all-devouring. To put it concretely, if the postmodern claim on this point is correct, then Carl Henry was engaged in the social construction of reality every bit as much as Stanley Grenz is.

Second (although this point is minor), for a writer who says a great deal about the importance of doing theology in community, Grenz has given us a book with a very high proportion of *individual* self-references: "*my* proposal," for instance, is one of his favorite phrases. So I confess I am not certain what he means, in concrete terms, by his advocacy of theology as a communitarian activity.

Third, it is extraordinarily difficult to see on what ground Grenz moves from the church as the *locus* of theological reflection to the church as the *object* of theological reflection. To put the matter slightly differently, even if we agree that theology is properly a communitarian activity, it does not follow that the organizing doctrine of the resulting activity ought to be the community. That is an enormous leap, and logically and methodologically unjustified. Why should it not be, say, God, or Christology, or the cross?

Fourth, it is difficult to avoid the conclusion that this emphasis on the church has blinded Grenz to what the gospel itself is about. Paul does not resolve in Corinth to preach nothing but the church, but nothing but Christ crucified. Tied to this astonishing silence in a book that purports to tell us how to renew the *evangelical* center is a failure to think through and articulate a host of related matters. Can we maintain agreement on what the solution is, for instance, if we cannot agree as to what the problem is? So can we come to agreement about the atonement (Rom. 3:21-26) if we cannot agree on the wrath of God and human guilt (Rom. 1:18–3:20)? At what point do biblically faithful Christians *confront* and *contradict* the world in its current opinions, instead of reshaping the "gospel" so as to parrot the world's agenda? There is very little hint of the perennial urgency of this task in Grenz's volume.

Fifth, although he says some useful things about the influence of parachurch movements (which many are saying these days), the chapter on ecclesiology is a disappointment. It is not that evangelicals have no ecclesiology, but that we have several of them, to some extent mutually contradictory. And one of the reasons for this state of affairs is that one of the characteristics of evangelicalism is that soteriology is elevated above ecclesiology—or, to put the matter differently, soteriology is more determinative of the shape of ecclesiology than the reverse. Traditionally, it is Roman Catholicism that elevates ecclesiology above soteriology. I cannot detect that Grenz is even aware of the danger.

Sixth, Grenz does not give us a rationale for jumping from Plantinga's argument that belief in God is properly "basic" to the conclusion that the community is properly "basic" or that the "specifically Christian experience-facilitating interpretive framework" is properly basic. Unless I am misunderstanding him, Grenz is using "basic" in a manner rather different from Plantinga's usage. In any case, appeal to Plantinga makes a thoughtful reader long for reflection on a related matter. While Plantinga (rightly) rejects foundationalism, his appeal to God as properly "basic" introduces a kind of "soft" foundationalism, a warranted belief for the Christian community, a kind of nonfoundationalist's foundationalism. Plantinga happily talks of this God in extratextual terms: what he means by "basic" is more than what Grenz means. I suspect this matter needs more thought and care.

(6) I shall end with three irritants, with an ascending order of seriousness.

First, here and there the jargon is so thick and fuzzy that I am uncertain if anything substantial or precise is being said. "We listen for the voice of the Spirit who speaks the Word through the word within the particularity of the hearer's context, and who thereby can speak in all things, albeit always according to the Word who is Christ" (211). "This divine eschatological world is the realm in which all creation finds its connectedness in Jesus Christ (Col. 1:17) who is the *logos* or the Word (John 1:1), that is, the ordering principle of the cosmos as God intends it to be" (247).

Second, although I agree that coherence is one of the important elements of any responsible epistemology, for the life of me I cannot see that coherence is less important in modernist epistemology than in postmodern epistemology. To level the charge against Grudem is particularly misjudged. The reason why Grudem thinks it is possible to organize a systematic theology from almost any point is precisely because in his view the truth behind theology, and which theology is meant to discover and expound, is so superbly coherent that the internal ties will eventually take you to the whole anyway. Whether or not this is the best way of thinking about these things is not the point. The point is that coherence is far from being the peculiar preserve of postmodern epistemology. Moreover, to make coherence the ultimate test of a system is shortsighted. Tolkien gives us a very coherent world, but it is not a world so objectively true that it may usefully serve as the proper object of faith. Tolkien in *The Lord of the Rings* is certainly not claiming extratextual referentiality!

Third, Grenz has raised the fine art of sidestepping crucial questions to an annoying level. Recall that Grenz asks the obvious questions, "[C]an Christian theology make any claim to speak 'objective truth' in a context in which various communities offer diverse paradigms, each of which is ultimately theological? . . . Does the move to nonfoundationalism entail a final and total break with metaphysical realism?" (245). That is precisely what must be asked: Can we talk about objective reality, objective truth? But

instead of answering the question, he judges that it is "both improper and ultimately unhelpful" (245). It would be better to ask, "How can a postfoundationalist theological method lead to statements about a world beyond our
formulations?" (245). And that leads him to his Pannenberg-inspired references to the eschatological world, leaving unanswered the question about
whether we can say anything objective about this world. In any case, what,
precisely, is the relationship between our "statements" and this "world
beyond our formulations"? If the expression "world beyond our formulations" is taken in an absolute sense, we cannot say anything about it, so we
may as well stop trying. But if the expression imposes some important limitations that are not absolute, then we are obligated to tease out, as best we
can, the relationships between that world and our statements of it. But that
brings us back to truth claims, and so Grenz punts. Again, he tells us, we must
not ask, "Which religion is true?" but "What end is most ultimate, even if
many are real?" (280-281). Hence Grenz argues (as we have seen):

> The communitarian reminder that the goal of all social traditions is to con-
> struct a well-ordered society (although the various communities might well
> differ from each other as to what that society entails) suggests that the truth
> question is better formulated: Which theologizing community articulates an
> interpretive framework that is able to provide the transcendent vision for
> the construction of the kind of world that the particular community itself
> is in fact seeking? Hence, rather than settling for the promotion of some
> vague concept of community, the communitarian insight leads to the ques-
> tion, Which religious vision carries within itself the foundation for the com-
> munity-building role of a transcendent religious vision? Which vision
> provides the basis for community in the truest [sic!] sense? (281).

But on what ground do Christians claim that their vision for community-
building is best? Isn't that a merely communitarian conclusion? Would, say,
a Muslim community concur? What is the next move? Do we establish merely
sociological criteria to measure our respective communities? But aren't those
sociological criteria merely social constructs? Grenz is trying to have his cake
and eat it. He cannot have it both ways.

Renewing the Center is a bit of a disappointment. Quite apart from its
stance, with which, transparently, I have sometimes disagreed, it has the fla-
vor of the amateurish about it. Nevertheless the questions Dr. Grenz is asking are important. No one reading this review article has the right to hunker
down in traditional modernist epistemology and feel justified in mere cultural conservatism. To the extent that he has exposed the folly of that route

in several of his books, Dr. Grenz has done all of us a considerable service. But it does not seem to have struck him that, just as thoughtful Christians should not permit their epistemology to be held hostage by modernism, so they should not permit their epistemology to be held hostage by postmodernism. There are alternatives, deeply Christian alternatives. Dr. Grenz could serve all of us well with his fluent pen. But he needs to take stock and rethink several matters of fundamental importance before he goes any farther down this trail.

PART TWO

TRUTH, FOUNDATIONALISM, AND LANGUAGE

3

TRUTH DEFINED AND DEFENDED[1]

Douglas Groothuis

"What is truth?" said jesting Pilate; and
would not stay for an answer.
—FRANCIS BACON

TRUTH AND THE EVANGELICALS

In his popular book *A New Kind of Christian*, Brian McLaren sketches a defense of postmodernism for Christians. The book received an "Award of Merit" in the category of "Christian Living" for the 2002 *Christianity Today* book awards. McLaren portrays postmodernism as the only way forward for an irrelevant and hopelessly modernistic evangelicalism. Instead of synthesizing the work of postmodernist-friendly writers through a simplified nonfiction work, McLaren weaves a story in which Dan, a disillusioned Christian considering leaving the pastorate, is strengthened in his faith through his lively interaction with Neo, the winning and winsome protagonist of postmodernism.[2] The narrative format makes the material more stimulating for those not inclined to read weightier treatises and also allows the writer to insinuate and suggest controversial ideas through his spokesman, without stating these ideas plainly through developed arguments. In one significant exchange, Neo tells Dan that

> the old notions of truth and knowledge are being, hmm, I was going to say
> "deconstructed," but we don't need to get into all that vocabulary. The old

---

[1] Adapted and expanded from a forthcoming book by Douglas R. Groothuis, to be published by InterVarsity Press. © by Douglas R. Groothuis. Used by permission of InterVarsity Press, Downers Grove, Illinois 60515.
[2] Stanley Grenz, Leonard Sweet, and Nancey Murphy are all favorably mentioned in the footnotes.

notions are being questioned. New understandings of truth and knowledge that might improve on them haven't been fully developed yet. So, Dan, I'm not saying in any way that truth isn't important. But I am saying that truth means more than factual accuracy. It means being in sync with God.[3]

While Neo claims that truth is "more than factual accuracy," the rest of the book questions whether truth concerns factual accuracy at all. Neo describes modernity—the bogeyman—as "an age aspiring to absolute *objectivity*, which, we believed, would yield absolute certainty and knowledge" at the expense of poetry, narrative, religion, and the arts. It was also "a *critical* age." If you believe in "absolute, objective truth, and you know this with absolute certainty, then of course you must debunk anyone who sees differently from you."[4] Neo believes that evangelicals have taken on the worldview of modernity (despite its criticisms of religion) in that they underscore the notion of objective, absolute, and knowable truth and the need to refute those who disagree with it. This modernistic hangover, according to Neo, must be soundly rejected.

The postmodernist "deconstruction" of objective truth and rationality, on which Neo does not directly elaborate, amounts to this: truth does not lodge in statements that correspond to reality. That modernist notion needs to be deconstructed or reduced to its "true" elements. Truth is a matter of perspective only; it is something that individuals and communities construct primarily through language. If this postmodernist view is accepted, objective truth is ruled out in principle. Truth dissolves into communities, ethnic groups, genders, and other contingent factors. No one "metanarrative" (or worldview) can rightly claim to be a true and rational account of reality. That would be arrogant and impossible.

Neo resonates with this postmodernist model when he attacks the factuality (or truthfulness) of Scripture itself. The Bible contains history, but lacks the modern "concern for factual accuracy, corroborating evidence, and absolute certainty."[5] Dan claims that we should read the Bible "less like scholars and more like humble seekers trying to learn whatever we can from it." We should be less critical and read it in a "postmodern fashion," which is "postanalytical and postcritical."[6] Neo also asserts that the Bible is not our "foundation"[7] nor is it "authoritative" in the modern sense. It is rather a col-

---

[3] Brian D. McLaren, *A New Kind of Christian: A Tale of Two Friends on a Spiritual Journey* (San Francisco: Jossey-Bass, 2001), 61.
[4] Ibid., 17.
[5] Ibid., 56.
[6] Ibid.
[7] Ibid., 53.

lection of useful stories to guide us.[8] The old theological distinctions between liberals and conservatives (who fuss over biblical inerrancy and authority) no longer matter. Seizing the postmodern moment is what matters most.[9]

Since McLaren has already diluted the notion of truth, he must redefine the nature of Scripture to fit these conceptions. The older liberals held to a classic correspondence view of truth and claimed that many biblical statements—particularly those truth-claims related to history and science—failed to correspond with reality.[10] On the other hand, the Christians attracted to postmodernism change the very concept of truth itself and then apply their new concept of truth to the Scriptures. The Bible is then relieved of the pressure to exhaustively conform to an objective and given reality outside itself and outside the perspectives of its readers. The Bible is now "true" in the sense that it is found meaningful by the believing community, that it gives us great narratives, and that it inspires us spiritually. Perfect agreement with fact is no longer an issue. Realizing this, for McLaren and those he represents, means becoming "a new kind of Christian."

In his survey of "the younger evangelicals," Robert Webber dedicates a chapter to their views of apologetics. Here, as with the McLaren volume, one finds a suspicion of viewing Christian truth as objective, propositional, and defensible through compelling rational defense. Webber cites key propositions from Carl F. H. Henry's *magnum opus,* the six-volume *God, Revelation, and Authority* (1976–1983) and summarily announces that younger evangelicals—the cutting edge of the movement, to his mind—simply do not have that focus. These are the statements he cites:

10. God's revelation is rational communication conveyed in intelligible ideas and meaningful words, that is, conceptual verbal form.
11. The Bible is the reservoir and conduit of divine truth.
12. The Holy Spirit superintends the communication of divine revelation, first, by inspiring the prophetic apostolic writings, and second, by illuminating and interpreting the scripturally given Word of God.[11]

Webber, himself considerably older than those he writes about, nevertheless concurs with their rejection of a heavily propositional understanding of

---

[8] Ibid., 52.
[9] Ibid., 148; see also 145.
[10] For a classic critique of the older theological liberalism, see J. Gresham Machen, *Christianity and Liberalism* (1923; reprint, Grand Rapids, Mich.: Eerdmans, 1990).
[11] Cited in Robert E. Webber, *The Younger Evangelicals: Facing the Challenge of the New World* (Grand Rapids, Mich.: Baker, 2002), 97.

Christian truth. Apparently, the old view of truth must go, even as it was articulated by one of the stalwart intellectual pioneers and towering theologians of the evangelical movement.

Some recognize that an objective view of truth is already on the way out and are lamenting it. The American pollster George Barna has reported that only 9 percent of "born again Christians" possess a biblical worldview. He defines such a worldview in the following way:

> A biblical worldview was defined as believing that absolute moral truths exist; that such truth is defined by the Bible; and firm belief in six specific religious views. Those views were that Jesus Christ lived a sinless life; God is the all-powerful and all-knowing Creator of the universe and He stills rules it today; salvation is a gift from God and cannot be earned; Satan is real; a Christian has a responsibility to share their [sic] faith in Christ with other people; and the Bible is accurate in all of its teachings.[12]

Barna further reports that "among the most prevalent alternative worldviews was postmodernism, which seemed to be the dominant perspective among the two youngest generations (i.e., Busters and Mosaics)."[13] These findings drove Barna to write a very basic book on the Christian worldview called *Think Like Jesus,* which he hopes will combat evangelical illiteracy concerning the fundamentals of the Christian faith.[14]

On a more academic note, in their volume *Beyond Foundationalism: Shaping Theology in a Postmodern Context,* Stanley Grenz and John Franke appropriate ideas from the descriptive sociology of Peter Berger and Thomas Luckmann to explain Grenz and Franke's concept of truth. From within the discipline of the sociology of knowledge, Berger and Luckmann write of the "social construction of reality" through language. Berger and Luckmann do not make philosophical claims about the nature of truth, but describe how beliefs are formed and how they function in various social contexts. Strictly speaking, the sociology of knowledge is not about *knowledge* in the philosophical sense (which is a kind of rationally privileged belief), but merely about how beliefs gain plausibility in various cultural settings.[15]

Nevertheless, Grenz and Franke adopt this notion of constructing reality through language for theological purposes. While they grant that there is

---

[12] George Barna, "A Biblical Worldview Has a Radical Effect on a Person's Life," Barna Research Online, December 1, 2003, http://www.barna.org/cgi-bin/PagePressRelease.asp?PressReleaseID=156&Reference=F. Last accessed, February 23, 2004.

[13] Ibid.

[14] George Barna, *Think Like Jesus: Make the Right Decision Every Time* (Nashville: Integrity, 2003).

[15] Peter Berger makes this point in *A Rumor of Angels: Modern Society and the Rediscovery of the Supernatural* (Garden City, N.Y.: Anchor, 1970), chapter 2.

a "givenness to the universe apart from the human linguistic-constructive task" (even postmodernist maven Richard Rorty grants this), they do not consider language as rightly or wrongly relating to an objective reality (the classic correspondence view of truth defined and defended below). Rather, they make the rather remarkable statement that, "The simple fact is, we do not inhabit the 'world-in-itself'; instead we live in a linguistic world of our own making."[16] Furthermore, they claim that there is no "objectivity" understood as "a static reality existing outside of, and cotemporally with, our socially and linguistically constructed reality; it is not the objectivity of what some might call 'the world as it is.'"[17] Instead, "objectivity" concerns only what God will eventually bring about in the future, eschatologically.[18] (This echoes themes from Jürgen Moltmann and Wolfhart Pannenberg, neither of whom affirms biblical inerrancy.)[19] Grenz and Franke, therefore, deny that language can truthfully connect with an extra-linguistic reality outside of itself—the objective world as it now is.[20] This is a significant and momentous departure from any kind of theological realism (the claim that theological statements in harmony with Scripture reflect an objective reality) and the correspondence view of truth (more on this below).

These brief examples should suffice to show that something philosophically significant is afoot among purported evangelicals. The received concept of truth is being challenged and often left behind in favor of postmodern models. This chapter will not systematically identify and challenge questionable statements made by postmodernist-leaning Christians about the nature of truth and how truth relates to Scripture. This will be addressed in other chapters of this book. Rather the present chapter defends a concept of truth that is challenged by those who journey down the postmodern road away from objective truth. This vision of truth is both ancient and logically compelling. Nevertheless, many evangelicals are brushing it aside with little critical engagement. At worst, some evangelicals seem to abandon—or at least

---

[16] Stanley J. Grenz and John R. Franke, *Beyond Foundationalism: Shaping Theology in a Postmodern Context* (Louisville: Westminster John Knox, 2000), 53.

[17] Ibid.

[18] This claim is illogical. If language cannot *now* represent the objective world, why think that language can now represent a *future* world? If language is socially constructed in essence, it remains a construct in reference to future claims as much as it does to present claims. Moreover, the authors want us to believe that their statements about eschatological reality are true *right now*. If so, these words must be more than mere social constructions. If so, it also follows that we do not—as they claim—inhabit a "linguistic world of our own making," but that we have some cognitive claim on the "world-in-itself." So, their perspective seems self-contradictory: they presuppose a view of truth that they explicitly deny.

[19] For a critique of Pannenberg's and Moltmann's eschatology and overall worldview, see, Carl F. H. Henry, *God, Revelation, and Authority* (1976–1983; reprint, Wheaton, Ill.: Crossway, 1999), vol. 6, chapter 1.

[20] For further analysis of this, see R. Scott Smith's chapter in this volume, "Language, Theological Knowledge, and the Postmodern Paradigm."

marginalize—this venerable view of truth simply because many postmodern people are questioning or abandoning it. Here the wisdom of Pascal should chart our course:

> When everything is moving at once, nothing appears to be moving, as on board ship. When everyone is moving towards depravity, no one seems to be moving, but if someone stops, he shows up the others who are rushing on by acting as a fixed point.[21]

THE TRUTH QUESTION

The question of truth has at least two core components. First, what is the nature of truth itself? What does it mean for something—a belief or statement—to be true as opposed to false or nonsensical? These sorts of questions address the metaphysics or "being" of truth. Truth-claims can be made about pedestrian facts (Is it raining today?) or about ancient and consequential worldviews (Which of the many religions is true, if any of them?). Second, since contradictory truth-claims greet us in the religious realm (and elsewhere), truth-claims need to be tested in various ways. This invokes the field of epistemology, or the study of how we know what we know. While this chapter will not address epistemology directly,[22] no epistemology works independently of a theory of truth. Therefore, a rational theory of truth is required for a rational and truth-seeking epistemology, whether applied to philosophy, theology, or any other discipline.

MEANING AND TRUTH

Before assessing the four leading theories of truth, a word is in order on the matter of meaning. For a statement to be true or false—however we understand the concepts of truth and falsity—it must be meaningful; that is, it must put forth an understandable truth-claim. It must stake out a share of reality conceptually, and it must be intelligible. For example, the statement "colorless green ideas sleep furiously" is neither true nor false, because it doesn't advance any statement about anything. The statement may be grammatical, but it is, nonetheless, meaningless. The statement "God is three-in-one" (made by Christians) is meaningful. The statement "God is not three-in-one" (made by Muslims) is meaningful.[23] The statement "There is no God" (made

---

[21] Pascal, *Pensees*, ed. Alban Krailsheimer (New York: Penguin, 1966), fragment 699/382, page 247.

[22] J. P. Moreland and Garrett DeWeese deal more directly with epistemology in their chapter, "The Premature Report of Foundationalism's Demise."

[23] Some have taken the doctrine of the Trinity to be contradictory, but few have claimed it was meaningless.

by atheists) is meaningful. The statement, "There are many gods" is meaningful.[24] Of course, these statements cannot all be true, nor can they all be false. At most only one of these statements can be true.

One must discern the meaning of any given statement—that is, interpret it correctly—if that statement's truth claim is to be discerned and assessed. The refutation of a misinterpreted statement leaves the truth or falsity of that statement untouched. This holds true for entire worldviews as well. Many have misinterpreted the meaning of certain aspects of Christianity and have wrongly attributed to it claims for which it is not guilty. By failing to discern the meaning of Christianity's claims, some have thus rejected it unfairly.[25] In fact, any worldview that is caricatured and then criticized on that basis has not been fairly interrogated. The infamous straw man may raise his ugly head.

THE CORRESPONDENCE THEORY OF TRUTH

Although it can become quite technical in some of its details, the correspondence view of truth—often roughly referred to synonymously as realism[26]— is commonsensical and is employed at least implicitly by anyone who affirms something about reality. Aristotle got to the heart of the matter centuries ago:

> To say of what is that it is not, or of what is not that it is, is false, while to say of what is that it is, and of what is not that it is not, is true; so that he who says of anything that it is, or that it is not, will say either what is true or what is false.[27]

A belief or statement is true only if it matches with, reflects, or corresponds to the reality to which it refers. For a statement to be true it must be factual. Facts determine the truth or falsity of a belief or a statement. This is the nature and meaning of truth. A statement is never true simply because someone thinks it or utters it. We may be entitled to our own opinions, but we are not entitled to our own facts. That would make truth far too easy to achieve, as with relativism. Creating an acoustic blast is one thing; speaking a true statement is another. Believing a statement is one thing; that statement's being true is another. In this sense, truth is an achievement. Not all

---

[24] See Douglas Groothuis, "Meaning," in *Encyclopedia of Empiricism,* ed. Don Garrett and Edward Barbanell (Westport, Conn.: Greenwood, 1997).

[25] On this see Philip J. Sampson, *Six Myths About Christianity and Western Civilization* (Downers Grove, Ill.: InterVarsity Press, 2000).

[26] Not all who hold to some version of realism are happy to endorse what is called the correspondence view of truth, but these differences are fairly technical and do not affect the material that follows. See Alvin I. Goldman, *Knowledge in a Social World* (New York: Oxford University Press, 1999), 60.

[27] Aristotle, *Metaphysics,* book 4, chapter 7.

truth-candidates are elected by reality. Some are defeated. Not all statements hit their targets. Some are off the mark. Noted epistemologist Alvin Goldman likens the relationship of beliefs to truth to betting on a horse race. Whether we bet, or on what horse we bet, is up to us. Who wins the race is not up to us. "Once you form a belief . . . its 'success' or 'failure' is not up to you; that is up to the world, which in general is independent of you."[28] In other words, "only the world confers truth and falsity."[29] A true statement, then, is a "descriptive success," which means that it is faithful to reality.[30] Another way of explaining this is that truth-claims are intentional. This means that they are *about* something or *pertain* to something. They are *directed* at a state of affairs, and, if they are true, they capture that state of affairs conceptually. "God exists" is a statement about God's being there as opposed to being absent. God, then, is the intentional object of the intentional statement "God exists." If a statement fails to find its intentional object, it is false. An example of a statement that fails to find its intentional object (and therefore is false) is, "Albert Gore won the 2000 U.S. presidential election."[31]

TRUTH-MAKERS

Things become somewhat more tricky when we speak of the truth or falsity of statements made in the future tense; that is, when we make predictions about things that do not yet exist. This is not abstruse metaphysics with no purchase on the present. We want and need to know if certain promises are true, particularly those relating to cosmic history and personal immortality. In these cases, we can't claim that a statement such as, "Jesus will come again," is true on the basis that it *now* corresponds to a present or past objective event, since (as of March 2004 when I write this) the event of the Second Coming is future. This differs from the statement, "Jesus lived in ancient Palestine," since that is a past event of objective history. Yet in the case of the Second Coming, the claim is meaningful—it stipulates an intelligible state of

---

[28] Goldman, *Knowledge in a Social World,* 20. In some limited cases, however, one can make a belief or statement true by something one does or says. For instance, if I say, "I am speaking now," my saying this makes the statement true. Similarly, performative utterances make their contents true, as when a minister says, "I now pronounce you husband and wife." (Technically, this is called a "performative utterance.") Or, predictions can help make statements come true, as when someone says to a tennis player that she will win the match, and this, in fact, helps give her the courage to win the match. See Goldman, *Knowledge in a Social World,* 21. But in the cases of the truth of worldviews concerning matters of God, humanity, salvation, and eternity, these kinds of conditions do not obtain.

[29] Ibid., 21.

[30] Ibid., 60.

[31] On statements as intentional in relation to intentional objects, see J. P. Moreland and William Lane Craig, *Philosophical Foundations of a Christian Worldview* (Downers Grove, Ill.: InterVarsity Press, 2003), 136-137.

affairs—and it is certainly true that either Jesus will come back or he won't. Only one of these antithetical realities will happen. So, the statement is not exempted from the condition of being either true or false.[32] The particular truth-value of the statement "Jesus will come again" is still, however, according to the Christian worldview, based on its correspondence to God's perfect knowledge and infallible plan for the world. In addition, the predictive statement will, at some unknown time in the future, correspond to the actual event of the Second Coming by being fulfilled in history.

The truth of moral and logical principles does not correspond to reality in the same way as do statements about observable empirical facts. The law (or principle) of noncontradiction, for instance, is true, not because it corresponds to any one slice of reality (such as my brown desk), but because it corresponds to all of reality. The fact that nothing can be itself and not itself in the same way and in the same respect (A is not non-A) is a universal condition or requirement of existence. It is true at all times and at all places, and must be so. It is a necessary truth; it cannot be false. The truth of the law of noncontradiction further corresponds to the workings of God's mind. God is a God of truth and not of falsehood. God does not contradict himself and cannot deny himself. He knows all things truly and knows that neither his being nor his creation can contain logical contradictions.

Moral statements are also true because they match reality. The statement, "Adultery is wrong" is true because the statement corresponds to the objective, universal, and absolute moral law laid down by God in accordance with his character and the character of his creation. It, therefore, applies to all of reality—to all marriages. We don't verify the wrongfulness of murder in the same way as we verify an individual fact of history (such as the historicity of Christ), but this statement and all meaningful statements about morality are true or false, depending on whether or not they match the moral law. Another way that the truth of moral statements obtains is that they refer not only to the moral *law,* but to objective states of *value.* That is, acts of adultery have the objective moral property of wrong-ness (because they violate the moral law) whenever they occur. On the other hand, acts and attitudes of love in marriage—and in other divinely sanctioned relationships—have the moral value of being good (because they obey the moral law) whenever they occur.[33]

---

[32] Some philosophers debate whether or not a statement about contingent truths concerning the future are true or false before the events they predict occur, but I will not take that up here. For a view that all statements are always either true or false (with a fatalistic implication), see Richard Taylor, *Metaphysics,* 4th ed. (New York: Prentice Hall, 1990).

[33] See Moreland and Craig, *Philosophical Foundations,* 137-138. This paragraph assumes moral objectivism and God's character as the source of the objective moral law.

TRUTH-BEARERS

Truth, then, is an exclusive property that is not shared by all assertions. But what exactly possesses this property? What is a truth-bearer? A truth-bearer must be a unit of conceptual meaning. To grasp this, we need to distinguish sentences from propositions. A sentence may be written, spoken, or thought in the mind (without an external linguistic indicator). Declarative sentences, unlike questions or commands, stake claims on reality by stipulating that such-and-such is the case. A proposition is what a declarative sentence asserts; that is, what it means. Different sentences in the same language may have the same propositional content, such as "Jesus is the Lord" and "the Lord is Jesus." If a sentence is translated faithfully from one language to another—say, from New Testament Greek to English—both sentences mean the same thing; that is, they assert the same proposition. Language cannot get on without propositions, since so much of language involves targeting facts with words.

Therefore, propositions, we might say, are the ultimate bearers of truth; but since our declarative statements and thoughts are propositional by nature, they too, in a derivative sense, are truth-bearers. In a more existential sense, persons may be truth-bearers as well, since persons hold beliefs and make them known through words in speech and writing.[34]

THE BIBLICAL VIEW OF TRUTH

The Bible does not relate a technical view of truth, but it does implicitly and consistently advance the correspondence view in both Testaments. If the Bible presented its own unique, idiosyncratic view of the basic nature of truth— one not generally shared by other worldviews—this would insulate and iso- late the Bible from any assessment of its truth-claims by outsiders, thus making the point of any work of apologetics impossible. Further, if Scripture offered a particular Christian take on the basic meaning of truth, Christianity would be "true" by definition, but only in a trivial sense.[35] Any other world- view could claim its own view of truth and be exempt from criticism.

The Hebrew and Greek words for truth are rich in meaning, but have at their core the idea of conformity to fact. In another sense, God is true to his truth, meaning that he is faithful and will not lie (Heb. 6:18). God is a God

---

[34] The God of the Bible is the ultimate truth-bearer, since he is an infallible and all-knowing mind, who also brings about truths in ways impossible for any other personal being.

[35] See Moreland and Craig, *Philosophical Foundations*, 131. There is a specific Christian understanding of truth broadly understood, but this includes the commonsensical or classic view of truth as correspondence to reality. See Douglas Groothuis, *Truth Decay: Defending Christianity Against the Challenges of Postmodernism* (Downers Grove, Ill.: InterVarsity Press, 2000), chapters 3 and 4.

of truth (Ps. 31:5), whose word is truth (John 17:17). The Holy Spirit is "the Spirit of truth" (John 14:17; 15:26; 16:13) and so will teach us all things. Jesus, the Son of God, is "full of grace and truth" (John 1:17), and declared himself to be "the way, the truth, and the life" such that no one could come to the Father apart from him (John 14:6). The prophets (Jer. 8:8), Jesus (Matt. 24:24), and the apostles (1 John 4:1-6) warn of those who pervert the truth of God through errors and lies. Hence, all of Scripture puts God's revealed objective truth at the solid center of spiritual and ethical life and faithfulness. God's Truth must be learned (Acts 17:11), meditated upon (Psalm 119), and defended (Jude 3; 1 Pet. 3:15-17). Error, whether theological or moral, must be addressed in love (2 Cor. 10:3-5; 2 Tim. 2:24-26), whether this concerns the false beliefs of unbelievers or the false beliefs of errant Christians.[36]

Versions of the correspondence view of truth have been held by the majority of ancient (Plato, Aristotle), medieval (Augustine, Anselm, Aquinas), modern (Descartes, Locke, Hume, Leibniz, Russell), and contemporary (John Searle, William Alston, Alvin Goldman, and Thomas Nagel) philosophers. Nevertheless, two other theories of truth deserve some attention.

DOES TRUTH EXIST? POSTMODERNIST CHALLENGES

Is all this protracted musing on one's orientation to truth, the worth of truth, and the need to courageously seek truth just pseudo high-minded bombast? Is it pretentious philosophizing that is out of touch with contemporary realities? Is the imperious and singular search for Truth something we should shed in favor of opening up the field to many truths? Perhaps it is a will-o'-the-wisp, nothing more than nonsense on very high and deep-rooted stilts. I have addressed the case against the classical view of truth in another work,[37] but a few salient points cry out for attention, lest any attempt to defend the Christian worldview as true end up firmly planted in mid-air.[38]

The case against the concept of truth as it has been explained above is an ancient one. The ancient philosopher Protagoras claimed that "man is the measure of all things" instead of being measured by them. Socrates, of course, didn't take this lying down. Instead, as related in Plato's *Theaeteus,* he quickly dismantled the claim by asking Protagoras a series of philosophically embarrassing questions. Protagoras was a teacher, but who has anything to learn

---

[36] For much more on the biblical view of truth, see Groothuis, *Truth Decay,* chapter 3.

[37] See Groothuis, *Truth Decay,* chapter 4.

[38] Greg Koukl and Francis Beckwith use this expression to describe relativism in their book, *Relativism: Feet Firmly Planted in Mid-Air* (Grand Rapids, Mich.: Baker, 2000). The phrase originally comes from Francis Schaeffer.

from an authority if we determine truth and falsity by mere opinion? Moreover, does not Protagoras disagree with those who deny his proposition? But how can he? "Man is the measure of all things" means that each man is his own measure and there is no measurement apart from his own judgment. And so on.[39] Despite this ancient refutation of Protagoras, his spirit is reincarnated (with a few twists) in a host of postmodernist thinkers.

In recent decades, various philosophers and sociologists have articulated postmodernist views of truth. In a nutshell, postmodernism holds that truth is not determined by its connection with objective reality, but by various social constructions devised for different purposes. Put another way, various cultures have their own "language games," which describe reality very differently. However, we cannot adjudicate which language game or which linguistic "map" correlates more correctly with reality, since we cannot get beyond our own cultural conditioning. There is no objective reality apart from our languages and concepts. To say we know the objective truth is to set up a "metanarrative" that is intrinsically oppressive and exploitative (Jean-François Lyotard). Various "interpretive communities" (Stanley Fish) determine their own truth. Texts, whether religious or otherwise, do not have any fixed, objective meaning; therefore they are neither true nor false in themselves (Jacques Derrida). Truth is what one's colleagues will let one get away with (Richard Rorty) or what the power structures deem to be so (Michel Foucault). Finally, there is no "God's eye view" of anything; therefore, there is no objective truth.

Postmodernist claims come in various forms, and should be evaluated individually, but, since they all reject the correspondence view of truth, they are all subject to several general criticisms.[40] First, metanarratives are not oppressive merely by virtue of being comprehensive truth-claims (or worldviews). At some level, everyone has a worldview or a take on how the world is and how it works. These views may or may not be oppressive toward those who do not hold the worldview. That is a question of the intellectual content (or truth claims) of the worldview in question. The Marxist worldview historically has been very oppressive and un-liberating, despite propaganda to the contrary. The Wahhabi version of Islam, the ideology of Osama bin Laden and his destructive followers, fueled the atrocities of September 11, 2001, and

---

[39] For a very clear treatment of this, see Ronald Nash, *Life's Ultimate Question: An Introduction to Philosophy* (Grand Rapids, Mich.: Zondervan, 1999), 232-250.

[40] For detailed analysis of Derrida, Foucault, Fish, and Rorty, see Millard J. Erickson, *Truth or Consequences: The Promise and Perils of Postmodernism* (Downers Grove, Ill.: InterVarsity Press, 2001).

similar horrors globally. The Christian worldview, while frequently distorted, is not intrinsically oppressive given its ethic of incarnation, love, and justice.

Second, postmodernist pronouncements on rejecting objective truth tend to contradict themselves. These pronouncements claim to be applicable to reality itself, not merely to their own language game or constructed map; yet this is just what postmodernists themselves claim cannot be done. For example, the claim that all metanarratives are oppressive is itself a metanarrative or large-scale explanation of reality. Because of these contradictions, therefore, these kinds of claims are self-refuting and false. Moreover, while deconstructionists of various stripes claim that texts have no fixed and objective meaning, they still object when others "misinterpret" their own writings. But this approach presupposes a *proper* interpretation—based on the author's intended meaning—which becomes the objective standard by which to judge interpretations. If so, the central claim about the endless plasticity of texts cannot be true.[41]

Third, right-thinking people judge certain acts—such as racism, female genital mutilation, rape, child abuse, the murderous terrorist attacks on America on September 11, 2001—as objectively evil, as atrocities, and not as merely relative social constructions. If such assessments are correct, then the postmodern view cannot be sustained logically, since there are no objective moral facts in their view, only endlessly differing interpretations. As some have unwisely said, "One person's terrorist is another person's freedom fighter." This may be so on a descriptive level—there are differing opinions on the moral status of the perpetrators of violence—but it makes no argument about the moral status of the persons involved.

Fourth, by emphasizing the irresolvable diversity of truth-claims, postmodernism provides no reliable criteria to *test* these claims against reality. Instead, it succumbs to a kind of intellectual indifference. Truth is what you (or your culture) make it, nothing more. This stance thwarts the fundamental concern for truth essential for Christian theology, apologetics, and ethics. Although postmodernists have no objective criteria by which to evaluate truth-claims, they nevertheless still make objective moral judgments—even in spite of themselves. After *The New York Times* editorialized against postmodernism in the wake of the terrorist apocalypse of September 11, 2001,[42] Stanley Fish claimed in an op-ed piece later in the same newspaper that his postmodern view did, in fact, allow him to make moral judgments against

---

[41] See Millard J. Erickson, *Postmodernizing the Faith: Evangelical Responses to the Challenge of Postmodernism* (Grand Rapids, Mich.: Baker, 1998), 156.
[42] Edward Rothstein, "Attacks on U.S. Challenge Postmodern True Believers," *New York Times*, September 22, 2001.

such acts. However, he admitted that he had no objective criteria by which to level such judgments, and that none were available.[43] If so, his judgments are nothing more than subjective assertions of value posited within an objective value vacuum.

Although no major religion adheres to the postmodern view of truth, this frame of mind has affected the way in which many people view religious expression. Particularly in nations with religious freedom (especially the United States), the default position for many citizens is that religion is a matter of choice, taste, and preference. One finds a religion that suits him or her, or one is born into a religion that defines who one is. Dialoging about one religion being true or another false is beside the point. All are "true" in the postmodern sense because they give meaning and direction to people's lives. However, when it comes to certain Muslim beliefs on the duty to die in a jihad against the Western "infidels," postmodernist "tolerance" may begin to crack open. This indicates that a total relativism concerning religious beliefs is difficult to sustain.

The postmodernist view also bears on the increasing tendency of some to create their own religions (or "spirituality") by mixing and matching elements of several religions, however incompatible these may be. If spiritual truth is a matter of social or individual construction, then one need not be constrained by logical consistency or by adherence to a received tradition (say Buddhist, Jewish, Christian, or Islamic). There is an element of pragmatism here as well. If it "works" for someone to combine elements of Hinduism (the practice of yoga) and Christianity (church attendance, the golden rule, and prayer), one need not worry about intellectual consistency or spiritual fidelity to an ancient tradition or revealed authority.[44] But this smorgasbord approach lacks intellectual integrity because it makes religious belief something to use instead of something to discover and live by. A genuine truth-seeker should think twice about adopting this kind of nonchalant and self-serving approach and instead pursue something more likely to uncover truth.

Postmodernism often erodes religious confidence. What results is a free-floating spirituality largely devoid of certainty or sustained convictions. The sheer number of religious options combined with the intellectual superficiality of much contemporary religious expression encourages a less committed and less thought-out kind of religious believing. This is seen in the shift from

---

[43] Stanley Fish, "Condemnation Without Absolutes," *New York Times,* October 15, 2001.
[44] On the worldview and dangers of yoga, see Douglas Groothuis, *Confronting the New Age* (Downers Grove, Ill.: InterVarsity Press, 1988), 76-83; and Brad Scott, "Yoga: Exercise or Religion?" *Watchman Expositor* 18, no. 2 (2001); available online at www.watchman.org/na/yogareligion.htm.

"religion" to "spirituality." Religion is deemed as structured, authoritative, exclusive, and rigid. Spirituality, on the other hand, is more customized, subjective, inclusive, and open to pragmatic experimentation. Sociologist Robert Wuthnow speaks of Americans moving from an orientation of "dwelling" within an established religious worldview and set of practices to a spirituality of "seeking," wherein they "negotiate among competing glimpses of the sacred, seeking partial knowledge and practical wisdom."[45] This tentativeness is reflected in one's language about spiritual concerns. When one holds strong convictions on religious matters she will speak of them (or of the most important ones) in terms of "knowledge," "certainty," and other cognitively strong notions. This is what sociologist Peter Berger calls "firm objectivations," which are "capable of supporting world views and ideas with a firm status of objective reality within the consciousness of their adherents."[46] Yet when a strong social consensus making certain religious beliefs plausible breaks down, religious language also loses its intellectual strength. Instead of the "knowledge of God," one speaks of "beliefs," "opinions," or "feelings." Rather than speaking of faith as a way of confident knowing, the "leap of faith" is referred to, along with "religious preference."[47] These kinds of tentative references reveal what Berger calls "the deobjectivation of the religious tradition."[48] Deobjectivation is an ugly sociological word, but it indicates a common tendency exhibited by those suffering under the pressures of postmodern pluralism.

COHERENCE THEORIES: NOT COHERENT

Coherence theories of truth argue that what makes a statement or belief true is its coherence or consistency with one's other beliefs. If my "web of belief" is large and internally consistent—that is, if none of my beliefs contradict each other—my beliefs are true. A belief is false if it fails to cohere with the rest of my beliefs. In other words, truth is simply defined as logical coherence. The main problem with this view is that a set of beliefs held by fallible human beings may be coherent, but false.[49] Suppose all the evidence in a murder case

---

[45] Robert Wuthnow, *After Heaven: Spirituality in America Since the 1950s* (Berkeley: University of California Press, 1998), 3.

[46] Peter Berger, *Facing Up to Modernity: Excursions in Society, Politics, and Religion* (New York: Basic Books, 1977), 174.

[47] Ibid.

[48] Ibid.

[49] In a theological sense, one could say that coherence is the meaning of truth, if one means that whatever is true coheres with the mind of God, since God knows all things with perfect consistency. But this fact does not eliminate correspondence as the meaning of truth, since all true statements correspond with facts, which are either in the mind of God or pertain to other states of affairs.

indicates that the defendant is guilty, but the evidence has been rigged against an innocent person. Then the evidence fails to make its case precisely because it fails to hook up with reality. Further, it is possible for two worldviews to be internally consistent logically (that is, their core affirmations do not contradict each other) and still contradict each other regarding core truth-claims. Even if Islam and Christianity were both internally consistent, they could not both be true in essential beliefs, since Christianity is trinitarian and incarnational and Islam is not. Moreover, two contrasting but internally consistent scientific theories may describe and explain the same phenomena in very different ways. Both geocentrism and heliocentrism may be formulated in logically consistent forms. Yet both cannot be true.

Worse yet for coherence theories, one may hold to the correspondence view of truth in such a way that all one's beliefs cohere with this non-coherence view of truth. On the coherence view, therefore, the correspondence theory—a view that contradicts the coherence theory—would then be true. Of course, this indicates that something is badly amiss with the coherence account of truth.

Coherence or logical consistency cannot be what makes a truth-claim true, although logical coherence is a necessary and negative test for truth. That is, if a worldview contains core beliefs that contradict each other, that worldview must be false. For example, if a worldview claims that all is one (nondualism or monism) and then turns around and equally affirms that there are individuals souls that are reincarnated, that worldview contains a central contradiction and, therefore, must be false. The logical test of coherence concerns epistemology (theory of knowledge), not the nature of truth per se.[50]

PRAGMATIC THEORIES: NOT USEFUL

Pragmatic theories of truth have been advanced (in somewhat different forms) by American philosophers such as Charles Peirce, William James, and John Dewey. Richard Rorty, although considered a postmodernist by many, is an heir to the pragmatist legacy as well, and has influenced at least one evangelical writer significantly.[51] The general pragmatic view of truth deserves some attention given its popularity and because of the philosophical confusions it often brings.[52] To simplify a bit, the general pragmatist claim is that

---

[50] For more critical analysis of the coherence view of truth, see Moreland and Craig, *Philosophical Foundations*, 142-144.

[51] See Philip Kenneson, "There Is No Such Thing as Objective Truth, and It's a Good Thing, Too," in *Christian Apologetics in the Postmodern World*, ed. Timothy Phillips and Dennis Okholm (Downers Grove, Ill.: InterVarsity Press, 1995), 155-170.

[52] This section of the chapter cannot do justice to the different views of truth given by Peirce, James, and Dewey. For a detailed treatment, see Gertrude Ezorsky, "Pragmatic Theories of Truth," in *The Encyclopedia of Philosophy*, ed. Paul Edwards, 8 vols. (New York: MacMillan, 1967), 6:427-430.

a belief is true only if it produces desirable or beneficial effects in the long run. Something is true because it works in various ways found to be favorable. This theory of truth dispenses with considerations beyond some kind of utility. According to William James, a belief's "cash value in experiential terms" is all that counts.[53] One should remember that the pragmatic *definition* of truth differs radically from the claim that some truths may be verified or falsified by experience or evidence. The ways that truth is discovered or verified concern *epistemology*. The pragmatic view of truth under consideration claims that truth *is* what works in some way (it is a metaphysical claim), not that the actual living of life demonstrates some things already to be true and some things already to be false (an epistemological claim).

Defining truth in terms of positive outcomes is untenable for several reasons. Bertrand Russell, among others, provides some helpful reflections on the central claims of the pragmatic view of truth, particularly that of William James. These criticisms are apropos for the navigator of the contemporary postmodern intellectual landscape as well, since when one drops the correspondence view of truth, pragmatic considerations loom large in the selection and maintenance of religious belief.

According to Russell, James requires that a belief be deemed true when its effects are good; that is, when it "works." If this idea is to be useful (which is only fitting, given the pragmatist's view of truth) one must know two things before one knows if a belief is true: (1) what is good; (2) what the effects of this or that belief must be. We must know these things before we have determined whether a belief is true, "since it is only after we have decided that the effects of a belief are good that we have a right to call it 'true.'"[54] But this is deeply problematic. One must measure beliefs by usefulness, yet in many cases we just don't know ahead of time what the usefulness of a belief will be. Russell gives the example of believing that Columbus came to the New World in 1492. According to pragmatism, we cannot just look this up in a book. We have to determine its effects on us. But how can we know what this effect might be ahead of time?[55]

Added to this is the problem of knowing after the fact how beneficial one's beliefs have been. Beliefs have consequences, no doubt; but determining just what the causal connections are between beliefs and effects, and whether or not they are beneficial may be difficult in many cases. Russell gives

---

[53] William James, *Pragmatism and Four Essays from the Meaning of Truth* (Cleveland: Meridian, 1967), 133.
[54] Bertrand Russell, *A History of Western Philosophy* (New York: Simon & Schuster, 1945), 817.
[55] Ibid.

an example: "It is far easier, it seems to me, to settle the plain question of fact: Have Popes always been infallible? than to settle the question whether the effects of thinking them infallible are on the whole good."[56]

Moreover, what does it mean for an idea to "work"? Arthur Lovejoy pointed out that James seems to confuse two senses of what it means for an idea to work. One view is that a theory is verified if it makes true predictions about events. There is nothing objectionable about that. Those who predicted that George W. Bush would win the 2000 presidential election were proved right when he was so elected. In that sense, their prediction worked by being factually verified (which, of course, presupposes the correspondence view of truth). But "working" may simply mean that the individual effects of believing that Bush would be elected are deemed valuable to the individual. Certainly, optimism lifts the soul, but optimistic thoughts are either true or false (in light of the facts), irrespective of how happy or fulfilled they may make anyone.[57]

Russell disputes James's contention that the *meaning* of truth simply is found in its ability to produce desirable states of affairs. This ignores the common understanding of the meaning of truth. Consider the difference between two statements: (1) Other people exist, and (2) It is useful to believe that other people exist. If James's view of truth were correct, (1) and (2) would have an identical meaning; they would be synonymous. That is, they would express the same proposition. But they clearly do not. Therefore, the meaning of truth cannot be a belief's usefulness, even though some beliefs are more useful or fruitful than others.[58]

Furthermore, a belief may "work" and not be true. A woman may believe she lost a large sum of money due to being disorganized. Taken aback, she reforms her life, gets organized, and becomes a successful businesswoman. Later, however, she discovers that the money she thought she lost was in fact stolen by a roommate. Her belief that she lost the money was false, however fruitful the consequence of that false belief may have been.[59]

What makes a belief *true,* according to the correspondence theory, is that it matches reality. So, what makes it true that Columbus existed? It is true because a certain person named Columbus lived in the fifteenth century. This

---

[56] Bertrand Russell, "William James's Conception of Truth," in *Philosophical Essays* (1910; reprint, New York: Simon & Schuster, 1966), 118-119. This essay utterly devastates James's notion of truth and applies to many postmodern accounts of truth as well.
[57] Arthur Lovejoy, "The Thirteen Pragmatisms, II," *Journal of Philosophy* 5 (1908): 29-39; cited in Ezorsky, "Pragmatic Theories of Truth," 428.
[58] Russell, "William James's Conception of Truth," 119.
[59] The inspiration for this example comes from Winfried Corduan, *No Doubt About It* (Nashville: Broadman & Holman, 1997), 60-61.

fact is what makes my belief that he lived in the fifteenth century true. The effects of this belief are irrelevant to its truth-value. But James claims that "On pragmatic principles, if the hypothesis of God works satisfactorily in the widest sense of the word, it is 'true.'"[60] In fact, James thought that various and conflicting religious beliefs could "work" and thus be "true" on the pragmatic theory.[61] Those postmodern evangelicals who abandon the correspondence idea of truth often appeal to the meaningfulness of Christian community—its language, symbols, traditions, and fellowship—instead of any apologetic method that might verify the objective truth of Christianity over against rival worldviews.[62] If so, the postmodernist evangelical would have very little persuasive to say to a member of another religious group (say, a Mormon) who finds that group meaningful and "true" in a pragmatic sense. Russell's comments on this pragmatic conception of religion are on target:

> This simply omits as unimportant the question whether God really is in His heaven; if He is a useful hypothesis, that is enough. God the Architect of the Cosmos is forgotten; all that is remembered is belief in God, and its effects upon the creatures inhabiting our petty planet. No wonder the Pope condemned the pragmatic defense of religion.[63]

Russell bet his life on the proposition that God did not exist, and, having rejected pragmatism, he was clear on the meaning of that proposition.[64] While Russell's naturalism was untrue, his view of truth itself might be instructive to evangelicals sliding down the postmodernist slope.

G. K. Chesterton compactly dispensed with pragmatism as a theory of truth by discerning a paradox within it that related to truly human needs with respect to truth. He observes that the pragmatists are correct in affirming that humans should attend to those truths that bear on their lives: "that there is an authoritative need to believe the things that are necessary to the human mind. But I say that one of those necessities precisely is a belief in objective truth." While the pragmatist tells us to disregard anything absolute, it is the concept of absolute truth that is most necessary to thought. Thus, the pragmatist, who professes to have a humanly oriented and highly relevant philosophy, "makes nonsense of the human sense of actual fact."[65]

---

[60] James, *Pragmatism*, 192.
[61] Ibid., 177-193.
[62] This perspective is increasingly evident in the work of Stanley Grenz in recent years. For a critique of some of his statements to this effect, see Groothuis, *Truth Decay,* chapter 5.
[63] Russell, *History of Western Philosophy,* 818.
[64] For Russell's positive views of truth, see his *Problems of Philosophy* (1912; reprint, New York: Oxford University Press, 1959), chapter 12.
[65] G. K. Chesterton, *Orthodoxy* (1908; reprint, New York: Doubleday, 1990), 36, 37.

Martin Buber, the Jewish theistic philosopher, voiced the same concern:

> One can believe and accept a meaning or value, one can set it as a guiding light over one's life if one has discovered it, not if one has invented it. It can be for me an illuminating meaning, a direction-giving value only if it has been revealed to me in my meeting with Being, not if I have freely chosen it for myself from among the existing possibilities and perhaps have in addition decided with some fellow creatures: This shall be valid from now on.[66]

It is a revelation from a source beyond ourselves that gives the requisite meaning and bearing to our lives. That alone has real value for belief and behavior.

In light of these objections, it should be evident that the pragmatic theory does not describe the nature of truth, nor can it slake the soul's deepest thirst for reality. However, if a belief is true to reality, it should produce effects in keeping with its promises. A true worldview should be livable; it should not commit one to perpetual intellectual and moral frustration. If it does, something is amiss. But this concern is one of several *tests* for truth (in the area of epistemology). Pragmatic results do not *determine* the truth of a belief. Therefore, the pragmatic theory of truth is false and should be rejected—by evangelicals and anyone else serious about matters of truth and falsity.

What is more, any view of truth that makes truth somehow dependent on our culture as a whole or on our minds or wills makes truth something that we (either collectively or individually) create and control. This is the case for all views of truth that abandon correspondence as the essence and meaning of truth. This is the supreme danger of postmodernism—in the church or outside of it. This disregard for reality encourages what Russell called "cosmic impiety":

> The concept of "truth" as something dependent upon facts largely outside human control has been one of the ways in which philosophy hitherto has inculcated the necessary element of humility. When this check is removed, a further step is taken on the road towards a certain kind of madness—the intoxication with power.[67]

Russell is on to something deep and rich—a truth about truth and untruth. When people untether themselves from any responsibility to get reality right, to be true to the truth come what may, they forfeit the humility of being

---

[66] Martin Buber, *The Eclipse of God* (New York: Harper & Row, 1952), 70.
[67] Russell, *History of Western Philosophy*, 828.

beholden to a reality outside of themselves—a reality which may prove one right or prove one wrong, but which one does not command. One must rather obey—or disobey. Whether one is an atheist or a theist or anything else, cosmic piety means submission to the truth of the cosmos—and whatever may be beyond it as well.

CORRESPONDENCE VINDICATED

Examined against the standard of the correspondence theory of truth, the coherence, pragmatic, and all noncorrespondence theories of truth clearly fall short. A set of beliefs may be internally coherent and not match reality. A set of beliefs may produce some good outcomes (at least in this life) and fail to connect with reality in important ways. A culture may construct beliefs that grant it meaning and significance—e.g., the idea that if one perishes in an Islamic jihad one goes directly to paradise—yet those beliefs may be false in light of the facts. We are, then, left with the reality of the truth—truth that is recalcitrant and resistant to any coercion. Christians, of all people, must swear allegiance to the notion that truth is what corresponds to reality—and we must do so unswervingly whatever the postmodern winds of doctrine may be blowing in our faces. Whenever postconservative evangelicals depart from the correspondence view of truth—which is both biblical and logical—and thus sink into the postmodernist swamps of subjectivism, pragmatism, or constructivism, they should be lovingly but firmly resisted. Nothing less than the integrity of our Christian witness is at stake.

4

THE PREMATURE REPORT OF FOUNDATIONALISM'S DEMISE

J. P. Moreland and Garrett DeWeese

ONE UNIFYING THEME OF postconservative theology is the conviction that foundationalist epistemology is passé. We believe that this assessment is wrong and that the rejection of foundationalist epistemology is a serious mistake. In this chapter we will examine the reasons postconservatives give for abandoning foundationalism and will find them wanting. Then we will make a positive case for a modest foundationalism that we believe is clearly superior to the postconservative communitarian/coherentist alternative, showing that, in the important test case of perception, such an account explains how we are able to have knowledge of external reality that is not mediated by social or linguistic conventions.

I. THE "DEMISE" OF FOUNDATIONALISM?

As they assert "the demise of foundationalism," Stanley Grenz and John Franke observe with irony, "How infirm the foundation."[1] Rodney Clapp claims that foundationalism has been in "dire straits" for some time, avowing that "few if any careful thinkers actually rely on foundationalist thinking," even though they cling like addicted smokers to "foundationalist rhetoric." Says Clapp, evangelicals "should be nonfoundationalists exactly because we are evangelicals."[2] Nancey Murphy is concerned to justify a "postmodern" theological method in the face of "a general skeptical reaction

---

[1] Stanley J. Grenz and John R. Franke, *Beyond Foundationalism: Shaping Theology in a Postmodern Context* (Louisville: Westminster John Knox, 2001), 38. Grenz and Franke use the phrase "the demise of foundationalism" ten times in the first fifty-four pages (part 1) of the book.
[2] Rodney Clapp, "How Firm a Foundation: Can Evangelicals Be Nonfoundationalists?" in *Border Crossings: Christian Trespasses on Popular Culture and Public Affairs* (Grand Rapids, Mich.: Baker, 2000), 19-32.

to the demise of foundationalism in epistemology."[3] There is no need to multiply examples. What prompts the postconservative rejection of foundationalist epistemology?

The Postmodern Context

Postconservative theology represents an attempt to learn from postmodern critiques of modernism and to develop a theological method which takes seriously those critiques. The defining motif of postmodernism, in the famous slogan of Jean-François Lyotard, is "incredulity toward metanarrative."[4] The result is an aggressive pluralism that refuses to privilege any culture, any canon, any moral code, or any philosophical or theological system. The only intolerable claim in the postmodern ethos is the (modernist) claim to objective truth. But since foundationalist epistemology, allegedly fathered by René Descartes, aims at justifying objective truth claims, it too is intolerable.

Postconservatives seem to have swallowed this line of reasoning, and so seek an epistemology and a corresponding methodology that is anti-foundationalist. Whether the result will be more palatable in the postmodern context remains to be seen. But in our view, the question of the *adequacy* of anti-foundationalist epistemology is more important than its *acceptability*. To understand the reasons offered by postconservatives for rejecting foundationalism, we must begin with an understanding of foundationalism itself.

Foundationalism

A significant aspect of our self-understanding is that we are creatures who believe things. Our beliefs may be categorized as either true or false, and at least some of our true beliefs count as knowledge.

Traditionally—and rightly, we believe—knowledge has been taken as "justified true belief." For an item to count as knowledge, mere true belief is not enough. Accidentally true beliefs can't count as knowledge; they must be *justified* or *warranted*.[5] Justification or warrant, then, is what converts true belief to knowledge.

A *belief* is an intentional mental state whose object is either (i) an object in the external world; or (ii) such an object, a specific proposition, and the

---

[3] Nancey Murphy, *Anglo-American Postmodernity: Philosophical Perspectives on Science, Religion and Ethics* (Boulder, Colo.: Westview, 1997), 131-132.

[4] Jean-François Lyotard, *The Postmodern Condition: A Report on Knowledge* (Minneapolis: University of Minnesota Press, 1984), xxiv.

[5] While there are technical distinctions between the concepts of justification and warrant, those will not concern us here. For details, see Alvin Plantinga, *Warrant: The Current Debate* (Oxford: Oxford University Press, 1993).

relation of correspondence between them. In the former case, I may believe a field to be rectangular. The object of the belief is the field itself. I need not see the field *as* a field (for example, I may mistakenly think that it is a lawn) to have such a belief. In the latter case, the mental state is sometimes described as an affirming attitude toward a proposition, for to believe something is just to believe that it is true. My mental state is about the field itself, the proposition *that the field is green,* and it includes the judgment that the proposition succeeds in corresponding to the state of affairs (the grass's being green) in the external world. A belief may be said to be true or false in a derivative sense depending upon the truth or falsity of the propositional content of the belief.

Beliefs typically have *grounds.* To say that a belief is grounded is to say that it depends upon, arises from, or is supported by something else. That something else is, in Paul Moser's terms, an indicator that the belief is true.[6] Beliefs have positive epistemic status, or are *justified,* if and only if they have the right kind of grounds.

Foundationalism refers to a family of theories about what kinds of grounds constitute justification for belief, all of which theories hold the following theses:

(1) A proper noetic structure is *foundational,* composed of properly basic beliefs and non-basic beliefs, where non-basic beliefs are based either directly or indirectly on properly basic beliefs, and properly basic beliefs are non-doxastically grounded, that is, not based on other beliefs;

(2) The basing relation which confers justification is irreflexive and asymmetrical; and

(3) A properly basic belief is a belief which meets some Condition C, where the choice of C marks different versions of foundationalism.

Classical foundationalism, of which the Cartesian project is the paradigm example, holds that Condition C is indubitability: the ground of the belief must guarantee the truth of the belief. It is recognized in nearly all quarters that classical foundationalism is too ambitious.[7] Even granted that there are some indubitable beliefs, there simply aren't enough of them to ground our entire noetic structure. Further, it certainly seems that certain beliefs which

---

[6] Paul K. Moser, *Knowledge and Evidence* (New York: Cambridge University Press, 1989), 47.

[7] Two powerful critiques of *classical* foundationalism are Alvin Plantinga, "Reason and Belief in God," in *Faith and Rationality: Reason and Belief in God,* ed. Alvin Plantinga and Nicholas Wolterstorff (Notre Dame, Ind.: University of Notre Dame Press, 1983); and Nicholas Wolterstorff, *Reason Within the Bounds of Religion* (Grand Rapids, Mich.: Eerdmans, 1976).

are not indubitable may legitimately be held as properly basic, for example, beliefs grounded in perception, memory, or testimony. And more: classical foundationalism is motivated largely by the belief that certainty is a necessary condition of knowledge, or that one must know that one knows in order to have knowledge. But these analyses are either too strict or lead to an infinite regress, leading in either case to the skeptic's lair.

The past three decades have witnessed the development of various versions of foundationalism which avoid the criticisms leveled against the classical version. Among contemporary epistemologists, modest foundationalism of some form is the "dominant position."[8]

Modest foundationalism holds that Condition C is something weaker than indubitability: the ground of the belief must be truth-conducive. Thus, in a modest foundationalism, at least some properly basic beliefs are defeasible (subject to being shown to be false by subsequent evidence). Further restrictions on Condition C will mark the difference between different versions of modest foundationalism.

Anti-Foundationalism

Recognition of the failure of classical foundationalism has unfortunately led many thinkers to assume that *no* form of foundationalism can succeed. For some, the dismissal of modest foundationalism along with its classical cousin is motivated by a suspicion that a reasonable account of properly basic belief cannot be given—that is, that Condition C cannot be successfully cashed out. But for others, we suspect, the dismissal is due more to prior theoretical commitments. We will now examine three theoretical commitments that lie behind a number of postconservative rejections of foundationalism. In the next section we will suggest what we believe to be a satisfactory Condition C and show how such a foundationalism works.

The three theoretical commitments that appear in postconservative writings are these: (i) rejection of the correspondence theory of truth in favor of an epistemic or deflationary theory of truth; (ii) rejection of metaphysical realism in favor of a theory of socially or linguistically constructed reality; and (iii) rejection of the referential theory of language in favor of a "semiotic" theory in which linguistic signs refer only to other signs and never to the world as it is. Not every thinker who might accept the "postconservative" label accepts all three of these, to be sure, but these three are so closely linked and

---

[8] Michael R. DePaul, "Preface," in *Resurrecting Old-Fashioned Foundationalism*, ed. Michael R. DePaul (Lanham, Md.: Rowman & Littlefield, 2001), vii.

appear so frequently that we shall take them as jointly constituting the theo-retical ground for postconservative anti-foundationalism.[9]

It turns out on inspection that all three commitments are minority posi-tions in contemporary analytic philosophy, and the arguments to be found in contemporary postconservative writings for these commitments (and there are not many such arguments) are rather uninformed philosophically. We will discuss these three beginning with the third.

Rejection of the Referential Theory of Language. One tradition in phi-losophy of language, found in Plato's *Cratylus* and in St. Augustine's *Confessions,* holds that words bear some kind of metaphysical link to their referents. This view is rightly rejected. The association of certain words with concepts on the one hand, and real-world referents (particulars that fall under the concepts) on the other, is indeed conventional (with the possible excep-tion of onomatopoeic words).

But acknowledging the conventional nature of language does not, as is apparently assumed by postconservatives, undermine the ability of compe-tent language-speakers to refer to the world. To be sure, post-structuralism and deconstructionism claim that signifiers point only to other signs and never to the world as signified, that language simply does not relate to the world.[10] However, recent philosophy of language has devoted considerable effort to developing sophisticated theories of reference, with impressive results.[11] We do not have space here to expand on this; suffice it to say that there is good theoretical grounding for our commonsense belief and every-day experience that human beings are in fact able to refer to the world by means of language.

Rejection of the Correspondence Theory of Truth. According to the cor-respondence theory, a proposition is true just in case what it represents to be the case is in fact the case. Truth is a property of a proposition, and a propo-sition is made true by a fact. Something about the way the world is determines the truth of a proposition, so truth is determined by a relation between a

---

[9] So Grenz and Franke speak of the dramatic retreat of "Foundationalism, allied as it was with metaphysical realism and the correspondence theory of truth. . . ." And a few pages later they assert, "The simple fact is, we do not inhabit the 'world-in-itself'; instead, we live in a linguistic world of our own making. . . . Human reality is 'socially constructed'" (*Beyond Foundationalism,* 38, 53).

[10] For an exposition and critique of the postmodern view, see Kevin J. Vanhoozer, *Is There a Meaning In This Text? The Bible, the Reader, and the Morality of Literary Knowledge* (Grand Rapids, Mich.: Zondervan, 1998), 61-65.

[11] See, for example, Gareth Evans, *Varieties of Reference,* ed. John McDowell (Oxford: Clarendon, 1982); Saul Kripke, "Speaker's Reference and Semantic Reference," in *Contemporary Perspectives in the Philosophy of Language,* ed. Peter A. French, Theodore E. Uehling, Jr., and Howard K. Wettstein (Minneapolis: University of Minnesota Press, 1977), 6-27; Michael Devitt and Kim Sterelny, *Language and Reality: An Introduction to the Philosophy of Language* (Cambridge, Mass.: MIT Press, 1987), 15-86.

proposition and the *world*. The correspondence theory thus is a *realist theory* of truth.

Epistemic theories of truth claim that whether a statement is true depends on whether we have the right kind of reasons for asserting or believing the proposition—whether the proposition is *justified* for us. Thus truth is determined by a relation between a proposition and *us*. (Coherence theories of truth, scientism, and postconservative approaches that make truth relative to what is accepted by a social community are all epistemic theories.)

Deflationary theories deny that truth is a property. Certain deflationary theories claim to give a logical analysis that is purported to show that adding ". . . is true" to a statement (e.g., "The proposition *that grass is green* is true") does not attribute a real property to the proposition, but merely restates it. Other versions claim that when we say, "That's true," of a proposition, we are performing a "speech act"—that is, merely endorsing or consenting or agreeing to an assertion. Thus truth is determined by what we want to *do* with a proposition. (The pragmatic theory of truth turns out to be a deflationary theory, as do those postmodern approaches which identify assertions of truth with attempts to exercise power.)[12]

How should we decide which kind of theory of truth is correct? Several lines of reasoning lead us to reject epistemic and deflationary theories. To begin with, in rejecting deflationary accounts, we note three things. First, the purported logical analyses of sentences containing ". . . is true" do not do what it is claimed they do—they do not analyze the *meaning* of ". . . is true" but only analyze the *use* of the phrase. There is a significant difference, and a theory of truth must first of all give an account of the concept itself, what we *mean* by "is true," not merely how we *use* the concept. Second, all pragmatically oriented theories falter on the recognition that (i) some truths have no pragmatic use (e.g., "There is no largest prime number"); (ii) some truths are unknowable to us (e.g., it is either true or false that "The number of protons in the universe is even," but apart from divine revelation that is not something any person can ever know); and what is worse, (iii) some falsehoods have pragmatic value (e.g., "I did not have sexual relations with that woman . . ."). Third, it would come as a great surprise to millions of competent language speakers to learn that when they added ". . . is true" to a proposition, they were merely reasserting the original proposition and not making a further claim about the proposition itself. Such a counterintuitive

---

[12] For a thorough discussion, see Richard L. Kirkham, *Theories of Truth: A Critical Introduction* (Cambridge, Mass.: MIT Press, 1997).

result should not be accepted in the absence of compelling arguments, and the absence of such arguments is notable.

This counterintuitive result applies as well to postmodern assertions that claims of truth are merely disguised exercises of power. Now, it might be the case that sometimes, insisting on the truth of a proposition (or an ideology) is in fact an attempt to gain or exercise power. But it does not at all follow that in a frank exchange between persons of goodwill, a spirited claim of "Yes, it's true!" is in any way a disguised power play. If we reflect honestly on the occasions when we ourselves have claimed truth for one or another proposition, the postmodernist claim seems patently false.

We also reject epistemic accounts of truth because they seem to conflate the issues of (i) knowing (or justifiably believing) that a proposition is true, and (ii) a proposition's being true. Justification is a very important issue in epistemology, the subject of a very vigorous debate among professional epistemologists. But why should we think that the concept of truth can be equated to the concept of justification? Indeed, many theories of justification are concerned to show that justification is truth-conducive—that is, if we have the right kind of reasons or evidence for holding a belief, then the belief is likely true. Epistemic theories of truth make the truth of a proposition a matter of our having the right kind of reasons for believing it. But that can't be correct: we often have justified *false* beliefs, beliefs about the world which turn out not to be the case.[13]

Finally, some postconservatives level the following sort of argument against the concept of objective truth. In the words of Philip Kenneson:

> To say that truth is not out there is simply to say that where there are no sentences there is no truth, that sentences are elements of human languages, and that human languages are human creations. Truth cannot be out there—cannot exist independently of the human mind—because sentences cannot so exist, or be out there.[14]

But this is to confuse sentences with propositions. The former are individual utterances or inscriptions in a particular language; the latter are abstract, non-linguistic conceptual structures that exist independently of anyone's thoughts. Propositions may well exist (in God's mind) even if there are no human minds. Further, propositions may be the contents of the thoughts of many dif-

---

[13] For a thorough defense of a "minimal correspondence" theory of truth, see William P. Alston, *A Realist Conception of Truth* (Ithaca, N.Y.: Cornell University Press, 1996).

[14] Philip D. Kenneson, "There's No Such Thing as Objective Truth, and It's a Good Thing, Too," in *Christian Apologetics in the Postmodern World*, ed. Timothy R. Phillips and Dennis L. Okholm (Downers Grove, Ill.: InterVarsity Press, 1995), 159.

ferent people at different times. Propositions have the property of being true or false. A sentence is true or false derivatively, depending on the truth-value of the proposition that the sentence instantiates. Since the correspondence theory of truth is formulated in terms of propositions, not sentences, arguments such as Kenneson's are simply irrelevant.

We believe that biblical teaching makes the most sense in light of the correspondence theory of truth.[15] The Old and New Testament terms for truth are, respectively, 'emet and alētheia. The meaning of these terms and, more generally, a biblical conception of truth are broad and multifaceted: fidelity, moral rectitude, being real, being genuine, faithfulness, having veracity, being complete.[16] Two aspects of the biblical conception of truth appear to be primary: faithfulness, and conformity to fact. Arguably, the former presupposes a correspondence theory. Thus, faithfulness may be understood as a person's actions corresponding to the person's assertions or promises, and a similar point could be made about genuineness, moral rectitude, and so forth.

Whether or not this first aspect of a biblical conception of truth presupposes a correspondence theory, there are numerous passages in the second group—conformity to fact—that do. Two interesting classes of texts, with numerous examples of each, fall within this second group. First, there are hundreds of passages that explicitly ascribe truth to propositions (assertions, and so forth) in a correspondence sense. Thus, God says "I the LORD speak the truth; I declare what is right" (Isa. 45:19). Second, there are numerous passages that explicitly contrast true propositions with falsehoods. Repeatedly, the Old Testament warns against false prophets whose words do not correspond to reality (e.g., Deut. 18:22, "When a prophet speaks in the name of the LORD, if the word does not come to pass or come true, that is a word that the LORD has not spoken"), and the ninth commandment warns against bearing false testimony, that is, testimony that fails to correspond to what actually happened (Ex. 20:16).

Finally, what becomes of a claim such as "Jesus is Lord"? According to Kenneson, it is meaningless to say that such a claim is objectively true:

> Truth becomes internal to a web of beliefs; there is no standard of truth independent of a set of beliefs and practices. . . . Under the new paradigm,

---

[15] See Norman L. Geisler, "The Concept of Truth in the Inerrancy Debate," *Bibliotheca Sacra* 137 (October/December 1980): 327-339; Norman L. Geisler, ed., *Inerrancy* (Grand Rapids, Mich.: Zondervan, 1980); Douglas R. Groothuis, *Truth Decay: Defending Christianity Against the Challenges of Postmodernism* (Downers Grove, Ill.: InterVarsity Press, 2000).

[16] See R. Laird Harris, Gleason L. Archer, Jr., and Bruce K. Waltke, eds., *Theological Wordbook of the Old Testament*, 2 vols. (Chicago: Moody, 1980), 1:52-53; Colin Brown, ed., *New International Dictionary of New Testament Theology*, 5 vols. (Grand Rapids, Mich.: Zondervan, 1978), 3:874-902.

this sentence translates into something like "'Jesus is Lord' is consistent with the convictions and actions of Christians, but not with those of others." . . . It simply does not make sense to think of reality as it is in itself, apart from human judgments.[17]

We do not believe that this view can be reconciled with the biblical data or with evangelical convictions.

Rejection of Metaphysical Realism. Metaphysical realism is, simply, the view that there is an objective reality that exists irrespective of subjective beliefs or linguistic constructs. Grenz and Franke allow, "There is, of course, a certain undeniable givenness to the universe apart from the human linguistic-constructive tasks. Indeed, the universe predates the appearance of humans on the earth." But then they immediately go on to say, "To assume that this observation is sufficient to relegate all the talk of social construction to the trash heap, however, is to miss the point. The simple fact is, we do not inhabit the 'world-in-itself'; instead, we live in a linguistic world of our own making."[18]

It is difficult to know what to make of such claims. Grenz and Franke offer no argument, and one looks in vain for arguments for such claims in other postconservative writers. They seem to regard the claim as self-evident; to assert it is to prove it. But it is far from self-evident. For we can readily acknowledge that we use language to communicate concepts, that many—perhaps even most—concepts are learned by means of language, and that it is difficult to think clearly of something for which we lack an adequate vocabulary. We can even agree that certain facts are linguistically or socially constructed.[19] For example, what counts as a unit of economic exchange in America (a dollar bill) depends on American social conventions. But none of that entails that we do not or cannot apprehend many aspects of the world in itself. And it most certainly does not entail that an objective world does not exist.

Summary

We find it rather disappointing that postconservative writers uniformly reject foundationalism, and generally do so with very little argument. The three the-

---

[17] Kenneson, "There's No Such Thing as Objective Truth," 163-164.
[18] Grenz and Franke, *Beyond Foundationalism*, 53.
[19] For helpful accounts of the phenomenon of social construction that distinguish between what is socially (subjectively) constructed and what is ontologically (objectively) real, see John R. Searle, *The Construction of Social Reality* (New York: Free Press, 1995); and Ian Hacking, *The Social Construction of What?* (Cambridge, Mass.: Harvard University Press, 1999).

oretical commitments that can be discerned in their writings, which might undercut foundationalism, are either themselves highly suspect, or only do so in the case of extreme versions, as straw men that represent no contemporary foundationalists. A modest foundationalism, according to which some foundational beliefs are defeasible, is left untouched.

II. A MODEST FOUNDATIONALISM

Earlier, we characterized grounds of a belief as indicators of the truth of a belief,[20] and claimed that the right kind of grounds provides justification for a belief. Thus, the grounds should be understood as epistemic rather than causal or pragmatic. That is, the relevant kind of grounds will relate to the *truth* of beliefs, and not to the *cause* (e.g., hallucinatory drugs or a brain lesion) or the *usefulness* of a belief. What is of interest here is an account of the non-doxastic grounds, or evidence, which provides justification for properly basic beliefs.

Many foundationalists have wanted to say at this point that for evidence to be truth-conducive it must reliably indicate the truth of the proposition for which it is evidence; it is locating the reliability that sets one reliabilist against another. Possibilities include agent reliabilism, process reliabilism, social doxastic process reliabilism, and evidence reliabilism. This is not the place to discuss each version of reliabilism, and since it seems to us that a certain form of evidence reliabilism is the best version, it is that version that we'll develop.

Basic Evidence

Evidence reliabilism claims that a properly basic belief is a belief grounded in a particular kind of basic evidence. Now, not just any kind of evidence may play the role of basic evidence, for although the modest foundationalist is willing to accept some defeasible beliefs as properly basic beliefs, he is not willing to countenance just any sort of belief! A reasonable solution is provided by *modal reliabilism about evidence*—the doctrine that there is a qualified modal tie (viz., necessity) between basic evidence and the truth.[21] The reliable tie between basic evidence and the truth must be modal and not merely contingent (for example, nomological—governed by natural law—or

---

[20] Moser says that a truth indicator "provides indication for one that a proposition is true in the sense that it makes the proposition *probably true to some extent* for one" (Moser, *Knowledge and Evidence*, 50, emphasis his).

[21] See, for example, George Bealer, "A Theory of the A Priori," *Pacific Philosophical Quarterly*, 81:1 (March 2000): 1-30. The term "modal" stands for "necessary" (necessarily, two is an even number), "contingent" (it is contingent that Jefferson City is the capital of Missouri), or "impossible" (it is impossible that there be square circles).

causal), for that would open the position to such familiar counterexamples as contingently reliable clairvoyance.

We propose a modal characterization of basic evidence as the first approximation of a definition:

> *If* E *is a basic source of evidence, then necessarily, for anyone in ideal cognitive conditions, beliefs formed on the basis of* E *would be mostly true.*

Let us call someone in ideal cognitive conditions an ideal cognizer. A basic source of evidence, for example, one's sense of sight, delivers (sensory) evidence to a cognizing subject. We need not imagine this ideal cognizer to be God himself; a person with ideally functioning human cognitive and perceptual equipment would qualify. To the degree that we fail to be ideal cognizers—noetically flawed as we are by the Fall and by the absence of pure epistemic virtues—*we* will fail to get truth in every case. But as we approach such conditions, and if we restrict ourselves to suitably elementary beliefs grounded in basic evidence, we can approximate the ideal.

This characterization, then, is relativized to ideal cognizers. And it requires only that most, not all, deliverances of *E* be true, thus allowing for the possibility that even for an ideal cognizer a particular deliverance of basic evidence may be false (hence, basic evidence is possibly defeasible). Further, it is a simple conditional, not a biconditional, so it characterizes but does not define what constitutes a basic source of evidence.

But a crucial question needs answering at this point: What explains why a putative basic source has such a modal tie to the truth? Surely one cannot simply define a modal tie into existence! It is in answer to this question that the idea of theory enters. We assume that a particularist (as opposed to a methodist) approach to this question is correct, and that we can reflect theoretically on our own cognizing without thereby becoming guilty of viciously circular reasoning.[22] If this is so, then we may examine our own basic (non-doxastically grounded) beliefs and discern their evidential grounds. We may introspect our own cognitive states and assess our own intellectual virtues. We may compare track records of the deliverances of different putative basic sources. We may form hypotheses about the way these sources function in belief formation. We then engage in theorizing about the world, and finally, on the basis of our best comprehensive theory of the way the world is, we are

---

[22] For argument, see John Greco, *Putting Skeptics in Their Place: The Nature of Skeptical Arguments and Their Role in Philosophical Inquiry* (New York: Cambridge University Press, 2000).

able to explain why certain kinds of evidence are indeed basic sources.[23] And so we arrive at the following ("df" means "by definition"):

> E is a basic source of evidence $=_{df}$ (i) necessarily, for anyone in ideal cognitive conditions, beliefs formed on the basis of E would be mostly true, and (ii) E's modal reliability is explainable by the best available comprehensive epistemological and metaphysical theory of the world.

We believe this definition can take account of such generally recognized basic sources of evidence as introspection and rational intuition.[24] If that is correct, then we have an account of what it is for a source of evidence to be modally reliable, or basic, and of how to extend that account to other candidate basic sources such as perception, memory, and testimony. When applied to perceptual beliefs, our version of modal reliabilism implies that our perceptual experience is the ground for the truth of perceptual beliefs, and our reliabilist account of this is a second-order theory of why this is the case.[25] In the next section we will show in more detail how this works in the case of perception, such that perceptual beliefs are properly basic.

Briefly, we want to show how this view of modally reliable evidence meets certain objections commonly lodged against reliabilist theories. First, a common criticism leveled at reliabilism is that it falls prey to the widely discussed "generality problem." The problem is this: A reliable process, say, seeing a tree in a field, can also be described (more generally) as a process of seeing a tree, or seeing a landscape, or seeing; and (more specifically) as a process of seeing an oak in a pasture, or seeing an oak with new foliage in a cow pasture, or seeing an oak on an early spring morning in Jones's pasture, and so forth. The challenge is to say just which process is reliable and why. The critic suggests that in the end, the reliabilist cannot simply explain the reliability of *types* of doxastic processes, but will need to explain the reliability of each *token* (a particular example of a type) process. But an evidence reliabilism escapes this criticism, since it is evidence and not a process that is basic. For example, one's evidence for a perceptual belief *just is* that perception (more on this below); one's evidence for a memory belief *just is* that memory, and so on.

Second, reliabilism is criticized on the basis of thought experiments that

---

[23] We would need much more space to argue for the criteria to determine which theory is "best." Suffice it to say that simplicity is not the sole—nor indeed the most important—criterion. Such theoretical virtues as explanatory power, empirical adequacy, and fecundity are crucial as well.

[24] Much of the work on intuition as basic evidence (with some extension to perceptual experience) has been done by Bealer, "Theory of the A Priori."

[25] Thus, although we use the term "reliabilism," our theory is really a second-order theory. This differs from other forms of reliabilism, which are first-order theories.

supposedly show that reliabilism will either rule out doxastic processes that we know are reliable, or will allow in processes that we know are not reliable.[26] But as just noted, modal reliabilism about evidence does not claim that evidence justifies a doxastic process, but rather that it justifies beliefs. Further, the modality involved in the definition of basic evidence is metaphysical necessity, not nomological necessity. But the thought experiments assume at best a nomological possibility. So these criticisms miss the mark.

A final criticism suggests that any particular cognizer might simply fail to form any beliefs on the grounds of reliable evidence.[27] But by relativizing the definition of evidential reliabilism to ideal cognizers, we escape this criticism as well.

III. AN ONTOLOGICAL MODEL OF THE KNOWING SUBJECT AND RELEVANT MENTAL STATES

So far, we have laid out what we believe to be the best version of modest foundationalism, one which accepts defeasible basic beliefs in the foundation. On reflection, it seems clear that perceptual beliefs offer an important test case of the foundationalism we propose. The reason is that, if modest foundationalism is correct in accepting defeasible beliefs as properly basic, then perceptual beliefs seem to be the most important candidate class of putatively basic (but defeasible) beliefs. So we need to show how our best comprehensive theory of the world will be able to explain why perceptual experience is in fact basic evidence. If we can do so, we will have shown that we have every right to take our perceptual beliefs as basic (subject to certain restrictions), and we will have shown that our access to the world is not, after all, mediated by or subsequent to our linguistic structures, or our linguistic community, or our conceptual framework, or, indeed, by anything external to our minds. In this section, then, we shall unpack an ontological model of epistemically relevant mental states and the knowing subject. The model will show that perceptual experience is indeed modally reliable, and will explain that modal reliability in terms of a comprehensive theory of perception and the knowing subject. We do not offer such a comprehensive theory here, but we provide some crucial aspects of such a theory relevant to the nature of the knowing subject and the ontology of acts of perception.

It is often the case that postconservative pronouncements fail to have accompanying arguments for them, and we do not know of a single case in

---

[26] This sort of argument is made by Moser, *Knowledge and Evidence*, 202-203.
[27] This argument is made by Greco, *Putting Skeptics in Their Place*, 178.

which a postmodernist or postconservative has developed a model of the mind according to which assertions such as "all perception is theory-laden and takes place from within a standpoint (conceptual scheme, language game, social web)" is given any clarity whatever so that the reader can make sense of how this is supposed to take place. For example, Grenz claims:

> At stake in the new outlook, therefore, is a more profound [*caveat emptor:* note the rhetorical work this word does as a substitute for argument] understanding of epistemology. Recent thinking has helped us see that the process of knowing, and to some extent even the process of experiencing the world, can occur only within a conceptual framework, a framework mediated by the social community in which we participate.[28]

Such assertions have degenerated into un-illuminating mantras, and in those rare cases in which they do conjure up a picture of what they assert, the picture that comes to mind is of sad little perceptions saddled with the task of carrying theories on their backs! We hope to provide a remedy to this dialectical gap in what follows.

The Idea Theory and a Postmodern Model

Postmodernism is not unfairly characterized as a linguisticized version of Bertrand Russell's (foundationalist!) neutral monism, the postmodern version of which takes language (the group's linguistic behavior, etc.) as basic, and views both "reality" and "the self" as linguistic constructions. But a more charitable way to describe postmodernism, and one apt for our purposes, is to see it as a linguisticized, quasi-Kantian version of Descartes's Idea Theory of perception.

To understand the Idea Theory, and the postmodern adaptation of it, a good place to start is with a commonsense, critical-realist view of perception. According to critical realism, when a subject is looking at a red object such as an apple, the red object itself is the direct object of the sensory state. What one sees directly is the apple itself. True, one must have a sensation of red to apprehend the apple, but on the critical-realist view, the sensation of red is to be understood as a case of being-appeared-to-redly and analyzed as a self-presenting property. What is a self-presenting property? If some property F is self-presenting, then it is in virtue of F that a relevant external object is

---

[28] Stanley Grenz, *Revisioning Evangelical Theology: A Fresh Agenda for the Twenty-first Century* (Downers Grove, Ill.: InterVarsity Press, 1993), 73-74. Indeed, if Grenz's claim about the role of community mediation is accepted, it's hard to understand how epistemology can help us see anything. There will only be "seeing as" or "seeing that," but no "simple seeing." But more on these points later.

presented directly to a person, and F presents itself directly to the person as well. Thus, F presents its object directly, though by being grounded in F, and F presents itself directly and in an ungrounded way.[29]

This is not as hard to understand as it first may appear. Sensations, such as being-appeared-to-redly, are an important class of self-presenting properties. If Jones is having a sensation of red while looking at an apple, then having the property of being-appeared-to-redly as part of his consciousness modifies his substantial self. When Jones has this sensation, it is a tool that presents the red apple directly to him in virtue of having the sensation, and the sensation also presents itself to Jones directly and ungrounded in anything else. What does it mean to say that the sensation presents the apple to him directly by grounding that presentation? Simply this: it is *in virtue of* the sensation that Jones sees the apple. The *in virtue of* locution is primitive and unanalyzable. It is not efficient causality, as the following examples illustrate: The proposition "Grass is green" is true *in virtue of* grass being green. Grass is green *in virtue of* instantiating the property of being green. The earth exists now *in virtue of* God's sustaining power.[30] In both cases—the truth of "Grass is green" and the current existence of the earth—there is a metaphysical ground for the relevant feature. Similarly, Jones's direct awareness of the apple's redness is grounded in the sensation—being-appeared-to-redly—that he has.

Moreover, by having the sensation of red, Jones is directly aware of both the apple and his own awareness of the apple. For the direct realist, the sensation of red may indeed be a tool or ground that Jones uses to become aware of the apple, but he is thereby directly aware of the apple, with nothing mediating that awareness. His awareness of the apple is direct in that nothing stands between Jones and the apple, not even his sensation of the apple. That sensation presents the apple directly; though as a tool, Jones must have the sensation as a necessary condition for seeing the apple.

According to Descartes's Idea Theory, one's ideas (in this case, sensations) stand between the subject and the object of perception. Jones is directly aware of his own sensation of the apple and indirectly aware of the apple in the sense that it is what causes the sensation to happen. On the Idea Theory, a perceiving subject is trapped behind his own sensations and cannot get outside them to the external world in order to compare his sensations to their objects

---

[29] See J. P. Moreland, "The Knowledge Argument Revisited," *International Philosophical Quarterly* 43 (June 2003): 219-228.
[30] For an excellent discussion of *in virtue of* and related ontological distinctions, see William F. Vallicella, *A Paradigm Theory of Existence: Onto-Theology Vindicated* (Dordrecht, Netherlands: Kluwer Academic Publishers, 2002).

in order to see if those sensations are accurate. On this view, the mind may be likened to a bucket. Thoughts, sensations, and other mental states are "in" the mind as something is in a container, e.g., as apples are in a bucket. The *self* or *I* is, in a somewhat unclear way, trapped behind one's mental states and must experience the world *through*, that is, *mediated by*, one's ideas.

The postmodern and postconservative twist on the Idea Theory replaces Descartes's ideas with language. Language is like glasses that mediate objects, and objects are perceived indirectly by way of one's language (standpoint, social context, thoughts, conceptual structures).

In a certain sense, postmodernists and their postconservative adapters believe that people are trapped behind something in the attempt to get to the external world. However, for them, the wall between people and reality is not composed of sensations, as it was for Descartes; rather, it is constituted by our linguistic practices. Our language serves as a sort of distorting and, indeed, creative filter. We cannot get outside our language to see if our talk about the world is the way the world is. In fact, it may be superfluous even to talk about an external world. Many postmodernists claim that the "external world" is just a construction. On this view, intentionality—a mental state's "ofness," "aboutness," or "directedness" toward an object (even if the object does not exist, e.g., a fear *of* Zeus)—actually causes something to happen *to the object*. Intentionality causes the object to have some of its properties or parts. So, for example, by looking at an apple, the mind creates the apple's color, but the apple itself is colorless when not being perceived. Or, more extremely, it creates the object whole cloth. In fact, the "self" itself is, for some postmodernists, a construction of language. There is no unified, substantial ego. The "self" is a bundle of social roles, such as being a wife, a mother, a graduate student, an insurance salesperson; and these roles are created by the linguistic practices associated with them. For many postmodernists, then, consciousness and the "self" are social, not individual.

For those who have taken the postmodern turn, there is no "simple seeing." All seeing is "seeing as" or "seeing that" and, thus, an act of perception turns out to be a mental *judgment* of some sort. All perception, they claim, is theory-laden, experienced *from within* or *behind* a standpoint of some sort. To get clear on this, we need to distinguish two kinds of knowledge.

1. *Knowledge by acquaintance.* This happens when we are directly aware of something; for example, when I see an apple directly before me, I know it by acquaintance. One does not need a concept of an apple or knowledge of how to use the word "apple" in English to have knowledge by acquaintance of an apple. A baby can see an apple—and so have knowledge

by acquaintance of it—without having the relevant concept or linguistic skills. This form of knowledge includes "simple seeing," and is denied by post-modernists. We will postpone our critique of the denial of simple seeing and, in fact, will defend its reality by presenting and arguing for our model below.

2. *Knowledge by judgment.* This breaks down into mere conceptual knowledge and propositional knowledge. The former includes "seeing as," i.e., seeing an object *as* falling under or satisfying a concept. Examples include seeing an apple as being red or as being Joe's favorite fruit. This form of knowledge requires the subject already to have acquired the relevant concept. Usually, postmodernists reduce concepts to language and language to linguistic behavior; so to see something as F requires one first to have learned certain linguistic practices, and in this way, knowledge by acquaintance is reduced to judgmental knowledge, and this is further reduced to know-how. (How one does this without seeing social linguistic practices as being something or other is not clear. Zeno's regresses lurk near!) Propositional knowledge is knowledge that an entire proposition is true (or satisfies a postmodern surrogate for truth, e.g., is accepted by one's community). For example, knowledge that "the object there is an apple" requires having a concept of an apple and knowing that the object under consideration satisfies the concept.

A postmodernist does not take an act of seeing to be directly about an object (e.g., an apple). Instead, he takes it to be about one's own concept of or word for the object that stands between the subject and whatever is "out there" (if anything is). In this way a postmodernist reduces propositional attitudes such that they turn out to be about the contents of consciousness (and this is often further reduced to behavioral know-how regarding the relevant linguistic item, e.g., the word "apple"), and not about the external world. A propositional attitude involves a mental "attitude"—a state of thinking, fearing, hoping, wondering, believing—and a mental content—that P, e.g., that the apple is red. For the postmodernist, a propositional attitude such as "thinking that P" (that the apple is red) is a mental attitude of thinking directed toward a mentally internal object, viz., a proposition (more likely, toward a sentence in English, or "mentalese," a supposedly unique mental language in the brain), which is internal to the subject. "Thinking that P" is to have the attitude of thinking directed toward the proposition "that P." This is solipsism with a vengeance, Kantianism gone mad. By contrast, those of us who are direct realists would take "thinking that P" to be a mental attitude of thinking directed immediately toward the external state of affairs P (the apple's being red) in virtue of the subject having the proposition "that P" (the thought that the apple is red) in his mind.

Further, for the postmodernist there is no such thing as thinking without language, and, in fact, thinking is simply linguistic behavior in which one correctly uses words according to the linguistic practices of one's social group. But for two reasons, this just seems to be wrong. First, if a person cannot think temporally and epistemically prior to acquiring language, then one would never be able to *learn* language in the first place or be able to find an entry point into a language game as a first-person subject. Children *must* think temporally and epistemically prior to learning their community's language.

Second, language is neither necessary nor sufficient for thinking. It is not necessary, for the reason just given. Nor is it sufficient. One can have linguistic perceptions (sounds, sensory experiences of scribbles) without having any associated thought, for example, when one perceives a language one has not learned. Moreover, a linguistic sign (for example, the "internal" sound or visual sensation "the President") can occur to one in an idle sensory experience with no associated meaning at all, or with a potentially infinite set of meanings the subject assigns to it (the President of the United States, of the PTA, of the American League . . .). In all these cases, having a chunk of language is not sufficient for having the relevant thought.

Finally, postmodernists reject the idea that there are universal, transcultural standards, such as the laws of logic or principles of inductive inference, for determining whether a belief is true or false, rational or irrational, good or bad. Consequently, there is no predefined rationality. Postmodernists also reject the notion that rationality is objective on the grounds that no one approaches life in a totally objective way, without bias. Thus, objectivity is impossible, and observations, beliefs, and entire narratives are theory-laden. There is no neutral standpoint from which to approach the world, and thus observations, beliefs, and so forth are perspectival constructions that reflect the viewpoint implicit in one's own web of beliefs. Regarding knowledge, postmodernists believe that there is no point of view from which one can define knowledge itself without begging the question in favor of one's own view. "Knowledge" is a construction of one's social, linguistic structures, not a justified, truthful representation of reality by one's mental states. For example, knowledge amounts to what is deemed to be *appropriate* according to the professional certification practices of various professional associations. As such, knowledge is a construction that expresses the social, linguistic structures of those associations, nothing more, nothing less.

There is great confusion in the postmodern rejection of objective rationality on the grounds that no one achieves it because everyone is biased in some way or another. As a first step toward a response to this claim, we need to draw a distinction between psychological and rational objectivity. Psychological objectivity is the absence of bias, a lack of commitment either way on a topic, while rational objectivity is the ability to distinguish between good and bad reasons for a belief, and to hold beliefs for good reasons.

Do people ever have psychological objectivity? Yes, they do, typically in areas in which they have no interest or about which they have not thought deeply. Note carefully two things about psychological objectivity. For one thing, it is not necessarily a virtue. Psychological objectivity is virtuous if one has not thought deeply about an issue and has no convictions regarding it. But as one develops thoughtful, intelligent convictions about a topic, it would be wrong to remain "unbiased," that is, uncommitted regarding it. Otherwise, what role would study and evidence play in the development of one's approach to life? Should one remain "unbiased" that cancer is a disease, that rape is wrong, that the New Testament was written in the first century, or that there is design in the universe, if one has discovered good reasons for each belief? No, of course one should not—and it is doubtful that one can—when in possession of evidence for or against the proposition in question.

For another thing, while it is possible to be psychologically objective in some cases, most people are not psychologically objective regarding the vast majority of the things they believe. In these cases, it is crucial to observe that a lack of psychological objectivity does not matter, nor does it cut one off from presenting and arguing for one's convictions. Why? *Because a lack of psychological objectivity does not imply a lack of rational objectivity, and it is the latter that matters most, not the former.*

To understand this, we need to be clear on the notion of rational objectivity. One has rational objectivity just in case one can discern the difference between genuinely good and genuinely bad reasons for a belief, and one holds to the belief for genuinely good reasons. The important thing here is that bias does not eliminate a person's ability to assess the reasons for something. Bias may make it more difficult, but it doesn't make it impossible. If bias made rational objectivity impossible, then no teacher—atheist, Christian, or whatever—could responsibly teach any view the teacher believed on any subject! Nor could the teacher teach opposing viewpoints, because he would be biased against them! In fact, if incompetence is understood in terms of presenting a subject matter in a biased fashion, then the greater one's knowledge and beliefs about a subject area, the more incompetent one would be to teach it!

A Direct-Realist, Foundationalist Model

In our description and critique of a postmodernist model, we have already presented certain features of our foundationalist, direct-realist model.[31] Above we argued that "simple seeing" is real and is temporally and epistemically prior to having thoughts, beliefs, concepts, or language. We make a distinction between a sensation and a belief (thought, etc.). A sensation is a non-propositional/conceptual experience possessed by an experiencing subject. If a person has a red sensation, then the person is appeared to in a red-type way. The person has a certain sensory property within his consciousness, namely, being-an-appearing-of-red. Sensations do not contain beliefs or, put somewhat differently, "simple seeing" does not require "seeing as" or "seeing that." If one sees a red apple, then one has a sensation-of-red, i.e., one is appeared to in a red-type way. If one sees the object *as* red, then one possesses the concept *being red,* and applies it to the object of perception. This concept grounds the subject's ability to learn how to use the word "red." Finally, if one sees *that* this is a red apple, then one accepts the proposition that (and, thus, has the perceptual belief that) this object is a red apple. In order to have a sensory experience of something, one need not have concepts or propositions in one's mind. By contrast, a belief includes the acceptance of a proposition and is the way something seems to a subject when he thinks about the belief in question. According to a traditional view, sensations are not propositional, beliefs are.

We have been talking about sensations, but it is important to note at this point that being-a-sensation-of is a species of the genus being-an-awareness-of. For our purposes, sensations are types of awarenesses that (contingently in embodied persons) involve the five senses, but other forms of direct awareness would be rational awarenesses of abstract objects and their relations (propositions and the laws of logic, numbers and the laws of mathematics, or other universals and their relations; for example, that necessarily, something cannot be red and green all over at the same time), direct awareness of one's own self, and one's mental contents in introspective awareness (awareness of spiritual or aesthetic or moral objects).[32]

The questions that need to be addressed are: What are sensations, concepts, and propositions, and in what sense are they in the mind? And what is

---

[31] For a closely related treatment of these issues, see Dallas Willard, "How Concepts Relate the Mind to Its Objects: The 'God's Eye View' Vindicated?" *Philosophia Christi* 2:1:2 (1999): 5-20.
[32] For a statement and defense of properties as universals, see J. P. Moreland, *Universals* (Chesham, Buckinghamshire, England: Acumen; Montreal: McGill-Queen's University Press, 2001).

the ontology of an act of perception such that light is shed on a direct-realist theory of perception?

Two topics must be discussed before we answer these questions, because each topic provides needed materials for developing and justifying our model.

First, there are two aspects of knowledge of which any model of the mind must give an account:[33] (i) transcendence toward an object (a mental state such as seeing or thinking is directly about its object, e.g., one is directly seeing the apple or thinking about London); and (ii) community of mental states (we may all have the same sensation, belief, or thought in our minds—e.g., the sensation of redness, the thought that London is beautiful—though each one of us will have our own "having of the mental state": I have my own individual thinking of London, you have yours; we each have the same thought "that London is beautiful," but we each have our own thinking that thought). Put differently, mental states like sensations or thoughts are universals—there are kinds of mental states (pain-type sensations, a kind of thought that amounts to thinking that London is beautiful)—and several people can have a particular instantiation of the universal at once (several people can be in the same pain-type state at the same time).

Second, we need to be clear on five metaphysical notions: *substance, property, exemplification, event/mode.*[34] Our exposition of these will be brief and only take into account what is necessary for present purposes. A *substance,* such as an individual human person or a dog, is a particular that has properties, that is not possessed by something more basic than it, and that can gain a new property and lose an old one and remain the very same substance. A *property,* such as being red, is a universal that can be exemplified by or present in several things at the same time; e.g., several apples can all have the very same redness in them at once. *Exemplification* is a relation (nexus) that is primitive and unanalyzable. When a substance like an apple has a property like being red, the apple exemplifies redness. Exemplification is a non-spatial relation in virtue of which a property is "in" a particular, but the "in" is not a spatial, container "in." Redness is not "in" an apple by being

---

[33] See Dallas Willard, "Wholes, Parts, and the Objectivity of Knowledge," in *Parts and Moments: Studies in Logic and Formal Ontology,* ed. Barry Smith (Munich: Philosophia Verlag, 1982), 379-400; cf. Dallas Willard, "Knowledge," in *The Cambridge Companion to Husserl,* ed. Barry Smith and David Woodruff Smith (Cambridge: Cambridge University Press, 1995), 138-167; J. P. Moreland, "Naturalism, Nominalism, and Husserlian Moments," *The Modern Schoolman* 79 (January/March 2002): 199-216.

[34] For a readable treatment of these and other relevant philosophical distinctions, see Garry DeWeese and J. P. Moreland, *Philosophical Tools for Christians* (tentative title) (Downers Grove, Ill.: InterVarsity Press, forthcoming, 2005); cf. J. P. Moreland and William Lane Craig, *Philosophical Foundations for a Christian Worldview* (Downers Grove, Ill.: InterVarsity Press, 2003). Ordinarily, the term "event" is used in talking about specific mental states. And while it is strictly true that all temporal modes are events but not conversely, we shall use the two interchangeably. We do so because we believe that such mental events are, in fact, best analyzed as modes of the self in a realist version of intentionality.

spatially contained inside the apple or by being spatially present at the same place as the apple. The redness is "in" the apple in that redness enters the being of the apple; the apple has redness "in" it in that the apple exemplifies redness and redness enters the very being of the apple.

A sufficient condition for being an event is a substance having, gaining, or losing a property at or through a given time. The apple's being red or changing from green to red on Tuesday is an event. When a substance undergoes the event of having a property, that event is a *mode* of the substance. A substance's having a property at a time is a mode of the substance. It is modified by the property and the mode is a particular, dependent part of the substance. The particular mode cannot exist without the substance existing, though the substance could exist without the mode. A temporal mode is a state of affairs, namely, a substance's having a property at a given time. For example, when an apple comes to have the color red, or a chunk of clay comes to have the shape of being round, then the apple or the clay is modified by having redness or roundness, respectively. The having of redness by the apple is a mode of the apple. The particular apple's having redness is not repeatable. It is a particular exemplification of redness by this particular apple. The apple could exist without being red, but this particular instance of redness could not exist in some other apple. Redness could exist in another apple, but that would constitute a different instance of redness, a different mode in a different apple.

With these two topics in mind, what are sensations, concepts, and propositions, and how are they in the mind? Sensations, concepts, and propositions are mental universals that have intentionality and that may be exemplified by several minds at the same time. A sensation of seeing red is the mental property being-an-appearing-of-red; the relevant concept is the property being-a-concept-of-red. A proposition is a structural property that constitutes the meaning of a sentence and that in the relevant case has a structure that mirrors the subject, copula, and predicate of an indicative sentence. The proposition *that the apple is red* is the property that-the-apple-is-red. Just as the property being-water is a structural property built out of the properties being-hydrogen and being-oxygen, among other things, so the property that-the-apple-is-red includes, among other things, the property of being-a-concept-of-red.

How are sensations, concepts, and propositions in the mind? Sensations, concepts, and so forth are "in" the mind the way properties are exemplified by substances. When a mind changes from having the sensation of being red to entertaining the thought that snow is white, that mind first exemplifies the sensory property being-a-sensation-of-red, and, second, the propositional property that-snow-is-white. Thoughts are in the mind in the same way that properties are in substances; namely, minds exemplify thoughts. Individual mental events, a particular sensation or thought, are modes. As modes, they involve the having of the relevant mental property by a subject. The community of thought is akin to the fact that the unity of the class of red apples obtains in virtue of each exemplifying the same property, redness. Each apple has its own mode, its own having-of-redness, but the redness of one apple is identical to that of another. Similarly, each mind has its own event/mode of sensing red, but the sensation being-an-appearing-of-red is a universal exemplified by, embedded "in," each sensory event in each mind so modified.

According to this model, thoughts or sensations are not spatially contained inside the mind or in some other way between the subject and the object like a set of glasses. And the model has a way of capturing the truth in the notion that perception is theory-laden without having to embrace this view as it is normally understood, and thereby cutting the subject off from cognitive access to the external world. Concepts, thoughts, conceptual schemes, and so forth are not glasses *through and behind which* the subject is cut off from reality and which, indeed, constitute in Kant's sense their own phenomenological object. No, concepts, thoughts, and conceptual schemes serve as a sort of swiveled neck brace that directs the subject's attention but does not cut off the object from the subject by standing between them. Many of the perceptual "puzzles," like the infamous duck/rabbit, are precisely cases where either the concept of-being-a-duck or of-being-a-rabbit direct one's perceptual orientation such that certain things are noticed and others disregarded, certain things are brought to the perceptual foreground and others relegated to the background, while the diagram itself is the direct object of the various sensory states directed upon it. In this way, concepts, thoughts, and conceptual schemes may influence perception, but they do not determine what one sees nor are they necessary conditions for seeing in the first place.

So much for a broad-brush presentation of our foundationalist, direct-realist model of the self and its various epistemic states. A major argument for this view is the presentation of paradigm cases of knowledge and perception—sensory or otherwise—that the reader can recognize as being a regular part of his own experience of objects and of himself as a knowing subject. These cases form what is called the phenomenological argument.

The phenomenological argument focuses on a careful description and presentation of specific cases to see what can be learned from them about truth. As an example, consider the case of Joe and Frank. While in his office,

Joe receives a call from the university bookstore that a specific book he had ordered—say, Richard Swinburne's *The Evolution of the Soul*—has arrived and is waiting for him. At this point, a new mental state occurs in Joe's mind—the thought that Swinburne's *The Evolution of the Soul* is in the bookstore. Now Joe, being aware of the content of the thought, becomes aware of two things closely related to it: the nature of the thought's intentional object (Swinburne's book being in the bookstore) and certain verification steps that would help him to determine the truth of the thought. For example, he knows that it would be irrelevant for verifying the thought to go swimming in the Pacific Ocean. Rather, he knows that he must take a series of steps that will bring him to enter a specific building (the university bookstore) and to look in certain places for Swinburne's book. So Joe starts out for the bookstore, all the while being guided by the proposition *that Swinburne's* The Evolution of the Soul *is in the bookstore.*

Along the way, Joe's friend Frank joins him, though Joe does not tell Frank where he is going or why. They arrive at the store and both see Swinburne's book there. At that moment, Joe and Frank simultaneously have a certain sensory experience of seeing Swinburne's book *The Evolution of the Soul.* But Joe has a second experience not possessed by Frank. Joe experiences that his thought matches, corresponds with, an actual state of affairs. He is able to compare his thought with its intentional object and "see"—be directly aware of—both the book and the correspondence relation itself. In this case, truth itself becomes an object of Joe's awareness.

The example just cited presents a case of experiencing truth in which the relevant intentional object is a sense perceptible one, a specific book being in the bookstore. But this need not be the case. A student, upon being taught *modus ponens* (the logical form "If P, then Q; P; therefore, Q"; for example, "If it is raining outside, then it is wet; it is raining; therefore, it is wet"), can bring this thought to a direct awareness of specific cases of logical inferences and "see" or be directly aware of those cases and of the truth of *modus ponens* itself. Similarly, a person can form the thought that he is practicing denial regarding his anger toward his father, and through introspection he can be directly aware of his anger and directly see whether or not this thought corresponds with his own internal mental states.

In each case, the relevant thought directs the subject's subsequent intuitive noticings,[35] but in no way cuts the subject off from a direct awareness of the relevant entities. In each case, *there is linguistically and conceptually*

---

[35] What is subsequent is a series of a certain sort of mental act, "intuitive noticings" in which the subject searches for further evidence.

independent access to the external world—the real world—and not a Kantian phenomenological construction.[36]

And just here we can see the modal tie between the evidence of perception and truth. In general, it is possible to be aware of the modal status of a relation between two objects. For example, if one attends to a situation in which Plato is taller than Socrates, one may see that the *taller-than* relation between them is not necessary to the existence of either (e.g., Plato and Socrates could exist and still be themselves even if Socrates were taller than Plato). By contrast, the relation *brighter-than* between the colors yellow and red is a necessary link between them (yellow and red are necessarily such that yellow is brighter than red).

Similarly, through introspection, a person can be directly aware of the correspondence of a perceptual belief to its intentional object, and then one may also be able to be aware of the modal nature of the connection between perceptual evidence and truth. That is, given certain forms of perceptual evidence, a proposition appropriately grounded in that evidence cannot fail to be true. In perceptual situations in which a perceiver is having a hallucination or an illusion of some sort ("seeing" a red apple when no apple exists; seeing a red apple as a yellow grapefruit), our view implies that there must be some difference, however slight it may be, between the perceptual evidence in these problematic cases and the comparable evidence in veridical (accurate, truthful) cases.

Of course, we are not able in every case to compare a perceptual belief with its intentional object, due, perhaps, to cognitive or environmental conditions that fail to be ideal (e.g., if Joe forgot his glasses and can't quite make out the title of the book on the rack, but thinks it is *probably* Swinburne's, or if he misremembered the title and thought he was looking for *The Soul of Evolution*). But as we approach the state of an ideal cognizer, it is clear that the tie between perceptual beliefs and the world will be necessary.

IV. BIBLICAL INERRANCY

Finally, we want to show that the notion of modal reliabilism about evidence comports with biblical inerrancy. If we can show that the foundationalist model we have proposed easily accommodates the doctrine of inerrancy, then evangelicals who hold to inerrancy will have an additional reason to favor our model.

---

[36] For a technical, precise, and powerful critique of postmodernism along the lines we have adopted, see R. Scott Smith, *Virtue Ethics and Moral Knowledge: Philosophy of Language After MacIntyre and Hauerwas* (Burlington, Vt.: Ashgate, 2003). For Smith's analysis of postconservatives specifically, see his chapter in the present volume.

Our claim is that inerrancy as a property of the Bible makes the Bible a basic source of evidence. So beliefs formed on the basis of reading the Bible are properly basic in a way that is isomorphic or parallel to the way beliefs formed on the basis of seeing a red apple are basic.

To see how the argument goes, consider again the case of visual perception. As we have described the process, we form beliefs directly upon the perceptual evidence of seeing ordinary physical objects; we don't infer their presence or properties from other beliefs about, say, a sense-datum (and certainly not upon beliefs about how our linguistic community uses words!). As discussed in the previous section, it is easy to explain how human visual perception is indeed modally reliable (with certain familiar restrictions), and that is because our best comprehensive theory explains how the experience of seeing actual objects in the world serves as basic evidence and so grounds properly beliefs about what one is seeing.

Now, in the case of the Bible, the argument is isomorphic or parallel. We form beliefs directly upon reading the Bible. In at least some instances, we don't infer those beliefs from other beliefs (although often, especially when engaging in the particular discipline of exegesis, that is what we do). For example, let's say we read in Romans 5:8, "But God demonstrates his love for us in this: while we were still sinners, Christ died for us." We may simply find ourselves believing "God loves me," or "God has demonstrated his love for me," or "Christ died for me," without having inferred those beliefs from anything else. So it seems that Scripture is indeed serving as evidence, and that it does so for very many people. Now, we could be mistaken in the things we find ourselves believing; an ideal cognizer might believe something different. But as we apply the techniques of exegesis, as we gain theological understanding, as we acquire the moral and intellectual virtues, we approach at least marginally closer to the ideal.

Further, our best comprehensive theory includes evidence for belief in the existence of a certain kind of God, and for the belief that this God would have communicated with us. And within our best comprehensive theory of the world is embedded the doctrine of biblical inerrancy, based on a priori theological arguments that God's communication to us would be completely truthful.[37] So biblical inerrancy explains why the Bible is a basic source of evidence.

It is worth calling attention to the fact that in our argument for the proper

---

[37] The existence of a priori arguments for biblical inerrancy does not preclude the existence of broadly inductive arguments for inerrancy that provide defeaters for alleged inductive evidence against inerrancy and that provide additional positive grounds for biblical inerrancy. See J. P. Moreland, "The Rationality of Belief in Inerrancy," *Trinity Journal NS* 7 (Spring 1986): 75-86.

basicality of beliefs based on the modal reliability of visual perception, even though the experience of visual perception played a crucial role in establishing the proper basicality of visual perception, the premise that visual perception is modally reliable did not itself figure in the argument, so the argument is not circular. Similarly, although beliefs formed on the evidential basis of reading the Bible play a role in the argument for the proper basicality of the Bible, the premise that the Bible is inerrant did not figure in the argument, so this argument is not circular either. That is, we are not asserting that the Bible is inerrant simply because it says it is. And since beliefs grounded in basic evidence are justified, the property of inerrancy, which explains why the Bible can be basic evidence, is that which renders Scripture *on its own* sufficient to justify belief.

V. CONCLUSION

We have examined and found wanting the postconservative anti-foundationalist epistemology. We have made an argument to the effect that modest foundationalism is the correct general theory of justification in epistemology, and modal reliabilism about evidence is the best form of modest foundationalism. We have offered in some detail a model of the knowing subject that explains why perception is indeed a basic source of evidence. And finally, we have offered a summary of an argument to the conclusion that inerrancy is the property of the Bible which makes it a basic source of evidence, and have shown that such an argument comports well with the overall structure of the foundationalism we propose.

If we are correct about all this, then it seems that those postconservative theologians and philosophers who reject foundationalism will be rejecting as well an effective way to incorporate the doctrine of biblical inerrancy into their theologizing, and will need to do a lot of work to justify why their theological claims should be taken as meaningful for anyone outside the Christian community.

5

LANGUAGE, THEOLOGICAL KNOWLEDGE, AND THE POSTMODERN PARADIGM

R. Scott Smith

INTRODUCTION

It has become commonplace among conservative Christians to hear that the modernist (read: Enlightenment) picture of theological knowledge, as well as its justification, is badly flawed and ought to be discarded in favor of a post-modern, holistic alternative. The attacks usually focus on Cartesian founda-tionalism, a view about how beliefs are justified, characterized in such a way that our foundational beliefs require one-hundred-percent certainty. It is upon such indubitable foundations that the "edifice" of knowledge, theological and otherwise, is erected. And, as Nancey Murphy points out, that foundation for conservative Christians has been authoritative, inerrant Scripture.[1]

Though many postconservative, postmodern Christians (e.g., Murphy, Stanley Grenz, and John Franke) hold to this view of foundationalism, J. P. Moreland and Garrett DeWeese have dealt with it adequately in the previous chapter as the caricature it is. But that is not the only argument against foun-dational knowledge, for Murphy's main point is that even for "chastened" foundationalists (who do not require certainty in the foundations), the foun-dations end up "hanging from the balcony."[2] What does she mean by this? Basically, she means that no beliefs (or observations, for that matter) are exempt from the influence of theories. There simply is no theory-neutral observation or belief. So the so-called foundational beliefs end up being partly

---

[1] Nancey Murphy, *Beyond Liberalism and Fundamentalism: How Modern and Postmodern Philosophy Set the Theological Agenda* (Harrisburg, Va.: Trinity Press International, 1996), 15-16.
[2] Nancey Murphy, *Anglo-American Postmodernity* (Boulder, Colo.: Westview, 1997), 92.

supported by higher-level theoretical beliefs after all. If that is the case, then the foundationalist picture of how justification proceeds, from bottom to top, from foundational beliefs to levels of inferred beliefs, simply is misguided and misleading.

Like Murphy, Brad Kallenberg—an evangelical philosophical theologian, defender of Stanley Hauerwas, and former student of Murphy's at Fuller—also maintains this position that we cannot have epistemic access to the real world. Arguably, Hauerwas himself draws this same conclusion. So do Grenz and Franke, as well as another highly influential philosopher, Alasdair MacIntyre. What is it that stands between the "real" world and us? It is language, such that, as Grenz and Franke say, "we do not inhabit the 'world-in-itself'; instead, we live in a linguistic world of our own making."[3]

This view of the relation of language and world underlies Murphy's second argument against foundationalism, and I think it is the central contention driving the postmodern thought of these postconservative authors. Foundationalism presupposes what postmodernists deny, namely, an ability to know things as they really are, apart from language use. Murphy explains that there have been two types of foundationalism among Protestants: universal experience for liberals; and universal, enscripturated truth for conservatives. Both appeal to universal truths that we may know, but these authors deny the ability to know such truths.

This stance has led to certain apparent rhetorical advantages. If foundationalism is in dire disrepair, and if it does require certainty, then the postconservative, postmodern stance does not force us to have to prove (with certainty) our theological beliefs. If we cannot know things as they really are, then this position leads to a certain "humility of knowledge," and in the postmodern climate in much of academia, not to mention in witnessing, this is an attractive position to take. In short, the postconservative view reduces the pressure of having to prove to challengers that our theological claims (such as that Scripture is inerrant) are certain. We still can maintain our beliefs, but we do not have to prove them.

It therefore becomes crucial that we examine this postmodernist claim that we are inside language and cannot get outside of it to know reality (i.e., the world as it really is, independently of how we talk about it). To do this, I will bring into the "conversation" the postmodernists' "voices," so that we may carefully see just what they believe. Then I will evaluate their views to

---

[3] Stanley J. Grenz and John R. Franke, *Beyond Foundationalism: Shaping Theology in a Postmodern Context* (Louisville: Westminster John Knox, 2001), 53.

see if we should accept their position. After that, I will draw out a few hopefully illuminating implications of our findings, (1) by revisiting this second challenge to foundationalism; and (2) by applying their view of the language-world relationship to several essential Christian doctrines.

THE INTERNAL RELATION OF LANGUAGE AND WORLD

To approach the view of the postmodernists, I will begin with Nancey Murphy's alternative to foundationalism, which she calls epistemological holism. I will draw Alasdair MacIntyre into the conversation to show how Murphy uses his epistemological and linguistic views. After that, I will interweave selections from Kallenberg, Hauerwas, and Grenz and Franke to illustrate this overall view.[4]

Murphy and MacIntyre

For Murphy, foundationalism should be replaced by a postmodern holist view of epistemic justification. She draws upon W. V. O. Quine's "image of knowledge as a web or net," such that "there are no sharp distinctions between basic (foundational) beliefs and nonbasic beliefs."[5] Not only do the beliefs in the web reinforce each other in a variety of kinds of connections among themselves as well as to the whole, they also work in a top-down manner. For example, in philosophy of science, there are no data that are simply given; rather, all "facts" are made "by means of their interpretation" in light of other theoretical assumptions.[6]

Yet Quine provides too circumspect a view of what counts as knowledge to allow for how we can justify claims of other disciplines in which Murphy is interested, such as theology and ethics. And there could be competing webs of beliefs, which raises the specter of relativism. So, Imre Lakatos allows Murphy to unpack her own views of philosophy of science and later apply them to theology and ethics when considered as sciences in their own right.[7] For our purposes, we will focus on her appeal to the holist views of Alasdair MacIntyre. This move will allow her to develop an account of theological and ethical knowledge, as well as a broader theory of rationality.

For MacIntyre, rationality is found only within traditions, which are his-

---

[4] For a detailed exposition of MacIntyre, Hauerwas, and Kallenberg's linguistic views, see chapters 1 through 3 of my *Virtue Ethics and Moral Knowledge: Philosophy of Language After MacIntyre and Hauerwas* (Burlington, Vt.: Ashgate, 2003).

[5] Murphy, *Anglo-American Postmodernity*, 27.

[6] Ibid.

[7] This is the burden of Murphy's *Theology in the Age of Scientific Reasoning* (Ithaca, N.Y.: Cornell University Press, 1990), as well as the focus of chapter 9 of *Anglo-American Postmodernity*.

torically extended, socially embodied arguments about the nature of the good.[8] Traditions critically involve a historical dimension, and they are tied to communities or forms of life. MacIntyre thinks there are no theory-independent facts, for "facts . . . were a seventeenth-century invention."[9] Also, standards of rationality "emerge from and are part of a history in which they are vindicated by the way in which they transcend the limitations of and provide remedies for the defects of their predecessors within the history of that same tradition."[10]

According to Murphy, MacIntyre claims that specific types of claims (e.g., theological or scientific) make sense only in terms of historical reason.[11] This is what Murphy calls diachronic justification, or how we justify modifications within a tradition. A second aspect of justification is synchronic, and here we can see how MacIntyre provides a means to rationally assess why one tradition is rationally superior to a rival, even though rational standards are internal to a tradition. This involves the comparison of traditions' languages, such that "a tradition is vindicated by the fact that it has managed to solve its own major problems, while its competitor has failed to do so, and by the fact that it can give a better account of its rival's failures than can the rival itself."[12]

Seeing the rational superiority of one tradition over another depends upon people in one tradition learning the language of another as a second first language.[13] This can be done only by participation within that alien tradition, so that they learn the grammar of that language. In this way, they can see the epistemic resources available in another tradition to help solve the problems internal to their own.

Traditions provide the context within which we "see" the world. We can think and perceive only by means of the categories and stories found in traditions, for there is no independent reality against which we may compare a text.[14] Nor can we compare reality with our favored conceptual scheme, for we do not have "some sort of direct insight into the nature of reality."[15]

So Murphy advocates a shift away from foundationalism to an epistemological holism. A second shift for her involves language. For Murphy,

---

[8] Alasdair MacIntyre, *After Virtue*, 2nd ed. (Notre Dame, Ind.: University of Notre Dame Press, 1984), 222.
[9] Alasdair MacIntyre, *Whose Justice? Which Rationality?* (Notre Dame, Ind.: University of Notre Dame Press, 1988), 357.
[10] Ibid., 7.
[11] Murphy, *Anglo-American Postmodernity*, 58.
[12] Ibid., 59.
[13] E.g., see MacIntyre, *Whose Justice? Which Rationality?* chapter 19.
[14] Murphy, *Anglo-American Postmodernity*, 140.
[15] Ibid., 127.

modern views of language, which are representational or expressivist, also are reductionistic because, first, they focus on "atomic" propositions apart from their narrative context. Second, they focus on the individual and what he or she intended by a certain expression, rather than the "move" that person made in the context of a social setting.

In sharp contrast, she argues that these modern views of language are seriously flawed. Liberal Protestant theology makes use of expressivist religious language, and such language describes an inner state of the speaker. But Murphy contends that this view requires too sharp a separation between the cognitive and expressive functions of language. Consider the doctrine of creation. If this is just an expression of one's sense of dependence upon God, what is the importance of such a statement if one is not in fact dependent upon God in a propositional sense? Furthermore, if theological statements are just expressions of inner states of a speaker, why should that description be of interest to anyone else?[16]

Per Murphy, conservative Protestant theology, with its use of scriptural foundationalism and propositional, referential language, also faces severe problems. First, the language of scriptural foundationalism cannot secure the connection between these propositions and a reality beyond our experience. Second, this view of "religious language needs to be criticized for its neglect of the self-involving character of religious discourse."[17]

Instead, Murphy embraces the holism found in the later Wittgenstein and J. L. Austin. Holism in this sense is found in at least two ways. For her, sentences have their meaning in their narrative context. Translation of a proposition into any other language simply will not preserve its meaning, for meanings are not universal. Also, meanings are not a matter of a first-person awareness or intention; rather, meaning is a matter of use in a linguistically shaped form of life, the whole in which words have their meaning. Such uses are a matter of publicly observable behaviors, both verbal and nonverbal.

Murphy is right to point out, like Austin, how we *do* certain things as speakers with our uses of various utterances and not just make true (or false) statements as representations of reality. Since speech acts "are more complex than modern philosophers imagined, the array of criteria for assessing them must be more complex than the single criterion of truth or falsity."[18] Some other criteria for the assessment include "conventional appropriateness or inappropriateness, ingenuousness or its opposite, accuracy or inaccuracy, fair-

---

[16] Murphy, *Beyond Liberalism and Fundamentalism*, 81.
[17] Ibid.
[18] Ibid., 117.

ness or unfairness."[19] So representation and expression are essential, but by no means the only, dimensions of what we do with language.[20] If meaning is a matter of use and not of a person's intention (construed as a private mental awareness), it is no wonder that *ostension,* which has been used in traditional accounts of meaning, simply becomes relatively unimportant.

Just what is ostension, and why do postconservatives see it as being problematic? In the traditional account, ostensive definition involves our noticing and directing our attention to what we are aware of, e.g., a painful feeling, and then applying a term ("pain") to refer to that feeling. The meaning of that term is fixed by an inner "pointing" (a directing of our awareness to that term and the feeling to which "pain" refers). But on Murphy's postconservative account, as well as that of others that use the later Wittgenstein's private language argument, an individual, private language user *could* be mistaken when using a term to refer to something, if meaning and proper use is a matter of one's own private awarenesses. In order to tighten the connection between cognition and proper term usage, postconservatives think meaning needs to be fixed by language use in a social, linguistically formed community, where others can check up to see if we use terms properly.[21]

Her debt to Austin and the later Wittgenstein runs deeper still. Language and life (i.e., behavior) are inextricable,[22] such that language is not *about* the world, as it would be if it were a reflection or representation of reality. Rather, language is *in* the world. She indicates that "the biblical narratives *create* a world, and it is within this world that believers are to live their lives and understand reality."[23]

Kallenberg and Hauerwas

If we draw upon Brad J. Kallenberg, whom Murphy mentored at Fuller and whose book she highly recommends,[24] we may see his use of Wittgenstein and how language is "in" the world. In his view, language and world are *internally* related. We do not somehow get outside language to know how things are from some supposedly neutral standpoint. Rather, "the connection between

---

[19] Ibid.

[20] Ibid., 112.

[21] It is true that I can misread a quote from a book and not even be aware of it, whereas others present can recognize the error and correct me. So, there is some truth to this part of the view. But, does that mean that meaning is a third-person, social matter, and not primarily a first-person one? For more discussion of Wittgenstein's use of the private language argument, as well as how Kallenberg and MacIntyre use it, see chapters 1 and 2 of my *Virtue Ethics and Moral Knowledge.* For my critique, see chapter 5.

[22] Ibid., 127.

[23] Murphy, *Anglo-American Postmodernity,* 120 (emphasis added).

[24] See Brad J. Kallenberg, *Ethics as Grammar* (Notre Dame, Ind.: University of Notre Dame Press, 2001). See Murphy's endorsement on the jacket.

'language and reality' is made by definition of words, and these belong to grammar, so that language remains self-contained and autonomous."[25] Accordingly, "it is in language that it is all done."[26] Or, in Kallenberg's terms, "language does not represent reality, it *constitutes* reality."[27]

Why does he think this? On Kallenberg's view, it is the penchant in philosophy for theoretical explanations, which chiefly occurs in metaphysics, that leads to philosophical confusion, something from which Wittgenstein sought to cure us. According to Kallenberg, theorizing separates language and world, since theories offer an explanation of the world, expressed in language, which supposedly can refer to and stand apart from that world. But this is a confusion, for if "all explanations are framed in language, we have no extra-linguistic means for explaining, validating, or justifying the way we use language."[28]

Kallenberg rejects the view that language can correspond to reality because

> [t]here is no way to talk about what language gets compared with without *talking* about it; there is no criterion for knowing I've got the right "this" (this effect, this referent, this object, this sensation, this word) unless language is already in place. Therefore, the "meaning" of a word can only be determined by its place in the linguistic system.[29]

If we cannot transcend language and match up words with their objects as they really are in the real, extra-linguistic world, then to talk of such correspondence with reality is pernicious and misleading. Wittgenstein expresses the idea well when he remarks that "the connection between 'language and reality' is made by definition of words, and these belong to grammar, so that language remains self-contained and autonomous."[30]

This does not mean that the way the world is has no bearing on how we talk, for on Kallenberg's view, a community's language is internally related to its world. But talking of the objective world would perpetuate the old confusion that somehow we can separate world and language. So, for instance, Murphy asserts consistently that "laws of nature are always *statements* of relations among variables within a closed or isolated system,"[31] and that the

---

[25] Ludwig Wittgenstein, *Philosophical Grammar*, ed. Rush Rhees, trans. Anthony Kenny (Berkeley and Los Angeles: University of California Press, 1974), §55.
[26] Ibid., §95.
[27] Kallenberg, *Ethics as Grammar*, 234.
[28] Ibid., 180.
[29] Ibid., 182.
[30] Wittgenstein, *Philosophical Grammar*, §55.
[31] Murphy, *Anglo-American Postmodernity*, 30 (emphasis added).

"irreducibility of concepts [such as mental to physical] entails the irreducibility of laws."[32]

In similar fashion, we may see how Hauerwas also accepts this internal relation of language and world. For Hauerwas, the Christian life is not just one of decision making, but more importantly, it is one of vision, of seeing the world "rightly," or, as it ought to be perceived. How do we do this? We do not just go out and look at the world, for having vision requires that we accurately "see" the world, morals, us, and more. To do this requires having stories, which are ways of knowing.[33] But most of all, to have vision, we must know a certain language:

> The moral life is . . . not just the life of decision but the life of vision—that is, it involves how we see the world. Such "seeing" does not come from just perceiving "facts," but rather we must learn how the world is to be properly "seen" or better known. Such learning takes place by learning the language that intends the world and our behavior as it ought to be that the good might be achieved.[34]

We cannot just go out and read "facts" of the world, for there are no facts (at least that we may know) independent of linguistic expression. So, how can we come to know the world? For Hauerwas, we cannot just go out and look, for "we come to know the world as we learn to use our language."[35] To see rightly requires being formed by a community's language, which for believers is that of the Bible, or Gospels.

Such a language is always that of a community, for "we have to follow interpersonal rules in a public language."[36] Descriptions of our actions cannot be up to us as individuals, for "the beliefs and convictions we use to form and explain our behavior are not of our own making. To be a moral self is to be an inheritor of a language of a people."[37] Often in ethics we think of the actions of individual agents, but "action and agency by their very nature are socially dependent."[38] The meaningfulness of terms that are used to describe actions depends upon the language (or grammar) of the community. Further, verbal and non-verbal behaviors are primarily public, and they are

---

32 Ibid., 20.
33 Stanley Hauerwas, *Vision and Virtue* (1974; reprint, Notre Dame, Ind.: University of Notre Dame Press, 1981), 71.
34 Ibid., 20.
35 Ibid., 17.
36 Stanley Hauerwas, *Character and the Christian Life* (1975; reprint, Notre Dame, Ind.: University of Notre Dame Press, 1994), 18.
37 Ibid., 33.
38 Ibid., 102.

meaningful if they "fall under some description which is socially recognizable as the description of an action."[39]

If we always work within language, how do we know truth and reality? Hauerwas explains that "to know reality truthfully requires the ability to discriminate between true (good) and false (bad) stories."[40] We cannot achieve some neutral, language-independent, objective standpoint from which we may find a "story of stories." Even so, truth can be realized, but now it is always from a particular standpoint, which is when people form their lives by a truthful narrative. The story of Jesus is the true story, and it enables Christians to see reality (the world, themselves, and situations) as they are.[41]

If we cannot achieve a vantage point outside of all languages, then we cannot adjudicate from any such standpoint between contending stories. If that is so, then "truth" and "truthfulness" do not have anything to do with correspondence between a proposition and a state of affairs in the world, for we cannot know any such thing. As Kallenberg puts it, "'truthful' names the community that is able to shape a people who, in Wittgenstein's words, can 'see the world rightly.'"[42] The same follows for the behaviors that show the truthfulness of the Christian story. There is no "story of stories" (not even the gospel), no universal "meta-story" that stands outside all particularity that serves as a judge over all stories or that gives meaning to these concepts.

Grenz and Franke[43]

Stanley Grenz and John Franke's core presuppositions bear a close family resemblance to those of Murphy, MacIntyre, Kallenberg, and Hauerwas. I will draw upon their *Beyond Foundationalism,* in which they seek to develop a theological methodology for our postmodern context, and in which they recognize that tradition and cultural contexts do influence theologizing.

According to Grenz and Franke, we do not have unmediated experiences, for they "are always filtered by an interpretive framework."[44] Indeed,

---

[39] Ibid., 101.

[40] Stanley Hauerwas, "Ethics and Ascetical Theology," *Anglican Theological Review* 61, no. 1 (January 1979): 97.

[41] Stanley Hauerwas, *A Community of Character* (Notre Dame, Ind.: University of Notre Dame Press, 1981), 96.

[42] Kallenberg, *Ethics as Grammar,* 156.

[43] I have written elsewhere on Grenz and Franke's views in "Christian Postmodernism and the Linguistic Turn," in *Christianity and the Postmodern Turn,* ed. Myron Penner (Grand Rapids, Mich.: Baker, forthcoming, 2005).

[44] Grenz and Franke, *Beyond Foundationalism,* 49.

It is simply not possible to step back from the influence of tradition in the act of interpretation or in the ascription of meaning. Interpretive communities that deny the reality of this situation and seek an interpretation unencumbered by the "distorting" influence of fallible "human" traditions are in fact enslaved by interpretive patterns that are allowed to function uncritically precisely because they are unacknowledged.[45]

Elsewhere they warn that insights that might be gained from sociology about the church as a community must not be allowed to "deteriorate into a new foundationalism."[46] Why might that be a concern?

Such degeneration occurs when speech about the church as community begins with some generic reality called "community," which can *supposedly be discovered through objective observation* of the world, and then proceeds to fit the church into this *purportedly* universal phenomenon as if the community of Christ were a particular exemplar of some more general reality.[47]

Just as we have seen in Murphy and others, foundationalism has led us astray into thinking we can have objective, unmediated observations of the real, objective world. But that simply cannot take place. Quite confidently, Grenz and Franke assert that "we do not live in a universe that is simply a given, external reality."[48]

Yet we live in "the" world, it seems, so what is it? Simply put, "we do not inhabit the 'world-in-itself'; instead, we live in a linguistic world of our own making."[49] Language becomes a primary focus for their theology, as language "provides the conceptual tools through which we construct the world we inhabit."[50] In their view, theology mainly is about "the world-constructing, knowledge-forming, identity-forming 'language' of the Christian community."[51]

Like the other authors I have considered, Grenz and Franke think that language and world are internally related. But they do not give up completely on objectivity. They wisely acknowledge that the linguistic construction of the world cannot extend to all creation. After all, the physical world predates the appearance of humans on it.[52] And Christians can know the world eschato-

---

[45] Ibid., 113.
[46] Ibid., 226.
[47] Ibid., 226-227; emphases added.
[48] Ibid, 271.
[49] Ibid., 53.
[50] Ibid.
[51] Ibid.
[52] Ibid.

logically, as God wills it to be in the future. Here they appeal to what they call *eschatological realism*. This is what the biblical authors describe as the world and community God is creating, which are yet to be realized, and this vantage point provides the world with its main sense of objectivity.

How does the construction of the Christian world take place? The other authors emphasize the proper, grammatical use of Christian language within the Christian community. But Grenz and Franke also wisely bring in the role of the Holy Spirit, who speaks through Scripture today to the many Christian communities, thereby constructing the new community, the church. Importantly, this provides them with a "reality hook," for though Christians are inside language, God the Spirit has broken through and given authoritative revelation in the written word of God and guides the construction of the church.

But if we cannot know some universal truth from an ahistorical vantage point, then it seems we are left with no essence to Christian language, and even the many "Christian" communities. While Grenz and Franke stress the local character of all theologies, including their historical and cultural contexts, nonetheless these local theologies may bear a family resemblance in at least three respects, and if so, they are indeed Christian.[53] Again, the Spirit plays a core role in uniting them:

> The Spirit continually speaks through the biblical text, illuminating subsequent generations to understand their present in light of the grand, *telic* narrative of God and guiding them in the task of living out in their own contexts the vocation all Christians share, namely, that of being the community of Christ in the contemporary world.[54]

We now have completed our survey of the role language plays in the thought of Murphy, MacIntyre, Kallenberg, Hauerwas, and Grenz and Franke. While some details vary among them, nonetheless there is a strong family resemblance between their views, the most important being that a language and its world are internally related. That is, a world is what it is in light of its relationship to the language that was (and is) used to construct it. We simply cannot get outside language and know foundational (read: universal, transcendent, objective) truths, and thus we are always working from within language, even when we do theology, despite the conservative Christian the-

---

[53] See page 25 of *Beyond Foundationalism* for their initial statement of this concept. But see also page 166, where they summarize what they will unpack in part 3: that all localized Christian theologies should be "trinitarian in content, communitarian in focus, and eschatological in orientation."

[54] Ibid., 259.

ological claim that Scripture provides that inerrant foundation for the edifice of theological knowledge. On this view, to appeal to such a notion simply perpetuates a confusion that we can get outside language and know how reality *truly* is. And it also just does not help us in dialoguing with outsiders to the Christian community, for to many such people, it will strike them as just another claim to know objective truth, when so many think that we cannot achieve such knowledge. But that does not mean that Scripture becomes relatively unimportant for these authors. Rather, it is the "norming norm," as Grenz and Franke put it, or the "grammar" for the Christian community. That is, Scripture is authoritative for all that we as Christians do and how we live.[55] Indeed, it is normative for all people, as our authors would claim. Let us now turn to assess these many claims.

ASSESSING THEIR VIEWS

There are several contributions from the views of these postconservative authors that we should note. I will rehearse a few of these briefly. First, Hauerwas and Kallenberg, at least, emphasize Christians being the people of God, and this stress focuses our attention on the importance of the body of Christ for our maturing in Christ. This focus is a healthy corrective from American society's obsession with living autonomously and highly individualistically. The focus in Murphy, Kallenberg, Hauerwas, and MacIntyre upon Christians developing godly habits of behavior, and not just doctrinal beliefs, is very helpful in our becoming more like Jesus.

Second, our authors' stress upon witnessing to the truth of the gospel story by our lives, especially lived in the context of a Christian community, is vital for a winsome witness to non-Christians today, who often question (or flatly deny) that we can know transcendent, universal religious truths. This is so important in a time in which many are looking for authentic lives. If we are to witness to the truth of the gospel, then we need to live out the faith in ways that will testify to the living reality of our Savior's being in our midst.

Third, they are right on target to draw our attention to our particularity, and how our "situatedness" can and does influence our beliefs. Grenz and Franke especially call us to consider the historical, cultural context of our theologizing, for we are indeed influenced by it. The extent to which we are influenced is, of course, a different matter.

Fourth, I think all of these authors' emphases upon how we do in fact

---

[55] Ibid., 57-92.

use our language are quite interesting and illuminating. We do shape our understanding of the world by the terms we use. I recall how the *Los Angeles Times* announced several years ago on its front page that it would now use the term "pro-choice" to refer to people who favor abortion and "anti-abortion" for those who disagree. By their favoring "anti-abortion" over "pro-life," they shaped and pitted the debate over abortion as between those who favor a good thing, choice, and those who are against something ("anti-abortion"), rather than as those who also have a positive stance ("pro-life").

And some things are *made* into what they are by how we use our language. A minister declares that a man and a woman are now husband and wife, which marries that couple and establishes a legally recognized relationship. Defendants are declared guilty or not guilty in the eyes of the law when the jury foreperson utters those words. Adoptions are finalized when the judge uses words to declare that to be the case.

Fifth, I must mention the apparent strength of their view by its appeal to "humility of knowledge." In this day and age, this appeal gains a hearing, for many people today have accepted the idea that we should be suspicious of universal truth claims. One factor that has influenced this attitude is the belief that there are no universal, objective moral truths, and so to appeal to them is in effect to oppress people and limit their autonomy. Another factor is what has played out in the use of science. For years, modern science has enjoyed enormous prestige, such as in medicine, and it has held out the hope that many diseases will be cured one day by science. This is the good side of science that promised an inevitable progress for the good of humanity. Yet that promise was shattered when science was used to create the atom bomb as a weapon of mass destruction, and also to perform hideous experiments upon Jewish captives in the Nazi concentration camps.

While the appeal to humility of knowledge seems to appeal to a virtue, it may not be a real advantage over a realist epistemology. As Moreland and DeWeese have argued, a chastened kind of foundationalism also may evince humility of knowledge by not requiring one-hundred-percent certainty in the foundations. So once again, I think the real issue surfaces—do we, or do we not, have access to an objective, real world?

These are some of the various strengths of their views, and I have not tried to be exhaustive. Now I will turn to address some concerns I have with their views, and these will focus on what I think is their core view—that we are inside language and cannot get out to know an objective world as it is in itself, and that instead we construct our worlds by our language use in our particular communities.

ARE WE ON THE INSIDE? THE ISSUE OF ACCESS[56]

Our authors attempt to take the view that we are inside language quite consistently; therefore I propose that we examine that view, and their claims, for consistency. That is, I aim to see just how consistent they are (or can be) on this view.

Let us start by considering their many, sweeping claims. Take, for example, Murphy's claims that there are no theory-neutral observations, or that in foundationalism, the foundations inevitably are partly supported by theoretical beliefs. Or consider MacIntyre's broad claims that we know there are no self-evident truths, that facts were a seventeenth-century invention, or that the standards for rationality are internal to traditions. Kallenberg, too, makes many such assertions and arguments, like his claim that language and world are internally related, and that there is conceptual confusion that metaphysical searches for "essences," or universals, have foisted upon us. Hauerwas likewise claims that we cannot just go out and read facts off the world, for we always know things from under a certain aspect. Yet he does know that the gospel is the true story, even if we cannot prove it as such within history. And finally, Grenz and Franke tell us that foundationalism is (at the least) in dire disrepair; that we live in a linguistic world of our own making; and that all theology is local. Indeed, we could recite many, many such claims.

The key question to ask, I think, is this: What *are* these claims? At one level, they are fascinating claims, and if right, we should embrace them. But, as I suggested, let us take their views seriously and consistently, and test these and other such claims by their own standards.

What, then, are these claims? On the one hand, it seems that these statements are claims made from within the community (or, more likely, communities) of these authors. That is, if language and world are internally related, and we cannot know any objective, universal, essential truth, then we cannot know any essence of language. But we have seen that at least Murphy, Kallenberg, Hauerwas, and Grenz and Franke all appeal to the Christian community and, thus, the Christian language, as their specific kind of language. So that should help specify the particular community out of which they write.

Or does it? If we take MacIntyre's admonishment seriously that there is no such thing as language as such, but only specific languages that are (or were) spoken and written in specific times and locations, then it is hard to see how a general appeal to Christian language will specify the relevant linguis-

---

[56] For a detailed examination of this line of argument, see chapter 4 of my book *Virtue Ethics and Moral Knowledge*.

tic community. Such specification will make all the difference, for if there is no essence to language, but only many languages, and if each one is internally related to its particular world, then we must know which community it is out of which any postconservative author writes.

But if we take MacIntyre's point seriously (and well we should, for our other authors do), then, as he asserts, there is no such thing as Latin-as-such; there is only Latin-as-was-written-and-spoken-in-the-time-of-Cicero-in-Rome. [57] Accordingly, it seems unjustifiable to simply refer to the Christian community and its language as being specific enough to pinpoint the relevant linguistic community. For despite commonalities, Christians are not a monolithic, homogeneous group. There are, for example, Baptists, Pentecostals, Methodists, Anglicans, Evangelical Free, and many more. And within each, there are other variations. For instance, within Baptists, there are Southern, Conservative, and American, to name a few. And within Southern Baptists, there is diversity, at least in terms of degree of adherence to the doctrine of inerrancy.

Additionally, there are variations in terms of geographic location, even just within the United States, not to mention the world. In other countries, there is diversity in other ways, such as the degree to which a local congregation is dominated by missionaries or indigenous leaders. Even within a local stateside congregation, there are sub-groupings or "cell groups," in terms of age, geographic location, or other life stages.

So which is the relevant community? If we take their view seriously that language and world are internally related, and that languages are discrete, then detailed specification of the relevant linguistic community will make all the difference, for it is that community's use of its particular language that makes its world. On this view, if taken consistently, the claims an author makes are claims made from a particular linguistic community and how it has shaped its world by how its members talk in it.

It is telling, therefore, when we see that none of our authors, with the possible exception of Murphy, informs us of the specific, discrete community out of which he or she writes. To her credit, in *Whatever Happened to the Soul?* Murphy informs her audience that she writes as a fellow Christian among other nonreductive physicalists at Fuller Theological Seminary.[58] She also writes as an Anabaptist, but that too surely must include differences among

---

[57] MacIntyre, *Whose Justice? Which Rationality?* 357.
[58] Even this specificity may not be sufficient, for surely there are subgroups within Fuller. In that case, it will not do to refer just to Fuller as the relevant community. Rather, which group within Fuller is the relevant one?

its local groups. But at least in the works I have referenced in this essay, none of the other writers specifies his local communal affiliation besides saying that he writes as a Christian.

Does Murphy's specification help her make her case? If languages are internally related to their respective worlds, then so what if that is how she and others at Fuller happen to talk? In reference to her Anabaptist affiliation, which specific community within that tradition is hers? Or so what if that is how the members of Kallenberg's specific community happen to talk? The same goes for all our other authors. The discrete, historically situated character of forms of life means that each one writes from a relatively small Christian community. On this view, languages are discrete and internally related to their own particular worlds, so other groups literally talk in different languages, and they inhabit different worlds. Even other Christians would talk their own languages, which may or may not share some of these authors' communities' specific presuppositions.

So one possible answer to the question "What are these claims?" is that they are just constructs of each author's discrete community's way of talking. But if so, then so what? Yet Murphy and others have explored a response to this point. Even if we do speak different languages, the community and tradition still matter since we can see the rational superiority of one tradition over another. Murphy has embraced the holism of Lakatos and MacIntyre precisely because of their ability to adjudicate between rival programs, or traditions, which boil down to different languages, with their own related worlds. So let us see if MacIntyre's work can provide the solution Murphy and others expect.

Like MacIntyre, or his exemplar, Aquinas, Murphy somehow must have learned and mastered many different languages (such as the languages of science, theology, ethics, philosophy of language, and more, and in both their modern and postmodern versions), or else we would have to deny her scholarly grasp of her material. And indeed, Murphy presents impressive credentials, with doctorates in both theology and philosophy of science. But on MacIntyre's account, linguistic mastery is what she needs in order to see the rational resources available in various traditions, and their rational superiority and inferiority. How does one gain such mastery?

To master a language as a second first language, one has to learn it as an insider. It is not a simple matter of translation, for in translation we lose meaning. Becoming bilingual involves mastering a language's verbal uses as well as its gestures (that is, the nonverbal behaviors). But that presents a problem. How could Murphy master these languages? She did not live in the time of Locke, Descartes, or Kant, or the nineteenth-century theologians she cites so often, and that is significant, for on her view languages are highly particular. It therefore seems *impossible* for her to master languages of people groups who no longer are alive. Also, presumably, she does not speak (as a native) the language of representational theorists in language, nor of substance dualists, since those are not her communal affiliations.

Now at this point, Murphy could object that this point is irrelevant. We have today many liberal and conservative theologians, foundationalists, dualists, and reductive physicalists, so it does not matter if a past community, along with its world and language, no longer exists. But each of these generalized groupings has diverse characteristics. Again, the same issue resurfaces: Which is the relevant community? That we (her readers) know this is highly important, for if language use makes a world, then it makes all the difference that we know her relevant community.

But this brings to the surface another key issue, which gives rise to a second way to understand the sweeping claims of these authors. Murphy and the other authors have given us accounts of foundationalism and its degenerative state; the failures of representational views of language; the problems of dualism or reductive physicalism, etc.; as well as all of Murphy's suggested replacements. They have told us that language and world are internally related, and so on. In *which* world do these conditions obtain? And *what* are these claims? To be consistent, they must be constructions made by how people talk according to the language of a local, discrete community. They cannot be statements that are true in a sense of corresponding with an extra-linguistic reality, lest they undermine one of their core beliefs.

Therefore, why are there problems with foundationalism? It is because that is how they and their respective communities' members talk, according to their grammar. The same holds for all their views, including the assertion that we can rationally adjudicate between rivals. All these claims are moves within language-games in their respective ways of life, and as such they are meaningful only because that community's members have decided that such uses have meanings. Even the claim that one tradition is rationally superior to another is but a claim made from within a way of life and how its members have made its world. But so what? Why *should* anyone in a different community (even a different Christian community) talk as they do? There is no basis for commending any of our authors' views to those outside of their specific groups. They just say that outsiders should join with them and see "reality" as they do.

But surely this conclusion is drastically opposed to their apparent intentions in writing many lengthy, detailed books on these subjects. Murphy has not written these essays in such a way as to just state how her community talks. Her choices of publishers (e.g., Fortress, Trinity, Westview, and Cornell) indicate that she expects a far broader audience to understand her work. The same holds for Kallenberg, Hauerwas, and MacIntyre, who all publish regularly with large presses like the University of Notre Dame Press. Grenz and Franke chose Westminster John Knox, a large press, and Grenz has written with many other publishers.

Also, Murphy has argued that we *should* reject modern epistemological, linguistic, metaphysical, and theological views in favor of her constructionist ones. And all the others have made similar kinds of claims. But since they do not seem content with just telling us how they talk in their respective, local communities, then it seems far more likely that each one actually presupposes an epistemic access to the real world in itself, even though they all officially deny that that is possible.

In either case, their view is in serious difficulty. On the one hand, if their claims are just constructs made by how they talk within their very localized communities, then so what? On their view, why should anyone else (even a Christian) outside that specific community talk that way? Alternatively, they presuppose epistemic access to the real world in itself, a result that would destroy the core of their whole view.

APPLICATIONS

Now that I have developed a negative argument against their view, let us see what applications we may draw from it. First, as I argued above, their attack on foundationalism is just a result of how they talk within their particular communities. Following their own view consistently, they cannot be giving us a report of how things are in the *real* (i.e., objective, extra-linguistic) world. If that is the case (and I do not see how it can be otherwise), then all their charges are just the ways they happen to talk in their respective communities (which remain unspecified). But if there is not a real, objective problem (i.e., in the extra-linguistic world), then why should anyone outside their local communities accept (much less be concerned with) their claims?

Second, I now want to draw out some specific implications for their linguistic constructionism for core Christian doctrines. I will examine quickly the nature of God and the prospects for special revelation; the two natures of Christ; the crucifixion, resurrection, and atonement; justification and hamartiology; and finally, the Christian practice of witness.[59]

---

[59] See chapter 7 of my *Virtue Ethics and Moral Knowledge* for a more complete account of what this view will do to orthodox Christian doctrines.

The Nature of God and the Prospects for Special Revelation

Orthodoxy has held that God exists in his own right, that he is not dependent upon us for who and what he is. Conservative Christians also have held that God has revealed himself in his Son and in Scripture. While we may not be able to know God fully, what we know through the ways he has revealed himself is veridical.

But notice what happens to these doctrines on the postconservative views we have been considering. Just as we cannot know things as they are, in an objective sense, so we cannot know God as he is in himself. The reason is that we are inside language and cannot get outside to know reality as it truly is, i.e., apart from language. But let us suppose that God is not inside language. Could it not be the case that while we are inside language, God has broken through that barrier and revealed objective truth? He did this through Scripture, and he also did so in his Son, who lived among us and revealed the Father. Indeed, some may suggest that God participates in our language-games.[60]

This is a natural, attractive reply to my argument, so let us consider how it fares on the views of postconservatives themselves. Regardless of God's abilities to break through, we still are on the inside of language. Therefore, no matter how God tries to reveal himself and objective truth, we cannot know such revelation in itself. Accordingly, we make the revelation what it is for us by how we talk about it. The same goes for God himself. We cannot know God as he is in himself, so we must make God by how we use our language. But that result is plainly idolatrous on the terms of conservative Christians' own grammar, the Bible. If I am right, then that result alone ought to make us pause and give up these postconservative views.

The Two Natures of Christ

Consider now God's revelation in Christ, the perfect God-man. As God, he would know all truth from (literally) a God's eye view. As a human, however, Jesus would be inside language. Even worse, he would know both situations to be true at the same time! That resulting mental makeup would seem to be radically schizophrenic and unlivable. Surely such a person would not compel our worship, but that seems to be the kind of Savior we end up with on postconservative views.

---

[60] This comment was made to me by a Fuller graduate at my presentation on Murphy's views at the western regional meeting of the American Academy of Religion, March 21, 2004, at Whittier College, California.

The Crucifixion, Resurrection, and Atonement

Pivotal to Christian theology, the faith rises or falls on the resurrection. Paul certainly realized this in 1 Corinthians 15, for if the dead have not been raised, then our faith is worthless. But Christ has been raised. Likewise, the crucifixion and death of Christ are essential to the faith, for without it our sins have not been atoned for. Orthodox Christians have held that the crucifixion, resurrection, and atonement are real, historical events.

But what are they on the postconservative view? As Hauerwas points out, though the gospel is the true story, there is no way within history to prove it as such. But even worse, events too are things we cannot know as they truly are. Just like the other things we have examined, events take on their character by the way we talk in our communities. Our language use makes them what they are. So what are these particular events? They are what they are due to how Christians have talked and made their world. They are "true" simply because of that.

If that is so, then there are worlds in which Jesus is not the Savior, such as the Muslim world(s), or Buddhist one(s). That Jesus is the Savior in Christian world(s) is due to how Christians talk. But the Bible teaches that Jesus is the only way to God (Acts 4:12), so this conclusion undermines what Scripture clearly teaches.

It also follows that there are worlds that simultaneously exist in which God foreknows all possible future contingents (e.g., in a Christian community that talks the language of Molinism and middle knowledge), and yet others in which God cannot know that which in principle cannot be foreknown (as in a Christian community where the language of open theism is spoken). In both kinds of communities, the members say that God is omniscient, yet how that term is used in each community varies. If language use makes a world, and languages are discrete, so that there is no essence to Christian language, but many "Christian" languages, then it follows that, at the same time, God may know all future contingents and *not* know them.

Now some may reply that though this is true, it is not a problem, because within the open theist world, God is omniscient in the way its members use that term, while within the Molinist world, God is omniscient in terms of how Molinists talk. The problem I have raised only arises if we assume we can somehow get a viewpoint apart from language to see that we have (apparently) contradictory views of God.

While that is a possible reply, I do not think it is a good one. For one, I already have argued that postconservatives most likely presuppose an epistemic access to a language-independent world in order to deny that such a view is possible. For another, the issues surrounding the specificity of community resurface here. If a language and a world are internally related, then how members use their language within their communities makes their particular world, including, as I argued above, God. But then there would be Christian communities in which God himself (and not just their respective views of God) has different properties, and we would know that, even within a community on a postconservative understanding. Hence, I do not see how we as Christians plausibly can maintain such a view, when our "grammar" (i.e., on postconservatives' own views) is the Bible, and the Bible plainly teaches that God always is the same in his essential attributes. The Christian God must be identical to himself in all communities, but that conclusion does not follow from the postconservatives' own views.

Our Sinfulness and Justification

The same result follows for the doctrines of hamartiology and justification. Why are we sinners? Because that is how Christians have made their world by how they talk. And how is it that we are justified? Yes, it is by faith in Christ, but this is so because of how Christians have made their world. We set up the conditions we all face, and the solution as well! But these conditions clearly seem to be beyond our abilities to establish or control. Furthermore, these conclusions contradict Scripture, which clearly teaches the universal sinfulness of all people (e.g., Rom. 3:10, 23) as well as the universal offer of the gospel to all people(s) (Matt. 28:19), as truths that are not dependent on our use of language within our communities to make them so.

Witnessing and the Authentic Jesus

Last, I will consider the doctrine of witness. I think this is one of the attractive points of postmodern, postconservative theology. Postconservatives such as Hauerwas and Kallenberg call our attention to the need to live out the faith in community in such a way that outsiders may see the authentic Jesus in our midst. We thereby witness by our lives, and not so much by propositional arguments, which supposedly appeal to universal, ahistorical reason, which we have seen is an Enlightenment fiction on this view.

Hauerwas gives several illustrations of this kind of witness,

> . . . in which people are faithful to their promises, love their enemies, tell the truth, honor the poor, suffer for righteousness, and thereby testify to the amazing community-creating power of God. . . . This church [the confessing one] knows that its most credible form of witness (and the most "effec-

tive" thing it can do for the world) is the actual creation of a living, breath-
ing, visible community of faith.[61]

We could augment this list of intelligible acts of witness with Christians' loving one another; their giving to those who ask of them; and so forth.

All these actions are exceedingly powerful in their Christian witness. Jesus
did say, "by this all men will know that you are my disciples, if you love one
another" (John 13:35, NIV). The problem, though, arises because of the postconservative understanding of the nature of behaviors in linguistic forms of
life. Verbal and nonverbal behaviors are tied to a form of life and are endowed
with meaning *by a particular community.* It would seem, then, at least at first
glance, that such behaviors (which amount to bodily movements) alone will
not necessarily communicate what Hauerwas and others think they will.

Moreover, the very claim that these behaviors are intelligible to outsiders
is itself just a claim made from *within* Hauerwas's way of life (whichever one
that is). It is a sweeping universal claim, but its truthfulness is due just to how
his community has made its world by its language. So the same issues resurface. We do not see Hauerwas specify in sufficient detail which Christian
community he speaks from, but it cannot be some *generalized* Christian body,
unless he be guilty of the same kind of theoretical confusion that metaphysi-
cians supposedly have created. So his claim is just a particular claim made
true by how some discrete "Christian" group has used its language to create
its world. Included in that world are the outsiders, who gain their form as
such due to how Hauerwas's community has described them, including their
having the ability to see that the Christian virtues are the truthful way to live.
*Therefore, this assertion of the intelligibility of Christian behaviors to out-
siders is utterly question begging.* By insisting upon the intelligibility of the
truthfulness of these actions, Hauerwas presupposes that outsiders have a
point of contact with Christian language. But that presupposition contradicts
his notion that the Christian world stands in a strictly internal relation to its
language.

Furthermore, a Christian way of living is not the only way to live out the
virtues he depicts as being so clear in their witness. If this is so, then their witness to the unique truthfulness of the gospel may not be as clear as Hauerwas
thinks. Muslims likely would stress the importance of telling the truth, and
for that matter, so might atheists. There is no inherent reason they would not
want to keep their promises, although their reason for so doing might be dif-

---

[61] Stanley Hauerwas and William H. Willimon, *Resident Aliens* (Nashville: Abingdon, 1989), 46-47.

ferent from what we would expect of a Christian. And the Christian way of living out these virtues may not be the only way to do so. For instance, Jews would likely honor the poor, and, again, so might secularists.

Additionally, non-Christians may perform acts that would fall under these descriptions in ways different from Christians. For instance, consider that what counts as suffering for righteousness in one community might not be the same in another. What some Jehovah's Witnesses see as righteous behavior, and thereafter suffer for it, may not look the same in a Protestant Christian setting. Jehovah's Witnesses may encounter criticism from a Protestant Christian when doing door-to-door proselytizing, and for that they may think they have suffered for righteousness. Yet, from a Christian standpoint, they have not done so for the true gospel. On the other hand, a Christian may suffer for righteousness by going as a missionary to a people group, preach the gospel to them, and then be martyred by those very people. So, if each way of life makes its own world by its language, then there is no way for outsiders to distinguish between these alternative ways of acting and their corresponding meaningfulness.

So not only does Hauerwas's assertion beg the question, it also is not the case that these listed behaviors are limited to just the Christian community. They also need not be performed in the same way. Somehow their intelligibility as being truthful of just the Christian way of life presupposes some further standard, one that apparently is so apart from linguistic expression. Yet Hauerwas may reply and agree that, yes, others may act in certain ways that would fit these descriptions based upon how they use their language. However, he could contend that mature Christians will tend to live out *most or all* of these virtues, and *that* would be something uniquely truthful of the Christian community. Hence the consistent practice of these virtues could be intelligible to outsiders.

Perhaps Kallenberg can help strengthen this point. He thinks that Wittgenstein held to the idea that primitive reactions convey meanings *across* communal boundaries. Somehow these behaviors supposedly are prelinguistic, and they become the basis for language. Wittgenstein cites such reactions as grimacing when stuck with a pin, or a mother's caring for her crying child, as primitive reactions. Could therefore Hauerwas's aforementioned kinds of Christian behaviors count as primitive reactions, something that will communicate across linguistic boundaries and perhaps preserve this intelligibility of their Christian witness?

Unfortunately for Hauerwas, an appeal to primitive reactions will not help, for on his own account, *the virtuous behaviors he describes presuppose linguistic usage.* For instance, to see someone as an enemy requires that a self has been formed by use of language to take on that characteristic. The same holds for who counts as the poor, and what counts as a promise, at least on his view of the relation of language and the world. And the same can be argued for what counts as truth telling, righteousness, or honoring someone. To make these extra-linguistic is tantamount to jettisoning the entire view that a world is internally related to language. That is, if these are exceptions and are pre-linguistic, then why should not other things be outside as well, such as the gospel, virtues, or other things? But to be consistent on Hauerwas's account, seeing someone as an enemy or as the poor or honoring someone all require the use of language. Once again, Hauerwas begs the question; on his own account, these intelligible, virtuous behaviors have been made so by how his linguistic community has made its world by its language.

Furthermore, there is a deeper issue at stake here. A supposed strength of the postconservatives' views is that they emphasize the importance of authentically living out the faith. The promise is that outsiders can see the authentic Jesus in the Christian community formed in the ways postconservatives propose. But is that even possible on this view's own terms? I do not see how, for if we cannot know things as they truly are, then neither can we know the real, authentic Jesus. The Jesus we can know on this view is just a construction of how Christians talk in their own community. But that result takes away one of the apparent strengths of this view.

EPILOGUE

So far, I have given a "negative" argument against Murphy, MacIntyre, Hauerwas, Kallenberg, and Grenz and Franke's views. Here I will not begin to sketch my own way of showing that we do indeed have access to the way things really are, apart from language or any other supposed barrier that stands between us and the real world.[62] Instead, I will build upon what Moreland and DeWeese have argued in the previous chapter—that is, a direct realist view, in which we can and do have epistemic access to reality.

We can and do get "outside" of language because we were never on the "inside." In fact, we come in contact with the real world every day. If that is the case, then Murphy's second argument against all kinds of foundationalism

---

[62] For an excellent article that develops the basis for our having knowledge of objective truth, see Dallas Willard, "How Concepts Relate the Mind to Its Objects: The 'God's Eye View' Vindicated," *Philosophia Christi* 2:1:2 (1999): 5-20. See also my "Hauerwas and Kallenberg, and the Issue of Epistemic Access to an Extra-linguistic Realm," *Heythrop Journal* (July 2004). At the end of that essay, I sketch some reasons why we can and do have such access. In *Virtue Ethics and Moral Knowledge*, I also develop some cases to show this same point (e.g., see chapter 5).

fails. That view held that the foundational beliefs are not theory-independent, because we cannot have any theory-independent, neutral contact with the objective, real world. But we can and do have such contact, and so this argument is defeated.

Now does this mean that my view suffers from a lack of epistemic humility, the supposed virtue of the approach taken by the authors I have considered? I do not think that needs to be the case at all. Postconservatives claim that their view allows for epistemic humility because they do not have to prove (with certainty) that the faith is true in an objective sense. But we do not need to have one-hundred-percent certainty to be justified in believing that we can and do come in epistemic contact with the objective, language- and mind-independent world. There are many things we know, such as that we exist, that Jesus is the only way to God, and that the postconservative view under consideration fails to meet its own criteria. We do not have to have certainty to know these things, as well as many, many other things. Instead, we can show humility by giving reasons for our beliefs, all the while acknowledging that it is *possible* we could be wrong. By that I mean that I *could* be mistaken. For example, it is possible that I am just a brain in a vat, and these sentences are just the result of the stimulation of "my" brain by a mad scientist. But then I want to ask the questioner, why should I believe that? If we have ample reasons for our beliefs, then the burden of proof is upon the one who challenges us. And we can walk humbly before our God, all the while having great confidence that we know the truth, and that we can (and should) commend it to others with compelling evidence.

PART THREE
THEOLOGICAL
METHOD

6

IS THEOLOGICAL TRUTH FUNCTIONAL OR PROPOSITIONAL? POSTCONSERVATISM'S USE OF LANGUAGE GAMES AND SPEECH-ACT THEORY

A. B. Caneday

INTRODUCTION

"The problem of the contemporary systematic theologian, as has often been remarked, is actually *to do* systematic theology."[1] For evangelicalism, David Tracy's observation is even more accurate today than three decades ago when he first expressed it. Pluralism's intensification has rendered evangelical theology introspective and preoccupied with theological prolegomena—how to do theology—and less active in actually doing theology. This has been true for more than two decades. Christian theologians have occupied themselves more with *methods* for doing theology than with *doing* theology, more with wondering *how* we may know God than with *knowing* God, and more with concern for *the impact of culture* upon forging Christian theological beliefs than with *the impact of Christian theological beliefs* upon transforming culture.

Preoccupation with methodological correctness by so many of the church's theologians for nearly a generation has yielded at least three effects. First, evangelical theology withers, blighting the church's worship, stunting spiritual growth, and gagging prophetic voices to the benighted world.[2]

---

[1] David Tracy, *Blessed Rage for Order: The New Pluralism in Theology* (1975; reprint Chicago: University of Chicago Press, 1996), 238, emphasis his.

[2] Several have narrated the demise of Christian theology. Though his criticism is not principally against preoccupation with theological method, for the effects of this preoccupation, see David F. Wells, *No Place for Truth: Or Whatever Happened to Evangelical Theology?* (Grand Rapids, Mich.: Eerdmans, 1993).

Second, evangelical theology accommodates our pluralistic culture even while engaging in cursory if not glib review and critique of it.[3] Third, methodological correctness tends to intimidate and shape Christian theological action, speech, and thought. Occupied with methodological correctness shaped by postmodernism concerns, some serve as "theological methods police" who detain for questioning those who have published works of Christian systematic theology on suspicion that they have engaged in methodological naïveté toward our postmodern culture.[4]

Chief among theological methods police is Stanley Grenz, who calls for and outlines a "revisioning" of theological method.[5] Against evangelical theological method grounded in Scripture as God's inerrant Word—a method that he perceives as grounded in Enlightenment and modernist foundationalism—Grenz, recently joined by John Franke, advocates a method that is nonfoundational and that rejects a propositional view of Scripture in favor of a functional view that centers upon experience rather than doctrine.[6] By "experience" they mean "encounter with God in Christ."[7] Roger Olson, an advocate of this theological shift, christened it *postconservative,* distinguishing it from evangelicalism but also from postliberalism, which is the source for Grenz's theological "rules of discourse" borrowed from George Lindbeck's cultural-linguistic theological method.[8]

Postconservatives welcome the triumph of postmodernism and the

---

[3] For a not so cursory critique of postmodernism, see D. A. Carson, *The Gagging of God: Christianity Confronts Pluralism* (Grand Rapids, Mich.: Zondervan, 1996).

[4] See, for example, the criticism of Gordon R. Lewis and Bruce A. Demarest, *Integrative Theology* (Grand Rapids, Mich.: Zondervan, 1996) and of Wayne Grudem, *Systematic Theology: An Introduction to Biblical Doctrine* (Grand Rapids, Mich.: Zondervan, 1994) by Stanley J. Grenz in his *Renewing the Center: Evangelical Theology in a Post-Theological Era* (Grand Rapids, Mich.: Baker, 2000), 77.

[5] Stanley J. Grenz, *Revisioning Evangelical Theology: A Fresh Agenda for the Twenty-first Century* (Downers Grove, Ill.: InterVarsity Press, 1993).

[6] Stanley J. Grenz and John R. Franke, *Beyond Foundationalism: Shaping Theology in a Postmodern Context* (Louisville: Westminster John Knox, 2001), 48. Grenz and Franke call Charles Hodge and Wayne Grudem "conservative modernists" (50).

[7] Ibid., 48.

[8] See Roger Olson, "Reforming Evangelical Theology," in *Evangelical Futures: A Conversation on Theological Method,* ed. John G. Stackhouse, Jr. (Grand Rapids, Mich.: Baker, 2000), 201. It is worth noting that when young evangelicals coined the term "the new evangelicalism" in the late 1940s, they retained the historic designation—"evangelical"—but distanced themselves from the separatism and quarrelsomeness so closely associated with fundamentalism. They did not overturn fundamentalist doctrine. Harold Ockenga stated, "Doctrinally, the fundamentalists are right, and I wish to be always classified as one" ("From Fundamentalism, Through New Evangelicalism, to Evangelicalism," in *Evangelical Roots,* ed. Kenneth Kantzer [New York: Thomas Nelson, 1978], 40). Olson, on the other hand, asks, "Are 'evangelical' and 'theologically conservative' synonymous? Are all evangelical theologians conservative? Most observers—both inside and outside the large and diverse subculture of North American evangelical Christianity—would probably answer yes. Evidence is growing, however, that some theologians who insist on wearing the label 'evangelical' (or cannot escape it even when they try) are shedding theological conservatism. A new mood, if not movement, in North American evangelical theology can be described as 'postconservative.' The best analogy is to 'postliberal' theology—the posture of theologians who see themselves moving beyond liberalism while preserving some of its qualities" ("Postconservative Evangelicals Greet the Postmodern Age," *Christian Century* 112 [May 3, 1995]: 480).

demise of all forms of foundationalism including the end of *conservative modernism* as they call it. Perceiving conservative evangelicals to be modernists who simply ground their beliefs upon Enlightenment foundationalism, postconservatives judge conservatives as engaging a naïve theological method that yields not *"systematic* theologies" but "encyclopedias of theological knowledge."[9] Grenz and Franke treat evangelical theology as if it were "a collection of isolated factual statements arising directly from first principles" and as if evangelicals made no distinction between "first-order" and "second-order" theological discourse.[10] They contend that "theology can no longer model itself after the foundationalist metaphor of constructing an edifice."[11] Grenz and Franke fault evangelicals for their appeal to Scripture as theology's "foundation" as if this metaphor for Scripture inextricably ties their beliefs to Enlightenment-modernist philosophical and epistemological foundationalism.[12] "Instead," Grenz and Franke assert, "we ought to view Christian doctrine as comprising a 'belief-mosaic' and see theology, in turn, as the exploration of Christian doctrine viewed as an interrelated, unified, whole."[13]

Grenz and Franke contend that evangelical theologians who view Scripture as the inerrant and sure foundation of theological truth are modernists, not simply affected by modernistic ideas. Consequently, they insist that evangelical theology needs more than correction. Evangelical theology—including its method of appeal to Scripture—needs to be overthrown because Grenz and Franke think that conservative evangelicals' confidence in Scripture's authority is actually grounded in the canons of Enlightenment foundationalism. So, "in contrast to the Enlightenment ideal that effectively took theology out of the church and put it in the academy," their proposal would return "theological reflection to its proper primary location within the believing community."[14] Not only do Grenz and Franke adopt a coherence view of truth that leads to their acceptance of nonfoundationalism, but they

---

[9] Grenz and Franke, *Beyond Foundationalism,* 50.

[10] "First-order" refers to the language of Scripture as God's revelation, and "second-order" refers to theological formulations of Scripture's teaching. Whether Grenz and Franke are correct is disputable. Other essays in this volume critique the Grenz-Franke model.

[11] Grenz and Franke, *Beyond Foundationalism,* 51.

[12] It seems that Grenz and Franke commit a word-meaning fallacy that Wittgenstein's "language games" exposes, namely, that the same words (in this case "foundation") may bear significantly different meanings depending upon the "language game" being played. Grenz and Franke, in this case, are not "playing by the rules" of the "language game."

[13] Grenz and Franke, *Beyond Foundationalism,* 51. As if recognizing that their rejection of the metaphorical use of "foundation" is rather harsh, Grenz and Franke say that "while we might view the Christian interpretive framework as in a certain sense foundational for theology, we could more properly speak of theology as the articulation of the cognitive mosaic of the Christian faith" (51). This concession appears directed to "Reformed epistemologists" such as Alvin Plantinga and Nicholas Wolterstorff (see *Renewing the Center,* 200-201).

[14] Grenz, *Renewing the Center,* 201; and Grenz and Franke, *Beyond Foundationalism,* 45-46.

also embrace a key element of postliberalism. They adopt Lindbeck's novel use of Ludwig Wittgenstein's metaphor of grammar as "language games" to support their claim that theology should be a community conversation. They also creatively employ "speech-act" theory at a macro level to advance their case that the Bible is "the primary voice in the theological conversation"[15] of the community.[16]

Regrettably, postconservatives, led by Grenz and Franke, have discarded viewing Scripture as *propositional* in favor of viewing Scripture as *functional*, as if the two were incompatible. In conjunction with subordinating Scripture to the primary voice among three sources for theology—Scripture, culture, and tradition—they have located doctrinal authority within the "language games" of the believing community rather than in the *linguistic practices* of the biblical canon. Moreover, they have identified the Spirit's contemporary use of Scripture rather than Scripture itself as that which regulates the community's theology. They reject the continuity evangelicals have historically observed between Scripture and Christian theology. Evangelicals have historically regarded their ongoing endeavor to confess properly, accurately, and to God's glory the faith once for all delivered to God's people as continuing in the tradition of the apostles and prophets of old. Though the best evangelical theologians have carefully distinguished between Scripture as God's authoritative Word and their own theological work as at best approximating the theological truths of God's revelatory Word, postconservatives object that conservative evangelicals have virtually fused the two into one. Postconservatives opt for a view of doctrine that, if consistent with the principles adopted, enables them to tolerate mutually exclusive beliefs as equally true.

Do we need to choose whether Christian doctrine bears a functional or a propositional role in the church? Is the postconservative separation between "first-order" and "second-order" discourse valid? Does Christian doctrine, as "second-order" discourse, simply have a functional role for the church? Is Scripture propositional in nature and foundational to Christian theology or not? This essay contends that evangelical theologians at their best have not naïvely equated their theological expressions with Scripture. Also, correctly understood, evangelical theologians have upheld that doctrine is both propositional and functional. The false disjunction in the title of this chapter is purposeful, fully cognizant of warnings against the fallacy of framing one's

---

[15] Grenz, *Renewing the Center*, 206.
[16] Speech-act theory consists of viewing our use of words as having three distinguishable but not separable linguistic acts: (1) utterance of words—merely speaking (locutionary act); (2) the function of words—promise, command, greet, etc. (illocutionary act); and (3) the effect words bring about—persuasion, conviction, etc. (perlocutionary act).

research questions disjunctively, excluding other options.[17] The title highlights the false disjunction postconservatives pose.

FROM PROPOSITIONAL TO NARRATIVE THEOLOGY

More than a decade ago Grenz began his theological project with *Revisioning Evangelical Theology.* As he lays out his revision of the theological task, he rejects what he calls "Evangelical Propositionalism."[18] He challenges the ideas of the Dean of Evangelicalism, Carl Henry, expressed in his multi-volume work—*God, Revelation and Authority.*[19] Whether Grenz adequately or correctly represents Henry's beliefs is disputable.[20] The designation "propositional revelation" (probably not coined by evangelicals) is not without its ambiguities and difficulties, which is why Henry qualifies his use of the expression.[21] Despite Henry's careful definition of "propositional revela-

---

[17] Cf., e.g., David Hackett Fischer, *Historians' Fallacies: Toward a Logic of Historical Thought* (New York: Harper & Row, 1970), 4.

[18] Grenz, *Renewing the Center,* 65ff.

[19] Carl F. H. Henry, *God, Revelation and Authority,* 6 vols. (1976–1983; reprint, Wheaton, Ill.: Crossway, 1999).

[20] See Rodney J. Decker, "May Evangelicals Dispense with Propositional Revelation?—Challenges to a Traditional Evangelical Doctrine," unpublished paper read at the annual meeting of the Evangelical Theological Society, Colorado Springs, November 2001. (Decker's article is available online at http://faculty.bbc.edu/rdecker/documents/prop_rev.pdf.) Critical assessment of Henry's defense of "propositional revelation" is warranted, for his claims need some nuancing.

However, more than nuancing is needed concerning Henry's claim that God's revelation is *univocal,* associating him rather closely with Enlightenment and modernist liberal theology. Michael Horton comments, "After judging that analogy has lost favor in Roman Catholic theology, Carl Henry remarks, 'The main logical difficulty with the doctrine of analogy lies in its failure to recognize that only univocal assertions protect us from equivocation; the very possibility of analogy founders unless something is truly known about both analogates.' In the next sentence, Henry cites his mentor Gordon Clark in support of this criticism of analogy. Many conservatives like Henry apparently share with liberal theology the assumption that language must be either univocal or equivocal, setting the bar for 'truth' so high that at some point a crisis must inevitably arrive in interpretation. 'The key question is: are human concepts and words capable of conveying the literal truth about God?' If so, these words and concepts must directly mirror the divine being, or they represent *untruth*" (*Covenant and Eschatology: The Divine Drama* [Louisville: Westminster John Knox 2002], 189). See also my chastening appeal to evangelical theologians concerning analogy in "Veiled Glory: God's Self-Revelation in Human Likeness—A Biblical Theology of God's Anthropomorphic Self-Disclosure," in *Beyond the Bounds: Open Theism and the Undermining of Biblical Christianity,* ed. John Piper, Justin Taylor, and Paul Kjoss Helseth (Wheaton, Ill.: Crossway, 2003), 156-158, 192-193, 196-199.

[21] Decker makes this clear:

First, Henry does not view the Bible as a digest of assorted logical syllogisms. He explicitly claims that "the truth of revelation is not a series of unrelated and disconnected propositions" (*GRA* [*God, Revelation, and Authority*], 1:233). It should also be noted that propositions are not the same as concepts. A concept (e.g., grace or sin) cannot be true or false. Only as one asserts a proposition regarding a concept can it be true or false. Third, propositional revelation is not invalidated by figures of speech, rhetorical questions, or imperatives. "Regardless of the parables, allegories, emotive phrases and rhetorical questions used by these writers, their literary devices have a logical point which can be propositionally formulated and is objectively true or false" (*GRA,* 3:453). Questions are not propositions in the technical sense, but rhetorical questions imply a judgment that can be stated in propositional form. Likewise, imperatives, though technically not propositions by their grammatical form, do not "cancel the fact that revelation is primarily correlated with a communication of propositional truth. Imperatives are not as such true or false propositions; but they can be translated into propositions (e.g., 'to kill is wrong') from which cognitive inferences can be drawn" (*GRA,* 3:417) (Decker, "May Evangelicals Dispense with Propositional Revelation?" 3).

tion" and his insistence that God's revelation is both *propositional* and *personal*, Grenz yields no substantial concession to evangelical theologians such as Henry.[22] Instead, he adopts an exaggerated and severe judgment of the work of evangelical theologians. He approves of Pinnock's assessment of evangelical theology: "Clark Pinnock . . . rejects as inflexible and undynamic the 'propositional theology that sees its function as imposing systematic rationality on everything it encounters.'"[23] Grenz continues:

> Taking his cue from the contemporary narrative outlook, he chides academic theology for looking for truth in doctrine rather than in the biblical story. Viewing revelation as primarily narrative, Pinnock sees the task of theology as expounding the story and explicating its meanings. Theology, then, is a secondary language whose propositions "live off the power of the primary story."[24]

Grenz offers no recognition that Pinnock overstates the case. Pinnock's division between "doctrine" and "the biblical story" foreshadows Grenz's separation of the same. Both fail to acknowledge that evangelical biblical theologians, who are engaged in narrative theology because their work is in the redemptive and historical narrative of Scripture, and who are engaged in self-criticism concerning the subtle influences of the Enlightenment and modernism upon their presuppositional beliefs, already offer chastening to systematic theological method. Furthermore, though Grenz perceives a dichotomy between beliefs that God's *revelation is propositional* and that God's *revelation is largely narrative* in form, he passes over crucial hermeneu-

---

Vanhoozer, who engages Henry's views more carefully and with more nuance than Grenz and other critics, seems to press Henry's comments on the Sixth Commandment too far. Vanhoozer says, "Henry thinks that *the primary concern of revelation* is 'the communication of truth.' Even divine commands, such as 'Thou shalt not murder,' can be 'translated into propositions' (e.g., 'murder is wrong') (477 [sic; 417]). This example of Henry's is instructive; in my view, *the primary purpose of a command* is not to state a universal truth (though I would agree that such a statement is implicit) but to direct human behavior. The question, then, is whether evangelical theology can correspond to the primary concerns of Scripture, whether this be the communication of truth or the regulation of action" (Kevin J. Vanhoozer, "The Voice and the Actor: A Dramatic Proposal About the Ministry and Minstrelsy of Theology," in *Evangelical Futures*, 70 n. 25; emphasis added). It appears that Vanhoozer shifts categories from "the primary concern of revelation" (which by Henry's illustrative use of the Sixth Commandment includes a full range of non-indicative statements) to "the primary purpose of a command." Henry's statements already account for Vanhoozer's qualification.

[22] For example, Grenz claims, "Despite good intentions, evangelical contextualizers all too easily can remain trapped in a view of propositional revelation that simply equates the divine self-disclosure with the Bible. . . . These theologians are likewise at risk of merely continuing the older enterprise of biblical summarization, with only a slight nod to the necessity of rephrasing theological propositions in contemporary language." Grenz singles out Millard Erickson as a theologian who "occasionally displays this conservative tendency" (*Revisioning Evangelical Theology*, 71-72).

[23] Grenz, *Revisioning Evangelical Theology*, 71. He cites Clark Pinnock, *Tracking the Maze: Finding Our Way Through Modern Theology from an Evangelical Perspective* (San Francisco: Harper & Row, 1990), 186.

[24] Grenz, *Revisioning Evangelical Theology*, 71.

tical questions and proceeds as if this disjunction were real. Thus he fails to engage evangelical scholars who have addressed the hermeneutical issues he passes over, including "the hermeneutical spiral, the pairing of 'distanciation' and 'fusing of horizons,' and asymptotic approaches to knowledge."[25]

For Grenz, his problem "with evangelical propositionalism . . . is not its acknowledgment of a cognitive dimension of revelation and consequently of the statements of theology."[26] The problem, he claims, is that because Western individualism has held evangelicals hostage, they have misunderstood "the social nature of theological discourse."[27] He presumes his premise that evangelicals have uncritically clothed themselves with the "Western mindset," which is also modernism, both of which evangelicals need to shed "if our theology is to speak the biblical message in our contemporary situation . . . and reclaim the more profound community outlook in which the biblical people of God were rooted."[28]

What, however, does Grenz mean? He answers, "Evangelicals are correct in asserting that the revealed truth of God forms the 'basic grammar' that creates Christian identity. . . . But this identity-creative process is not an individualistic matter occurring in isolation. Instead, it is a development that happens within a community."[29] Having set up this false disjunction, as if evangelical theology isolates individuals from a community, Grenz claims,

> We may view theology as the faith community's reflecting on the faith experience of those who have encountered God through the divine activity in history and therefore now seek to live as the people of God in the contemporary world. Ultimately, then, the propositions of systematic theology find their source and aim in the identity and life of the community it serves.[30]

What can deliver Grenz's communitarian Christian theology project from being reduced to one more religious belief current within an ocean of religious pluralism? Grenz and Franke look to a modification of Lindbeck's use of the concept of "language games." How can they retain the Bible as authoritative after reducing it to "the primary voice in the theological conversation"? Grenz and Franke appeal to "speech-act" theory. Does appeal to "speech-

---

[25] D. A. Carson, "Domesticating the Gospel: A Review of Grenz's *Renewing the Center,*" chapter 2 in this volume, 46.
[26] Grenz, *Revisioning Evangelical Theology,* 72.
[27] Ibid., 73.
[28] Ibid.
[29] Ibid.
[30] Ibid., 75-76.

act" theory save the postconservative project so that it can speak of anything objective? To these questions we now turn, respectively.

EVANGELICAL THEOLOGY AS COMMUNITY CONVERSATION

While Grenz surfs across the waves stirred by the deep currents of Enlightenment foundationalism and modernist epistemology, his survey of these currents bears an inveigling quality that fails to fathom the depths. As a key element in his proposal to postmodernize theology and to approach theology as a "community conversation," Grenz appeals first to Wittgenstein's "language games" and then to J. L. Austin's "speech-act theory."

Wittgenstein's "Language Games"

As Grenz and Franke adopt a nonfoundational theological method, they raise the question, "What would theology look like if it not only rejected the correspondence theory of truth, but sought to follow Wittgenstein and move beyond realism as well?"[31] They do not, however, directly appeal to Wittgenstein. Instead, they visit Lindbeck, who channels Wittgenstein's "language games" with a novel twist, if not a failure to "play by the rules."

The later work of Wittgenstein, climaxing in his *Philosophical Investigations*, corrected his earlier work on language and truth, *Tractatus Logico-Philosophicus*, in which he defended the "picture theory of meaning," that objects pictured by words and sentences determine their meanings. Later he corrected this belief that a word has an essential meaning and that it invariably pictures a particular object. He came to recognize that meanings of words and of sentences are determined by their uses within contexts.[32] He designated these wider contexts "language games." Wittgenstein simply discovered philosophically what is intrinsically true of language.[33] It is axiomatic that words and sentences derive their meanings from their uses within contexts. Biblical exegetes and scholars have long acknowledged the truth of what Saussure demonstrated linguistically and Wittgenstein showed philosophically.[34]

---

[31] Grenz and Franke, *Beyond Foundationalism*, 45.

[32] Ludwig Wittgenstein, *Philosophical Investigations*, trans. G. E. M. Anscombe (Oxford: Blackwell, 1953); idem, *Tractatus Logico-Philosophicus*, trans. D. F. Pears and B. F. McGuiness (London: Routledge & Kegan Paul, 1974).

[33] Wittgenstein built upon the work of Ferdinand de Saussure, *Course in General Linguistics* (New York: McGraw-Hill, 1959).

[34] Cf. the influences of James Barr, *The Semantics of Biblical Language* (Oxford: University Press, 1961); and Anthony C. Thiselton, "Semantics and New Testament Interpretation," in *New Testament Interpretation: Essays on Principles and Methods*, ed. I. Howard Marshall (Grand Rapids, Mich.: Eerdmans; Exeter, England: Paternoster, 1977), 78-79.

Regrettably, some take Wittgenstein's "language games" beyond his own conclusions, as David Clark observes:

> They say that because language functions in complex ways according to the grammatical rules that govern what can and cannot be said in a particular form of life, language may not refer at all. This means they relate the words 'truth' and 'meaning', not to reality, but to grammar. Meaning is not a function of a connection of language to reality, but of language to more language.[35]

Grenz and Franke trade upon this exaggerated use of Wittgenstein's work to claim his support for their cause:

> Coherentism and pragmatism provided ways to leave behind the foundationalist preference for the correspondence of truth. The means to overcome metaphysical realism, however, came from another source, the "turn to linguistics." . . . [S]ignificant for the quest for a nonfoundationalist epistemology via linguistics was the work of Ludwig Wittgenstein (1889–1951). In a sense, Wittgenstein completed the shift toward belief systems and the communal dimension of truth pioneered by the coherentists and the pragmatists. . . . Wittgenstein came to realize that rather than having only a single purpose, to make assertions or state facts, language has many functions, e.g., to offer prayer, make requests, and convey ceremonial greetings. This discovery led to Wittgenstein's important concept of "language games." According to Wittgenstein, each use of language occurs within a separate and seemingly self-contained system complete with its own rules. . . . Each use comprises a separate "language game," and each "game" may have little to do with the other "language games." . . . Like the move to coherence and pragmatism, adopting the image of "language games" entailed abandoning the correspondence theory of truth. But unlike these two earlier proposals it also opened the door for the questioning of metaphysical realism. According to Wittgenstein, meaning and truth are not related—at least not directly or primarily—to an external world of "facts" waiting to be apprehended. Instead, they are an internal function of language. Because the meaning of any statement is dependent on the context—that is, on the "language game"—in which it appears, any sentence has as many meanings as contexts in which it is used. Rather than assertions of final truth or truth in any ultimate sense, all our utterances can only be deemed "true" within the context in which they are spoken.[36]

---

[35] David K. Clark, *To Know and Love God: Method for Theology,* Foundations of Evangelical Theology, ed. John S. Feinberg (Wheaton, Ill.: Crossway, 2003), 377.

[36] Grenz, *Renewing the Center,* 194-195. Grenz offers only one citation of Wittgenstein's later work, and in doing so, his reference is confusing because his note refers to Ludwig Wittgenstein, *Philosophical Investigations,* §65, page 32 (it is actually page 31).

Grenz and Franke hyperextend Wittgenstein's "language games," for to agree with Wittgenstein concerning how words and sentences denote meaning does not require agreement with the postconservative notion that "meaning and truth are not related—at least not directly or primarily—to an external world of 'facts' waiting to be apprehended."[37]

Doctrine as "Rules of Discourse"

Grenz and Franke's use of Wittgenstein's "language games" is an adaptation derived from Lindbeck's "cultural-linguistic" approach that separates doctrine from Scripture. Lindbeck endeavors to find a via media between two types of theological method he finds deficient. On the one hand, associated with conservative evangelicals and with Henry in particular, he identifies the "cognitive-propositionalist" type that "stresses the ways in which church doctrines function as informative propositions or truth claims about objective realities."[38] On the other hand, he finds classical liberalism to be the "experiential-expressive" type that views doctrines as "noninformative and nondiscursive symbols of inner feelings, attitudes, or existential orientations," a type associated with Schleiermacher and classical liberalism.[39] As the via media, Lindbeck proposes the "cultural-linguistic" alternative model in which doctrines function as the believing community's "rules of discourse." He attempts to root his theological-methods model in Wittgenstein's concept of "language games." For Lindbeck, "Doctrines regulate truth claims by excluding some and permitting others, but the logic of their communally authoritative use hinders or prevents them from specifying positively what is to be affirmed."[40] Christian doctrines are like community rules:

> For example, the rules "Drive on the left" and "Drive on the right" are unequivocal in meaning and unequivocally opposed, yet both may be binding: one in Britain and the other in the United States, or one when traffic is normal, and the other when a collision must be avoided. Thus oppositions between rules can in some instances be resolved, not by altering one or both of them, but by specifying when or where they apply, or by stipulating which of the competing directives takes precedence.[41]

---

[37] Ibid. The qualifier in this statement, "at least not directly or primarily," proves that Grenz and Franke extract more from Wittgenstein's "language games" than is acceptable.

[38] George A. Lindbeck, *The Nature of Doctrine: Religion and Theology in a Postliberal Age* (Philadelphia: Westminster, 1984), 16.

[39] Ibid., 21.

[40] Ibid., 19.

[41] Lindbeck, *Nature of Doctrine*, 18.

The following example illustrates how the "rules-of-discourse view" functions:

> Consider the assertion, "We are saved by grace alone." The propositionalist will take this as a *factual* claim about the mechanism of salvation. The experiential-expressivist will understand it as the *symbolic expression of an experience* of the power of God in salvation. On Lindbeck's view, the meaning of the doctrine can be expressed in a *rule* like, "Christians should always speak and act upon their salvation in a way that expresses gratitude to God, not pride in their own accomplishment."[42]

Doctrine as "rules of discourse" supplants Scripture as "rule of faith and practice" (which historically has been the church's source of doctrine). "Scripture in tradition" displaces *sola Scriptura*.[43] Lindbeck exploits Wittgenstein's "language games" that locate meanings of a word or a sentence within their respective contexts, to locate meaning of doctrine within a community's "rules of discourse." Is it legitimate to transfer Wittgenstein's metaphor of "language games" from grammar to doctrine?

According to Lindbeck, a community's doctrines, like rules of grammar, function as norms by which adherents know how to think about and live within the world as a member of a given believing community. Doctrines are "teachings regarding beliefs and practices that are considered essential to the identity or welfare of the group." And thus "they indicate what constitutes faithful adherence to a community."[44] In other words, the doctrine of a given Christian community (whether Lutheran, Reformed, Catholic, or other) functions as the "rules of the belief game" within that community for how to think, how to speak, and how to live.

Lindbeck, however, takes Wittgenstein's "language games" beyond their proper conclusions.[45] Whereas Wittgenstein's "language games" concern what determines meanings of words and sentences, Lindbeck stretches the "language games" metaphor. Believing that rules of grammar do not say anything true or false about reality outside the language those rules govern, he claims each rule is "true" only within the framework of the rules that comprise that language. Having made the shift of categories, with ease Lindbeck applies his concept of "rules of grammar" to "doctrine as grammar."

---

[42] Thanks to Michael Horton ("Yale Postliberalism: Back to the Bible?" in *A Confessing Theology for Postmodern Times,* ed. Michael S. Horton [Wheaton, Ill.: Crossway, 2000], 196) for pointing out this example from William Placher, "Postliberal Theology," *The Modern Theologians,* vol. 2, ed. David F. Ford (Oxford: Basil Blackwell, 1989), 120. See Horton's essay for a critique of Lindbeck's proposal.
[43] Kevin J. Vanhoozer, "The Spirit of Understanding: Special Revelation and General Hermeneutics," in *First Theology: God, Scripture, and Hermeneutics* (Downers Grove, Ill.: InterVarsity Press, 2002), 222.
[44] Lindbeck, *Nature of Doctrine,* 16.
[45] See David Clark's comments at note 35 above.

So, his interpreters conclude that Lindbeck views doctrinal statements as making "true" or "false" claims only within the "language game" of the particular Christian community within which those statements are made. "True" and "false" are categories that are not suitable to particular doctrinal statements, for the elements that comprise the whole are "true" or "false" only intrasystematically.[46] Doctrines are "true," then, as "parts of a total pattern of speaking, thinking, feeling, and acting."[47] So, according to Lindbeck, doctrines do not make "first-order" claims of truth, which is to say, as interpreters including Grenz and Franke read him, they make no claim about objective reality. Instead, functioning as rules of grammar, Christian doctrines make second-order assertions. As such, Christian doctrines function to regulate how Christians of a particular believing community are to speak about God; Christian doctrines do not function to make actual assertions about God.[48] So to claim that Jesus Christ really is God is not a claim about objective reality; it is only a claim about what Christians believe and what is correct for Christians to confess within their own community.[49]

As he argues his case in *The Nature of Doctrine*, Lindbeck has led numerous readers to understand him to jettison a correspondence theory of truth for a coherence theory because particular doctrines have no necessary correspondence to reality; they only cohere with other doctrines within the system of belief, that is, intrasystematically.[50] "Correspondence to reality is at a different level."[51]

---

[46] Lindbeck, *Nature of Doctrine*, 80.

[47] Ibid., 64.

[48] Ibid., 69.

[49] Vanhoozer comments, "Let us assume that this account of meaning is broadly correct. Does it follow that what theologians should describe is the use of Scripture *today* rather than the use to which words and sentences were put by those responsible for the final form of the biblical text? To replace *sola Scriptura* with 'Scripture in tradition'—which is to say, with community conventions—is to use the wrong strategy at the worst time" ("The Spirit of Understanding," 222).

[50] The clarity of Lindbeck's argument, or the lack thereof, has recently come to greater light in an exchange with Avery Cardinal Dulles. See Dulles, "Postmodernist Ecumenism: A Review of *The Church in a Postliberal Age*. By George A Lindbeck. Edited by James J. Buckley. Grand Rapids, Mich.: Eerdmans, 2003," *First Things* 136 (October 2003): 57-61. See "George Lindbeck Replies to Avery Cardinal Dulles," *First Things* 139 (January 2004): 13-15. Lindbeck's correction of Dulles's misunderstanding is instructive for both conservative and postconservative evangelical interpreters of Lindbeck's cultural-linguistic approach to doctrine. Lindbeck acknowledges that because of certain "deficiencies, it has been easy to suppose that the second, intrasystematic kind of 'truth' is an alternative to rather than a condition for propositional or ontological truth. When this happens, readers falsely conclude—with delight in the case of postmodern relativists, but, more to my liking, with sadness in the case of Cardinal Dulles—that 'for Lindbeck, the truth of Christianity . . . is predominantly intrasystemic.' A corrected formulation, in contrast, simply notes that special attention to the intrasystematic (and categorical) *conditions* for affirming ontological truth is inseparable from a cultural-linguistic perspective on a religion such as Christianity. It most emphatically does not imply that the realities which faith affirms and trusts are in the slightest degree intrasystematic. They are not dependent on the performative faith of believers (as if, for example, Christ rose from the dead only in the faith of the Church), but are objectively independent."

[51] Horton interprets Lindbeck as saying, "So Christianity is the one true 'gigantic proposition,' and other religions are thoroughly incommensurable with it, just as German is incommensurable with Japanese. Thus, a non-Christian religion is not false but meaningless" ("Yale Postliberalism: Back to the Bible?" 200).

Lindbeck's broadening of Wittgenstein's "language games" metaphor is dubious, and it is doubtful that Wittgenstein intended his concept to be so exploited, but full assessment of Lindbeck's proposal lies outside this essay.[52]

Evangelical Community Constructs the World

Evangelical theologians at their best distinguish between *Scripture* as God's Word and *interpretation of Scripture* as entailing theological formulations. To the degree that evangelical theologians view their understanding of Scripture as fused into one with God's revelation, as if their knowledge of God and of his ways were already perfected and absolute, postmodern epistemological correctives are helpful. So evangelicals use the designations "first-order" and "second-order" as helpful distinctions between God's revelatory Word and the church's theological expressions derived through the interpretation of Scripture, respectively.[53]

However, since Grenz has been working to "revision" evangelical theology, not only has he adopted Lindbeck's two categories—first-order and second-order—but he has also filled these categories from Lindbeck's novel use of Wittgenstein's "language games" discussed above. Nevertheless, Grenz wants to advance a step beyond where Lindbeck's proposal goes. Furthermore, Lindbeck is not pleased with postmodernists like Grenz, though he does not mention him, who reason that "for Lindbeck, the truth of Christianity . . . is predominantly intrasystemic."[54] Grenz claims that the "task of theology is not purely *descriptive* . . . but *prescriptive*."[55] What does he mean? He is not referring to what Christians *ought* to obey. Instead, he says, "The theologian seeks to articulate what *ought* to be the interpretive framework of the Christian community."[56]

Because Grenz and Franke adopt a coherence view of truth that leads to their acceptance of nonfoundationalism and to what they call "communitar-

---

[52] See ibid., 205; cf. Saul A. Kripke, *Wittgenstein on Rules and Private Language* (Cambridge, Mass.: Harvard University Press, 1982); cf. idem, *Covenant and Eschatology,* 311 n. 101.

[53] Regrettably, suiting the sharp cleavage he perceives between two camps within evangelicalism, Roger Olson claims that for "traditionalists," "traditional theological formulations are a first-order language of revelation. God revealed doctrines," but "reformists" (postconservatives) "tend to emphasize the human instrumentality in articulating doctrine, seeing it as a second-order language—in other words, as a human interpretation of divine revelation" (Roger Olson, "The Future of Evangelical Theology," *Christianity Today* 42 [February 9, 1998]: 42). Later in the same essay, Olson equivocates on his use of terms; he confuses first-order with "core doctrines" and "second-order" "with secondary doctrines" (47). David Clark distinguishes between summations of Scripture as "doctrine" (first-order) and interpretations of Scripture for contemporary culture as "theology" (second-order) (*To Know and Love God,* 88-89).

[54] Lindbeck, "George Lindbeck Replies to Avery Cardinal Dulles," 13.

[55] Grenz, *Renewing the Center,* 203.

[56] Ibid.

ian theology" after the order of Lindbeck's, they encounter a problem that poses devastating danger to their project. They ask:

> How can we seek truth in a multicultural world in which various communities offer diverse theological paradigms? In other words, does theology speak about anything objective, or does it content itself with merely articulating the interpretive framework of a specific religious tradition?[57]

Is the communal view of Grenz and Franke capable of reflecting reality beyond itself? Can Christian theology talk about a real world? Or, "Does the move beyond foundationalism entail a move away from metaphysical realism?"[58] Grenz and Franke regard this question "improper and ultimately unhelpful."[59] Instead, they would prefer the question, "How can a nonfoundationalist theological method lead us to statements about a world beyond our formulations?"[60] Their response is to take a cue from postmodern sociologists "who provide insight into the world-constructing role of society in general and language in particular."[61] They accept a basic postmodern antithesis: either we have full and absolute knowledge of a thing, or our knowledge of a thing is socially constructed with dubious connection with reality, which is the thing-in-itself.[62] Because of this, in the end, they have to answer the question, "Why give primacy to the world-constructing language of the Christian community?"[63] Grenz and Franke respond, "As Christians . . . we believe that the Christian theological vision is *true*. But on what basis can we make this claim?"[64] How can they avoid retreating to what they perceive to be the "foundationalist epistemology" of conservative-evangelical modernists? They simply assert their way out of their dilemma.

> [W]hich theological vision is able to provide the transcendent vision for the construction of the kind of world that particular theologizing community is in fact seeking? Which theological vision provides the framework for the construction of true community? We believe that Christian theology, focused as it is on God as the triunity of persons and on humankind as the *imago dei*, sets forth a helpful vision of the nature of the kind of commu-

---

[57] Grenz and Franke, *Beyond Foundationalism*, 51.
[58] Ibid., 52.
[59] Ibid.
[60] Ibid.
[61] Ibid.
[62] Carson, "Domesticating the Gospel."
[63] Grenz and Franke, *Beyond Foundationalism*, 54.
[64] Ibid.

nity that all religious belief systems in their own way and according to their own understanding seek to foster.[65]

As Lindbeck accepts the community tradition as a given, so Grenz and Franke accept it because it is there. In the end, then, Alister McGrath's criticism of Lindbeck's postliberal or cultural-linguistic approach to theology fits the Grenz-Franke model also.[66] The problem concerns the origin of doctrine. What is the source of the cultural-linguistic use of doctrine? Is it God's revelation, or is it human communal wisdom (in other words, religion)?

Rather than offer correctives to evangelical theology, Grenz and Franke (following Lindbeck) overreach in their criticism of what they call cognitive-propositional theology and endeavor to overhaul evangelical theology. Because they set up a false disjunction between propositional and personal revelation, they fail to give adequate consideration to theology that is both cognitive and propositional, and they discard propositional theology. Consequently they locate theological authority within the "language games" (linguistic practices) of the community of believers rather than in the "language games" of Scripture. So the Grenz-Franke model is subject to Vanhoozer's criticism of Lindbeck's approach:

> Lindbeck's cultural-linguistic model, by seeing theology's task as describing the grammar of the community's culture and language, ultimately runs the risk of reducing theology to cultural anthropology, in which talk about God *just is* talk about the community. Such reduction amounts to a failure to speak of God . . . and hence to a failure to preserve the reality of God, together with his divine initiatives. Failure to refer to the divine initiatives results, in turn, in the loss of the central point of the good news, which is to say, in the loss of the gospel itself.[67]

Scripture as Theology's Norming Norm and "Speech-Acts"

If doctrines function as community norms that direct adherents on how to think, speak, and live as Christians, what role does Scripture have? Grenz and Franke reply that Scripture functions to regulate theology's communitarian norm, but not in the way evangelicals view Scripture as the foundation for belief.

---

[65] Ibid.
[66] Alister E. McGrath, *The Genesis of Doctrine: A Study in the Foundations of Doctrinal Criticism* (Grand Rapids, Mich.: Eerdmans, 1997), chapter 2.
[67] Vanhoozer, "Voice and the Actor," 100.

Grenz claims that not until Charles Hodge and his contemporary Princetonian theologians did the church embrace a doctrine of Scripture as the foundation for Christian faith nor as "the central fundamental."[68] Simultaneously Grenz attempts to argue that Princeton's theologians attempted a novel move to establish a doctrine of Scripture as foundational to all Christian theology and that the view of the Bible as not inerrant got lost in the fray.[69] It seems that Grenz falls prey to a word-use fallacy that leads to category confusion. For him, the imagery of Scripture as "foundational" to all Christian theology necessarily links the evangelical belief with Enlightenment epistemology and modernist foundationalism and renders the evangelical view worthy of rejection. So, Grenz asserts, "a misunderstanding of Luther's principle of *sola scriptura* led many theologians to trade the ongoing reading of the text for their own systematic delineation of the doctrinal deposit that was supposedly encoded in its pages centuries ago."[70] He continues, "Thereby, the Bible was all too readily transformed from a living text into the object of the scholar's exegetical and systematizing prowess," an altogether revealing statement of Grenz's postmodern predilection.[71]

As if he had established a real and substantive change in how evangelicals understand *sola Scriptura* in the wake of nineteenth-century Princetonian theologians, Grenz remarkably appeals to the Westminster Confession (the Princetonians' own Confession) to ground his idea that "the Bible is the norming norm in theology."[72] So, as if recovering a treasure lost to evangel-

---

[68] Grenz, *Renewing the Center,* 69-80.

[69] Carson responds:
> A decade and a half ago, a small group of scholars, exemplified by Jack Rogers and Donald McKim, tried to convince the world that the Princetonians had transformed the historic doctrine of Scripture into an indefensible precisionism, an indefensible inerrancy. Their own historical errors were nicely put to rest by John Woodbridge and others, whose close knowledge of the primary sources dealt this revisionist historiography a death blow. The result is that no one of stature makes the same mistake today. But now Grenz is attempting his own wrinkle: the Princetonians may not have *changed* the doctrine but they *elevated* it from one article of faith to the foundation for faith. This sweeping claim probably cannot be sustained. The Princetonians had more to say about Scripture than some of their forebears, precisely because that was one of the most common points of attack from the rising liberalism of the (especially European) university world. But I suspect that even-handed reading of the evidence would not find Hodge or Warfield adopting a stance on Scripture greatly different from that of Augustine or Calvin, so far as its role in the structure of Christian theology is concerned ("Domesticating the Gospel," 69).

[70] Grenz, *Renewing the Center,* 206.

[71] Ibid. To view the Bible as "a living text" is hardly supported by Hebrews 4:12. The expression—a living text—reflects the postmodern treatment of texts, the way loose constructionists view the Constitution of the United States. Furthermore, to suggest that the modern period witnessed the rise of exegetical and theological prowess insults all those who went before.

[72] Ibid., 207. He cites Westminster Confession 1.10—"The supreme Judge, by which all controversies of religion are to be determined, and all decrees of councils, opinions of ancient writers, doctrines of men, and private spirits, are to be examined, and in whose sentence we are to rest, can be no other but the Holy Spirit speaking in the scripture." Does not the fact that chapter 1 of the Westminster Confession is "Of the Holy Scriptures" seem ironically contrary to Grenz's presumption that the Princeton theologians did not stand in the tradition on Scripture flowing from the Westminster Divines?

icals in the modern era, he appeals to "speech-act theory" to make effective for "the postmodern, postfoundationalist context" his particular view of how the Spirit speaks through Scripture to perform "the illocutionary act of addressing us."[73] His use of speech-act theory is novel; it is not at the ordinary hermeneutical level at which evangelicals employ it frequently and properly concerning interpretation of the biblical text. He quickly passes over the Spirit's speech-acts in Scripture to the church—the Spirit is teaching, reproving, correcting, and instructing (2 Tim. 3:16). He treats these speech-acts as "only parts of a larger whole, namely, the *goal* or *product* of the Spirit's speaking."[74]

Grenz and Franke say:

> We affirm with the church throughout its history that God has acted and spoken; the biblical texts bear witness to God's acting and speaking to the communities of faith in the biblical era. But God acts and speaks today too, and the Bible is the Spirit's chosen vehicle for speaking authoritatively to us.[75]

Similar to Lindbeck's novel use of Wittgenstein's "language games" metaphor, so Grenz and Franke appeal to Austin's speech-act theory to carry their agenda forward.

Austin distinguishes three kinds of acts accomplished by speech: (1) *saying* something (the locutionary act); (2) what we *do when saying* something (the illocutionary act); and (3) what we *accomplish when saying* something (the perlocutionary act).[76]

While other evangelicals engage speech-act theory at its linguistic level (as crucial to interpretation of texts), Grenz and Franke merely summarize Austin's concepts and then bypass the hermeneutical level of the Scripture's *objective speech-acts* to address instead the Spirit's *subjective speech-acts* by using Scripture within the community of believers.[77] Thus, they skip over *accessible* speech-acts in Scripture, to which the church has historically turned for its theological beliefs, to get to *inaccessible* speech-acts in the

---

[73] Ibid.

[74] Ibid; emphasis his.

[75] Grenz and Franke, *Beyond Foundationalism*, 73. For a better articulation of how the Bible, a closed canon, is authoritative to the contemporary church, see N. T. Wright, "How Can the Bible Be Authoritative?" *Vox Evangelica* 21 (1991): 7-32.

[76] J. L. Austin, *How to Do Things with Words* (Cambridge, Mass.: Harvard University Press, 1962), esp. Lectures 8-10, 94-131.

[77] For excellent discussions of how speech-act theory enriches our understanding of biblical hermeneutics, see Kevin Vanhoozer, "The Semantics of Biblical Literature: Truth and Scripture's Diverse Literary Forms," in *Hermeneutics, Authority, and Canon,* ed. D. A. Carson and John D. Woodbridge (Grand Rapids, Mich.: Zondervan, 1986), 53-104; and Vanhoozer, *Is There a Meaning in This Text? The Bible, the Reader, and the Morality of Literary Knowledge* (Grand Rapids, Mich.: Zondervan, 1998), 201-280.

Spirit's *use* of Scripture for us. Grenz and Franke do this because they reason, "If the final authority in the church is the Holy Spirit speaking through scripture, then theology's norming norm is the message the Spirit declares through the text."[78] Yet it is not the *text* of Scripture but the Spirit's *use* of Scripture that they feature in their view. So the theologian's hermeneutical work is not so much to hear what the text of Scripture says, but to hear what the Spirit has to say to the church by appropriating Scripture:

> Because the Spirit speaks to us through scripture—through the text itself—the ongoing task of the community of Christ is to ask continually, What is the Spirit saying to the church? (Rev. 2:11, etc.). We inquire at every juncture, What illocutionary act is the Spirit performing in our midst on the basis of the reading of this scripture text? What is the Spirit saying to us in appropriating this text? In short, we inquire, What is the biblical message?[79]

So, though Grenz and Franke mention the need to do "careful exegesis" of the biblical text in order to understand its "'original meaning,'" their appropriation of Austin's speech-act theory is not at the textual level of exegesis but at the level of the "Spirit's illocutionary act of appropriation" of Scripture for the contemporary church:

> Consequently, we must never conclude that exegesis alone can exhaust the Spirit's speaking to us through the text. Although the Spirit's illocutionary act is to appropriate the text in its internal meaning (i.e., to appropriate what the author said), the Spirit appropriates the text with the goal of communicating to us in our situation, which, while perhaps paralleling in certain respects that of the ancient community, is nevertheless unique.[80]

So, it is in "this process of listening to the Spirit speaking through the appropriated text, [that] theology assists the community of faith both in discerning what the Spirit is saying and in fostering an appropriate obedient response to the Spirit's voice."[81]

Assuming the veracity of social constructivism, Grenz and Franke claim that the Spirit appropriates the Bible to construct a new world. What world is this? It is the eschatological world God purposes for his creation as he has

---

[78] Grenz and Franke, *Beyond Foundationalism*, 74.
[79] Ibid.
[80] Ibid., 74-75.
[81] Ibid., 75.

revealed in the Bible. As through his speech-act "in the beginning" God created the world, so now God is creating a new world by the Spirit's perlocutionary act in using Scripture.[82]

Their appropriation of speech-act theory entails misappropriation, for Grenz and Franke focus upon the Spirit's appropriation of Scripture, which is hardly accessible as speech-acts, instead of focusing upon the Scriptures which are the Spirit's *accessible* speech-acts. Though they regard these *inaccessible* speech-acts of the Spirit to be "closely bound to the text," the Spirit's world construction does not reside in the text. This is so because the biblical text is not the Spirit's creative speech itself; Scripture is just the instrumentality of the Spirit's creative speech. So it is outside Scripture that "the Spirit performs the perlocutionary act of creating *world.*"[83] Thus, however closely linked the Spirit's present inaccessible speaking may be with Scripture, Grenz and Franke locate the Spirit's present speaking outside the canon. They do so because the new world the Spirit creates in his perlocutionary act "is not simply the world surrounding the ancient text itself. It is the eschatological world God intends for creation as disclosed in the text."[84] In fact, they say that the Spirit's perlocutionary act of world construction "does not lie in the text itself."[85] They dislodge the perlocutionary act from the locutionary and illocutionary acts. By the Spirit's appropriation of the biblical text the "Spirit performs the perlocutionary act of creating a world through the illocutionary act of speaking, that is, of appropriating the biblical text as the instrumentality of divine speaking."[86]

Their appropriation of speech-act theory, then, is to move beyond what Scripture says and means (textually accessible) to God's acts and speech today (textually inaccessible). But if "God acts and speaks today," how can we access these speech-acts? Is not our access to God's speech-acts only through God's Word, the text of Scripture? Scripture is where God's speech is accessible to his people. If, as they claim to agree with Hans Frei, the "location of meaning" is in the biblical narrative, not residing in an event within ancient history that lies behind the text, why do Grenz and Franke not focus upon the text of Scripture as the location of the Spirit's speech-acts instead of locating meaning in the Spirit's appropriation of Scripture for the contemporary community of believers?[87] If liberals and many evangelicals locate the mean-

---

[82] Ibid., 77.

[83] Ibid.

[84] Ibid.

[85] Ibid.

[86] Ibid., 78.

[87] Ibid., 73; cf. Hans Frei, *The Eclipse of Biblical Narrative: A Study in Eighteenth and Nineteenth Century Hermeneutics* (New Haven, Conn.: Yale University Press, 1974), 280-281.

ing of the biblical text behind the text, do not Grenz and Franke shift the location of meaning too? The postconservative project, guided by Grenz and Franke, turns the Bible into something other than what it actually is just as much as some evangelicals have unwisely done when they attempt to locate God's revelation—the real locus of God's revelation and authority—somewhere other than in the text of Scripture.

CONCLUSION

If the location of Scripture's meaning is in the text, surely the Spirit's speech-acts—locutionary, illocutionary, and perlocutionary—are all resident in Scripture. For this reason, Vanhoozer offers an approach to theological method with his "canonical-linguistic" proposal that is superior to Grenz and Franke's adaptation of Lindbeck's cultural-linguistic method.[88] Vanhoozer summarizes the three features of his approach:

> (1) The Scripture principle—the way in which one identifies the Bible as the Word of God—should be formulated in terms of divine communicative action [speech-acts]. (2) The canonical-linguistic approach conceives theology as the practice of indwelling the biblical texts, of looking along the texts so as to understand the judgments they embody, hence to learn canonical wisdom. (3) Doctrine is instruction or direction on how to participate fittingly in the ongoing drama of redemption.[89]

Thus, rather than locate the perlocutionary aspect of the Spirit's speech-acts outside the text of Scripture within the contemporary church, does not the Spirit's word that makes all things new reside in Scripture itself? The Bible itself, as God's revelation, is God's interaction with us. Scripture conveys God's speech-acts to us.

Furthermore, Vanhoozer's approach better accounts for the place of

---

[88] Vanhoozer, "Voice and the Actor," 61-106. Against the Grenz-Franke assumption that modernist epistemological foundationalism is to blame for any view of Scripture as foundational to Christian theology, Vanhoozer contends that we can "take the canon as our theological foundation without succumbing to epistemological foundationalism" (86).

[89] Ibid., 101. Vanhoozer identifies his canonical-linguistic approach as "postpropositionalist because it rejects the picture theory of meaning. Instead, it insists with speech-act theory that language is a form of action and that propositions may be used to do more than picture the world" (75). No one should confuse Vanhoozer's view with the *post*conservative view of Grenz and Franke when he states that his view "is better described as postconservative rather than postliberal" (77). He carefully defines his terms. "The present approach is postconservative theology because it transcends the debilitating dichotomies between referring and expressing, between propositional and personal revelation, between God saying and God doing, precisely by focusing on the Bible as a set of divine communicative acts. God in Scripture is doing many things with words, not simply conveying information, nor even revealing himself. The approach is post*conservative* in that it maintains there is something in the text that is both indispensable and authoritative, namely, the divinely intended meaning" (76). Even though Vanhoozer may be hyperbolizing these alleged "debilitating dichotomies" to make his point, it is evident that he is not a postconservative in the same vein as Grenz.

God's people. For Vanhoozer, the doctrines of the "community of faith" do not set the "rules of discourse." Authority does not reside in how Christian readers of Scripture use Scripture; doctrinal authority derives from how the biblical authors, authorized by God's Spirit, use terms such as "God," "grace," and "salvation."[90] Vanhoozer's approach preserves Scripture as the church's foundation of faith, retains the correspondence theory of truth, and reclaims the priesthood of individual believers as capable of doing theology rightly. He portrays proper interplay between Scripture and Christians:

> Right theological judgment is the product of human cognitive action that has been nurtured by divine canonical action concerning right covenantal relations. The canon is nothing less than a unique and indispensable framework—the spectacles of faith, as Calvin put it—that enables us faithfully to imagine (to see and to taste) the world as it is in Christ, the "wisdom of God" (1 Cor. 1:24), or in other words, as it really is.[91]

Is this not the way forward rather than the way marked out by Grenz and Franke? If some evangelical theologians imply that the Bible comes to us in the wrong form and is more useful and effective if given the shape of their theological formulations, have not Grenz and Franke also reshaped the Bible through their adaptation of Lindbeck's cultural-linguistic approach?

Is it conceivable that postconservatives such as Grenz and Franke have not engaged postliberalism *radically* enough, that is, at its biblical-theological roots? Authentic evangelical faith chastened by insights of postliberal biblical theology need not lead to the theological method postconservatives have mapped out following the postliberal lead of Lindbeck who, though building upon the biblical-theological and hermeneutical work of Brevard Childs, Hans Frei, et al., took steps that evangelicals need not and should not take. Positively, for example, Erich Auerbach correctly distinguishes biblical narrative from other literature, such as Greek epic: "Far from seeking, like Homer, merely to make us forget our own reality for a few hours, it [Scripture] seeks to overcome our reality: we are to fit our own life into its world, feel ourselves to be elements in its structure of universal history."[92]

---

[90] Ibid., 77.
[91] Ibid., 85.
[92] Erich Auerbach, *Mimesis: The Representation of Reality in Western Literature* (Princeton, N.J.: Princeton University Press, 1968), 15.

The theologian's task is far more than transposing Scripture into atemporal truths. The theologian's assignment is not to reshape, for example, the four Gospels to fit the form of the New Testament Letters because these seem more manageable and usable for preaching, teaching, and catechetical instruction. Rather, the task is to uphold Scripture as God's Word that grounds the church's beliefs today as it did in the days when the Spirit authorized the writing of Scripture through the apostles and prophets of old. Scripture is indispensable to the existence and life of the church. Scripture is God's speech-acts by which he formed the church and by which he accomplishes his purposes of judgment and of salvation in the world.

Does not the warp and woof of the biblical text with its variety of literary genres, from narrative to letter, weave the fabric of Christian theology that should occupy the church's theologians? Does not the Christian theologian's task stand in continuity with that of Moses and of Isaiah and with that of Jesus and of Paul who did theology for God's people? Surely, what the Bible yields is not raw data that need to be shaped into theology. It is already theology in its own right.[93] It is already theology done by God's authorized theologians for God's people.

Does not Scripture's use of Scripture teach us how we are to read and to use Scripture to shape and to ground the beliefs and behavior of God's people? Isaiah's historical-cultural context differs from that of Moses. Nevertheless, Isaiah employs Moses' exodus motif effectively for his own generation, shaping and grounding the faith and expectation of God's salvation for generations beyond him. Likewise, Jesus and Paul stand in continuity with Isaiah and with Moses who precede them, so that they open the Scriptures as God's revelation that functions to provide directly the theological beliefs God's people are to embrace. Should not Christians always be striving to embrace the first-order language of God's revelation as their own in such a manner that their own second-order formulations of things believed asymptotically move toward the fullness of Scripture's first-order form and content? This is the hermeneutical spiral in which Christians, theologians or not, find themselves as they immerse themselves in God's Word.

All that God discloses to us in Scripture comes to us with its own theological categories and structures for understanding God and his ways. Therefore, should not the first work of the church's theologians be *biblical theology,* with the Bible's message altering us, forging our theological cate-

---

[93] Cf. Wright, "How Can the Bible Be Authoritative?" 7-32.

gories, shaping our understanding of the world we inhabit, and changing the world itself? Surely the theologian's task is to embrace the Bible's covenantal categories and structures for understanding God and his ways, for interpreting and explaining the world in which we live, for transforming us to live in this present world, and for preparing us to inhabit the world for which we hope in Christ, rather than to draw upon contemporary culture as a source for theology.

7

POSTCONSERVATISM, BIBLICAL AUTHORITY, AND RECENT PROPOSALS FOR RE-DOING EVANGELICAL THEOLOGY: A CRITICAL ANALYSIS

Stephen J. Wellum

INTRODUCTION: BEING "BIBLICAL" IN OUR THEOLOGY

At the heart of evangelical theology is the attempt to be *biblical,* to "take every thought captive to obey Christ" (2 Cor. 10:5). But what does it mean to be "biblical" in our theology? How does one know that one's theological proposals are faithful to Scripture, and thus biblically warranted? That question might seem strange to ask, especially for evangelicals, since many of us, at least in the past, have seemingly believed that the task of doing theology is fairly obvious and straightforward. However, in recent days, let alone in the past, many have begun to acknowledge that the task of *doing* theology in a "biblical" way is not at all obvious. Many acknowledge today that it is a bit more complicated than we have thought, and thus self-conscious reflection on these matters is crucial for the doing of evangelical theology today, especially for those of us who believe that constructing a center for evangelical theology is both a possibility and a necessity. In fact, in my view, there are at least three reasons why critical reflection on how we *do* theology as evangelicals is so important today.

First, probably the most basic and important reason is this: the glory of God and the cause of the gospel demand it. Surely, at the core of Christian discipleship is the attempt to live under the Lordship of Christ and to have his Word rule and reign over us, both individually and corporately, to the praise of his glory. Being clear about theological method helps us in this task.

Indeed, it is precisely because of our commitment to the Lordship of Christ and the full authority of Scripture that we must reflect seriously on both how to read Scripture properly and how to apply it to our lives in a faithful, godly manner.

A second reason concerns the disconcerting yet true observation that diverse and even contradictory theological proposals *all* claim to be "biblical." But how can this be? Is the Bible like a wax nose that can be twisted to fit with a variety of viewpoints, even conflicting readings of Scripture? But if all theologies are *not* equally biblical, which most of us would want to affirm, then on what basis may we argue that *our* way of doing theology, *our* theological beliefs are more *biblical* than someone else's?[1] On what basis may we argue that it is possible to construct a center for evangelical theology that is *true* to Scripture and thus *true* to "the faith that was once for all delivered to the saints" (Jude 3)?

This last set of questions coupled with our present cultural and intellectual context, namely the rise of postmodernism, leads to a final reason why thinking about theological method is so crucial for evangelicals today. In fact, it is primarily this third reason that I want to address in this chapter. In light of the rise of postmodernism, the question *Whose theology is more "biblical" or more "true"?* is viewed with disdain and suspicion. Why? For the simple reason that postmodernism, at its heart and for all of its diversity, is a mindset that is tightly linked to a denial that humans can know truth in any objective, universal sense. At this point, *post*modernism is often contrasted with modernism, which reflects much of the spirit of the Enlightenment—a spirit, interestingly enough, that borrowed much from Christianity in regard to its commitment to truth, but then sought rationally to ground truth in "the turn to the human subject." Thus, for example, like historic Christianity, modernism believed that truth was objective and universal and that reason could discover truth by research and investigation. However, unlike Christianity, it sought to discover truth apart from dependence upon God and his spoken Word. Instead of following the Christian motto of "faith seeking understanding" and underscoring the priority of divine revelation, modernism sought to follow the agenda of "I understand in order to believe." In this sense, then, modernism sought to subsume all truth claims, whether philosophical or religious, under the "authority" of human reason independent of God's Word.

---

[1] I was first confronted with the question of what it means to be "biblical" as a student of Kevin J. Vanhoozer during the 1980s at Trinity Evangelical Divinity School. For his response to this question see his article, "The Voice and the Actor: A Dramatic Proposal About the Ministry and Minstrelsy of Theology," in *Evangelical Futures,* ed. John G. Stackhouse, Jr. (Grand Rapids, Mich.: Baker, 2000), 61-106.

Postmodernism, on the other hand, is best viewed as modernism that has
veled its road to its logical end and is thus much more epistemologically
f-conscious of its starting points and conclusions.[2] In this sense, postmod-
ism takes seriously the Enlightenment project centered in the autonomous
: but then, ironically, concludes that if the Enlightenment view is correct,
th could never be objective and universal, at least for the human subject.
ıy? The simple reason is that finite human beings and communities are too
:orically situated and sociologically conditioned to ever yield a "God's eye
point of view," that is, an objective and universal viewpoint. Truth, in the end,
cannot be what modernism hoped it was; rather it must be perspectival, provisional, local, and ultimately, what the community most values—pragmatic.
Of course, if postmodernism is "true," in contrast to the beliefs of modernism, then any claims of individuals or communities to know "the truth"
is necessarily wrong—an interesting irony indeed. Postmodernism, at its
heart, is a distrust of anyone who says, "That's the way it is" or "This is the
truth," and as such, it tends to lead to a full-blown pluralism and mitigated
skepticism. Thus, to think that one can answer the question *Whose theological proposal or way of doing theology is more "biblical" or more "true"?* is
viewed as both naïve and oppressive. Indeed, for many today, even to ask
such questions begs the question since it already assumes a "modernist"
understanding of reality and truth, namely a foundationalism in epistemology and a corresponding realism in metaphysics.[3]

Obviously the implications of this mindset for evangelical theology and,
in particular, theological method are vast. For, ultimately, what is at stake is
whether Christian theology, in any kind of historic, normative, and objective
sense, is even possible. In the end, debates today over theological method are
really entire worldview debates, and as such, evangelicals have no option but

---

[2] D. A. Carson, *The Gagging of God* (Grand Rapids, Mich.: Zondervan, 1996), 19-22, makes this exact
point.

[3] The literature on postmodernism is legion. For evangelical treatments of the subject, both popular and
more academic, see David K. Clark, *To Know and Love God: Method for Theology,* Foundations of
Evangelical Theology, ed. John S. Feinberg (Wheaton, Ill.: Crossway, 2003); William Lane Craig and
J. P. Moreland, *Philosophical Foundations for a Christian Worldview* (Downers Grove, Ill.: InterVarsity
Press, 2003), 71-170; David S. Dockery, ed., *The Challenge of Postmodernism,* 2nd ed. (Grand Rapids,
Mich.: Baker, 2001); Millard J. Erickson, *Truth or Consequences: The Promise and Perils of
Postmodernism* (Downers Grove, Ill.: InterVarsity Press, 2001); Douglas Groothuis, *Truth Decay:
Defending Christianity Against the Challenges of Postmodernism* (Downers Grove, Ill.: InterVarsity Press,
2000); Kevin J. Vanhoozer and J. Andrew Kirk, eds., *To Stake a Claim* (Maryknoll, N.Y.: Orbis, 1999);
Kevin J. Vanhoozer, *Is There a Meaning in This Text?* (Grand Rapids, Mich.: Zondervan, 1998); Nancey
Murphy, *Anglo-American Postmodernity* (Oxford: Westview Press, 1997); Roger Lundin, Clarence
Walhout, and Anthony C. Thiselton, *The Promise of Hermeneutics* (Grand Rapids, Mich.: Eerdmans,
1999); Anthony C. Thiselton, *Interpreting God and the Postmodern Self* (Edinburgh: T & T Clark, 1996);
Stanley J. Grenz, *A Primer on Postmodernism* (Grand Rapids, Mich.: Eerdmans, 1996); D. A. Carson,
The Gagging of God; Brian Ingraffia, *Postmodern Theory and Biblical Theology* (Cambridge: Cambridge
University Press, 1995); Gene E. Veith, Jr., *Postmodern Times* (Wheaton, Ill.: Crossway, 1994).

to think afresh about how we are to do theology in light of our present context. In fact, it is precisely for this reason, given the rise of postmodernism, that many postconservatives, among others, are calling for a rethinking and re-visioning of how evangelicals should do theology. Repeatedly, postconservatives are warning us that we cannot do theology as we have done it before since the former way of doing theology, especially among conservative evangelicals, has too uncritically embraced the now rejected and outdated "foundationalist" epistemological project. Correspondingly, postconservatives are challenging us to rethink and recast how we ought to do theology in the wake of the postmodern critique, not only so that we will gain a hearing by our cultured despisers, but also so that we may speak clearly to our post-theological generation with understanding, clarity, and precision.[4]

Certainly, most evangelicals, including "traditionalists,"[5] agree that we must constantly rethink how better to do theology in any era, let alone this postmodern one. And obviously the questions raised by our postmodern situation are of utmost importance for the elucidation and defense of the gospel today. However, as with any proposal, we must first listen to it by giving it a sympathetic hearing: we must first listen before we can speak. But with that said, we must also adopt the spirit of *caveat emptor*—"Buyer beware." As heirs of the Reformation, we must always embrace the attitude of *semper reformandum*—"always reforming"—but not uncritically. After all, our doing of theology is not merely an academic exercise; it is first and foremost done as an act of worship to our triune God and in obedience to his Word. In that light, the remainder of the chapter will be broken into two parts. First, similar to other chapters, I will describe and then critically evaluate, at least in a preliminary fashion, the new, revised theological method envisioned by current voices within the postconservative movement as they challenge us to

---

[4] This has certainly been the cry of many postconservatives. For example, see Roger E. Olson, "Postconservative Evangelicals Greet the Postmodern Age," *Christian Century* 112 (May 3, 1995): 480-483; idem, "Postconservative Evangelical Theology and the Theological Pilgrimage of Clark Pinnock," in *Semper Reformandum: Essays in Honour of Clark H. Pinnock,* eds. Stanley E. Porter and Anthony R. Cross (Carlisle, England: Paternoster, 2003), 16-37; Stanley J. Grenz, "From Liberalism to Postliberalism: Theology in the Twentieth Century," *Review and Expositor* 96 (1999): 385-410; idem, *Revisioning Evangelical Theology: A Fresh Agenda for the Twenty-first Century* (Downers Grove, Ill.: InterVarsity Press, 1993); Henry H. Knight III, *A Future for Truth: Evangelical Theology in a Postmodern World* (Nashville: Abingdon, 1997); Timothy R. Phillips and Dennis L. Okholm, eds. *The Nature of Confession: Evangelicals and Postliberals in Conversation* (Downers Grove, Ill.: InterVarsity Press, 1996); Gary Dorrien, *The Remaking of Evangelical Theology* (Louisville: Westminster John Knox, 1998). But it is not only postconservatives who have argued for the need to rethink theological method in light of postmodernism. See Michael S. Horton, *Covenant and Eschatology* (Louisville: Westminster John Knox, 2002); Kevin J. Vanhoozer, "Voice and the Actor;" idem, *First Theology* (Downers Grove, Ill.: InterVarsity Press, 2002); Richard Lints, *The Fabric of Theology* (Grand Rapids, Mich.: Eerdmans, 1993).

[5] This is Roger Olson's term to refer to "conservatives" in contrast to "reformists" (i.e., postconservatives). See his article, "The Future of Evangelical Theology," *Christianity Today* 42 (February 9, 1998): 40-48.

take seriously our postmodern situation. Second, I will provide some brief personal reflections on what evangelicals must both reject and affirm in regard to the doing of evangelical theology in light of postconservative proposals. Obviously, postconservatism is not a monolithic movement, and as a result it is impossible to capture all the nuances of its proponents in regard to theological method. That is why I have chosen to focus on a particular proposal, namely the Grenz/Franke proposal, as representative of postconservatism in general. It is to this specific proposal that I now turn.

EVANGELICAL THEOLOGICAL METHOD FOR A POSTMODERN WORLD: THE GRENZ/FRANKE PROPOSAL

Without doubt Stanley Grenz (and now John Franke) is one of postconservativism's most prolific and important thinkers, who, for more than a decade, has been at the forefront of warning and challenging evangelicals to rethink their understanding of the nature of theology, especially in light of the postmodern critique of the Enlightenment project associated with modernism.[6] Grenz has written numerous books and articles on these matters, but probably the best summation of his proposal is found in his work, coauthored with Franke, *Beyond Foundationalism: Shaping Theology in a Postmodern Context*.[7] In what follows I will attempt to summarize Grenz and Franke's creative and complex proposal by asking three diagnostic questions before I turn to a number of critical reflections.

How Do Grenz/Franke Understand Postmodernism and Its Importance for Doing Theology?

Even though Grenz and Franke admit that "postmodernism" is notoriously difficult to define, they understand the heart of it as "the rejection of certain central features of the modern project, such as its quest for certain, objective,

---

[6] See Robert E. Webber, *The Younger Evangelicals: Facing the Challenges of the New World* (Grand Rapids, Mich.: Baker, 2002), 83-106, who views Grenz and Franke as key theologians who epitomize the postconservative movement.

[7] Stanley J. Grenz and John R. Franke, *Beyond Foundationalism: Shaping Theology in a Postmodern Context* (Louisville: Westminster John Knox Press, 2001). See also the following books and articles for an elaboration of his view, along with some of John Franke's materials: Stanley J. Grenz, "Nurturing the Soul, Informing the Mind: The Genesis of the Evangelical Scripture Principle" in *Evangelicals and Scripture*, eds. Dennis L. Okholm, et al. (Downers Grove, Ill.: InterVarsity Press, 2004), 21-41; idem, *Renewing the Center: Evangelical Theology in a Post-Theological Era* (Grand Rapids, Mich.: Baker, 2000); idem, "Articulating the Christian Belief-Mosaic" in *Evangelical Futures*, 107-136; idem, *Revisioning Evangelical Theology*; idem, *Primer on Postmodernism*; John R. Franke, "Reforming Theology: Toward a Postmodern Reformed Dogmatics," *Westminster Theological Journal* 65 (Spring 2003), 1-26; idem, "Postmodern Evangelical Theology: A Nonfoundationalist Approach to the Christian Faith," in *Alister E. McGrath and Evangelical Theology*, ed. Sung Wook Chung (Grand Rapids, Mich.: Baker, 2003), 280-309; idem, "Scripture, Tradition and Authority: Reconstructing the Evangelical Conception of *Sola Scriptura*," in *Evangelicals and Scripture*, 192-210.

and universal knowledge, along with its dualism and its assumptions of the inherent goodness of knowledge."[8] Ultimately, they summarize their understanding of postmodernism by adopting the now famous description of Jean-François Lyotard, "incredulity toward metanarrative"[9]—that is, postmodernism rejects any claim to universality.[10] For Grenz and Franke, even though there are negative elements of postmodernism (e.g., deconstructionism), overall they view it as basically a positive movement. In fact, they argue that postmodernism is not only the cultural context theologians must interact with, it is also a more hospitable environment for the doing of Christian theology in contrast to modernism's restrictions. Thus, freed from the constraints of the Enlightenment project, postmodernism, they argue, "has actually been responsible for the renewal of theology as an intellectual discipline,"[11] and as such, it has spawned numerous helpful theological research programs.

Specifically, there is one aspect of postmodernism that Grenz and Franke find very helpful for the doing of theology, namely the epistemological shift from "foundationalism" to a "chastened rationality." For them, this entails two significant points: first, the rejection of the Enlightenment project to ground knowledge in basic beliefs that are universal, objective, indubitable, and discernable to any rational person; and second, the acceptance of "the transition from a realist to a constructionist view of truth and the world."[12] In this they agree with many postmodern thinkers that "humans do not view the world from an objective vantage point but structure their world through the concepts they bring to it, such as language."[13] And in line with other post-Kantian thinkers, they affirm that there seems to be no way that humans can get "behind" or "above" our language to "check and see" if it corresponds to the way things really are. That is why they accept the assertion of many postmoderns that "human languages function as social conventions that describe the world in a variety of ways depending on the context of the speaker. No simple one-for-one correspondence exists between language and

---

[8] Grenz and Franke, *Beyond Foundationalism*, 21-22; cf. Grenz, *Renewing the Center*, 184-199.

[9] Jean-François Lyotard, *The Postmodern Condition,* trans. Geoff Bennington and Brian Massumi (Minneapolis: University of Minnesota Press, 1984), xxiii-xxiv.

[10] For further development of this understanding of postmodernism, see Stanley Grenz, "The Universality of the 'Jesus-Story' and the 'Incredulity Toward Metanarratives,'" in *No Other Gods Before Me? Evangelicals and the Challenge of World Religions,* ed. John G. Stackhouse, Jr. (Grand Rapids, Mich.: Baker, 2001), 85-111.

[11] See Grenz and Franke, *Beyond Foundationalism*, 22. In their assessment of postmodernism, Grenz and Franke disagree with many evangelicals who fear that postmodernism is antagonistic toward Christianity.

[12] Ibid., 23. For more on the terms foundationalism, chastened rationality, realism, and nonrealism see David Clark, *To Know and Love God,* 133-164, 259-294, 353-383; Craig and Moreland, *Philosophical Foundations,* 71-170; W. Jay Wood, *Epistemology* (Downers Grove, Ill.: InterVarsity Press, 1998), 77-174.

[13] Grenz and Franke, *Beyond Foundationalism*, 23.

the world, and thus no single linguistic description can serve to provide an objective conception of the 'real' world,"[14] including theological descriptions.

How, then, has the advent of these two affirmations of postmodernism impacted our understanding of theological method? It would seem that a chastened rationality and a constructionist view of truth would be detrimental to evangelical theology as historically conceived. But Grenz and Franke disagree, and below we will discover their proposal in light of their acceptance of these two points. However, before we turn to their proposal, it is important to point out two observations they make regarding theological method that they believe the arrival of postmodernism has unveiled. The first observation, an ironic one indeed, is that the postmodern situation has shown that "although for a hundred years conservative and liberal theologians have seemingly been going their separate ways, both have actually been responding, albeit in different ways, to the same agenda, the agenda of modernity."[15] How so? In this way: both classical liberalism *and* conservative theology were "modernist" and "rationalistic" in their approach to theological method, although in different ways. Thus, for example, liberalism was "modernist" in that it sought for an unassailable foundation, not in Scripture, but in human religious experience.[16] In this regard, liberalism in its approach to Scripture and theology was "extratextual" in that universal religious experience served as the foundation and grid by which Scripture was read and doctrines were formulated.[17] However, on the other hand, conservative theology was also "modernist" in its approach. It too sought an unassailable foundation, not in universal religious experience but in an inerrant Bible "as the source book of information for systematic theology."[18] Grenz and Franke state their claim as follows:

> Like their liberal antagonists, conservative theologians also searched for a foundation for theology that could stand firm when subjected to the canons of a supposedly universal human reason. Conservatives came to conclude that this invulnerable foundation lay in an error-free Bible, which they

---

[14] Ibid.

[15] Ibid., 10.

[16] For Grenz and Franke, a paradigmatic example of classical liberalism is Friedrich Schleiermacher.

[17] For more on viewing theological positions on a spectrum of extra- versus intratextual see David F. Ford, ed., *The Modern Theologians,* 2nd ed. (Oxford: Blackwell, 1997), 1-15.

[18] Grenz and Franke, *Beyond Foundationalism,* 13. Grenz and Franke have in their sights the Princeton theologians—Charles Hodge, B. B. Warfield, J. Gresham Machen—as well as evangelical theologians such as Carl F. H. Henry, Gordon Lewis, Bruce Demarest, and Wayne Grudem (see 13-15, 35-37). On their treatment—indeed in my view, misunderstanding—of the post-Reformation Scholastics and Princetonians see Paul Kjoss Helseth's "Are Postconservative Evangelicals Fundamentalists?" chapter 9 in this volume; cf. Carl R. Trueman, "It Ain't Necessarily So," *Westminster Theological Journal* 65 (Fall 2003): 311-315; and Richard A. Muller, *Post-Reformation Reformed Dogmatics,* 4 vols. (Grand Rapids, Mich.: Baker, 2003).

viewed as the storehouse for divine revelation. Hence, the great Princetonian theologian, Charles Hodge, asserted that the Bible is "free from all error, whether in doctrine, fact, or precept." This inerrant foundation, in turn, could endow with epistemological certitude, at least in theory, the edifice the skilled theological craftsman constructed on it. For indeed, rather than offering merely a personal opinion on any matter under consideration, the adept theologian claimed that he was only restating in a more systematic form what scripture itself says.[19]

But there is a second point that postmodernism has revealed, namely that the task of doing theology is much more complicated than we once thought; the process of moving from biblical text to theological formulation is something that evangelicals have not taken seriously enough. This is not to say that Grenz and Franke think that evangelicals have been completely unreflective on theological method or that they do not have one. Rather, their point is that evangelical theology has too closely aligned itself with a "modernist" epistemology as evidenced in our commitment to "objectivism" and "rational propositionalism." That is why, according to our authors, most conservative evangelicals, even to this day, have viewed the theological task in the Princetonian tradition, namely as purely an objective "science" whose task is merely to collect and organize, in an inductive manner, the "propositions" of Scripture, in any order, thus giving "the appearance of being elaborate collections of loosely related facts derived from the Bible"[20] which are then put into an eternal, timeless system. But with postmodernism's refutation of foundationalism, evangelicals' indebtedness to this "objectivist" and "rationalistic" approach must be rejected. What, then, are we to replace it with? It is to our authors' alternative proposal that we now turn.

What Is Grenz and Franke's Alternative Proposal for Doing Evangelical Theology?

I will briefly summarize their overall proposal in three steps.

1. *Theology Must Employ a Nonfoundationalist Epistemology*. In light of the postmodern demise of "foundationalism," Grenz and Franke believe that the best epistemological alternatives for theology are a linking of coherentism, pragmatism, and the later-Wittgenstein's notion of language-games— all of which are nonfoundationalist in orientation. First, coherentism rejects

---

[19] Grenz and Franke, *Beyond Foundationalism*, 34.
[20] Ibid., 50.

the foundationalist assumption that a "justified set of beliefs necessarily comes in the form of an edifice resting on a base. . . . [n]o beliefs are intrinsically basic and none are instrinsically superstructure."[21] Instead, coherentism asserts that beliefs are more like a mosaic or web, each belief interdependent and supported by its relationship to other beliefs within the mosaic, and justified, not by a belief's correspondence to reality, but in its overall fit with other held beliefs.[22] Second, pragmatism affirms, like coherentism, that the truth of any belief is not correspondence to reality, but whether a belief advances "factual inquiry." Truth, in other words, emerges over time as we engage in prediction followed by testing, observation, and experimental confirmation.[23] And, third, the linguistic turn in philosophy entails that language is no longer viewed in a realist way, that is, as "mirroring" or "picturing" reality, but is viewed as a social affair governed by various "language-games."[24] Thus, meaning and truth are viewed as one's ability to use the language-game correctly in a particular context, and thus, what counts as justification for beliefs is *internally* determined by the language-game itself, not by its correspondence to reality.

Given these three commitments, how, then, do Grenz and Franke apply these nonfoundationalist philosophical resources to the doing of theology? Interestingly, they do so by developing the insights of German theologian Wolfhart Pannenberg and Yale theologian George Lindbeck. From Pannenberg, they accept and employ his coherentist model as well as his view that truth is historical and eschatological. All truth, they affirm along with Pannenberg, "ultimately comes together in God, who is the ground of the unity of truth," and theology's task, then, is "to bring all human knowledge together in our affirmation of God" even though "our human knowledge is never complete or absolutely certain."[25] Thus, truth, in its absolute fullness, is known only in the future. Presently, truth, including *all* theological statements, is provisional, and thus theological statements should be treated as hypotheses to be tested according to coherentist and pragmatic procedures.

From Lindbeck, Grenz and Franke adopt and utilize his view that theological statements and doctrines are not "true" in the sense that they say anything about a reality external to the language; rather they function in a Kantian

---

[21] Ibid., 39. For more on coherentism see Wood, *Epistemology*, 113-125; Craig and Moreland, *Philosophical Foundations*, 121-127; Clark, *To Know and Love God*, 156-161.
[22] See Grenz and Franke, *Beyond Foundationalism*, 38-39.
[23] See ibid., 40-41. For more on pragmatism see Craig and Moreland, *Philosophical Foundations*, 144.
[24] For more on the later-Wittgenstein and his understanding of "language games," see Clark, *To Know and Love God*, 376-380; John S. Feinberg, "Noncognitivism: Wittgenstein," in *Biblical Errancy*, Norman Geisler, ed. (Grand Rapids, Mich.: Zondervan, 1981), 163-201; cf. Grenz and Franke, *Beyond Foundationalism*, 42.
[25] Grenz and Franke, *Beyond Foundationalism*, 44; cf. Wolfhart Pannenberg, *Systematic Theology*, trans. Geoffrey W. Bromiley, 3 vols. (Grand Rapids, Mich.: Eerdmans, 1991–1998), 1:21-60.

"regulative way," that is, as rules of grammar establishing the "language-game" of Christian thinking, speaking, and living. Thus, theological statements or doctrines are not making any "first-order" truth claims (i.e., asserting something objective about reality as if we had access to the "world-in-itself"). Instead, they are merely "second-order" assertions (i.e., rules for speech about God).[26] Both Lindbeck and our authors call this approach "intratextual" in contrast to "extratextual." By this they mean that theology has the task of using its language to "redescribe reality within the scriptural framework,"[27] rather than either translating Scripture into extra-scriptural categories or erroneously assuming, as the conservatives thought, "that theological statements (doctrines) make first-order truth claims (that is, they assert that something is objectively true or false)."[28] In the end, to be "intratextual," our authors contend, entails that the text "absorbs the world, rather than the other way around."[29]

But if so, it must still be asked: Do our authors believe that there is anything "foundational" for Christian theology, given their nonfoundational approach? The answer to this question leads us to the second step of their revisionist proposal for doing evangelical theology.

2. *Theology Must Affirm the "Basic" Nature of the Christian Interpretative Framework.* The language of "basic" or "properly basic" is adopted from the work of Alvin Plantinga, Nicholas Wolterstorff, et al., who belong to the view known as "Reformed Epistemology."[30] Reformed epistemologists have argued two main points against "classic foundationalism." First, they have argued that the whole agenda of classic foundationalism is internally incoherent, and second, that belief in God is not merely a derived or non-basic belief, but a "properly basic" belief, and thus, a person who believes in God is within his *rational* rights to do so, even though he might not be able to furnish specific arguments for his belief.[31] However, in a parallel but different way, Grenz and Franke employ the language of "basic" to

---

[26] Grenz and Franke, *Beyond Foundationalism,* 45-46; cf. George A. Lindbeck, *The Nature of Doctrine* (Philadelphia: Westminster, 1984). For a critique of Lindbeck's theory, see Alister E. McGrath, *The Genesis of Doctrine* (Oxford: Basil Blackwell, 1990).

[27] Grenz and Franke, *Beyond Foundationalism,* 46.

[28] Ibid., 45; cf. Lindbeck, *Nature of Doctrine,* 30-45, who labels the approach of liberalism as "experiential-expressivist," that of conservative theology as "cognitive-propositionalist," while he dubs his own view "cultural-linguistic."

[29] Grenz and Franke, *Beyond Foundationalism,* 6.

[30] For more on Reformed Epistemology, see Alvin Plantinga and Nicholas Wolterstorff, eds., *Faith and Rationality* (Notre Dame: University of Notre Dame Press, 1983); Alvin Plantinga, *Warranted Christian Belief* (Oxford: Oxford University Press, 2000); cf. also Craig and Moreland, *Philosophical Foundations,* 160-169.

[31] See a summary of these arguments in Nicholas Wolterstorff, *Reason Within the Bounds of Religion,* 2nd ed. (Grand Rapids, Mich.: Eerdmans, 1984); cf. Plantinga and Wolterstorff, *Faith and Rationality.*

answer the question, Is there anything in Christian theology that may be considered *basic* or *foundational*? Their answer is affirmative: "the Christian-experience-facilitating interpretative framework, arising as it does out of the biblical narrative."[32]

But what exactly is the "Christian-experience-facilitating interpretative framework"? And by labeling it "basic," do they mean "first-order" in the sense that Scripture gives us true, objective knowledge of God and this world (reality), yet is never exhaustive? Historically, evangelicals have argued that Scripture is both "basic" and "first-order" so that Scripture serves as the theologian's interpretative framework from which second-order theological reflection is grounded. But is this what Grenz and Franke are affirming? Are they merely saying what evangelicals have always affirmed, and if so, then what is exactly new about their proposal? Unfortunately, this does *not* seem to be what they are affirming, for at least two reasons.[33]

First, our authors seem to view the "Christian interpretative framework" *not* as Scripture alone. Instead they view it as a *combination* of our experience of being encountered redemptively in Jesus Christ by God and of being placed in a community of believers who have experienced similar event(s) in their lives and who together interpret their experiences "cast in the categories drawn from the biblical narrative as well as from its explication in the didactic sections of scripture."[34] It is, then, this *combination* of things that serves as *the* Christian interpretative framework. In this sense Christians are identified as Christians because we share in common a particular experience of being encountered by God in Christ and we interpret that experience, not as nineteenth-century liberalism did in terms of a "single, universal, foundational religious experience that supposedly lay beneath the plethora of religious experiences found in various religious traditions,"[35] but in terms of an

---

[32] Grenz and Franke, *Beyond Foundationalism*, 49.

[33] In a recent exchange between John Franke, Carl Trueman, and Richard Gaffin, Franke is unclear in his use of the language of "first-order." See Franke, "Response to Trueman and Gaffin," *Westminster Theological Journal* 65 (Fall 2003): 331-343. Franke acknowledges that theology is a "second-order" discipline based upon the "first-order" commitments of the Christian faith, namely "the primary stories, teachings, symbols, and practices of the Christian community" (338). He even says that "the language of the Christian story narrated and expounded in Scripture" is first-order (338). But unless he contradicts himself, nowhere does he seem to mean that Scripture is first-order in the sense that it serves as our *foundation* for theology and that it gives us, under inspiration of the Spirit, a true and objective, yet finite knowledge of God, ourselves, and this world (a realism) from which theological reflection is grounded. Rather, he argues for an indirect identity between God's revelation and Scripture, following Karl Barth's dialectic of veiling and unveiling, so that the Spirit's inspiration of Scripture is not viewed as a past event that produced an infallible and inerrant text that serves as the objective foundation for our theology, but an ongoing dynamic activity (see 340-343). Given this, I can only conclude that Franke is using the language of "first-order," not in its historic sense, but in a pragmatic, primacy sense.

[34] Grenz and Franke, *Beyond Foundationalism*, 48.

[35] Ibid.

interpretative framework that arises out of the biblical narrative, but which is not reduced to it and which serves as an "identity-constituting narrative."[36]

Second, in contrast to traditional evangelical theology, Grenz and Franke are emphatic that they do not view the "basic" nature of the Christian interpretative framework as either a return to a renewed foundationalism or an affirmation that this interpretative framework is first-order. They state:

> The cognitive framework that is "basic" for theology is not a given that precedes the theological enterprise; it does not provide the sure foundation on which the theological edifice can in turn be constructed. Rather, in a sense the interpretative framework and theology are inseparably intertwined. Just as every interpretative framework is essentially theological, so also every articulation of the Christian cognitive framework comes already clothed in a specific theological understanding. In fact, every such articulation is the embodiment of a specific understanding of the Christian theological vision; each embodies a specific understanding of the world as it is connected to the God of the Bible.[37]

In other words, the "interpretative framework" which includes Scripture is already theological in nature, and thus second-order. That is why they insist that "the theologian's task is not to work from an interpretative framework to a theological construct,"[38] as if theology were working from Scripture to theology. Instead, as our authors insist, "the theological enterprise consists in setting forth in a systematic manner a properly Christian framework as informed by the Bible for the sake of the church's mission in the contemporary context."[39]

Now if I understand our authors correctly, their proposal is denying that theology moves from first-order language (Scripture alone) to second-order description (theological formulation). As noted, it is at this point that they seriously depart from traditional evangelical theological method.

---

[36] Ibid. Grenz and Franke labor hard to distinguish their view from classical liberalism. They acknowledge that they are similar in their emphasis on the role of "religious experience." However, they claim that their view differs in two areas. First, "religious experience" is *not* a new foundation, i.e., a single, universal experience that lies beneath the plethora of religious experiences found in various religious traditions. Second, "religious experience" never precedes interpretation; rather, "experiences are always filtered by an interpretative framework—a grid—that facilitates their occurrence" (49), thus emphasizing the nonfoundational nature of their view.

[37] Ibid., 49-50.

[38] Ibid., 50. See Richard Lints, *Fabric of Theology,* who takes an opposite approach. Lints, in my view, rightly argues that theology, at its heart, is about moving from interpretative framework (Scripture, first-order) to theological vision (theology, second-order). See also Kevin J. Vanhoozer, "From Canon to Concept: 'Same' and 'Other' in the Relation of Biblical and Systematic Theology," *Scottish Bulletin of Evangelical Theology* 12 (1994): 96-124; and Horton, *Covenant and Eschatology,* who argue for a view of theology similar to Lints.

[39] Grenz and Franke, *Beyond Foundationalism,* 50.

Furthermore, they seem to imply erroneously that evangelicals tend to equate their theology (i.e., doctrinal formulations and confessional statements) with Scripture to such an extent that their theology becomes a *de facto* substitute for Scripture.[40] Instead, Grenz and Franke assert that all theological formulations are only particular, contextual expressions of the Christian faith, not the Christian faith itself. But is this understanding of evangelical theology correct?

On the one hand, evangelicals have rightly acknowledged that even though Scripture is first-order, even though it is fully authoritative, we must still interpret the text, which inevitably means that we are involved in a kind of "hermeneutical spiral."[41] We approach the text with assumptions and biases, but as we read and study the text, it, by the work of the Spirit, in relation to a believing community, is able to correct our readings. Thus, by hard work, listening to others (i.e., the role of tradition), prayer, and in obedience to God's Word, we are able to understand Scripture more correctly and accurately. On the other hand, evangelicals have rarely claimed that our theological constructions (including our confessions) are as authoritative as the text itself. But we have affirmed what Grenz and Franke seem unwilling to affirm, namely, that if our exegesis, exposition, and theological reflections *accurately reflect* what Scripture teaches, then we can say that our interpretation is true and biblical. Of course, this never entails that our theological formulations can ever act as a substitute for Scripture. We are always driven back to the text, again and again, to reformulate and rethink our doctrinal positions precisely because theology is second-order language. But given the fact that Scripture is first-order language due to its divine inspiration, our theology is always rooted and grounded in a "revelational foundation"—a Word-revelation that allows us to understand God, ourselves, and this world truly (i.e., objectively), but never exhaustively.[42] But this, sadly, seems to be what Grenz and Franke are denying.

Why do they opt for this way of revisioning theology? It is due to their double conviction that all "foundationalisms" have been rejected, including a "revelational foundationalism," and that conservative evangelicals, in the past and present, have mistakenly viewed Scripture and theology through an outdated "modernist" grid. In particular they have in their sights Charles

---

[40] See Franke's incredible assertion in this regard in "Response to Trueman and Gaffin," 338-339.

[41] See Grant R. Osborne, *The Hermeneutical Spiral* (Downers Grove, Ill.: InterVarsity Press, 1991). See also the helpful reflections by D. A. Carson in this regard in *Gagging of God*, 93-137.

[42] This is not to say that all biblical language is merely referential, but nor is it merely intrasystemic in a nonrealist sense. Rather, language is a divine gift, created by God, to allow us to know him and his world, even though our language will never yield an omniscient perspective. It yields a true, yet finite and never exhaustive knowledge.

Hodge (and those who follow in his wake) as a classic paradigm example of a "modernist" who described Scripture as "a storehouse of facts" and who viewed the theological task as merely putting Scripture in its "proper order and relations."[43] In my view, Hodge's understanding of theological method is unfortunate and should be rejected, even though it is debatable whether he actually followed this method in practice. In this regard, then, Grenz and Franke are right in pointing out that theology is more than merely collecting, arranging, and organizing the facts or propositions of Scripture. In addition, they are correct to observe that knowledge, including theology, is not merely a collection of isolated factual statements arising directly from first principles since, as they correctly state, "our beliefs form a system in which each belief is supported by its neighbors and, ultimately, by its presence within the whole . . . we ought to view Christian doctrine as comprising a 'belief-mosaic' and see theology, in turn, as the exploration of Christian doctrine viewed as an interrelated, unified whole."[44] But to fail to distinguish a "biblical foundationalism" from a classical, Enlightenment one is simply a mistake of gigantic proportions. In the end, it leads them to think differently about the theological task and to view theology along the lines of a coherentist, pragmatic, and nonrealist vision, instead of as a more realist vision grounded in a first-order, true, and objective revelational foundation.[45]

But a crucial question still remains: Given this revisionist model of theology, what happens to the question and status of truth, especially in a religiously pluralistic world? In order to answer that question, let us turn to the third and last step of their proposal.

3. *Theology Must Answer the Question of Truth Along Communitarian and Pragmatist Lines.* Given what our authors have proposed, it is now legitimate to ask, as they themselves ask, "Does theology speak about anything objective, or does it content itself with merely articulating the interpretative framework of a specific religious tradition?"[46] An important question indeed! In fact, I dare say that this is *the* crucial question facing Christian theology

---

[43] Charles Hodge, *Systematic Theology,* 3 vols. (Grand Rapids, Mich.: Eerdmans, 1952), 1:19.

[44] Grenz and Franke, *Beyond Foundationalism,* 51.

[45] Interestingly, Grenz and Franke choose Charles Hodge as their paradigm example of a "conservative modernist," but they never interact with the Dutch tradition of Reformed theology, namely Abraham Kuyper, Herman Bavinck, Geerhardus Vos, and Cornelius Van Til, and now John Frame, Kevin Vanhoozer, and Michael Horton. Herman Bavinck, for example, strongly rejected the methodology of Charles Hodge long before postmodernism entered the radar screen, but he maintained simultaneously the view that Scripture is the sole "foundation" for the doing of theology along with a realist epistemology and metaphysic, grounded not in natural theology but in a solidly theological worldview argument. See Bavinck, *Reformed Dogmatics: Prolegomena,* trans. John Vriend (Grand Rapids, Mich.: Baker, 2003), 1:59-112.

[46] Grenz and Franke, *Beyond Foundationalism,* 51.

today, given the rise of postmodernism and our interaction with a religiously pluralistic world. What is their response? Sadly, they think that this way of asking the question is "both improper and ultimately unhelpful,"[47] so instead they want to ask, "How can a nonfoundationalist theological method lead us to statements about a world beyond our formulations?"[48]

Their response is that they admit that there is "a certain undeniable givenness to the universe apart from the human linguistic-constructive task."[49] However, they view this "givenness" as not the objectivity of what some think of as "the world-in-itself," since, in their view, humans do not have access to this noumenal reality. But is there any sense in which we may speak of "objectivity"? Yes, they argue, in the sense of a future world, "the world as God wills it to be"[50]—an eschatological world that is still to come, which, they contend, "is far more real—objectively real—than the present world, which is even now passing away (1 Cor. 7:31)."[51] So, it seems, in the present, our authors think that we must content ourselves with an epistemological and metaphysical nonrealism, but we can anticipate, in the future, an eschatological realism. Whether one can make sense of this I will address below, but for Grenz and Franke this entails that the task of the Christian community—through its theological language, by the work of the Holy Spirit in, among, and through them, speaking through Scripture—is to *construct* a world that begins to reflect God's own will for creation, as centered in Jesus Christ.[52] However, they quickly add, the constructivist role of theology is always provisional, local, and second-order as we attempt to listen to God's Spirit speaking to us through the three sources for theology: the biblical narrative, the tradition of the church, and contemporary culture.

But a fundamental question still remains: "Why give primacy to the world-constructing language of the Christian community?"[53] Is it because it is *true*? Obviously, our authors cannot state it this way since that would assume an implicit "foundationalism." So how do we address the pressing question of the "truth" of the language of theology? In a consistent fashion, Grenz and Franke believe that we must wed communitarian and pragmatist insights. We must attempt to show that the Christian theological vision of a "true" community, rooted in the triune nature of God, is "the kind of com-

---

47 Ibid.
48 Ibid., 52.
49 Ibid., 53.
50 Ibid.
51 Ibid.
52 See ibid.
53 Ibid., 54.

munity that all religious belief systems in their own way and according to their own understanding seek to foster" and that the Christian vision provides "the best transcendent basis for the human ideal of life-in-relationship."[54] In other words, in our apologetic debate with other competing linguistic constructions of the world, we must ask, "Which religious vision carries within itself the ground for community in the truest sense?"[55] And it is the conviction of our authors that "no other religious vision encapsulates the final purpose of God. . . . Other religious visions cannot provide community in its ultimate sense, because they are *theologically* insufficient. They do not embody the fullest possible understanding of who God actually is."[56]

However, as in other areas of their proposal, one begins to wonder whether these statements are consistent with their overall nonfoundationalist approach. After all, how does one determine what the "true" community is? On what grounds will other competing linguistic constructions of various religious communities (Islam, for example) accept our Christian linguistic construction as a "truer" view of community than theirs? Does Grenz's question not implicitly assume a kind of foundationalism and realism? I will have more to say on this below, but before I do, I want to turn to our third and last diagnostic question in describing the Grenz/Franke proposal.

What Role Does Scripture Play in Grenz/Franke's Proposal for Theological Method?

In our last diagnostic question, I want to probe deeper in regard to the role Scripture plays in Grenz and Franke's revisionist proposal for doing evangelical theology. I have already argued that for Grenz and Franke, Scripture is *not* first-order language, as traditionally conceived; rather it is the "Christian interpretative framework" which is "basic" for Christian theology—a combination and interweaving of Scripture, experience, tradition, and so on—the "language game" of the Christian community. In fact, they are forthright in confessing that they believe there are three *sources* for theology—Scripture, tradition, and culture—and ultimately, it is the Spirit who speaks through all three of them, although the Spirit's speaking through Scripture is the "norming norm" of the church. Let us unpack exactly what they mean by this in five steps.

First, we may begin with what they do *not* mean. Clearly, they reject what

---

[54] Ibid. See the development of this argument in Grenz, "The Universality of the 'Jesus-Story' and the 'Incredulity Toward Metanarratives,'" 102-111.
[55] Grenz, "The Universality of the 'Jesus-Story' and the 'Incredulity Toward Metanarratives,'" 108.
[56] Ibid., 109.

evangelicals have historically meant by *sola Scriptura*—that Scripture serves as first-order language, the final authority for all Christian theology and praxis. They state their opposition this way: "Scripture does not stand alone as the sole source in the task of theological construction or as the sole basis on which the Christian faith has developed historically. Rather scripture functions in an ongoing and dynamic relationship with the Christian tradition, as well as with the cultural milieu from which particular readings of the text emerge."[57] Additionally, Scripture, as the "norming norm" must *not* be viewed as a "storehouse of facts" or "propositions"—i.e., propositional revelation—by which theology merely gathers, arranges, and orders the propositions of Scripture in a proper way.[58] Furthermore, they do not view Scripture as a book that is authoritative *in itself* as God's breathed-out Word[59] in the sense that Scripture is objective, basic, and self-authenticating apart from the faith of the church and the instrumentality of the Spirit.[60]

So, second, what then do they mean? What authority does Scripture have as the "norming norm" of the church? For them, the Scripture is authoritative due to the fact that "it is the vehicle through which the Spirit speaks."[61] They state, reminiscent of Karl Barth, that, ". . . the authority of the Bible is in the end the authority of the Spirit whose instrumentality it is. As Christians, we acknowledge the Bible as scripture in that the sovereign Spirit has bound authoritative, divine speaking to this text. We believe that the Spirit has chosen, now chooses, and will continue to choose to speak with authority through the biblical texts."[62] But why do Christians believe this? It is certainly *not* because the Bible in itself, as an inspired text, is God's Word in a self-attesting way, say Grenz and Franke, but rather it is due to the fact that the church has experienced the power and truth of the Spirit of God through these writings. Thus, as our authors argue, "they [the church] knew these documents were 'animated with the Spirit of Christ.'"[63] Thus, on the one hand,

---

[57] Ibid., 112.

[58] See Grenz and Franke, *Beyond Foundationalism*, 60-63.

[59] See ibid., 65-66 on their treatment of 2 Timothy 3:16. They argue that *theopneustos,* "God-breathed," emphasizes the surpassing value of the Spirit-energized Scriptures, not some purported pristine character of the autographs. But is that really the point of the text? No. The point is that the resultant product of the Spirit's supernatural work is nothing less than God's Word, not merely in a dynamic sense in that the people of God "knew these documents were 'animated with the Spirit of Christ'" (66), but in an objective sense. See B. B. Warfield, *The Inspiration and Authority of the Bible* (Philadelphia: Presbyterian & Reformed, 1948), 131-166, 245-296; cf. Paul D. Feinberg, "The Meaning of Inerrancy," in *Inerrancy,* ed. Norman L. Geisler (Grand Rapids, Mich.: Zondervan, 1980), 276-283.

[60] See Grenz and Franke, *Beyond Foundationalism*, 64-68, 102-105, 114-115.

[61] Ibid., 65; cf. Stanley J. Grenz, "The Spirit and the Word: The World-Creating Function of the Text," *Theology Today* 57 (October 2000): 357-374.

[62] Grenz and Franke, *Beyond Foundationalism,* 65; cf. Franke, "Response to Trueman and Gaffin," 340-343.

[63] Grenz and Franke, *Beyond Foundationalism,* 65.

they agree with Protestant theology that the text produced the community. But, on the other hand, they also defer to the Catholic tradition by asserting that "the community preceded the production of the scriptural texts and is responsible for their content and for the identification of particular texts for inclusion in an authoritative canon to which it has chosen to make itself accountable."[64] In this sense, then, Scripture is a product of the community of faith that produced it. But what unifies the relationship between Scripture and community is the work of the Spirit, who "appropriates" the biblical text and speaks to us through it. That is why, our authors confidently affirm, "following the lead of the church of ages, we too look to the biblical texts to hear the Spirit's voice."[65]

Third, given that the authority of Scripture is the Spirit speaking through the Scriptures, it still must be asked: In what sense is the Bible the forming source for our theological construction? Their answer is this: The "biblical message" is the norming norm in theology. They state, "As noted earlier, it is not the Bible as a book that is authoritative, but the Bible as the instrumentality of the Spirit; the biblical message spoken by the Spirit through the text is theology's norming norm."[66] But what is the relationship between the "biblical message" and the text itself? Thankfully they reject the classic liberal view that the biblical message lies somehow "behind" the text. Unfortunately, however, they are reluctant to posit a "one-to-one correspondence between the revelation of God and the Bible, that is, between the Word of God and the words of scripture,"[67] in the sense that evangelicals have traditionally affirmed that the Bible *is* the Word of God. For Grenz and Franke, ultimately to say "the Word of God" is to have both a Christological and pneumatological focus.[68] But with that said, how are we to think of this crucial relationship? They ultimately conclude that the relationship is somewhat fluid. Yes, the "biblical message" is the norming norm for theology, but "in saying this we must be careful not to posit a nebulous, ethereal 'something' standing behind the text to which we have at best only limited access. Rather, the biblical message is in some important sense bound to the canonical text itself."[69] But how? Grenz and Franke's explanation involves the employment of three crucial proposals.

(1) They adopt Nicholas Wolterstorff's "appropriated discourse"

---

[64] Ibid., 115; cf. Franke, "Scripture, Tradition, and Authority," in *Evangelicals and Scripture,* 192-210.
[65] Grenz and Franke, *Beyond Foundationalism,* 66.
[66] Ibid., 69.
[67] Ibid., 70-71.
[68] See ibid., 71.
[69] Ibid., 72.

model.[70] In this model, Wolterstorff proposes that a crucial way for conceiving of the relationship between God's speech and Scripture is not only in terms of "deputized discourse," that is, God enlisted the prophets, for example, to bring a message to the community, but also in terms of "appropriated discourse," that is, God "appropriates" the discourse of the biblical authors as his own, without necessarily agreeing with them at every point. Obviously, for Wolterstorff the problem arises in trying to lay out the criteria for determining what God agrees with in his appropriation and what he does not agree with.[71] Grenz and Franke never address this issue, though one assumes that they would appeal to the Spirit speaking through the text to the community.

(2) However, in contrast to Wolterstorff, they adopt a "textual-sense interpretation" over against an "authorial-discourse interpretation." In an authorial-discourse view, God's speaking is tied to the text by the intention of the biblical authors which is discovered, in the language of speech-act theory, by attending to the illocutionary acts of the biblical authors. However, Grenz and Franke, contrary to much of traditional hermeneutics, reject this approach for a textual-sense interpretation. In this view, the meaning of the biblical text is found in the text but not necessarily directly tied to the author's intent, since once the author creates the text it takes on a life of its own. Appealing to philosopher Paul Ricoeur, they state it this way: "although an author creates a literary text, once it has been written, it takes on a life of its own. The author's intention has been 'distanced' from the meanings of the work, although the ways in which the text is structured shape the meanings the reader discerns in the text. In a sense, the text has its own intentions, which has its genesis in the author's intention but is not exhausted by it."[72]

(3) In light of the above two points, Grenz and Franke now answer the question, "What does it mean to declare that the Spirit speaks through scripture?"[73] Their answer is this: the Spirit speaks through Scripture by "appropriating the biblical text."[74] But they are very clear that in "appropriating the text," the Spirit's intention is *not* simply and totally tied to the author's intention in the text. In an amazing admission, they write:

> . . . the Spirit's illocutionary act of appropriation does not come independently of what classical interpretation called "the original meaning of the

---

[70] See Nicholas Wolterstorff, *Divine Discourse* (Cambridge: Cambridge University Press, 1995).
[71] See a helpful critique of Wolterstorff's proposal in Horton, *Covenant and Eschatology*, 156-164.
[72] Grenz and Franke, *Beyond Foundationalism*, 74.
[73] Ibid., 73.
[74] Ibid., 74.

text." . . . At the same time, the Spirit's address is not bound up simply and totally with the text's supposed internal meaning. Indeed, as certain contemporary proponents of "textual intentionality" (e.g., Paul Ricoeur) remind us, although an author creates a literary text, once it has been written, it takes on a life of its own. The author's intention has been "distanced" from the meanings of the work, although the ways in which the text is structured shape the meanings the reader discerns in the text. In a sense, the text has its own intention, which has its genesis in the author's intention but is not exhausted by it.

Consequently, we must never conclude that exegesis alone can exhaust the Spirit's speaking to us through the text. Although the Spirit's illocutionary act is to appropriate the text in its internal meaning (i.e., to appropriate what the author said), the Spirit appropriates the text with the goal of communicating to us in *our* situation, which, while perhaps paralleling in certain respects that of the ancient community, is nevertheless unique.

Further, in appropriating the biblical text, the Spirit speaks, but the Spirit's speaking does not come through the text in isolation. Rather, we read the text cognizant that we are the contemporary embodiment of a centuries-long interpretive tradition within the Christian community (and hence we must take seriously the theological tradition of the church). And we read realizing that we are embedded in a specific historical-cultural context (and hence we must pay attention to our culture). In this process of listening to the Spirit speaking through the appropriated text, theology assists the community of faith in discerning what the Spirit is saying and in fostering an appropriate obedient response to the Spirit's voice.[75]

Fourth, what, then, is the *goal* of the Spirit's speaking through the appropriated biblical text? Our authors respond by arguing that the goal of the Spirit's speaking, what they describe as the perlocutionary effect, is to create a "world," that is, to project a way of being in the world, a mode of existence, and a pattern of life—ultimately, God's eschatological world, that which he intends for creation.[76] But, once again, it is crucial to remember that for our authors, this projected "world" "does not lie in the text itself, even though it is closely bound to the text"[77]; rather, it is the Spirit who creates this "world," specifically a "communal world," through the text.[78] The Bible narrates the primary paradigmatic events that shape the identity of the Christian community, and the Spirit appropriates the biblical narrative, connecting us with our narrative past and linking us to our glorious future, so

---

[75] Ibid., 74-75.
[76] See ibid., 76-77.
[77] Ibid., 77.
[78] See ibid., 75-83.

that in speaking through the text, the Spirit forms in us a communal interpretive framework that creates a new world. In this way, the Spirit leads us
to view ourselves and all reality in light of a specifically biblical interpretive
framework so that we might thereby understand and respond to the challenges of life in the present as the contemporary embodiment of a faith community that spans the ages.[79]

Fifth, and last, how, then, should we read Scripture? What should our
hermeneutics be? Their answer is that we must read Scripture as a "theological text." At its heart, this kind of reading is *not* to use the Bible as that which
provides "raw materials for erecting a systematic theological edifice."[80]
Instead, our reading of the Bible is "to discern the Spirit's voice through the
appropriated text"[81] as centered in "the biblical message as a whole, that is,
in the overarching goal and purposes of God to create an eschatological world
as indicated by scripture in its entirety."[82] Obviously, in this theological reading, we must respect the integrity of the text within its own world, while at the
same time acknowledging that a distance stands between our world and the
world of the text. Thus, to read theologically is to listen for the Spirit's voice
in Scripture not merely through exegesis, but also to us in our present context,
as the Spirit creates a new world in the reader's present.[83] And furthermore,
we are to read Scripture in such a way that we look for "converging patterns
present throughout the documents . . . above all, we read the texts in light of
their convergence in the pattern that centers on God's work in Jesus Christ and
the subsequent sending of the Spirit, that pattern that Christians believe lies at
the heart of the Bible as a whole."[84] In this sense, we are to read the diverse
texts of Scripture as a single voice. However, our authors are emphatic that
the singularity of voice is *not inherent in the texts themselves,* nor is it ulti-

---

[79] See ibid., 81, where the authors summarize the perlocutionary effects of the Spirit's speaking. They
state, "The Bible not only recounts paradigmatic stories of 'long ago' but also declares God's intention
for the world. In scripture we find a vision of a future, new creation in which humans live in harmony
with each other, with God, and with all creation (e.g., Rev. 21:1–22:5). In addition to connecting us with
our narrative past, therefore, the Spirit constructs our communal identity by linking us to this glorious
future. The Spirit speaks to us through the text—appropriates the biblical vision of the divinely intended
new creation—so that we might view our situation in light of God's future and as a result open ourselves
and our present to the power of that future, which in fact is already at work in us and among us (e.g.,
Rom. 8:9-30). By narrating our foundational past and disclosing our glorious future, the Bible provides
a paradigm of life as the believing community and as participants in that fellowship. That is, scripture
mediates a specifically Christian 'interpretative framework.' . . . Through the appropriated biblical text,
the Spirit forms in us a communal interpretive framework that creates a new world. The Spirit leads us
to view ourselves and all reality in light of an unabashedly Christian and specifically biblical interpretive
framework so that we might thereby understand and respond to the challenges of life in the present as
the contemporary embodiment of a faith community that spans the ages."

[80] Ibid., 84.
[81] Ibid.
[82] Ibid., 86-87.
[83] See ibid., 87-89.
[84] Ibid., 90.

mately dependent on the church's decision to shape the canon; rather it rests upon the "singularity of the Spirit who speaks through the texts."[85]

This approach, they assert, has the benefit of opening up an ongoing conversation involving the interplay of the three sources of theology: Scripture, tradition, and culture. Since the Spirit speaks through all three, we carefully listen for the voice of the Spirit who speaks through Scripture, in light of his speaking through the tradition of the church, and within the particularity of culture. To be sure, Grenz and Franke add the cautionary note that the Spirit's speaking that occurs in tradition and culture will not be a speaking against the text, but they do not concede that the text is more "foundational" than tradition or culture, even though it is the "norming norm" of the church. In fact, for them, tradition, culture, and Scripture are not different moments of communication; rather they are but one speaking. And thus, Grenz and Franke assert, we do not engage in different listenings, but only one.[86] In the end, they affirm, in the famous slogan, "all truth is God's truth."[87]

But, it must be asked, what keeps this theological reading of Scripture from subjectivism? Interestingly, they ask themselves this question: "Does this link between Spirit and Word make the authority of the Bible dependent on our hearing the voice of the Spirit in its pages?"[88] Their answer: a theology of Word and Spirit need not lapse into subjectivism, as long as it does not place the individual ahead of the community. They state, "The Bible remains objectively scripture because it is the book of the church. From its inception, the community of Christ—following the lead of the ancient Jewish community (e.g., Neh. 8:1-8)—has been a people who gather around the text to hear the Spirit's voice speaking through it. And throughout the ages this community has testified that the sovereign Spirit has spoken—and continues to speak—through the pages of the Bible."[89] In this sense, then, a theological reading of Scripture must always take place within a communal setting—not only in light of the faith community that precedes us, but also in light of our own local congregational setting. In the end, they assert, "our goal is to hear what the Spirit is saying to this particular congregation and to these particular believers who share together the mandate of being a fellowship of believers in this specific setting."[90]

---

[85] Ibid.
[86] See ibid., 163.
[87] See ibid., 161.
[88] Ibid., 67.
[89] Ibid., 68.
[90] Ibid., 92.

CRITICAL REFLECTIONS ON THE GRENZ/FRANKE PROPOSAL

What should we think of this very creative and challenging proposal which, in general, is an excellent representative of postconservative thinking on the subject of theological method? Does it help us do theology better in light of our current cultural context? Or is it held captive to it? Does it help us answer better what it means to be "biblical"? Or is it ultimately adverse in this regard? Certainly within the limitations of this chapter, I cannot do justice to it. As one might have noticed, Grenz and Franke's discussion, indeed any discussion of theological method, interfaces with so many difficult and crucial areas—postmodernism, epistemology, Scripture, hermeneutics, historical theology—that my reflections will of necessity be simply that, reflections.

Positive Reflections

First, Grenz and Franke are to be commended for challenging evangelicals to take seriously the doing of theology in a post-theological age. They are certainly not the first to do so, but they represent a strong reminder that our doing theology today must address the issues of the day. Theology and theological method does not have the luxury of merely repeating slogans from the past; it must be done afresh by the people of God to address current issues, otherwise we will fail in our high calling before the Lord. As Martin Luther reminded us many years ago, we must fight the battles of our day—where the world and the devil are that moment attacking—for unless we do, we are not being faithful soldiers of our Lord Jesus Christ.[91]

Second, this proposal challenges evangelicals to rethink our theological method afresh. Our authors are to be applauded for challenging us to be more self-conscious about this important subject. Even though I find much of their presentation of conservatives quite misleading—especially their characterization of "traditionalists" as "modernists" without any careful distinctions made between various kinds of foundationalisms, or of other conservative traditions that do not fit their sweeping generalizations,[92] or even their treat-

---

[91] Cited in Francis A. Schaeffer, *The God Who Is There*, in *The Complete Works of Francis A. Schaeffer*, 2nd ed., 5 vols. (Wheaton, Ill.: Crossway, 1985), 1:11. The same point is made in John M. Frame, *The Doctrine of the Knowledge of God* (Phillipsburg, N.J.: Presbyterian & Reformed, 1987), 76-88; Horton, *Covenant and Eschatology*, 220-276; David F. Wells, "The Nature and Function of Theology," in *The Use of the Bible in Theology: Evangelical Options*, ed. Robert K. Johnston (Atlanta: John Knox Press, 1985), 175-199.

[92] Here I am thinking of the Dutch Reformed tradition and its heirs who attempt to do theology in a different way than Charles Hodge, but who operate with the same view of Scripture, a commitment to epistemological realism, and appreciation for both tradition and culture without treating them as sources of theology. See, for example, the works of Herman Bavinck, Abraham Kuyper, Geerhardus Vos, John Frame, Richard Gaffin, Richard Lints, and Michael Horton.

ment of contemporary evangelical theologians[93]—they do remind us of some crucial areas that many evangelicals need to rethink, such as: (1) we must not view the theological task *merely* as an inductive collecting, organizing, and arranging of texts, a kind of proof-texting approach apart from reading and applying Scripture in light of its own internal categories and structure;[94] (2) we need to be careful that we do not conceive of propositional revelation in such a way that we do not do justice to all the language and literature of Scripture;[95] (3) we must read Scripture canonically, not merely atomistically;[96] (4) we need to be reminded of our own historical located-ness and the importance of listening to the past in our theological construction and the hermeneutical-spiral nature of interpretation; (5) the demise of classical foundationalism entails that we rethink traditional theological method, especially the agenda of natural theology, which has sought to move from the axioms of either universal reason or experience to Scripture and then to theology.[97]

Third, I applaud their desire to be "intratextual" in their approach to theology. Generally speaking, as noted earlier, we may conceive of two different approaches to the doing of theology—extratextual and intratextual. To be extratextual means that Scripture must be read through an extratextual ideological or philosophical grid that we bring to the text. In the worst-case scenario, complete priority is given to some modern or postmodern secular worldview, and Christianity is valid only insofar as it fits in with that worldview. Christian faith and practice is found true or acceptable only when it conforms to the criteria that is external to it and claims superiority over it. An excellent example of this is that of classical liberalism or contemporary pluralism.[98] That certainly is *not* how evangelicals should do theology or be

---

[93] In particular I am thinking of Wayne Grudem, but the same could be said for Carl Henry and others. Are we really to think that Grudem does not take seriously tradition and culture or that he thinks the chosen order of theological reflection upon Scripture is merely arbitrary? After all, he is heavily indebted to the Reformed tradition of Bavinck, Vos, Frame, Gaffin, et al. My own view of Grudem's chapter on methodology is that it is not adequate (even though I do not think that was a main focus of his book), but his statement that we can go to Scripture and "look for answers to *any* doctrinal questions, considered in *any sequence*" (*Systematic Theology* [Grand Rapids, Mich.: Zondervan, 1994], 32) is due to the conviction that Christian theology, precisely because it is grounded in God's Word, is an interrelated "mosaic," to use the authors' terminology. Grudem, I am sure, would agree with Grenz and Franke when they view theology not as "a collection of isolated factual statements arising directly from first principles," but rather as a whole worldview, a package deal, and that as such, to speak of any point already implies and has entailments for other points of theology.

[94] For a better way of developing this point see Horton, *Covenant and Eschatology;* Lints, *Fabric of Theology.*

[95] For a better analysis of this point see Kevin J. Vanhoozer, "The Semantics of Biblical Literature: Truth and Scripture's Diverse Literary Forms," in *Hermeneutics, Authority, and Canon,* ed. D. A. Carson and John D. Woodbridge (Grand Rapids, Mich.: Zondervan, 1986), 53-104; cf. idem, *Is There a Meaning in This Text?*

[96] On this point see Lints, *Fabric of Theology;* and Horton, *Covenant and Eschatology.*

[97] Once again, for a better development of these ideas see Horton, *Covenant and Eschatology.*

[98] See Hans W. Frei, *Types of Christian Theology* (New Haven: Yale University Press, 1992), 28-55.

"biblical," and our authors rightly reject this approach, as should all evangelicals. Intratextual, on the other hand, means that priority is given to the language, self-description, categories, form, and structure of Scripture and thus our doing of theology and whole understanding of the world is, as Calvin stated, viewed through the "spectacles" of Scripture.[99] To be intratextual does not imply that in the doing of theology the task is simply one of repeating Scripture, for Scripture must be *applied* to every aspect of our lives, both individually and corporately. But it does entail that to do *Christian* theology requires that God's Word is our final authority, the grid or interpretative matrix or metanarrative by which we view everything—our beliefs, doctrine, life, and practices. In the end, it is doing theology intratextually—that is, starting with the language, literature, form, and structure of Scripture itself as redemptive-historical revelation, progressively disclosed—that is required in order to attach the predicate "biblical" to our theology.[100]

Now even though I agree with the overall "intratextual" approach of Grenz and Franke, it is necessary to distinguish their approach, which is more indebted to the influence of postliberalism at this point, from the intratextual approach I would take, which conceives of Scripture as divinely authorized discourse, the sole authority for Christian faith and practice. Thus, in my view, they are correct to emphasize the need for the canonical Scriptures to be the "norming norm" for our theological reflection. They are also right in affirming that the task of theology is to re-describe reality within the scriptural framework so that all of life is viewed from an "unabashedly Christian and specifically biblical interpretive framework so that we might thereby understand and respond to the challenges of life in the present as the contemporary embodiment of a faith community that spans the ages."[101] However, given their proposal, I question whether they can fulfill these aspirations in such a way that the full authority of Scripture is maintained, at least as historically conceived, and a transcendental condition for the possibility of doing a normative theology is given.[102] It is to those concerns that I now briefly turn.

---

[99] See John Calvin, *Institutes of the Christian Religion,* ed. John T. McNeill, 2 vols. (Philadelphia: Westminster, 1960), 1:69-74.

[100] For a development of some of these ideas see Carson, *Gagging of God,* 141-314; cf. Horton, *Covenant and Eschatology;* Lints, *Fabric of Theology;* Vanhoozer, "Voice and the Actor."

[101] Grenz and Franke, *Beyond Foundationalism,* 81.

[102] The term "transcendental" comes from the thought of Immanuel Kant. It refers to the task of discovering the preconditions for something to be possible. In the case of Kant, he was attempting to discover the transcendental conditions for the possibility of knowledge. In the context of this chapter, the term is being used to state my conviction that the necessary precondition for the possibility of a normative, objective, truth-telling theology is the self-disclosure of the triune God in Scripture by which Scripture alone is viewed as our final, first-order authority for our faith and practice.

Negative Reflections

First, I am not convinced that Grenz and Franke's overly positive interpretation of postmodernism in regard to Christian theology and evangelical theological method is correct. Certainly, I agree with them that postmodernism has been helpful in pointing out the inherent problems of modernism, namely its hubris in thinking that finite human beings are self-sufficient, autonomous subjects who can discover, on their own apart from God and his revelation, truth in the metanarrative sense of universality and objectivity. Christian theology, at its best, has always criticized modernism for this very point.[103] However, I am a bit amazed that our authors do not seem to recognize that postmodernism starts from exactly the same starting point that modernism does, namely human autonomy, instead of God and his revelation. In the end, Christian theology must be neither modern nor postmodern. To be sure, modernism was no friend of the gospel, but neither is postmodernism.[104] Both have legitimate points to make, when viewed from a Christian worldview perspective; but both, taken as a whole, also stand opposed to the gospel and biblical Christianity. Michael Horton states it well when he comments:

> Too often in contemporary theology, despite the now almost universal repudiation of modernity, method assumes a remarkably modern critical stance. Although antifoundationalist "foundations" are presupposed in the place of modern ones, in the thriving (if scorned) industry of methodological theology, the distinct voice of scripture and that "great conversation" which is tradition is still postponed. In other words, theology is increasingly absent from the discipline of theology.[105]

Second, I find it difficult to fathom how our authors link evangelical theology's acceptance of an "error-free Bible as the incontrovertible foundation of their theology"[106] with an Enlightenment foundationalism.[107] A scriptural foundationalism is *not* grounded in the finite human subject as both modernism and postmodernism attempt to do, but instead it is rooted and grounded in the Bible's own presentation of the triune God—to use the

---

[103] For example, see the works of Francis Schaeffer, Carl F. H. Henry, Cornelius Van Til, Herman Bavinck, et al.

[104] On this point see Ingraffia, *Postmodern Theory and Biblical Theology;* and Horton, *Covenant and Eschatology,* 20-45. Both authors correctly argue that postmodernism both misunderstands historic Christian theology and simultaneously stands over against biblical thought and the entire Christian worldview.

[105] Horton, *Covenant and Eschatology,* 4.

[106] Grenz and Franke, *Beyond Foundationalism,* 23-24.

[107] See, for example, Peter Hicks, *Evangelicals and Truth* (Leicester, England: InterVarsity Press, 1998), 140-197, who clearly distinguishes the two and argues for a theological base for truth, realism, and objectivity based on revelation.

famous words of Francis Schaeffer, the God who is there. Knowledge, grounded in the one who is the Creator and sovereign Lord, the one who exhaustively knows all things, and additionally, the one who has created human beings in his image and who has disclosed himself to us, is certainly *not* the same kind of "foundationalism" as found in modernism. This is simply a mistake.

Third, I am puzzled by Grenz and Franke's adoption of coherentism, pragmatism, and epistemological and metaphysical nonrealism as resources for evangelical theological method. No doubt human beings are finite, linguistic creatures. And I agree that we, as human beings, cannot get outside of our own heads to check out "reality" from an omniscient perspective. I also agree that not all language is referential (even though some of it is), for language has many uses, including an identity-forming and world-constructing function, as well as an idolatrous world-constructing use! But to admit all of this does not entail a commitment to accept the entire nonrealist viewpoint, especially from a Christian worldview commitment. No doubt, given the post-Kantian, finite, autonomous starting point of much of postmodern thought, it is not hard to understand why certain postmodern perspectives adopt nonrealism and, correspondingly, perspectivalism.[108] But that an evangelical theology would adopt such commitments is not only unnecessary but also disturbing.

For after all, a Christian view of God, creation, and the world, including the creation of human beings and language, must acknowledge that language is a God-given gift, designed in such a way that we are able to know God truly, as well as ourselves and this world, though never exhaustively. Why should we think that because our knowledge of God comes through revelation and then through our senses, reason, and linguistic means, it cannot be knowledge of God as he really is or of reality as it really is, but only a matter of linguistic construction? That is simply an unscriptural concept. As John Frame rightly reminds us, "In Scripture, reality (God in particular) is known, and our senses, reason and imagination are not barriers to this knowledge; they do not necessarily distort it. Rather, our senses, reason, and imagination are themselves revelations of God—means that God uses to drive His truth home to us. God is Lord; He will not be shut out of His world."[109] Thus, all things being equal, the human subject, though never omniscient, can objectively know this world at a finite level. God is not only the creator of the human subject and the object (world), but he has also revealed himself truthfully in nature and Scripture. To be sure, Christian theology, in defending a

---

[108] For a helpful discussion of perspectivalism see Clark, *To Know and Love God*, 133-164.
[109] Frame, *Doctrine of the Knowledge of God*, 33.

"design plan" to language, does not ignore the fact that the Fall has affected both our cognitive faculties and the environment so they are not always in perfect working order. But even though language may be problematic in some regards, it is still designed, even in this fallen order, to lead us to know God and his world, a knowledge that is true and objective even though finite and now fallen.[110]

Moreover, it seems to me that there are some internal problems in our authors' defense of a present nonrealism and a future eschatological realism. On the one hand, if God knows all things past, present, and future infallibly (I assume they would affirm this), then why can we not say that what we know, as a subset of his knowledge based upon his revelation, truly reflects both the knowledge of him and of this world in the present, not merely in the future? For after all, Grenz and Franke seem to assume that there are truths that we may know now that are not merely constructed, such as the fact that God is bringing about the eschatological reality of the new creation. If we may know that truth now, then why not other truths? On the other hand, given their view, why should we think that the future will yield an epistemological and metaphysical realism if in the future we will still remain finite creatures? After all, there is no evidence that we will gain a "God's eye viewpoint" in the new creation; so if there is no realism now, then why would there be realism in the future?

Fourth, and probably one of the most serious implications of Grenz and Franke's adoption of nonfoundationalism, is the problem they have in stating the truth question. After all, how does one attempt to demonstrate the truthfulness of the gospel in a postmodern and pluralistic world? An important question indeed! In their answer, they struggle to argue how we may show that Christianity is "true" in the face of world religions and competing worldviews. They assume that other worldviews will accept our understanding of what a "true" community is (which seems to imply a kind of realism and criteria outside of the system). But given their nonfoundationalism, I do not see how they will be able to make their case. In the end, their project leaves Christian theology apologetically defenseless, a self-contained linguistic system that is not able to demonstrate before a watching world why it is indeed true. Christian theology can and must do much better than this.

Fifth, I am convinced, for a number of reasons, that their view of

---

[110] For a defense of this understanding of a critical realism that includes a theological analysis of the relationship between God, the world, and human language, see Kevin Vanhoozer, *Is There a Meaning in This Text?* See also how this theological view is worked out in the domain of science in Alistair E. McGrath, *Reality: A Scientific Theology*, vol. 2 (Grand Rapids, Mich.: Eerdmans, 2002); cf. also Frame, *Doctrine of the Knowledge of God*, 11-88; and Clark, *To Know and Love God*, 353-383.

Scripture does not do justice to what the Bible claims for itself and, therefore, it greatly weakens the grounding for doing theology in any kind of normative fashion. In regard to the Bible's claim for itself, evangelical theology has affirmed that Scripture is nothing less than God's Word written, the product of God's action through the Word and by the Holy Spirit whereby human authors freely wrote exactly what God intended and without error.[111] One of the entailments of this view of Scripture for theology is that in order to be "biblical," we must allow our theology to attend to the language, shape, and form of Scripture as the "spectacles" by which we look at the world. Scripture, then, given its divine inspiration, is first-order language, fully authoritative, infallible, and inerrant, and that being the case, it serves as our foundation by which all second-order reflection is grounded, evaluated, and corrected. Ultimately, evangelical theology has argued, Scripture serves this role, not merely because it is the community's book, nor merely due to its being utilized by the Spirit in some dynamic sense, but precisely because it is what it claims to be, God's Word written, that is, divinely authorized discourse that gives us God's own interpretations of his own mighty actions.[112] Now, at least historically, this is what evangelicals have meant by biblical authority.[113] But does the view of Scripture proposed by Grenz and Franke live up to this expectation? I do not think so, for at least five reasons.

(1) Their understanding of first- and second-order language as applied to Scripture and theology does not treat Scripture itself as "first-order" and thus fully and finally authoritative. Rather it is the "Christian interpretive framework," which is a combination of Scripture, experience, and interpretation that is basic and foundational for them, but it is in the category of second-order.

(2) They deny that Scripture has an "inherent" authority due to its divine authorship or inspired character and thus it is not a self-authenticating or self-attesting text. Instead, they view the authority of Scripture in a *dynamic* man-

---

[111] For a summary statement and defense of what the Bible claims for itself, see my article, "The Inerrancy of Scripture," in *Beyond the Bounds*, ed. John Piper, Justin Taylor, and Paul Kjoss Helseth (Wheaton, Ill.: Crossway, 2003), 239-250; cf. also John M. Frame, "Scripture Speaks for Itself," in *God's Inerrant Word*, ed. John W. Montgomery (Minneapolis: Bethany, 1974), 159-177.

[112] For a development of this view of Scripture and its implication for understanding the nature of theology, once again see Horton, *Covenant and Eschatology*, 245-246. Horton argues that Scripture is "text" (first-order) and not "interpretation" (second-order), rather than thinking of it as God's own interpretation of his actions (Word-Act revelation). Thus, theology and doctrine may be viewed as truth claims (second-order), but contra Grenz and Franke, they may also give us direct statements of reality due to the fact that they accurately reflect Scripture, although their meaning is context-dependent and that context may well be described as the "grammar" (i.e., theological system). But, as Horton rightly observes, "theology involves both extrasystematic and intrasystematic truth claims, and this cannot be neatly organized into first order and second order, respectively" (246).

[113] For a description, explication, and preliminary defense of such a view, see Kevin J. Vanhoozer, "God's Mighty Speech-Acts: The Doctrine of Scripture Today" in *First Theology*, 127-158.

ner—the Spirit "appropriating" the text and speaking "through" it.[114] They seem to believe that if inspiration is viewed as a past event, then this implies that God has ceased to act and has become directly identical with the medium of revelation. They seem to echo Barth's concerns that God always remain only *indirectly* identical with the creaturely mediums of revelation, including Scripture, otherwise God's freedom will be compromised and human beings would be able to move from a position of epistemic dependency to one of epistemic mastery.[115] But surely there is something strange about saying that an inspired, objective text, the product of God's mighty action, would change the epistemic relationship between God and ourselves from that of dependency to mastery.[116] In the end, their view does not do justice to what the Bible claims regarding itself.

(3) Franke (and I am assuming Grenz) falsely identifies Barth's dialectic of veiling and unveiling with a Reformed distinction between archetypal and ectypal, or God's knowing all things exhaustively and infallibly (divine knowledge) and our knowing things finitely, yet truly.[117] In Reformed theology, this distinction has been used to acknowledge that even though Scripture is very much human and, as such, will never transcend its finitude, it is precisely because Scripture is God's own speech in human language that the language that *God* selects is appropriate for us so that we may know him, ourselves, and the world truly. Thus, all of biblical language in all of its diversity—because it is God who authorizes it—must be accurate and true, even though it does not give us access to the kind of knowledge that God has. Scripture, then, is sufficient for the purposes God intended.[118] However Franke does not view Scripture in this way, even though he appeals to this Reformed distinction. Instead he views the relationship between God's revelation and the creaturely medium, such as Scripture, in an *indirect* fashion. That is one of the main reasons why inspiration must now be construed in dynamic terms and revelation must not be understood apart from speaking

---

[114] See Darrell L. Bock, *Purpose-Directed Theology* (Downers Grove, Ill.: InterVarsity Press, 2002), 17-27, who makes a similar criticism. Bock states, "However, the fact that the Spirit inspires the Word and helped to create it suggests that the product *and its narrative, propositions and promises* possess authority not only in how the Spirit makes use of them but also in what they affirm. There is an authority in the text because it is Spirit-induced, whether or not that product is 'deputized' or 'appropriated'" (18), emphasis his.

[115] See Franke, "Response to Trueman and Gaffin," 340-343.

[116] On this issue and a better way to think of the relationship between Word and Spirit and God and biblical language, see John M. Frame, "God and Biblical Language: Transcendence and Immanence," in *God's Inerrant Word*, 159-177; idem, "The Spirit and the Scriptures" in *Hermeneutics, Authority, and Canon*, 217-235.

[117] See Franke, "Response to Trueman and Gaffin," 341-343.

[118] For an explanation and exposition of the Reformed position see Michael S. Horton, "Hellenistic or Hebrew? Open Theism and Reformed Theological Method," in *Beyond the Bounds*, 201-234; cf. idem, *Covenant and Eschatology*, 206-219.

of someone receiving revelation—hence, their view that Scripture is revelation and authoritative precisely because it is where the Spirit continually speaks *through* the text to us. In this account, our authors are attempting to affirm a nonfoundational understanding of Scripture and theology by means of a thoroughly pneumatological approach. But, as my next point will emphasize, this proposal leads to a Word-Spirit relation that is highly problematic: it views the Spirit as speaking and creating a world independently of Scripture's speaking, instead of maintaining a correct view that the Spirit's speaking is *always* the speaking of Scripture. But that leads me to my next point of criticism.

(4) Given their conception of the Word-Spirit relation, Grenz and Franke leave us with a hermeneutical subjectivism in regard to our knowing what the Spirit is seeking to communicate through Scripture to the church. Why? For this reason: they assert that "the Spirit speaking through the Scripture" refers to the *Spirit's* illocutions, but these are *not* identical with those of the biblical authors. That is why they say exegesis alone, while important and not completely divorced from the original meaning of the text, cannot discover what the Spirit is speaking.[119] This is further complicated due to their acceptance of a "textual-sense" interpretation model. Following Paul Ricoeur, since the text now takes on a life of its own, apart from the author's illocutions, a serious problem emerges: how does one know what the illocutionary acts of the Spirit are, especially when it is possible for the Spirit to speak independently of the human authors' illocutionary acts?[120] But if this is so, then how is Scripture really serving as our final authority for theological construction? Instead of arguing that Scripture itself, due to its divine inspiration, gives us a first-order interpretative framework that is found *in* Scripture, and in light of which we view the world and do our theology, so that "the Spirit's creating a world, then, is not a new illocutionary act but rather the perlocutionary act of enabling readers to appropriate the illocutionary acts inscribed in the biblical text,"[121] our authors have the Spirit speaking in relation to but apart from the actual illocutions of Scripture. But how, then, does one determine what the Spirit is actually speaking, except in the light of the *subjectivity* of the local community's hearing the Spirit's voice? And, furthermore, which community do we listen to?[122] Their proposal is even further compli-

---

[119] See, once again, Grenz and Franke, *Beyond Foundationalism,* 74-75.
[120] Vanhoozer, *First Theology,* 198, makes this same criticism. He rightly observes, "Grenz's account fails to explain how we can infer what illocutionary acts have been performed and to whom we should ascribe them. Consequently he leaves unanswered the fundamental question of how Scripture's actual *content* is related to the Spirit's accomplishing his further, perlocutionary, effects."
[121] Ibid.
[122] See Trueman, "It Ain't Necessarily So," 317-321, who makes the same point.

cated by arguing that the sources for theology are the Spirit's speaking through Scripture, tradition, and culture (not simply the Christian culture but the larger socially constructed world) in a nonfoundationalist way. No doubt our authors do not want to pit any of these three ways of speaking against one another, especially against Scripture. But is this merely a moot point?[123] Given their rejection of *sola Scriptura* and their acceptance of a nonfoundationalist epistemology, how can we actually "check and see" to know whether the world the Spirit is creating in and through our theological language belongs to the eschatological world? Or, conversely, how can we falsify a world of our own idolatrous making that contradicts the Bible's world? Appeal to tradition at this point simply pushes the problem back one step: Which tradition? Which community? For it is a sad fact of church history that there are a variety of church traditions on many central points of doctrine. So to whom do we listen since, I dare say, each community views itself as seeking to hear faithfully the same Spirit speak through Scripture, tradition, and culture?[124] In the end, I am convinced that their proposal leaves us with a hermeneutical subjectivism that will not sufficiently ground a normative evangelical theology in a pluralistic and postmodern world.

(5) For all of their stress on the importance of reading Scripture as a text and the necessity of a theological hermeneutic, which I basically agree with, unless their proposal is spelled out in greater depth and clarity, I do not see how they have helped us go about the actual practice of *doing* theology, namely, reading and applying Scripture to our lives. They warn us repeatedly that we must avoid "proof-texting" and read Scripture in all of its diversity according to the converging patterns that center in Jesus Christ. That is fine, as far as it goes, and most evangelicals would agree with that approach. But, given their view of Scripture, when they argue that the unity of the canon (i.e., singularity of voice) does *not* rest in the texts themselves, but in the Spirit who speaks through the texts,[125] we have the same serious problem mentioned above: how does one determine the Spirit's speaking if it is not *directly* related to the text itself? Do we hear the Spirit speaking through the text or where we *want* him to be heard? In contrast to our authors, what evangelical theology has argued and should argue is that when the Spirit speaks, it is always the speaking of Scripture. To maintain otherwise is to lead to the troubling conclusion that the church cannot know what God is saying through

---

[123] This is Daniel J. Treier's question in, "Canonical Unity and Commensurable Language: On Divine Action and Doctrine," in *Evangelicals and Scripture,* 214-216.

[124] See Vanhoozer, "Voice and the Actor," 85-87, who raises these same kinds of questions.

[125] See Grenz, *Beyond Foundationalism,* 90.

Scripture, and to shift the locus of authority from the text to the community and therefore from Scripture itself to the pragmatic preferences of the people. Horton states it well when he warns of the dangers of this kind of proposal: ". . . much of modern theology (*especially* Protestant theology) has turned repeatedly to 'what the Spirit is saying to us today' while neglecting or in many cases rejecting rather significant sections of scripture. This done, one can either turn to his or her own inner light or to an authoritative magisterium"[126]—or to a community of believers.

Overall Assessment

What is my overall assessment of the Grenz/Franke proposal? No doubt there is much that is helpful, challenging, and admirable about their view. They have stirred us from our dogmatic slumbers to think carefully and thoughtfully about evangelical theological method, especially in light of our current cultural context—and we must give them our thanks. However, as creative as their proposal is, at the end of the day, what I find surrendered is biblical authority—i.e., a text that is first-order and God-given through human authors which is our basis for how we interpret the world, ground our beliefs, and live our lives. Without that solid grounding, not in human reason and autonomy, nor in the community of God's people, but in Scripture itself, we have, in terms of theological method, surrendered the very transcendental condition for the possibility of doing theology in any kind of normative fashion. The burden of what it means to be "biblical" in our theology will be placed upon various community interpretations, throughout history, as we listen to the voice of the Spirit through Scripture; but that kind of subjectivity will greatly undercut the very doing of a normative evangelical theology. Ultimately, without the living God who discloses himself in an authoritative and reliable Word-revelation, theology loses both its *identity* and its *integrity* as a discipline and is set adrift, forever to be confused with sociology, philosophy, anthropology, and the like.[127]

CONCLUDING REFLECTIONS: EVANGELICAL THEOLOGICAL METHOD TODAY

Where do we go from here? Obviously the answer to that question would require a book in and of itself, but thankfully there are a number of evan-

---

[126] Horton, *Covenant and Eschatology*, 210.
[127] On this point see Kevin J. Vanhoozer, "Christ and Concept: Doing Theology and the 'Ministry' of Philosophy," in *Doing Theology in Today's World: Essays in Honor of Kenneth S. Kantzer*, ed. John D. Woodbridge and Thomas E. McComiskey (Grand Rapids, Mich.: Zondervan, 1991), 99-110.

gelical theologians who are providing excellent answers.[128] However, in a summary fashion, I offer three personal reflections, in light of the previous discussion, as to what I think is crucial for the doing of evangelical theology today.

First, evangelical theology must uphold the full authority of Scripture as God-given, first-order language that is "foundational" for all Christian thinking and living. It is at this point where I have to part company with the Grenz/Franke proposal and much of postconservative theology. In the current cultural climate, I am convinced that the crucial issue facing evangelical theology is the authority of Scripture and of the God who gave it. At the heart of postmodernism's problem, and the main reason for much of the fragmentation in contemporary theology, is an implicit denial of the God of Scripture, and thus a diminishing of the full authority of Scripture in theology and the church. But given the God of Scripture and the Scripture that he gives (2 Tim. 3:16), we must affirm that we do have a divine interpretation of reality including his own redemptive acts in history—which though not exhaustive is nonetheless true and objective. No doubt human beings never attain an omniscient view of things, even in the future. But because our finite knowing is a subset of God's comprehensive and infallible knowledge, human beings, as complicated as the hermeneutical task may be, still may have a true knowledge of this world and of God and his ways. That is why Christian theology has always affirmed, and I am convinced must continue to affirm, a "revelational foundation."

No doubt a "revelational epistemology" involves a commitment to both general and special revelation, but priority must always be given to special revelation, and in particular Scripture.[129] Why? For the simple reason that Scripture is God's own divine interpretation, through human authors, of his own redemptive acts that carries with it a true, objective, and authoritative interpretation of his redemptive plan. We do not have this kind of interpretation of the world in general revelation, but we do have it in Scripture. That is why Scripture must be viewed as first-order language—as the "spectacles" by which we view the world. In this sense, the Scripture is "foundational" for our theology. It is, in the words of postmodern jargon, our "metanarrative." Scripture, then, not only describes accurately a certain segment of history, namely redemptive history, but it also serves as our "interpretive framework" for viewing the world. Thus, theology must move from Scripture's own interpretative framework (first-order),

---

[128] In particular, but not limited to them, I am thinking of the works by Lints, Horton, and Vanhoozer, cited above.
[129] See Frame's reflections on this in *Doctrine of the Knowledge of God*, 62-75.

which is found *in* Scripture, to theological vision (second-order). Of course, as stated, this view only makes sense if Scripture is nothing less than God's Word written, which is precisely the claim Scripture makes for itself. I do not see how evangelical Christianity can exist and flourish without unreservedly embracing this claim and the entailments of it.

Second, to be "biblical," evangelical theology must take seriously the role of "biblical theology" in our theological proposals and formulations. In order to be "biblical" in our theology, our reading of Scripture must reflect what it is and claims to be. I have already stated that Scripture claims to be nothing less than *God's* self-revelation through human authors, and thus we are convinced that there is a unity to it, among all the diversity, so that we may view Scripture as a unified divine communicative act, declaring God's unfailing purposes and plan.[130] In addition, it is important to stress that when we approach the Bible in its own categories and structure, we observe that God's self-revelation, in word and act, also involves historical progression, along a redemptive-historical storyline, ultimately centered in Jesus Christ (cf. Heb. 1:1-2), and thus we must read Scripture accordingly.[131] This is precisely what Horton has recently proposed when he asserts that a proper theological *method* must be "redemptive-historical-eschatological," so that we are reading Scripture according to its own intrasystematic categories. In this sense, then, the content of Scripture must define our methodology so that our reading of Scripture will reflect what Scripture actually is.[132]

---

[130] On this see Vanhoozer, *First Theology,* 159-203; Horton, *Covenant and Eschatology,* 123-276.

[131] On this point see Lints, *Fabric of Theology,* 259-336; cf. Carson, *Gagging of God,* 141-335.

[132] See Horton, *Covenant and Eschatology,* 1-19, 147-276. For Horton the terms "eschatological" and "redemptive-historical" capture the heart of Scripture's own intrasystemic categories. By the term "eschatological" Horton means more than a mere locus of theology. Rather, it is a lens by which we read Scripture and do our theology. Scripture itself comes to us as a redemptive revelation, rooted in history, unfolding God's eternal plan worked out in time, and as such the very "form" and "shape" of Scripture is "eschatological." It is for this reason that Horton is rightly uncomfortable with a "cognitive-propositionalist" approach to theology. Scripture is more than a storehouse of facts or propositions, for Scripture unfolds for us a *plot,* a storyline, a divine interpretation of the drama of redemption, which is eschatological at heart and Christological in focus, and as such, our *doing* of theology must reflect this. By "redemptive-historical," Horton is referring to the Scripture's own presentation of itself as "the organic unfolding of the divine plan in its execution through word (announcement), act (accomplishment), and word (interpretation)" (5). Given that redemption is progressive and unfolding, so is revelation, as it is God's own interpretation of his action and of human response in actual historical contexts. For Horton, there are at least three important implications of grasping the nature of Scripture for theological method. First, epistemologically speaking, a redemptive revelation entails that even though God's knowledge is exhaustive and is progressively revealed to us over time, for us, our knowledge is always finite, incomplete, dependent upon God's first-order revelation, yet true if it corresponds to that revelation. Second, our reading of Scripture and our doing of theology must attend to the historical unfolding of redemptive history that is *organically* related to and ultimately centered on Jesus Christ. The very "form" and "shape" of Scripture reminds us that God did not disclose himself in one exhaustive act but in an organic, progressive manner; and in fact, it is this organic quality of revelation that serves to explain the diversity of Scripture. Theology, as a result, must be very careful not to proof-text without considering the redemptive-historical structure and progression in Scripture. Third, theology must avoid speculation. It must attend to what God has actually said and done.

In contemporary idiom, the theological discipline that attempts to trace out the historical unfolding of redemptive history is that of "biblical theology."[133] "Biblical theology" is keenly aware that God did not disclose himself in one exhaustive act but in an organic, progressive manner, tied to God's performative action in word and deed. Biblical theology, in the final analysis, is trying to do justice to Scripture's own intrasystematic categories, so that it learns to "think God's thoughts after him." No doubt Scripture is not simply a storyline. It consists of many literary forms; and in a variety of ways—through narrative, law, apocalyptic, psalms, wisdom literature, gospel, and letter—the Scriptures unfold a plot, which culminates in Jesus Christ. But, as Carson reminds us, "the fact remains that the Bible as a whole document tells a story, and, properly used, that story can serve as a metanarrative that shapes our grasp of the entire Christian faith."[134]

In light of this, it is important to reference the important work of Richard Lints. Lints has not only argued that the methodology of "biblical" systematic theology must read and apply Scripture along its redemptive-historical plot line, but he has also helpfully proposed that we read Scripture according to three horizons: textual, epochal, and canonical.[135] Thus, in reading any text we not only exegete it in terms of its syntax, context, historical setting, and genre (i.e., textual horizon), we also place that text in light of where it is in redemptive history (i.e., epochal horizon), and even, in the final analysis, in light of where it is in the canon (i.e., canonical horizon). It is only then that we read Scripture truly in a "biblical" manner—according to its truest, fullest, *divine* intention. In fact, to read the Bible as unified Scripture is *not* just one interpretive interest among others, but the interpretive strategy that best corresponds to the nature of the text itself, given its divine inspiration.[136]

---

[133] For more on the discipline of "Biblical theology," see Charles H. H. Scobie, *The Ways of Our God: An Approach to Biblical Theology* (Grand Rapids, Mich.: Eerdmans, 2003); T. D. Alexander, Brian S. Rosner, et al., *New Dictionary of Biblical Theology* (Downers Grove, Ill.: InterVarsity Press, 2000); Graeme Goldsworthy, *Preaching the Whole Bible as Christian Scripture* (Grand Rapids, Mich.: Eerdmans, 2000).

[134] Carson, *Gagging of God*, 194.

[135] See Lints, *Fabric of Theology*, 259-311.

[136] See the development of this in Vanhoozer, *First Theology*, 194-203. In addition to stressing the importance of a canonical reading, Lints has also argued that one of the important ways God has glued the diverse epochs of redemptive history together is by the "promise-fulfillment" motif, which then becomes crucial in one's reading of Scripture and doing theology. By this motif, biblical authors are able to see the unity of God's plan, among the diversity. What has been promised in the past now has come to fruition in the new. And, furthermore, one of the means by which God's redemptive-historical plan unfolds is by the use of God-given "typology." However, typology makes sense only if it is rooted in a strong view of divine providence and knowledge. For while the type does have significance for its own time, its greater significance is directed toward the future; it testifies to something greater than itself that is still to come. But the future antitype *will* surely come, not only because God knows, according to his plan, the relationship between the type and the antitype, but also because God will providentially bring it to pass so that the prophetic fulfillment of the original type is as certain as the God who providentially ordains that fulfillment (cf. 303-311).

Third, to be "biblical," evangelical theology must then seek to read and apply all that Scripture says, according to its own presentation, to all of life.[137] In other words, theology must do more than merely repeat Scripture; it must also move from biblical interpretation and exposition (i.e., biblical theology) to theological vision (i.e., systematic theology). No doubt it must do so in light of the wisdom of the past (i.e., tradition) but it must also seek to address the issues of our day (i.e., context). But it must always do so by being grounded in Scripture, which serves as our "spectacles" or "interpretive framework," our worldview, by which we seek to live and act, and by which we attempt to "think God's thoughts after him"—for the praise of his glory.[138]

The challenges of postmodernism to evangelical theology are great. How we respond will affect generations to come. In our rethinking how to *do* theology in this contemporary context, may our heart's desire be to take every thought captive to obey Christ (2 Cor. 10:5) so that we may be found faithful servants of our great God and Savior.

---

[137] See Frame, *Doctrine of the Knowledge of God*, 81-88, where he discusses the concept of "application." Horton and Vanhoozer speak of the application work of theology as "performance." In contrast to postliberal theology that attempts to have the text "absorb" the reader into it, they propose the metaphor of "performance." As Vanhoozer states, "Evangelical theology is God-centered biblical interpretation that issues in performance knowledge on the world stage to the glory of God. It therefore prepares us for life in the real world, where reality is defined by the gospel of Jesus Christ. Herein is the sum of Christian wisdom: to know how to live 'in Christ'" ("Voice and Actor," 106).

[138] Viewing theology as "thinking God's thoughts after him" is a beautiful summary of the entire theological task. Interestingly and sadly, Roger Olson not only caricatures such an approach as "rationalistic" but also rejects it outright. See his article, "Postconservative Evangelical Theology and the Theological Pilgrimage of Clark Pinnock," in *Semper Reformandum*, 26. For a defense of viewing theology as "thinking God's thoughts after him," see Greg L. Bahnsen, *Van Til's Apologetic: Readings and Analysis* (Phillipsburg: Presbyterian & Reformed, 1998), 220-260; cf. Bavinck, *Reformed Dogmatics: Prolegomena*.

8

POSTCONSERVATISM:
A THIRD WORLD PERSPECTIVE

Kwabena Donkor

POSTCONSERVATISM AS A MOOD in North American evangelical theology has been likened to postliberal theology.[1] In this case, postconservative theology evidences a desire on the part of its practitioners to hold on to some of the qualities of conservative evangelical theology while simultaneously attempting to move beyond the confines of conservatism. Roger E. Olson has been foremost among evangelical theologians in trying to delineate the theological and practical contours of the postconservative mood.[2] In recent articles he outlines the "conservative-postconservative" and "traditionalist-reformist" divides, and explicitly identifies "reformists" with "postconservatives."[3]

When the "conservative-postconservative" divide is viewed in the apparently larger context of the "traditionalist-reformist" dialectic, it seems that Thomas Oden's critique of Olson's basic taxonomy is quite instructive. According to Oden, the traditionalist/reformist distinction may not be the best way to characterize the distinction between conservatives and postconservatives, for he believes that a more penetrating characterization would result from an examination of underlying assumptions.[4] In my view, a care-

---

[1] Roger E. Olson, "Postconservative Evangelicals Greet the Postmodern Age," *Christian Century* 112 (1995): 480. As Olson describes it, postliberal theology describes the posture of those theologians who, while trying to move beyond liberalism, continue to preserve some of its qualities.

[2] See his "Postconservative Evangelicals Greet the Postmodern Age"; and idem, "The Future of Evangelical Theology," *Christianity Today* 42 (February 9, 1998): 40-44. See also Millard J. Erickson, *The Evangelical Left: Encountering Postconservative Evangelical Theology* (Grand Rapids, Mich.: Baker, 1997), 29-30. Here, Erickson depends on Olson's characterization of postconservatism. Indeed, the term "postconservative" is Olson's creation. See Olson's "Reforming Evangelical Theology," in *Evangelical Futures: A Conversation on Theological Method,* ed. John G. Stackhouse, Jr. (Grand Rapids, Mich.: Baker, 2000), 201.

[3] Olson, "Reforming Evangelical Theology," 203.

[4] Thomas C. Oden, "The Real Reformers Are Traditionalists," *Christianity Today* 42 (February 9, 1998): 45.

ful analysis of basic assumptions is a necessary exercise in this debate because the issues at stake are inherently methodological ones.[5] It may very well be that, upon closer examination, postconservatism does not simply involve the endorsement of the classic "Bebbingtonian" categories; rather, as Olson describes it, it ceases to make the defense of historic orthodoxy a primary objective.[6] Thus, might it be possible that postconservativism holds to the so-called defining features of evangelicalism in such a novel fashion that it puts the whole evangelical movement at risk? In this chapter I argue that postconservativism involves a paradigm shift that places it in conflict with the ethos of historic evangelicalism. I also explore the implications of the postconservative agenda for theological pluralism in general, and Third World religious thought in particular.

I. UNDERSTANDING POSTCONSERVATIVE THEOLOGY

To the extent that postconservativism is perhaps presently only a mood and not a full-blown theological movement, it is reasonable to conclude that its positions are still in the formative stages. As a general observation, however, the postconservative theological impulse derives from a sense that evangelicals must respond to the sea change in Western culture in order for evangelicalism to maintain its relevance. While several evangelical theologians have reflected on the contemporary cultural context, few have actually written programmatic theological responses. Two such programmatic proposals, written by Kevin J. Vanhoozer and Stanley J. Grenz, have been offered to evangelical scholars for study and reflection.[7] In this chapter I look at postconservative evangelical theology, primarily, through the eyes of Grenz, whose program, in my view, seems to depart the most from historical evan-

---

[5] While alluding to the need for methodological discussions in the current evangelical climate, Stephen Williams correctly observes that the matter of theological method inevitably raises the question of presuppositions. See Stephen Williams, "The Theological Task and Theological Method: Penitence, Parasitism, and Prophecy," in *Evangelical Futures*, 159.

[6] Olson, "Postconservative Evangelicals Greet the Postmodern Age," 480. According to Olson, postconservatives continue to hold to four defining features of evangelicalism, which David Bebbington has classically formulated as conversionism, biblicism, activism, and crucicentrism, but they no longer make it their chief role to defend historic orthodoxy.

[7] Kevin J. Vanhoozer, "The Voice and the Actor: A Dramatic Proposal About the Ministry and Minstrelsy of Theology," in *Evangelical Futures*, 61-106; Stanley J. Grenz, "Articulating the Christian Belief-Mosaic: Theological Method After the Demise of Foundationalism," in *Evangelical Futures*, 107-136. The essays presented here represent a rather concise statement of the authors' position on the subject since both of them, especially Grenz, have written extensively on the issue. For a more complete presentation of Grenz's ideas, see Stanley J. Grenz, *Revisioning Evangelical Theology: A Fresh Agenda for the Twenty-first Century* (Downers Grove, Ill: InterVarsity Press, 1993); Stanley J. Grenz, *Renewing the Center: Evangelical Theology in a Post-Theological Era* (Grand Rapids, Mich.: Baker, 2000); Stanley J. Grenz and John R. Franke, *Beyond Foundationalism: Shaping Theology in a Postmodern Context* (Louisville: Westminster John Knox, 2001).

gelicalism. I am nevertheless cognizant that, although postconservatism is only a mood at present, it is a diverse phenomenon.

Stanley J. Grenz: Theology as Articulating the Christian Belief-Mosaic

In characterizing theology as the articulation of the Christian belief-mosaic, Grenz is seeking to develop an evangelical theological method that in his view will be relevant to postmodern thought.[8] He begins this discussion by observing that the postmodern situation "calls for an evangelical theological method that proceeds nonfoundationally and in so doing takes seriously the postmodern situation characterized by the move away from both realism and the metanarrative."[9] Grenz's view of Christian doctrine as "belief-mosaic" highlights a fundamental concern in his approach. His use of the concept "belief-mosaic" synonymously with "web of belief" demonstrates the seriousness with which he takes the so-called demise of foundationalism and the credence he gives to coherentist epistemology.[10] In Grenz's approach, the starting point is the Christian community and not a Scripture principle.

The Community: "Basicality" for Christian Theology. For Grenz, since evangelical theology has a strong base in foundationalist epistemology, the demise of foundationalism with the dawn of postmodernism means that some kind of postfoundationalist epistemology needs to be worked out to ground a renewed evangelicalism. For this grounding, Grenz builds on what has been called "Reformed epistemology," which, while it questions strong foundationalism, does not deny the foundationalist insight of searching for a type of basic belief. The particular interpretation of reason given by Reformed epistemologists needs outlining: there is no such thing as universal reason, which means that there is not available to us a single, universal set of criteria by which we may definitively judge the epistemic status of all beliefs.[11] Reason is not a neutral instrument of reflection; it is rather "person specific" and "situation specific."[12] Instead of any given foundational cognitive datum, Grenz and Reformed epistemologists agree on constituting the believing community

---

[8] The concern to accommodate the postmodern situation in theological reflection has been expressed quite clearly as follows: "Two aspects of the postmodern ethos are especially important for theological method: the fundamental critique of modernity, and the attempt to live and think in a realm of chastened rationality characterized by the demise of modern epistemological foundationalism" (Grenz and Franke, *Beyond Foundationalism*, 19).

[9] Grenz, "Articulating the Christian Belief-Mosaic," 119.

[10] Ibid., 123. For a brief account of coherentists' rejection of foundationalism, see Grenz and Franke, *Beyond Foundationalism*, 38-40.

[11] Grenz, "Articulating the Christian Belief-Mosaic," 120.

[12] Ibid.

as the basic Christian belief for theological reflection. What is specifically basic is the Christian community as an experience-facilitating interpretive framework. The fundamental implication of this communitarian turn is that the believing Christian community becomes the matrix out of which theological expression is brought forth.[13] But Grenz is careful to point out that, although in his approach theological reflection issues from the community's experience, this is not a return to foundationalism as in the liberal approach. In the latter approach, it was supposed that a single, universal, foundational religious experience "lay beneath the plethora of religious experiences found in the various religious traditions."[14] In Grenz's approach, the experience of the Christian community is specific to it and indeed identifies it as such.

Recasting Theology. The distinguishing of Grenz's approach from the liberal one in terms of the specificity of experience that characterizes it points to other significant insights in the approach. What is important to Grenz about the believing community is the view that religious experience is a function of a cognitive interpretive framework that "sets forth a specifically religious interpretation of the world."[15] In other words, Grenz agrees with the basic insight of Lindbeck that religious experience does not precede interpretation (as was the case in liberalism), rather religious experience is "filtered by an interpretive framework that facilitates the occurrence."[16] Applying this insight to his recasting of evangelical theology, Grenz states, "In this sense, the specifically Christian experience-facilitating interpretive framework, arising as it does out of the biblical gospel narrative, is 'basic' for Christian theology."[17] Grenz makes a further distinction of this elevation of experience from the classical liberal approach. In Grenz's postconservatism, unlike in liberalism, there is no generic religious experience but, rather, tradition-specific religious experience.[18] From this perspective, Christian theology becomes an intellectual effort to "understand, clarify, and delineate" the community's interpretive framework. Since the community's interpretive framework that theology attempts to delineate is informed by the Bible's narratives, the theological enterprise is not simply *descriptive,* but *prescriptive* as well, i.e., articulating what *ought* to be the interpretive framework of the Christian community.

In accordance with Grenz's search for a coherentist theological method,

---

[13] Elsewhere, Grenz describes theology as "the believing community's reflection on faith." See Grenz, *Revisioning Evangelical Theology,* 81.

[14] Grenz, "Articulating the Christian Belief-Mosaic," 121.

[15] Ibid., 122.

[16] Ibid.

[17] Ibid.

[18] Ibid.

he does not see the interpretive framework as a given that precedes the theological enterprise, and from which foundation the theological house is built, yielding separable units of doctrines. That view would signal a return to foundationalism. Rather, an interpretive framework is given with, or clothed in, any specific theological understanding. Christian theology, therefore, embodies a specific interpretive framework of conceptualizing the world holistically, in connection with the biblical view of God. Hence, Grenz views Christian doctrine as a "web of belief." But theology, according to Grenz, should not only explicate the belief-mosaic but should also demonstrate "the explicative power of the Christian faith by indicating the value of the Christian worldview for illuminating human experience."[19] Theology, then, is conversational—a conversation between the doctrinal mosaic and human experience—involving what Grenz describes as an "interplay, or perichoretic dance, of an ordered set of sources of insight."[20] It is a conversation in which the faith community, by explicating the meaning of the sacred texts, rituals, etc., through which it expresses its understanding of the world, seeks to articulate what ought to be the Christian belief mosaic. Grenz appears to anticipate the apparent indeterminate nature of this community-based conversation by observing that it is not a conversation in which "anything goes."[21] Instead the conversation proceeds under the guidance or interplay of an ordered set of sources of insight. These sources of insight constitute the voices in the theological conversation.

Theology as Conversation. Grenz's constructive theological conversation has three voices. The first and primary voice is the *Bible*. Formally, Grenz gives primacy to Scripture in theological reflection, but he has a nuanced view of the Scripture principle. He argues that under the foundationalist presuppositions of modernity, Luther's *sola Scriptura* principle was deprived of its concern to bring Word and Spirit together in a living relationship.[22] The Bible was transformed from a living text into the object of the theologian's exegetical and systematizing effort. Consequently, the authority of Scripture became identified with its "stateable content,"[23] namely, the doctrines it teaches, but Scripture is normative, says Grenz, "because it is the instrumentality of the Spirit."[24] Grenz's point is that the "Protestant principle means that the Bible is authori-

---

[19] Ibid., 124.
[20] Ibid.
[21] Ibid.
[22] Ibid.
[23] Grenz and Franke, *Beyond Foundationalism*, 62.
[24] Grenz, "Articulating the Christian Belief-Mosaic," 125.

tative in that it is the vehicle through which the Spirit speaks."[25] Indeed, Grenz takes the point a step further to say that, in the end, the Bible's authority is the authority of the Spirit whose instrumentality it is.[26] Grenz employs insights from contemporary speech-act theory to explain how his reformulated Scripture principle may be understood in the postmodern, postfoundationalist context. The Spirit, through Scripture, performs the illocutionary act of addressing humans, as well as a concomitant perlocutionary act of creating an "eschatological world" consisting of a new community of renewed individuals. By applying speech-act theory categories of illocutionary and perlocutionary acts to the role of the Spirit in the use of Scripture, Grenz legitimizes the primacy he accords the community in theological reflection. By the Spirit's illocutionary act, contemporary believers are able to ascertain the meaning of the text for the present, and by his perlocutionary act a Spirit-formed community is established. The ongoing theological task, therefore, is to help the believing community hear the Spirit's voice through the biblical text.[27]

The second voice in theology as conversation is *tradition*. Tradition in this sense means giving any particular believing community a historical sense of participation in "the one faith community that spans the ages."[28] Tradition in this conception is "the history of the interpretation and application of canonical scripture by the Christian community, the church, as it listens to the voice of the Spirit speaking through the text."[29] Grenz's pneumatology runs through his whole methodological program. The Spirit forms the community and guides its ongoing reflection on the biblical message to the point that tradition, in Grenz's view, "is in many respects an extension of the authority of scripture."[30] As a resource for theological reflection, the theological heritage has value in helping the theologian avoid pitfalls as well as pointing out areas for fruitful reflection. It serves as a "hermeneutical context or trajectory"[31] for the theological enterprise. The characteristic mark of

---

[25] Grenz and Franke, *Beyond Foundationalism*, 65.

[26] Ibid.

[27] Grenz explains how the Spirit enables the contemporary Christian community to respond appropriately to its cultural context: "Through the appropriated biblical text, the Spirit forms in us a communal interpretive framework that creates a new world. The Spirit leads us to view ourselves and all reality in light of an unabashedly Christian and specifically biblical interpretive framework so that we might thereby understand and respond to the challenges of life in the present as the contemporary embodiment of a faith community that spans the ages" (Grenz and Franke, *Beyond Foundationalism*, 81).

[28] Grenz, "Articulating the Christian Belief-Mosaic," 126.

[29] Grenz and Franke, *Beyond Foundationalism*, 118. Grenz provides a concise definition of tradition in terms of its composition: "The Christian tradition is comprised of the historical attempts by the Christian community to explicate and translate faithfully the first-order language, symbols, and practices of the Christian faith, arising from the interaction among community, text, and culture, into the various social and cultural contexts in which that community has been situated."

[30] Ibid., 119.

[31] Ibid., 120

this trajectory is its vitality, involving as it does the dialectic of change and continuity.[32] It should be pointed out that in his portrayal of the nature of tradition and its role as theological resource, Grenz is intent on providing a nonfoundational conception of tradition.[33]

Finally, the *wider historical-cultural context* should inform theological construction. Grenz comes to this conclusion based in part on his analysis of insights from cultural anthropology.[34] He concludes that the quest for a culture-free theology is both theologically and biblically unwarranted, besides the fact that "all theology by its very nature as a human enterprise is influenced by its cultural context."[35] In particular, Grenz mentions the various disciplines of human learning; these may lead to deeper or wider awareness of what is involved in the Spirit's work of creating a new identity in the Christian person. More significant is the reason he gives for including the historical-cultural context as a resource:

> Our theological reflections can draw from the so-called secular sciences, because ultimately no discipline is in fact purely secular. Above all, because God is the ground of truth, as Wolfhart Pannenberg so consistently argues, all truth ultimately comes together in God. . . . Because the life-giving Spirit is present wherever life flourishes, the Spirit's voice can conceivably resound through many media, including the media of human culture. Because Spirit-induced human flourishing evokes cultural expression, Christians can anticipate in such expressions traces of the Creator Spirit's presence.[36]

So deep is Grenz's appreciation of the pneumatological basis of the Spirit's speaking in culture that for him "culture and biblical text do not comprise two different moments of communication (with tradition then forming a third); rather, they are ultimately one speaking."[37]

Acknowledging the role of culture in Christian theology is one thing, but the manner in which culture should be incorporated into the theological enterprise is a different matter altogether. Grenz contemplates the extant programs of correlation and contextualization and concludes that both are inadequate by themselves. Methods of correlation and contextualization function in a foundationalist manner, although they move in opposite directions. Whereas correlationists tend to universalize culture, contextualizers are more

---

[32] Ibid., 126.
[33] Ibid., 114.
[34] See his discussion in Grenz and Franke, *Beyond Foundationalism*, 130-147.
[35] Ibid., 151.
[36] Grenz, "Articulating the Christian Belief-Mosaic," 127-128.
[37] Ibid., 128.

often inclined to overlook the distinctiveness of every understanding of Christianity's message.[38] Grenz's nonfoundationalist approach is to hold the two models in tandem and thereby bring about an interactive process that is both correlative and contextual. What is perhaps noteworthy in Grenz's model is what it presupposes: "this model presupposes neither gospel nor culture—much less both gospel and culture—as preexisting, given realities that subsequently enter into conversation. Rather, in the interactive process both gospel . . . and culture . . . are dynamic realities that inform and are informed by the conversation itself."[39] Theology emerges out of this ongoing, interactive conversation between gospel and culture.

What Makes Theology Christian? Grenz is aware, and decidedly so, that his particular casting of evangelical theology makes all theology group- and situation-specific.[40] This observation is characteristically postmodern as Grenz would have it, yet it raises for him the question of what constitutes any particular local theology as "Christian." Grenz answers this question by identifying three motifs, which for him reflect what he calls the Christian "style."[41] The Christian style comprises a Trinitarian structure, a communitarian focus, and an eschatological orientation. In other words, theology is Christian not only when it adopts a Trinitarian understanding of the Being of God, but when the very explication of the community's belief structure is Trinitarian in nature. This means Christian theology is more than believing in the particular doctrine of the Trinity. It should allow the doctrines of God, Jesus Christ, and the Holy Spirit to frame theological discourse. Second, since it is one's presence in the Christian community that necessitates theological reflection, Community becomes the integrative motif, i.e., the theme around which all Christian theological foci should be understood and explored. Finally, the eschatological aspect of Christian theology, which Grenz identifies as its orientating motif, means that Christian theology does not deal with static realities, but realities that are linguistically and socially constructed, tending toward God's eternal *telos* for the creation. Thus Grenz asks, "How can Christian theology continue to talk about an actual world, even if it is only future, in the face of the demise of realism and the advent of social constructionism?"[42]

---

[38] Grenz and Franke, *Beyond Foundationalism*, 157.
[39] Ibid., 158.
[40] Grenz, "Articulating the Christian Belief-Mosaic," 129.
[41] Ibid.
[42] Ibid., 134.

II. SUMMARIZING POSTCONSERVATISM METHODOLOGICALLY

Why embark on a methodological analysis of postconservative theology? In the fluid theological situation we have today, methodological analysis is helpful to clarify assumptions, explore connections in thought, and bring legitimacy to the theological enterprise. Theologians do their work on the basis of a method, whether it is stated explicitly or not, and it is the exploration of the conceptual, theoretical, epistemological, and metaphysical commitments underlying the work that gives the approach its particular identity. This is an essentially fundamental theological exercise.[43]

In outlining the proposal by Grenz, many of his methodological commitments have already become evident. It is necessary, however, to give a unified view of postconservative theology by providing a methodological summary. The need for a conversation among evangelicals on method is well acknowledged, but just what a conversation on method entails is not all that clear. Commenting on the paucity of evangelical engagement in methodological discussions, John Stackhouse comments that evangelical discussions of methodology have often focused on the nature and interpretation of the Bible, whereas evangelical theology and methodology is more than exegesis.[44] The broadness of the methodological question is, however, clearly perceived by Stephen Williams, who observes that "the matter of theological method inevitably raises the question of presuppositions about the theological task, and I believe that, within evangelicalism, attending to the task means raising some broader questions than we often do. . . ."[45] At this point in this essay, I propose to summarize postconservative theology from the point of view of three aspects of method: the perceived *goal* of evangelical theology, the *presuppositions* with which it embarks on its theological formulations, and the *sources* that are admitted into its constructive work. When method per se is seen formally and primarily as *activity,* albeit, an intellectual activity, a structural analysis of it will reveal the components that I have highlighted above.[46]

---

[43] See Randy L. Maddox, *Toward an Ecumenical Fundamental Theology* (Chico, Calif.: Scholars Press, 1984), 109-112. Maddox argues that to bring legitimacy in theology a fundamental theological discipline is needed to "reflect upon the means by which theology executes its judgments concerning the legitimacy of particular theological formulations."

[44] John G. Stackhouse, "Preface," in *Evangelical Futures,* 9.

[45] Williams, "The Theological Task and Theological Method," 159.

[46] For a more complete discussion on the structural components of method, see chapter 3 of my *Tradition, Method, and Contemporary Protestant Theology* (Lanham, Md.: University Press of America, 2003).

The Goal of Postconservative Theology

J. I. Packer has made the point quite clearly that up until the opening of the nineteenth century, all mainline practitioners of the discipline variously called *first principles, theology, dogmatics, systematic theology,* etc., had a unified understanding of the aim of the discipline. Theology was understood to function as a science, "to give the world a body of analysed, tested, correlated knowledge concerning God in relation to his creatures in general and to mankind in particular."[47] Packer notes also that systematic theology of the older type, more specifically the older evangelical type, shares this goal of theology. There is no question that postconservative evangelical theology intends to alter this classical evangelical understanding of the goal of theology.

Grenz's view regarding the goal of theology is quite pragmatic.[48] When we discussed his position on theology as conversation, it was pointed out that for him, the goal of theology is to help the believing community hear the voice of God in the text. It is to facilitate the restoration of what Grenz otherwise calls "convertive piety"[49] by delineating the "Christian experience-facilitating interpretative framework" out of the biblical narrative.

It is quite clear that although in Grenz's view the cognitive element in theology is not denied, there is a decided shift away from a cognitivist approach to theology. Grenz's characterization of the eschatological motif that should inform Christian theology appears to diminish the cognitive aspect of evangelical theology, at least in the sense that Packer describes it. His preference for treating eschatology as *eschaton* rather than as *eschata* relates to this point.[50] What is more significant in the postconservative approach is not the fact that there is a shift in understanding about the goal

---

[47] J. I. Packer, "Is Theology a Mirage?" in *Doing Theology in Today's World,* ed. John D. Woodbridge and Thomas E. McComiskey (Grand Rapids, Mich.: Zondervan, 1991), 23. This should not be construed to mean that theology was a purely cognitive activity. As Packer points out, the classical exponents know that theology "yields genuine knowledge of God, first cognitive and then relational, being based on God's own revelation of truth about himself as the lover, seeker, and Savior of lost mankind" (18).

[48] Grenz provides the following concise working definition of theology's nature, task, and purpose: "Christian theology is an ongoing, second-order, contextual discipline that engages in critical and constructive reflection on the faith, life, and practices of the Christian community. Its task is the articulation of biblically normed, historically informed, and culturally relevant models of the Christian belief-mosaic for the purpose of assisting the community of Christ's followers in their vocation to live as the people of God in the particular social-historical context in which they are situated" (Grenz and Franke, *Beyond Foundationalism,* 16).

[49] Grenz, *Renewing the Center,* 334-339.

[50] Grenz and Franke, *Beyond Foundationalism,* 241. Grenz himself relies on Gerhard Sauter for this distinction. See Gerhard Sauter, *Eschatological Rationality: Theological Issues in Focus* (Grand Rapids, Mich.: Baker, 1996), 146-147. Grenz distinguishes *eschata* as the study of "last things" from the perspective of a conglomerate of future temporal occurrences from *eschaton* as the study of "last things" from an existential point of view without denying its futuristic aspects. Grenz chooses to treat eschatological realities theologically as *becoming* realities, tending toward God's *telos*. See Grenz and Franke, *Beyond Foundationalism,* 238-273.

of theology, but the reason for the shift and its implications. This discussion leads us to a consideration of the presuppositions of postconservative theology.

Presuppositions of Postconservative Theology

By presuppositions we mean fundamental hermeneutical principles that condition the whole theological enterprise.[51] For this purpose, we will examine two interrelated types of presuppositions: epistemological and ontological. Simply stated, these are respectively, fundamental assumptions about *how* we know and about *what* we know.

Epistemologically, postconservative theology signals a shift from the foundationalist epistemology of the older evangelical theology[52] to a post-foundationalist epistemology. This shift is rooted in a dynamic view of revelation. Grenz's dynamic revelation is centered in his communitarian starting point. We have already noted his indebtedness to Reformed epistemologists for this move. Formally, Grenz gives a primary place to Scripture by making it the genesis of the community's interpretive framework. However, because he does not make the interpretive framework a part of the given divine revelation that precedes the theological enterprise, but rather as something given with specific theological understandings, he effectively relocates revelation in the ongoing dynamism of the believing community.[53] Furthermore, not only does postconservative epistemology displace the ultimate genesis of doctrine from divine revelation, the communitarian emphasis makes this epistemology community-specific. In Grenz's writings, this epistemological specificity seems to be intended to distinguish the *Christian* community from other religious communities, but nothing would seem to prevent its use to legitimize distinctive communities within the wider Christian community.

The question as to whether theology makes first-order or second-order

---

[51] On the nature and significance of presuppositions see, David A. Powlison, "Which Presuppositions? Secular Psychology and the Categories of Biblical Thought," *Journal of Psychology and Theology* 12 (1984): 271; Paul Helm, "Understanding Scholarly Presuppositions: A Crucial Tool for Research," *Tyndale Bulletin* 44 (1993): 143-154.

[52] Packer notes the epistemological basis of the older type evangelical theology as "God's own self-disclosure to human beings in the *past*—an activity involving the giving of verbal messages and teachings through chosen agents and supremely through God's incarnate Son, Jesus Christ, and the embodying of this material in permanent form for us in the canonical Scriptures" (Packer, "Is Theology a Mirage?" 18-19).

[53] Vanhoozer appears to agree with Alister McGrath in criticizing approaches such as Grenz's that appear to locate the genesis of doctrine in the believing community rather than in divine revelation. See Vanhoozer, "Voice and the Actor," 77.

declarations bears directly on the issue of ontology.[54] On this issue, Grenz has expressed himself quite clearly:

> Theology is a second-order enterprise, and its propositions are second-order propositions. Theology formulates in culturally conditioned language the confession and world-view of the community of faith—of that people who have been constituted by the human response to the story of the salvific act of God in the history of Jesus the Christ. The assertion that theology speaks a second-order language is not intended to deny the ontological nature of theological declarations. Nevertheless, the ontological claims implicit in theological assertions arise as an outworking of the intent of the theologian to provide a model of reality, rather than to describe reality directly.[55]

Elsewhere, Grenz develops his idea on reality by speaking of "eschatological realism." Grenz clearly informs us that eschatological realism is his way of combining the insights of social constructionists with the concerns of critical realists.[56] By this notion, Grenz wishes to say that while Christian theology maintains a certain undeniable givenness to the universe, it is not that of a "static actuality existing outside of, and co-temporally with, our social and linguistically constructed reality. It is not the objectivity of what some might call the 'world as it is.' Rather, the objectivity set forth in the biblical narrative is the objectivity of the world as God wills it. . . ."[57] Under eschatological realism, Grenz acknowledges that there is a real universe "out there," but it is a reality that "lies 'before,' rather than 'beneath' or 'around' us. Ours is a universe that is in the process of being created, as many scientists acknowledge."[58] Again, it needs to be remembered that the framework for the creation of this ongoing eschatological reality in the present is the interpretive framework of the community.

---

[54] Wayne Proudfoot has noted that "First-order theology is executed when theologians claim to explain God and the world as they really are. Second-order theology emerges when the theologian realizes that her concepts are constructs of the imagination" (Wayne Proudfoot, "Regulae Fidei and Regulative Idea: Two Contemporary Theological Strategies," in *Theology at the End of Modernity: Essays in Honor of Gordon D. Kaufman,* ed. Sheila Greeve Davaney [Philadelphia: Trinity Press International, 1991], 107).

[55] Grenz, *Revisioning Evangelical Theology,* 78.

[56] Grenz, *Renewing the Center,* 20.

[57] Grenz, "Articulating the Christian Belief-Mosaic," 135-136. Grenz appears to build his ontology of eschatological realism in part on the petition of the Lord's Prayer, "Your will be done on earth as it is in heaven" (Matt. 6:10, NIV). One is left wondering whether ontology could be built legitimately on the Lord's petition, which appears to be ethical at its core. Furthermore, granted that such a construction is legitimate, does not the plea for the possible coincidence of the Lord's will in heaven and on earth (on earth as it *is* in heaven) undermine the characterization of present reality as *becoming?*

[58] Grenz and Franke, *Beyond Foundationalism,* 272.

Sources for Postconservative Theology

On the question of sources, Grenz speaks explicitly of the three pillars of theology: the biblical message, the theoretical heritage of the church, and the thought-forms of the historical-cultural context of contemporary people.[59] We discussed the sources for Grenz's postconservative theological method when we considered the three primary voices in his construal of theology as conversation. What needs to be pointed out presently is that sources are not employed in any sort of deductive, propositionalist-style theologizing. Rather, the use of sources is an intensely hermeneutical process, involving the interplay of the three-ordered set of sources of insight.

III. METHODOLOGICAL EVALUATION OF POSTCONSERVATIVE THEOLOGY

The combined effect of postconservatism's understanding of theology's goal, presuppositions, and sources may be quite far-reaching; first, for the discipline of theology itself within evangelicalism, and second, for its implication for the Third World, and indeed evangelization among other world religions.

A Prescription for Pluralism?

It seems that postconservatism would in principle admit to a certain measure of plurality. Grenz believes that with the dawn of postmodernism, all theology is "local" or "specific." But while admitting of plurality in postconservative theology, postconservatism does not welcome an ideology of pluralism. We must, however, ask: Does the pluralism that is structurally endemic to postconservative theology make evangelicalism worthwhile?

First, consider theology's goal. Traditionally, it is not unusual to break theology's goal into three formal tasks aimed at the achievement of the goal. Thus we distinguish constructive, apologetic, and critical tasks.[60] The demise of propositionalism in postconservative theology is accompanied by a corresponding deemphasis of doctrine. The result is that a careful look at postconservatism shows a fusion of the constructive and apologetic tasks as the critical task recedes into the background. As one reads the postconservative

---

[59] Grenz, *Revisioning Evangelical Theology*, 93ff.
[60] See E. Ashby Johnson, *The Crucial Task of Theology* (Richmond, Va.: John Knox Press, 1958), 60ff. According to Johnson, the constructive task provides the church with constructional formulations through which the church apprehends and communicates its message. On the other hand, the apologetic task enables the church to speak to the secular world in a fashion that can be appreciated and understood by the critic. Finally, the critical task is the tool by which theology is able to distinguish "good" theology from "bad" theology. See also John B. Cobb, "Theological Data and Method," *Journal of Religion* 32-34 (1953/1954): 213-214.

agenda, one is left wondering whether the question of heresy is even possible. On the one hand, the constructive effort does not seem to address the truth question directly, nor indeed can it. This is precisely because the goal of theology in postconservatism does not have to do primarily with truth. For Grenz, theology has a pragmatic concern: to delineate the Christian experience-facilitating interpretive framework. Regarding the truth question in Grenz, since he conceives a *prescriptive* component as an "ought" in his interpretive framework, it would be helpful for him to clarify, *formally,* how this "ought" is conceptualized.

On the other hand, the critical task, although not completely absent, lacks a strong critical principle. Grenz does recognize the critical task, yet there is no succinct statement or articulation of a critical principle.[61] The closest he comes to doing this is his discussion of the three motifs of Christian theology, but this hardly goes far enough to answer the question of heresy in theology. We pointed out earlier that postconservative epistemology is community-specific. The point has relevance for the truth question. How does one go about providing criteria for the assessment of competing truth claims?[62]

Second, consider postconservative epistemology. Postconservative theology takes it as axiomatic that evangelical theology should move beyond foundationalism.[63] It is for this reason that the search is on for a postfoundationalist (not necessarily anti-foundationalist) epistemology in evangelical theology, a term that appears to have been coined by J. Wentzel van Huyssteen.[64] On this issue, it is important to recall what is at stake. The rejection of foundationalism is a rejection of Enlightenment rationality, which in Lyotard's view constitutes a "totalizing" metanarrative.[65] Postfoundationalism is an attempt to find that safe place "somewhere between the modern and the postmodern . . . where reason rules but does not tyrannize, where we enjoy the temperate gains

---

[61] Grenz and Franke, *Beyond Foundationalism,* 18. The critical task for Grenz involves not only scrutiny of Christian beliefs and teachings for coherence with the biblical narratives, but also coherence with "the first-order commitments of the community" (ibid).

[62] Nancey Murphy discusses the issue of truth in the context of the Yale School's postliberal theology as represented by George Lindbeck. Murphy classes most postmodern formulations of the truth question as pragmatic theories of truth. In her estimation, these concepts of truth are inadequate substitutes of the correspondence theory of truth primarily because they provide no criteria for the assessment of such truth claims. See Nancey Murphy, "Philosophical Resources for Postmodern Evangelical Theology," *Christian Scholars Review* 26, no. 2 (1996): 197-198.

[63] See for example, Grenz, *Renewing the Center,* 184ff.; J. Wentzel van Huyssteen, "Tradition and the Task of Theology," *Theology Today* 55 (1998): 213-228; James K. A. Smith, "A Little Story About Metanarratives: Lyotard, Religion, and Postmodernism Revisited," *Faith and Philosophy* 18, no. 3 (2001): 353-368.

[64] Grenz, "Articulating the Christian Belief-Mosaic," 109. The term "postfoundational" is, as Grenz notes, van Huyssteen's preferred term for a nonfoundationalist epistemology.

[65] Jean-François Lyotard, *The Postmodern Condition: A Report on Knowledge,* trans. Geoff Bennington and Brian Massumi (Minneapolis: University of Minnesota Press, 1984), 37.

of the postmodern without suffering its extremes."[66] Postfoundationalism tries to avoid the deconstructionist attempt to dispense with reason itself[67] while at the same time rejecting modern rationality. The result for Grenz is "chastened rationality."[68]

The result of van Huyssteen's exploration in postfoundationalist epistemology reveals the conceptual pluralistic vulnerabilities to which postconservatism is exposed. Like Grenz, van Huyssteen's postfoundational rationality finds its resting place in tradition, understood in a sense similar to Grenz's community. But what kind of rationality is this? It is the community/tradition's communicative evaluations, responsible judgments, and problem-solving theory choices that constitute the true nature of rational reflection.[69] These constitute *research/tradition paradigms* whose application to the community's conceptual problems leads to what the tradition/community "could claim a very specific form of theoretical and experiential adequacy."[70] It is a pragmatic move that yields a pragmatic rationality. Van Huyssteen acknowledges that his approach lacks a clear and objective criterion for judging the experiential adequacy of competing traditions, yet he is not prepared to admit that this leads to a radical pluralism or even an easy pluralism. Maybe true. But what real advantage is there for evangelical theology in his conclusion that "cognitive agreement or consensus in theology is also, and maybe especially, unattainable, and that what Nicholas Rescher has called 'dissensus tolerance' could prove to be a positive and constructive part of theological pluralism"?[71]

It should be clear on the basis of this kind of postfoundationalist epistemology how the truth question is avoided, hence encouraging pluralism. First, within a particular community, the implication is that "in any appraisal of the rationality of a particular belief, theory, or research tradition, this belief, theory, or tradition is relative to its contemporaneous competitors, to prevailing doctrines of theory assessment, and to the previous theories within a research tradition."[72] Second, intersubjectively, this epistemology provides "a theory of rationality without first presupposing anything

---

[66] Van Huyssteen, "Tradition and the Task of Theology," 213.
[67] See Anton A. Van Niekirk, "Postmetaphysical Thinking Versus Postmodern Thinking," *Philosophy Today* 39 (1995): 177.
[68] Grenz, "Articulating the Christian Belief-Mosaic," 108.
[69] Van Huyssteen, "Tradition and the Task of Theology," 219.
[70] Ibid., 220. Notice that van Huyssteen has observed that his postfoundationalist epistemology relates closely to that of Andy F. Sanders, which has been called "traditionalist fallibilism." Ibid., 224.
[71] Ibid., 226.
[72] Ibid., 227.

about the truth or verisimilitude of those traditions we judge to be rational or irrational."[73]

Finally, consider postconservative ontology. Postconservatism displays a variety of positions on the question of ontology. While at this time a good number of postconservatives are said to reject ontological relativism,[74] methodologically, consistency demands a move beyond the correspondence theory of truth, since epistemologically we are made to lose an objective view to reality.[75] The move is from epistemology to ontology; and the loss of rational objectivity is the main point of postmodernity's "incredulity to metanarratives."[76] But has postmodernity's "incredulity to metanarratives," especially as formulated by Lyotard, been misread by evangelicals?

James K. A. Smith, in an insightful article, makes the point that the work of evangelical scholars such as Grenz, J. Richard Middleton, and Brian J. Walsh[77] involves a misreading of Lyotard. According to Smith, evangelicals have failed to realize that in the work *The Postmodern Condition: A Report on Knowledge,* Lyotard uses "metanarrative" critically, in the specific sense of scientific rationality's failure to understand its own status as myth/narrative.[78] In other words, Lyotard is not merely criticizing the universality of metanarratives or the *scope* of metanarratives as Grenz and others make it seem; rather Lyotard is concerned about scientific rationality's way of *legitimizing* its knowledge.[79] Indeed, in Smith's view, the Bible story is not a metanarrative in Lyotard's sense, although it makes universal claims of truth, since these claims are made not on the basis of some kind of *universal reason,* but on the basis of *faith.*[80] If Smith has read Lyotard correctly, then the point is this: "Lyotard relativizes [secular] philosophy's claim to autonomy, and so

---

[73] Ibid. Compare this with Grenz's proposed model to incorporate contemporary culture in theological reflection in which he explicitly states of the model, "this model presupposes neither gospel nor culture—much less both gospel and culture—as preexisting, given realities that subsequently enter into conversation. Rather, in the interactive process both gospel . . . and culture . . . are dynamic realities that inform and are informed by the conversation itself" (Grenz and Franke, *Beyond Foundationalism,* 158).
[74] Olson, "Postconservative Evangelicals Greet the Postmodern Age," 481. According to Olson, many postconservatives "opt for some version of critical realism, while others, such as Fuller professor Nancey Murphy, turn to philosophers such as Willard Van Orman Quine and Alasdair MacIntyre in developing a new philosophical orientation. A few have begun to explore the potential of postmodern antirealism."
[75] See Allan G. Padgett, "Christianity and Postmodernity," *Christian Scholars Review* 26, no. 2 (1996): 131. While Padgett does not seem to endorse common sense realism, he observes that "Christians will be (sophisticated) realists because they are theists. There is one God and therefore one world and one truth about that world (i.e., God's knowledge of the world)."
[76] Lyotard, *The Postmodern Condition,* xxiii-xxiv.
[77] J. Richard Middleton and Brian J. Walsh, *Truth Is Stranger than It Used to Be: Biblical Faith in a Postmodern Age* (Downers Grove, Ill.: InterVarsity Press, 1995).
[78] Smith, "Little Story About Metanarratives."
[79] Lyotard's point is that modernity's so-called universal reason cannot disengage itself from narratives as its ultimate ground and thereby divorce itself from myth. It cannot constitute itself into a supernarrative, standing over every other narrative to adjudicate the legitimacy of other narratives.
[80] Smith, "Little Story About Metanarratives," 355.

grants the legitimacy of a philosophy which grounds itself in Christian faith."[81] Consequently, evangelical realism need not be subjugated to a relativist view of reality. Mark Noll, raising the issue about the possibility of historical knowledge in traditional Christianity in the context of a postmodern world, observes that it is the very foundation of Christianity that is at stake in the crisis about realism.[82] He notes that the very existence of orthodoxy, both Catholic and Protestant, is defined by purportedly historical events concerning an omnipotent deity who created out of nothing, called Abraham to be the father of all nations, and delivered his descendants from slavery in Egypt in order to preserve his purposes. The story of Jesus' preexistence, incarnation and Virgin birth, and his death and resurrection are affirmed implicitly with a definite view of historical understanding.[83]

A Missiological Dilemma?

Conceptually, postconservative evangelical theology, in my view, seems to find itself in the unenviable position of having to be consistent with its methodological commitments and at the same time having to maintain a missiological voice as evangelicalism inherently demands. Fundamentally, the problem is how, in formulating evangelical theology along the lines of postmodernism's incredulity to metanarratives, postconservative theology can still maintain a legitimate apologetics. Clearly, postconservatism wishes to move beyond Lindbeck's postliberal cultural-linguistic approach, which for Grenz "potentially results in a 'sectarian' church, one that no longer assumes any role in the public realm."[84] Postconservatism intends to be intratextual/subjective. Postconservatism wishes to avoid what van Huyssteen has described as "the insular comfort of a nonfoundationalist isolationism, whereby what we see as our preferred tradition(s) can easily be transformed from being rationality's *destiny* to being more like rationality's *prison*."[85] These considerations have far-reaching implications for evangelism within the postconservative theological construct.

We have already observed that in van Huyssteen's postfoundational epistemology, traditions become *research paradigms* of relative experiential adequacy in their problem-solving ability. Applied to trans-contextual evaluation

---

[81] Ibid., 362. As Smith correctly observes, previously, a distinctly Christian philosophy "would have been exiled from the 'pure' arena of philosophy because of its 'infection' with bias and prejudice. . . . In this way the playing field is leveled and new opportunities to voice a Christian philosophy are created."

[82] Mark A. Noll, "Traditional Christianity and the Possibility of Historical Knowledge," *Christian Scholars Review* 19, no. 4 (1990): 392.

[83] Ibid.

[84] Grenz, *Renewing the Center*, 245.

[85] Van Huyssteen, "Tradition and the Task of Theology," 213-214.

of beliefs and viewpoints, van Huyssteen sees rationality's movement from "individual judgment to communal evaluation to intersubjective conversation."[86] In using these paradigms to appraise different traditions, van Huyssteen observes, "we should choose the theory or research tradition that we find the most compelling and that we judge to have the highest problem-solving adequacy for a specific problem within a specific context."[87] From this perspective, the Christian missionary urge in postconservative theology is a very pragmatic one: Christian theology is a better research paradigm.

An approach similar to van Huyssteen's is seen in Grenz's approach to the vexing question regarding the relationship between Christianity's unique claims and the religions of the world. After briefly outlining the options of exclusivism, inclusivism, and pluralism which, according to Grenz, are all framed by concern over the question of the final destiny of those outside the church, he transmutes the issue into the more pragmatic one of the role the religions play in the divine economy.[88] On the basis of his view that, biblically, God's overarching intent for creation may be summed in the word "community,"[89] and that the providential place of the religions may lie in the role they play in fostering community,[90] Grenz concludes that

> any religion can be assessed according to both the personal identity/social structure it fosters and the underlying belief system that sanctions the social order. The primary question in appraising any religion, therefore, concerns the extent to which religious beliefs and practices lead to a personal identity and to social structures that cohere with God's intent for human life.[91]

In this approach, the appropriate attitude to the religions is *dialogue,* and the process of critical appraisal as mentioned above is the context for determining the value of interreligious dialogue. Furthermore, in this appraisal process no religion, including Christianity, is allowed a privileged exemption.[92]

Yet, Grenz is concerned to maintain the finality of Christ for purposes of evangelization. The question is, in a pluralistic context where all religions tend to foster community, how do you maintain the finality of the Christian vision? Grenz's answer is to postulate a "transcendent community vision" which he claims is embodied in the Christian community by virtue of the rev-

---

[86] Ibid., 224.
[87] Ibid., 227.
[88] Grenz, *Renewing the Center,* 252-269.
[89] Ibid., 276.
[90] Ibid.
[91] Ibid., 278.
[92] Ibid.

elation of God in Jesus Christ. He maintains that "other religious visions cannot provide community in its ultimate sense, because they do not embody the highest understanding of who God actually is," but "through the incarnate life of Jesus we discover the truest vision of the nature of God."[93]

Obviously Grenz's approach to the missiological issue raises a few conceptual difficulties. How, for example, can Grenz maintain that the Christian vision of community embodies the highest understanding of who God *actually is*, when he says that "the ontological claims implicit in theological assertions arise as an outworking of the intent of the theologian to provide a model of reality, rather than to describe reality directly"?[94] Is not the claim that the Christian vision of community embodies the highest understanding of who God *actually* is a theological assertion? It would seem that on several fronts the postconservative approach to world religions faces a dilemma. I will look at this dilemma briefly from the African context.

Throughout Africa, there is a strong move to reinvent Christianity when it comes to evangelization, on the basis of a felt call for a Christian theology "with an African face."[95] Two main approaches are evident at this time: theology of adaptation and critical African theology.[96] Adaptation theology seeks to penetrate the mentality, culture, and philosophy of Africans and adapt the gospel to those values. Critical African theology, on the other hand, adopts a more radical and pluralistic approach, accusing theology of adaptation of *concordism*.[97] This is the theological context within which postconservative theology must conduct apologetics. It is not simply a "world religions" context in which Christianity is seen over against different religions, but an amalgam of Christian/world religions context in which the different world religions are believed to be "Christian" intrinsically. Both the theology of adaptation and critical African theology approaches create a dilemma for postconservative apologetics.

First, postconservatism's own postmodern epistemological commitments will seem to create a roadblock for evangelization. It is true that postconservatism seems resigned to dialogue instead of evangelization, but Grenz's pos-

---

[93] Ibid., 281-282.

[94] Grenz, *Revisioning Evangelical Theology*, 78.

[95] See John Parratt, *Reinventing Christianity: African Theology Today* (Grand Rapids, Mich.: Eerdmans, 1995), 13. For representative literature on the origins, progress, and attitudes of contemporary African theology see the following: Kofi Appiah-Kubi and Sergio Torres, eds., *African Theology En Route* (Maryknoll, N.Y.: Orbis, 1977); Kwesi A. Dickson, *Theology in Africa* (Maryknoll, N.Y.: Orbis, 1984); Gwinyai H. Muzorewa, *The Origins and Development of African Theology* (Maryknoll, N.Y.: Orbis, 1985); Rosino Gibellini, ed., *Paths of African Theology* (Maryknoll, N.Y.: Orbis, 1994).

[96] See Gibellini, *Paths of African Theology*, 16-22.

[97] Ibid. According to the critical African theologians, concordism "consists in confusing Christian revelation with the systems of thought that have historically served to express it" (18).

tulation of the transcendent community vision clearly intends evangelization. Yet critical African theologians appear to see quite clearly the undeniable pluralism of postmodern epistemology. It is true that the same argument can be made against conservative evangelical apologetics, but the case for Christianity's preeminence in the hands of postconservative theology is at best a weak one.[98]

Second, postconservatism's communitarian turn, in the African context, would seem to provide a catalyst for pluralism. In contemporary African theology, the theme of community has been identified as a particularly rich concept for developing a genuinely African theology.[99] The pluralistic problem would stem from the fact that whereas in the West the communitarian turn by and large involves different communities of the Christian faith, in the African context the turn revolves around traditional, religious, experience-constituting communities that are now deemed relevant for constructing a theology with an African face. The pluralistic potential should be obvious given the plethora of traditional African communities. At this point an observation needs to be made about the so-called comparative superiority of the Christian religion for fostering community in the African context vis-à-vis the traditional ancestral-based community construct. The report card from key African theologians in both the adaptation and critical camps is that Christianity has been disruptive of community/social order; hence they argue for the alleged need for a truly African theology.[100]

A final point regarding the dilemma I see postconservative apologetics facing in the African context concerns the nature of some traditional African communities. Most traditional African communities that pragmatically fostered wholesome communities still entailed aspects that would be deemed superstitious by biblical, Christian standards. Some of these elements, involving ancestral theology, are wont to be maintained by contemporary African Christian theologians.[101] Requiring these communities to purge themselves of these "errors," even in a dialogical setting, would seem to require the setting up of some "global" cognitive, propositional apparatus that would arise out-

---

[98] The insight of John Pobee that "'all evangelism is in some sense subversion' involving a change of loyalties from blood ancestors among whom Jesus historically and physically is not" could not apply to postconservative apologetics with the same force as it does to conservative evangelical apologetics. Cited by Ogbu U. Kalu, "Church Presence in Africa: A Historical Analysis of the Evangelization Process," in Appiah-Kubi and Torres, *African Theology En Route*, 20.

[99] See Parratt, *Reinventing Christianity*, 105-135.

[100] The phenomenon of independent churches throughout Africa, in spite of their theological inadequacies, is seen as a sign of Christian authenticity. See Kofi Appiah-Kubi, "Indigenous African Churches: Signs of Authenticity," in Appiah-Kubi and Torres, *African Theology En Route*, 117-125.

[101] See Parratt, *Reinventing Christianity*, 122-136.

side of the traditional community's interpretive framework, a move that would be fundamentally contrary to the postconservative ethos.

CONCLUSION

To sum up, I have tried to describe and evaluate postconservative evangelical theology from a methodological perspective primarily through the programmatic proposal of Stanley Grenz. I have examined the fundamental presuppositions on which the theology is being built in order to assess its compatibility with the older-type conservative evangelical theology. Although, materially, its proponents show a sincere desire to maintain the connection with conservative evangelicalism, its formal commitment to postmodern epistemological and ontological sensitivities seems to evidence the beginning of a paradigm shift. The implications of such a move for evangelical theology in general and for Third World evangelization in particular have been sketched. Clearly, the future direction of evangelicalism is at stake, and evangelical theology urgently needs an ongoing discussion and debate on these issues, especially from a methodological point of view.

PART FOUR

EVANGELICAL
HISTORIOGRAPHY

9

ARE POSTCONSERVATIVE EVANGELICALS FUNDAMENTALISTS? POSTCONSERVATIVE EVANGELICALISM, OLD PRINCETON, AND THE RISE OF NEO-FUNDAMENTALISM[1]

Paul Kjoss Helseth

I. INTRODUCTION

The Historiographical Consensus

It has become something of an article of faith in the historiography of American Christianity that the theologians at Old Princeton Seminary were scholastic rationalists whose doctrine of Scripture was shaped by the Scottish Common Sense Realism of the "Didactic Enlightenment" in America.[2] "The standard line," Roger Schultz notes, "is that in battling the skeptics of the Enlightenment, Scottish realists demanded an extreme (and unbiblical) standard of authority and certainty, and that the Princetonians incorporated this rationalistic element in their inerrantist doctrine of scripture."[3] According to the accepted wisdom, then, Old Princeton's doctrine of inerrancy—the taproot of what is considered to be its rather immodest dogmatism—"is not a

---

[1] This chapter is a revised edition of an essay published previously as, "'Re-Imagining' the Princeton Mind: Postconservative Evangelicalism, Old Princeton, and the Rise of Neo-Fundamentalism," *Journal of the Evangelical Theological Society* 45 (September 2002): 427-450. Material published previously is used with permission.

[2] According to Henry May, the Didactic Enlightenment was in part a counter-Enlightenment because it espoused "a variety of thought which was opposed both to skepticism and revolution, but tried to save from what it saw as the debacle of the Enlightenment the intelligible universe, clear and certain moral judgments, and progress" (*The Enlightenment in America* [New York: Oxford University Press, 1976], xvi).

[3] Roger Schultz, "Evangelical Meltdown: The Trouble with Evangel*histoire*," *Contra Mundum* 2 (Winter 1992); available online at http://www.visi.com/~contra_m/cm/columns/cm02_meltdown.html.

biblical doctrine, but rather a bastard ideology of the Enlightenment"[4] that was woven into the fabric of its highly innovative yet thoroughly modern and epistemologically naïve response to "an increasingly secular culture, on the one hand, and a rising liberal Christianity, on the other."[5]

The Postconservative Endorsement of the Historiographical Consensus

While a growing body of scholarship is establishing that Old Princeton's indebtedness to the naïve realism of the Scottish philosophy is more imagined than real, many evangelicals nonetheless endorse the broad outline of the standard critique.[6] Among those who resonate with the historiographical consensus are those ostensibly irenic individuals who presume that the essence of evangelicalism is found not in "propositional truths enshrined in doctrines," but rather in "a narrative-shaped experience"[7] that "is more readily 'sensed' than described theologically."[8] Believing that Christianity is primarily a life and only secondarily a doctrine, these evangelicals lament what Gary Dorrien calls "the fundamentalist evangelical establishment['s]"[9] enduring preoccupation with "questions of propositional truth,"[10] for such preoccupation, they contend, is evidence that much of evangelicalism has yet to move beyond the mindset engendered by the wrenching struggles of the fundamentalist-modernist controversy of the early twentieth century. Indeed, having wed themselves to Old Princeton's doctrine of inerrancy and thereby to the more divisive tendencies of a scholasticized theology,[11] conservative evangelicals, these postconservatives maintain, "have exaggerated the ratio-

---

[4] Ibid.

[5] Stanley J. Grenz, *Renewing the Center: Evangelical Theology in a Post-Theological Era* (Grand Rapids, Mich.: Baker, 2000), 73; cf. Gary Dorrien, *The Remaking of Evangelical Theology* (Louisville: Westminster John Knox, 1998), 13-47.

[6] See the literature cited in my articles on Old Princeton: Paul Kjoss Helseth, "B. B. Warfield on the Apologetic Nature of Christian Scholarship: An Analysis of His Solution to the Problem of the Relationship Between Christianity and Culture," *Westminster Theological Journal* 62 (Spring 2000): 89-111; idem, "'Right Reason' and the Princeton Mind: The Moral Context," *The Journal of Presbyterian History* 77 (Spring 1999): 13-28; idem, "B. B. Warfield's Apologetic Appeal to 'Right Reason': Evidence of a 'Rather Bald Rationalism'?" *The Scottish Bulletin of Evangelical Theology* 16 (Autumn 1998): 156-177; idem, "The Apologetical Tradition of the OPC: A Reconsideration," *Westminster Theological Journal* 60 (Spring 1998): 109-129.

[7] Roger E. Olson, "Postconservative Evangelicals Greet the Postmodern Age," *Christian Century* 112 (May 3, 1995): 481.

[8] Stanley J. Grenz, *Revisioning Evangelical Theology: A Fresh Agenda for the Twenty-first Century* (Downers Grove, Ill.: InterVarsity Press, 1993), 31; cf. idem, "Concerns of a Pietist with a Ph.D.," *Wesleyan Theological Journal* 36 (Fall 2002): 60-64, 70; Robert E. Webber, *The Younger Evangelicals: Facing the Challenges of the New World* (Grand Rapids, Mich.: Baker, 2002), 27, 31, 37.

[9] Dorrien, *Remaking of Evangelical Theology*, 10; cf. Grenz, *Revisioning Evangelical Theology,* 21-35.

[10] Grenz, *Revisioning Evangelical Theology,* 26.

[11] According to Jack Rogers and Donald McKim, the Princetonians developed a doctrine of Scripture "that would engender continuing strife on the American religious scene" (*The Authority and Interpretation of the Bible: An Historical Approach* [San Francisco: Harper & Row, 1979], 247).

nalistic dimension of Christian belief"[12] and thus have fallen prey to a kind of theological hubris—even bigotry—that threatens to plunge evangelicalism "back toward fundamentalism."[13]

Because they are convinced that all cognitive expressions of Christian experience *"reflect the particular cultural grid in which they were originally articulated,"*[14] and because they consequently agree with Alfred Lord Tennyson that "Our little systems have their day . . . and thou, O Lord, are more than they,"[15] postconservative evangelicals therefore advocate a "revisioning" of the theological task along the lines of "the postliberal research program."[16] Evangelicalism will become something more than "fundamentalism with good manners,"[17] they contend, only when evangelicals recognize that doctrines are not "timeless and culture-free" summaries of biblical truth that form the cognitive foundation of faith.[18] Rather, they are "reflection[s] on the faith of the converted people of God whose life together is created and shaped by the paradigmatic narrative embodied in scripture."[19] Doctrines, as such, are not to be afforded the same exalted status as the experiential "ethos" that unites the disparate elements of the evangelical community into a single body of faith.[20] Rather, they must be treated as those secondary reflections on Christian experience "that reflect and guide the converted community of God's people."[21]

---

[12] Dorrien, *Remaking of Evangelical Theology*, 195.

[13] Olson, "Postconservative Evangelicals Greet the Postmodern Age," 480, 482. The word "fundamentalism" is being used in this chapter in the largely negative sense in which it is used by Roger E. Olson in "The Future of Evangelical Theology," *Christianity Today* 42 (February 9, 1998): 40-48. As such, it is being used in the sense that has less to do with the affirmation of particular doctrines than it does with the dogmatic manner in which those doctrines are affirmed, for it describes a way of thinking about and doing theology that leads to a kind of gratuitous arrogance, i.e., to unwarranted "triumphalism, elitism, and separatism" (ibid., 47). On the "religious bigotry" of those who insist upon drawing distinct boundaries between theological views that are thought to be acceptable and unacceptable, see the comments of Robert Webber in *Between Peril and Promise*, ed. James R. Newby and Elizabeth Newby (Nashville: Thomas Nelson, 1984), 111. Interestingly, Webber's remarkably harsh intimation that evangelicals who are "enmeshed in modern categories of thought" articulate the faith in a more or less bigoted fashion itself borders on bigotry. It is, moreover, a fine example of special pleading. Unlike their modern counterparts who have an ahistorical understanding of the faith, the younger evangelicals, Webber argues, "are humbled by the complexity of truth, and they are gentle and generous toward those who differ. The younger evangelicals are not fighters intent on splitting churches. They are not dogmatic zealots or mean-spirited close-minded bigots. They seek to hold that which has always been held by all and affirm affection for those with whom they differ. Their love of the ancient and their return to tradition has given them this 'catholic spirit'" (*Younger Evangelicals*, 79, 81).

[14] Alan F. Johnson and Robert E. Webber, *What Christians Believe: A Biblical and Historical Summary* (Grand Rapids, Mich.: Zondervan, 1989), ix-x, emphasis theirs.

[15] Alfred Lord Tennyson, "In Memoriam."

[16] Cf. F. LeRon Shults, "Truth Happens? The Pragmatic Conception of Truth and the Postliberal Research Program," *Princeton Theological Review* 4 (February 1997): 26-36.

[17] Dorrien, *Remaking of Evangelical Theology*, 9.

[18] Grenz, *Revisioning Evangelical Theology*, 67.

[19] Olson, "Postconservative Evangelicals Greet the Postmodern Age," 481.

[20] Grenz, *Revisioning Evangelical Theology*, 30-35.

[21] Olson, "Postconservative Evangelicals Greet the Postmodern Age," 481.

*The Unsustainability of the Historiographical Consensus and
the Crumbling Foundation of Nonfoundational Theology*

Whatever the merits of postconservatism's move away from a "propositionalist understanding of the theological enterprise"[22] toward a "narrativist-communitarian model" of theology might be,[23] there is no disputing that postconservatives justify this transition in part by rejecting what they regard as the "Enlightenment foundationalist rationalism" of the Princeton Theology.[24] "Beneath and behind the postconservatives' approach to theology," Roger Olson argues, "lies a growing discontent with evangelical theology's traditional ties to what Wheaton historian Mark Noll describes as the 'evangelical Enlightenment,' especially common-sense realism."[25] While most postconservatives acknowledge that the Princeton theologians were not fundamentalists themselves,[26] they nonetheless argue that Old Princeton's scholastic rationalism—itself the necessary byproduct of the Princetonians' somewhat credulous endorsement of Scottish Realism[27]—was "mediated" to contemporary evangelicalism through the fundamentalism of the early twentieth century.[28] Turn-of-the-century fundamentalists endorsed Old Princeton's doctrine of inerrancy and thereby accommodated the legacy of Protestant scholastic rationalism, postconservatives contend, and this legacy, in turn, has been passed on to all those whose decidedly cognitive concerns lead them to seek "an invulnerable foundation for theology in an error-free Bible, viewed as the storehouse for divine revelation."[29] "Nowhere is neo-evangelicalism's genesis in fundamentalism more evident," Grenz concludes, "than in its theology. The fundamentalist acceptance of the Princeton understanding of inspiration . . . gave a particular nineteenth-century cast to neo-evangelicalism's emphasis on biblical authority."[30]

---

[22] Grenz, *Revisioning Evangelical Theology,* 67.

[23] Dorrien, *Remaking of Evangelical Theology,* 195.

[24] Grenz, *Renewing the Center,* 70; cf. Rodney Clapp, "How Firm a Foundation: Can Evangelicals Be Nonfoundationalists?" in *The Nature of Confession: Evangelicals and Liberals in Conversation,* ed. Timothy R. Phillips and Dennis Okholm (Downers Grove, Ill.: InterVarsity, 1996), 83-84.

[25] Olson, "Postconservative Evangelicals Greet the Postmodern Age," 481; cf. Grenz, *Renewing the Center,* 71; Mark A. Noll, *The Scandal of the Evangelical Mind* (Grand Rapids, Mich.: Eerdmans, 1994), 83-107.

[26] For example, see Roger E. Olson, *The Story of Christian Theology: Twenty Centuries of Tradition and Reform* (Downers Grove, Ill.: InterVarsity, 1999), 556-561; Grenz, *Renewing the Center,* 79. For a notable exception, see Webber, *Younger Evangelicals,* 81.

[27] For example, see Grenz, *Renewing the Center,* 73; Olson, *Story of Christian Theology,* 558; Dorrien, *Remaking of Evangelical Theology,* 23-28.

[28] Grenz, *Revisioning Evangelical Theology,* 65-72; cf. idem, "Concerns of a Pietist with a Ph.D.," 65-68; Webber, *Younger Evangelicals,* 31, 37.

[29] Grenz, *Renewing the Center,* 70; cf. 70-84.

[30] Ibid., 83. For a noteworthy response to this contention, see Kenneth J. Stewart, "That Bombshell of a Book: Gaussen's *Theopneustia* and Its Influence on Subsequent Evangelical Theology" (paper presented at the Wheaton Theology Conference, Spring 2001): 15-18. Stewart suggests that since 1950, "Evangelical thinking about the Bible has, without our realizing it, been in process of necessary recovery [*not* from the influence of Warfield and Old Princeton, but] from the exaggerated emphases of [Gaussen's] *Theopneustia.*"

It is the contention of this chapter that however warranted postconserva-tivism's repudiation of "evangelical propositionalism"[31] might be for any one of a number of different reasons, it cannot be justified by appealing to the scholastic rationalism of Old Princeton, simply because the Princeton theologians were not scholastic rationalists. While they certainly were the methodological disciples of Francis Turretin and consequently conceived of theology as that "science" having to do with God,[32] nevertheless they were not beholden for their epistemology to scholasticism or Enlightenment rationalism in a formative sense. For not only did they recognize that objective as well as subjective factors are of critical importance to the life of the mind, but they also based their theology on that combination of head and heart, of "cognitive-doctrinal" and "practical-experiential" factors that postconservatives themselves insist is of defining significance to the mainstream of the evangelical tradition.[33]

Thus, in order to challenge the viability of a major component of post-conservatism's justification for repudiating the "evangelical establishment's" conception of the theological task, what I undertake in the forthcoming discussion is an analysis of important scholarship that buttresses a point that I have attempted to make in other places, a point that calls into question the alleged philosophical connection between scholastic rationalism and the Princeton Theology.[34]

---

[31] Grenz, *Revisioning Evangelical Theology,* 65.

[32] Cf. Francis Turretin, *Institutes of Elenctic Theology,* 3 vols., trans. George Musgrave Giger, ed. James T. Dennison, Jr. (Phillipsburg, N.J.: Presbyterian and Reformed, 1992), 1:1-3.

[33] Grenz, *Renewing the Center,* 84, cf. 44-47; idem, *Revisioning Evangelical Theology,* 22-26; idem, "Concerns of a Pietist with a Ph.D.," 71-76; Olson, "Future of Evangelical Theology," 42. In a recent article, Mark Noll insists, "the difficulty with [Charles] Hodge's view of the spiritual life was not a neglect of lived religious experience, of the person, or of the affections. It was rather his predilection for affirming Christianity both as a set of scriptural doctrines and as a living connection with Christ, while yet never finding a way to bring these two affirmations into cohesive unity" ("Charles Hodge as an Expositor of the Spiritual Life," in *Charles Hodge Revisited: A Critical Appraisal of His Life and Work,* ed. John W. Stewart and James H. Moorhead [Grand Rapids, Mich.: Eerdmans, 2002], 191-192). It is the contention of this chapter that both of these affirmations are more or less unified in Hodge's understanding of "right reason." If this contention is essentially correct, then it follows that: (1) the weaknesses Noll cites in his analysis of Hodge's exposition of the spiritual life (cf. ibid., 205) are significantly less troublesome than they might otherwise appear to be; and (2) postconservatives who cite Hodge's alleged shortcomings as justification for advancing new theological methodologies or epistemologies must be on guard lest they fall prey to a kind of iconoclasm that pressures evangelicals to make what Richard J. Mouw calls, in this regard, "some false choices." With respect to this second point, Mouw worries about what he regards as "an iconoclastic spirit that often manifests itself in evangelical calls for new constructive theological initiatives." In short, he is not confident that recent evangelical efforts "to clear the way for new theological paths" will accomplish "much that is good," in part because these efforts appear to be based upon misrepresentations of the evangelical heritage. He suggests, "What some of my evangelical friends seem to be after in calling for such new moves [—including the moves toward a theological interpretation of the text and a combination of head and heart in religious epistemology—] seems already to be there in past evangelical thinkers who have helped me in my theological journey" ("Comments on Grenz Paper and 'The Word Made Fresh'" [presented at the annual meeting of the American Academy of Religion, Toronto, November 2002]: 2; cf. idem, "How Should Evangelicals Do Theology? Delete the 'Post' from 'Postconservative,'" *Books and Culture* [May/June 2001]: 21-22). For an example of iconoclasm, note that Robert Webber writes as if virtually all traditional evangelicals neglected the importance of the heart in religious epistemology. See *Younger Evangelicals,* 52-53, 103.

[34] Please see the articles cited in note 6 above.

That point, in short, is that Old Princeton's emphasis upon "right reason" and the primacy of the intellect in faith is not evidence that the Princeton theologians were covert, if not overt, rationalists, and the purveyors of a theology that was scholasticized by an "alien philosophy."[35] It is evidence, rather, that they stood in the mainstream of the Reformed tradition, and thereby in the mainstream of the evangelical tradition.[36] As such, the forthcoming discussion is a call, of sorts, for evangelicals to reassess the standard interpretation of the Princeton mind so that jaded conclusions are corrected and potentially troublesome consequences are avoided. When evangelicals undertake such an examination they will discover that a "superficial reading" of the Princetonians will make them appear "considerably more rationalistic" than they really were.[37] They will also conclude, as I do in the concluding section of this chapter, that conservatism's postconservative critics—having rejected a caricature of Old Princeton rather than the views of the Princetonians themselves—are themselves guilty of some of the worst features that they perceive in their conservative brethren.[38]

---

[35] This is the general theme of John Vander Stelt's *Philosophy and Scripture: A Study of Old Princeton and Westminster Theology* (Marlton, N.J.: Mack, 1978). The Dutch and Neo-Orthodox branches of the Reformed camp generally agree with this critique of Old Princeton, as do the postconservative scholars with whom I am familiar.

[36] Obviously, I think that the Reformed interpretation of the history of evangelicalism is largely correct. I recognize, however, that the issues involved are complex, which is why I like what Douglas A. Sweeney has to say about the matter: "When the historiographical wrangling ends and the dust settles, it may well be seen that 'Reformed' and 'Holiness' themes, indeed Calvinist/forensic/confessional and Arminian/realistic/revivalist themes, have been functioning dialectically all along (for better and for worse) in both evangelical history and evangelical historiography. In evangelical history, Arminianism and Wesleyanism (even Pentecostalism, though less directly) have arisen, not in seclusion, but from within Reformed Protestantism. They were not intended as radically new alternatives but as correctives to trends prevalent among other more established members of the Reformed family. Likewise in recent evangelical historiography, [Donald] Dayton and the Holiness camp have offered criticisms of and provided helpful correctives to trends prevalent within the more established Reformed paradigm" ("Historiographical Dialectics: On Marsden, Dayton, and the Inner Logic of Evangelical History," *Christian Scholar's Review* 23, no. 1 [1993]: 52). For an overview of the debate over the essential character of evangelicalism, see the entire issues of the *Christian Scholar's Review* 23, no. 1 (1993); and *Modern Reformation* 10, no. 2 (March/April 2001). See also the recent "Reflection and Response" involving Michael S. Horton and Roger E. Olson in *Christian Scholar's Review* 31, no. 2 (2001): 131-168.

[37] Peter Hicks, *The Philosophy of Charles Hodge: A Nineteenth-Century Evangelical Approach to Reason, Knowledge and Truth* (Lewiston, N.Y.: Edwin Mellen, 1997), 115. Richard Mouw concurs with this assessment. See his "Comments on Grenz Paper and 'The Word Made Fresh.'"

[38] Among these is the kind of dogmatism that breeds both fundamentalism and an inability to engage in genuine dialogue with those with whom they have serious theological disagreements. One of the more exasperating aspects of life under the "big tent" of contemporary evangelicalism is the tendency of postconservatives to call for dialogue with their conservative brethren without acknowledging that the kind of dialogue they are encouraging can take place only if conservatives concede from the start that postconservative assumptions are correct. See, for example, Michael Horton's "Response to Roger Olson's Reply," 165, 166, in which Horton, a confessional Protestant, chastises Olson for doing the very thing he (Olson) deplores in others, namely claiming the evangelical tent for his party. "By making his own heritage, which emphasizes the individual's experience, definitive for the whole of evangelicalism," Horton suggests, "[Olson] has pushed the rest of us to the margins." Obviously, the same could be said of many conservatives. The point, though, is that while the conservative has an epistemological basis for affirming a kind of dogmatism, the postconservative, as far as I can tell, does not. For a brief explanation of how the word "fundamentalism" is being used in this chapter, please see note 13 above.

II. Reassessing the Princeton Mind: The Augustinian or Non-Scholastic Nature of "Right Reason"

The Rogers and McKim Thesis: Simply False

Any attempt to reassess the standard interpretation of the Princeton mind must demonstrate at least a basic awareness of the Rogers and McKim thesis, in part because recent critiques—including those of postconservative and Neo-Orthodox theologians—cite their conclusions favorably.[39] In *The Authority and Interpretation of the Bible: An Historical Approach,* Jack Rogers and Donald McKim argue that the Princeton theologians were not the genuine heirs of the central Christian tradition that they claimed to be in part because their distinctively Reformed commitments were jettisoned by their philosophical assumptions. While the Princetonians were convinced that their view of the Bible was that of orthodox believers throughout the history of the church, in fact their doctrine of Scripture was shaped by their reverence for Turretin and their "uncritical acceptance" of the Scottish philosophy.[40] These factors not only led them to adopt "wholeheartedly the naïve inductive method of Bacon," but they also conspired to reverse in their thinking the Augustinian approach of "faith seeking understanding as a theological method."[41] Indeed, they had an "unbounded confidence" in the competence of human reasoning powers,[42] yet they failed to recognize that this confidence was fundamentally at odds with the theological commitments of the central Christian tradition:

> Despite the constant profession of faithfulness to Calvin and the Augustinian tradition, the Princeton theologians seemed never to fear that their minds had been affected by sin. Their later followers worked out the full implications of this faculty psychology. The Princeton men were sure that sin had made the emotions unreliable. But they held an almost Pelagian confidence that the mind was essentially undisturbed by sin's influence.[43]

According to Rogers and McKim, then, Old Princeton's understanding of the place of Scripture in the central Christian tradition was informed not by sound scholarly analysis but rather by tendentious historical scholarship that was colored by the assumptions of Enlightenment philosophy. This philoso-

---

[39] For example, cf. Grenz, *Renewing the Center,* 77; Olson, *Story of Christian Theology,* 566, 639 n. 23; Dorrien, *Remaking of Evangelical Theology,* 215 n. 19.

[40] Rogers and McKim, *Authority and Interpretation of the Bible,* 289.

[41] Ibid., 289, 296; cf. 269; 289-290.

[42] Ibid. 245; see also Lefferts Loetscher, *The Broadening Church: A Study of Theological Issues in the Presbyterian Church Since 1869* (Philadelphia: University of Pennsylvania, 1957), 70.

[43] Rogers and McKim, *Authority and Interpretation of the Bible,* 290.

phy lent itself to Old Princeton's narrow apologetical concerns, which culminated, as Rogers suggests in a later essay, in B. B. Warfield's rationalistic appeal "to the *natural man's* 'right reason' to judge of the truth of Christianity."[44] It also subverted the Princetonians' standing in the Augustinian tradition, for it turned them into scholastic rationalists who were indifferent to the role that subjective and experiential factors play in religious epistemology, and who, as a consequence, "self-consciously and carefully followed the Thomistic order that reason had to precede faith."[45]

An important piece of scholarship that challenges the assumptions behind this line of argumentation is the examination of Charles Hodge's philosophy by Peter Hicks. Although Hicks's analysis has yet to make much of an impact upon the historiography of the Princeton Theology, it makes a number of important points that call into question prevailing assumptions about Old Princeton, and which, as such, are relevant to the thesis of this chapter.[46] In *The Philosophy of Charles Hodge: A Nineteenth-Century*

---

[44] Jack B. Rogers, "Van Til and Warfield on Scripture in the Westminster Confession," in *Jerusalem and Athens: Critical Discussions on the Philosophy and Apologetics of Cornelius Van Til,* ed. E. R. Geehan (Phillipsburg, N.J.: Presbyterian & Reformed, 1980), 154, emphasis his.

[45] Rogers and McKim, *Authority and Interpretation of the Bible,* 296. In personal correspondence that is cited with permission, Stanley Grenz suggests that Old Princeton's theological method is problematic not primarily because of its "dependence" upon the Scottish philosophy ("although this is not to be discounted"), but because of its "indebtedness to the method of empirical science . . . inherited from the Enlightenment, which led [the Princetonians] . . . to model theology on the pattern of the natural sciences. This legacy in turn was passed on to neo-evangelicalism via fundamentalism," and neo-evangelicals then elevated this program "to normative status" (Stanley J. Grenz to Paul Kjoss Helseth, November 21, 2001). While I welcome Grenz's eagerness to downplay the significance of Scottish Common Sense Realism, I wonder if taking the focus off of the Scottish philosophy and placing it on Old Princeton's inductive method hurts rather than helps his critique. According to the historiographical consensus the Princetonians "modeled theology on the pattern of the natural sciences" *precisely because* their accommodation of Scottish Common Sense Realism jettisoned their commitment to the distinctive emphases of Reformed orthodoxy, including the noetic effects of sin. Although I disagree with this consensus, I nonetheless acknowledge that if the Princetonians in fact were "dependent" upon the Scottish philosophy, then their employment of an inductive method was extremely problematic, because it was then simply the practical outworking of warmed-over humanism. Thus, by downplaying the significance of Scottish Common Sense Realism, I wonder if Grenz is downplaying the primary reason for being opposed to an inductive method in the first place. As far as I can tell, the problem is not an inductive method *per se,* but an inductive method that has been bastardized by humanistic philosophical assumptions. What I am trying to establish in this chapter is that since the Princetonians themselves were not unduly influenced by such assumptions, one cannot repudiate their approach to doing theology by repudiating the methodological indiscretions of those who in fact have sacrificed the theological integrity of Old Princeton's method to the assumptions of an essentially humanistic philosophy. To state the matter clearly, I would suggest that if there is in fact a problem with "a propositionalist understanding of the theological enterprise," it is not to be found in the consistently Reformed understanding of the Princetonians, but in the latent humanism of their later-day friends, especially their later-day Arminian friends. On the relationship between humanism, Scottish Common Sense Realism, and the historiography of American Christianity, cf. Helseth, "'Right Reason' and the Princeton Mind," 19-21. For Richard Mouw's rather sympathetic comments on induction, cf. "Comments on Grenz Paper and 'The Word Made Fresh.'"

[46] According to John W. Stewart, Hicks's work addresses three important "lacunae" in the current scholarship about Hodge: first, "the degree to which Hodge may be characterized properly as a rationalist"; second, the nature of Hodge's relationship to Schleiermacher and other nineteenth-century romantic thinkers; and third, "Hodge's understanding—and eventual dismissal—of Immanuel Kant" (review of *The Philosophy of Charles Hodge* by Peter Hicks, in *The Journal of Presbyterian History* 77 [Spring 1999]: 64-65).

Evangelical Approach to Reason, Knowledge and Truth, Hicks argues that
although the Princeton theologians used ideas and expressions that were
"influenced by" the Scottish philosophy, "there is no indication in their
writings that they saw it as in any way binding, or that they saw [Thomas]
Reid, for instance, as the 'pure' form by which subsequent deviations were
to be tested."[47] Indeed, while they agreed with the Scottish philosophers
that truth exists objectively, that truth is a unity, and that we can have real,
though partial, knowledge of it, "it would seem from the evidence that the
Princetonians did not hold this position because Reid and his followers
taught it; rather, they accepted the Scottish philosophy because it concurred
with their fundamental epistemology."[48] At the foundation of their thinking about knowledge, Hicks suggests, was the conviction that "the basis of
epistemological realism" is "theological rather than philosophical."[49] That
is to say, while the Princetonians "[were] able to agree with the Scottish
philosophers that 'it is universally admitted that we have no foundation for
knowledge or faith, but the veracity of consciousness' [their] own conviction went one stage deeper: 'The ultimate ground of faith and knowledge
is confidence in God.'"[50] God, the Princetonians argued, is not only "the
creator and controller of the world and so guarantor of its ontological sta-
bility and epistemological coherence."[51] More importantly, he is the author
of our nature who has made us "capable of accurate belief about the external world and who would not let us be deceived."[52] For Hicks, therefore,
the Princeton theologians endorsed certain elements of the Scottish philosophy neither for purely speculative nor for merely apologetical reasons, but
rather because those elements were "a useful means of expressing principles that had their origin in [the Princetonians'] theological convictions."[53]
The Princeton theologians were "sophisticated theological realists" rather
than "naïve theological realists," Hicks concludes, and thus they were convinced that we can have real knowledge of God and of the external world
because God has condescended to make himself and the contents of his
mind known "in his works, in our nature, in the Bible, and in Christ," and
because "we have been made deliberately by the creator of the world, and

---

[47] Hicks, *Philosophy of Charles Hodge,* 206, 26.
[48] Ibid., 28.
[49] Ibid., 166.
[50] Ibid.
[51] Ibid., 167; cf. 206.
[52] Ibid., 168.
[53] Ibid. 167.

have been endowed with means of obtaining accurate information about that world."[54]

The Epistemological Context: The Unitary Operation of the "Whole Soul"

How, then, has God made us, and why can we legitimately conclude that Old Princeton's epistemological assumptions—"especially in the sphere of religion"[55]—in no way suggest accommodation to scholastic rationalism? One of the most important aspects of Hicks's analysis is his repeated assertion that Hodge did not divide the soul "into various faculties or aspects," but rather conceived of the soul as a whole or integrated "unit" that acts in all of its functions—its thinking, its feeling, and its willing—as a single substance.[56] While this "unified anthropology" was "very much at odds with the current faculty concepts that were based on two centuries of rationalism and Scottish Common Sense Philosophy," Hodge nonetheless insisted, following Scripture, that our intellects and our wills "are not detachable parts of us which can operate in isolation from each other," but rather are faculties or powers that act as a single unit in response to the governing disposition of the soul.[57] "The Scriptures do not contemplate the intellect, the will, and the

---

[54] Ibid., 191, 167. According to Hicks,

Naïve theological realism is the position of most unphilosophical people, past and present. If truth about God exists it may be known in essentially the same way as truth about anything else. Though it may be harder to believe, the statement "God loves you" is not radically different from the statement "John loves Mary." We know how to use the words involved. We accept God is different from John and that his love will be appropriately different, but the logic of the two sentences appears to be identical. In a parallel way our knowledge of God is accepted by the naïve theological realist as on the same model as our knowledge of John, or of the "numinousness" of a Gothic cathedral. We know what we mean by John, or the numinous, or God, and we know what we mean by saying we know, whether it is in the sense of being acquainted with, or being aware of, John, the numinous, or God.

Sophisticated theological realism would agree that there is a close relationship between ordinary knowledge and religious knowledge. But it would want to reverse the direction of the presentation. Granted, it would claim that in experience our knowledge of ordinary things provides the model for our knowledge of the divine, nevertheless in reality the reverse is the case. We can have knowledge because knowledge is something that has prior existence in God. Our knowledge is modeled on his knowledge. He is a God who knows, and he has created us able to know. We might cite as a parallel the case of divine love. For us experientially, human love is primary. We learn of it from our human parents, and then only later learn to project what we know on the human level on to God. But in reality love is primary in God; it can be experienced on the human level because the creator has chosen to incorporate into his creation aspects of what already existed in the divine being. So while our knowledge of love starts with the human and rises to the divine, the true movement is in the other direction. Our experience of love moves not from the real to the metaphysical, but from the copy or the derived to the original. The love of God is the reality that lies behind and the fulfilling of all that we have tasted in the lesser loving of our human experience (ibid., 191-192).

[55] Ibid., 107.
[56] Ibid., 175, 174; see, for example, Charles Hodge, "Free Agency," *Biblical Repertory and Princeton Review* 29 (January 1857): 115; idem, "My Son, Give Me Thy Heart," in *Princeton Sermons: Outlines of Discourses, Doctrinal and Practical* (London: Thomas Nelson, Paternoster Row, 1879), 131; idem, *Systematic Theology*, 3 vols. (New York: Charles Scribner's Sons, 1872–1873; reprint, Grand Rapids, Mich.: Eerdmans, 1982), 2:255.
[57] Hicks, *Philosophy of Charles Hodge*, 175, 17.

affections, as independent, separable elements of a composite whole," he argued. "These faculties are only different forms of activity in one and the same subsistence."[58]

It is this rejection of the faculty psychology, then, i.e., this conviction that our intellects and our wills "are neither independent nor distinct"[59] but are both expressions of an integrated whole that is "the thinking, feeling, and willing subject in man,"[60] that suggests at least three factors that are of critical importance to our analysis of the Princeton mind. In the first place, Hodge's unified anthropology suggests that he conceived of reason in a "broad" and not in a narrow sense,[61] and that he consequently acknowledged that a true or "right" understanding of whatever is apprehended by the mind involves more than just a movement of the rational faculty. Indeed, he recognized that since "[t]here is always an exercise of will in thought, and an exercise of feeling in cognition," a true or "right" understanding of what is rationally perceived involves "not mere intellectual apprehension. . . . It includes also the proper apprehension . . . [of an object's] qualities; and if those qualities be either esthetic or moral, it includes the due apprehension of them and the state of feeling which answers to them."[62] That Hodge conceived of cognition as an activity involving the whole soul is perhaps nowhere more succinctly manifest than in a sermon on knowing Christ. "The knowledge of Christ," he argued, ". . . is not the apprehension of what he is, simply by the intellect, but also a due apprehension of his glory as a divine person arrayed in our nature, and involves not as its consequence merely, but as one of its elements, the corresponding feeling of adoration, delight, desire and complacency."[63]

If Hodge's emphasis upon the unitary operation of the soul suggests that cognition is an activity involving both the intellect and the will, it also suggests that it is a moral rather than a merely rational enterprise. It also suggests, in other words, that the extent to which truth is apprehended by the mind and then followed in life is ultimately determined not by the rational power of the intellect alone, but rather by the moral character of the knowing agent. That this is the case, and that Hodge "combined both intellectual apprehension and moral response in the notion of knowledge,"[64] is clearly

---

[58] Hodge, *Systematic Theology*, 3:16; cf. Hicks, *Philosophy of Charles Hodge*, 173.

[59] Charles Hodge, "Excellency of the Knowledge of Christ Jesus Our Lord," in *Princeton Sermons*, 214.

[60] Hodge, *Systematic Theology*, 2:46.

[61] Hicks, *Philosophy of Charles Hodge*, 99.

[62] Hodge, "Excellency of the Knowledge of Christ Jesus Our Lord," 214; cf. idem, "Necessity of the Spirit's Teaching in Order to the Right Understanding of the Scriptures," in *Princeton Sermons*, 75-77; Hicks, *Philosophy of Charles Hodge*, 100, 107-108, 206.

[63] Hodge, "Excellency of the Knowledge of Christ Jesus Our Lord," 214.

[64] Hicks, *Philosophy of Charles Hodge*, 175.

revealed in his endorsement of the classical Reformed distinction between a merely "speculative" and a "spiritual" understanding of the gospel, the distinction that grounds his insistence that the teaching of the Spirit is necessary "in order to the right understanding of the Scriptures."[65] While Hodge was convinced that the unregenerate can entertain "correct intellectual convictions"[66] about the truth of Scripture because they can apprehend that truth in a "speculative" or merely rational sense, he nonetheless insisted that they cannot "come to the knowledge of the truth"[67] because they "cannot know the things of the Spirit."[68] They can neither discern the beauty nor taste the sweetness of the truth that they can rationally perceive,[69] in other words, because a moral defect "in the organ of vision"[70] prevents a "true" or "right" apprehension of the truth that is presented to their consciousness.[71]

The regenerate, on the other hand, can discern the "spiritual excellence"[72] of what is apprehended by their minds because they have the moral ability to "see and love the beauty of holiness."[73] Indeed, they can "know the things of the Spirit"[74] because they were infused with "a new spiritual principle" in regeneration,[75] and as a consequence they "embrace [the truth] with assurance and delight"[76] because they "see truth to be truth, to be excellent, lovely and divine."[77] That "right knowledge as well as right feeling . . . are inseparable effects of a work that affects the whole soul" and that certainly

---

[65] Hodge, "Necessity of the Spirit's Teaching in Order to the Right Understanding of the Scriptures," 75-77; idem, "Excellency of the Knowledge of Christ Jesus Our Lord," 214-215.

[66] Charles Hodge, "Indwelling of the Spirit," in *Princeton Sermons,* 77.

[67] Hodge, "Necessity of the Spirit's Teaching in Order to the Right Understanding of the Scriptures," 77, 76.

[68] Charles Hodge, "Delighting in the Law of God," in *Princeton Sermons,* 249.

[69] Cf. Charles Hodge, "Inability of Sinners," in *Theological Essays: Reprinted from the Princeton Review* (New York: Wiley & Putnam, 1846), 270; idem, *Systematic Theology,* 2:261.

[70] Hodge, *Systematic Theology,* 3:51.

[71] Cf. Charles Hodge, *The Way of Life,* introduction by Mark A. Noll (1841; reprint, Mahwah, N.J.: Paulist, 1987), 60; idem, *Systematic Theology,* 2:234; idem, "Inability of Sinners," 269-271.

[72] Hodge, "Necessity of the Spirit's Teaching in Order to the Right Understanding of the Scriptures," 76.

[73] Charles Hodge, "Regeneration, and the Manner of Its Occurrence," *Biblical Repertory and Princeton Review* 2 (1830): 285.

[74] Hodge, "Delighting in the Law of God," 249.

[75] Charles Hodge, "Regeneration," in *Princeton Sermons,* 136.

[76] Hodge, *Systematic Theology,* 3:71.

[77] Charles Hodge, "Evidences of Regeneration," in *Princeton Sermons,* 138. Note that there is a certain relationship between seeing and believing in Hodge's thought because of the internal work of the Spirit on the "whole soul" of a moral agent (cf. Helseth, "'Right Reason' and the Princeton Mind," 21-23). Note as well that while Hodge clearly affirmed the primacy of the intellect in faith, he was unyielding in his insistence that the whole soul is the subject of the Spirit's influence. As such, he rejected "what has been called the 'light system,' which teaches that men are regenerated by light or knowledge, and that all that is needed is that the eyes of the understanding should be opened. As the whole soul is the subject of original sin the whole soul is the subject of regeneration. A blind man cannot possibly rejoice in the beauties of nature or art until his sight is restored. But, if uncultivated, the mere restoration of sight will not give him the perception of beauty. His whole nature must be refined and elevated. So also the whole nature of apostate man must be renewed by the Holy Ghost; then his eyes being opened to the glory of God in Christ, he will rejoice in Him with joy unspeakable and full of glory. But the illumination of the mind is indispensable to holy feelings, and is their proximate cause" (*Systematic Theology,* 2:263).

leads to saving faith is made clear in a sermon on delighting in the Law of God.[78] Delighting in the Law of God, Hodge argued,

> is peculiar to the spiritual man, and is due to the influence of the Spirit. This influence is two-fold, or produces a two-fold effect. *First*, a subjective change in the state of the mind analogous to opening the eyes of the blind. It is such a change as imparts the power of spiritual vision, *i.e.*, the vision of the spiritual excellence of divine things. . . . *Second*, it produces a revelation of the truth, a presentation of it to the mind in its true nature and relations. This is a special work of the Spirit. . . . The effect of these operations of the Spirit is delighting in the law of God, which includes,
>
> 1. An apprehension of its truth and consequent conviction of its divine origin.
> 2. An apprehension of its excellence, of its purity, of its justice, and its goodness. It is seen to be right, to be morally glorious.
> 3. An experience of its power to convince, to sanctify, to console, to guide, to render wise unto salvation; an experience of its appropriateness to our necessities. It is seen to suit our nature as rational beings, as moral beings, as sinners.
> 4. An acquiescence in it, and rejoicing in it, as an exhibition of the character of God, of the rule of duty, of the plan of salvation, of the person and work of Christ, and of the future state. The Scriptures, therefore, are the treasury of truth; the store-house of promises; the granary of spiritual food; the never-failing river of life.[79]

Finally and most importantly, Hodge's emphasis upon the unitary operation of the soul suggests that he conceived of reason in an Augustinian rather than in a scholastic sense, and thus is not properly regarded as a scholastic rationalist. Although this contention certainly challenges the historiographical consensus, nevertheless it is largely confirmed by an unlikely source, namely, the historical analysis of the *Westminster Confession of Faith* by Jack Rogers. In *Scripture in the Westminster Confession: A Problem of Historical Interpretation for American Presbyterianism*, Rogers alleges that the Princeton theologians "did not develop an historically valid interpretation of Scripture in the Westminster Confession," in part because they failed to interpret the *Confession* in light of "the distinctively British background which . . . informed the thinking of the Westminster Divines and which created the

---

[78] Hodge, *Systematic Theology,* 3:36.
[79] Hodge, "Delighting in the Law of God," 249-250.

context in which they thought and wrote."[80] Whereas the Princetonians interpreted the Confession in light of the "Aristotelian and Scholastic" assumptions of "later Continental Reformed orthodoxy" and thus under-emphasized "the witness of the Spirit and the saving purpose of Scripture in their formulation of the doctrine of Scripture," the Westminster Divines, being "both Puritans and Calvinists," "placed primary empha-sis" on these "motifs" because they drew heavily on "an anti-Aristotelian Augustinianism"[81] that was "a deep-rooted tradition carried on in the Puritan party."[82]

One of the "principal threads" in this "anti-Aristotelian Augustinianism," Rogers argues, and thus one of the primary influences that distinguished the Westminster Divines from their more scholastic counterparts both in England and on the Continent, was "the presence of an Augustinian conception of 'right reason.'"[83] While those who followed Aquinas conceived of "right reason" as a faculty that "was implanted by God in all men, Christian and heathen alike, as a guide to truth and con-duct,"[84] those who followed Augustine insisted that the regenerate alone "may rise to an understanding of the truth"[85] because the regenerate alone have the moral ability to see revealed truth for what it objectively is, namely, glorious. Although those who followed Augustine acknowledged

---

[80] Jack B. Rogers, *Scripture in the Westminster Confession: A Problem of Historical Interpretation for American Presbyterianism* (Grand Rapids, Mich.: Eerdmans, 1967), 448, 438.

[81] Ibid., 438, 449, 220, 449, 438.

[82] Rogers and McKim, *Authority and Interpretation of the Bible,* 202.

[83] Rogers, *Scripture in the Westminster Confession,* 82, 438. According to Robert Hoopes, the author of the most extensive study on the concept of "right reason" to date, the concept of "right reason" was born in classical Greece when Socrates advanced the notion that "virtue and knowledge are identical" (*Right Reason in the English Renaissance* [Cambridge: Harvard University Press, 1962], 1). As an epistemological concept that was "assimilated by the early Church Fathers and redefined in the Christian context of sin and grace" (1), the concept was controlled by two formative convictions. Not only did it advance the notion that there is a realm of absolute or non-subjective truth that "includes both intellectual and moral truths" (4), but more importantly it recognized that in order for men to know this truth "they must themselves *become* good" (6). According to Hoopes, "wherever classical and Christian humanists speak of the achievement of true knowledge . . . they invariably speak of a certain transformation that must take place in the character of the knower before that knowledge can be attained. . . . Since Truth in its totality is at once intellectual and moral in nature, the conditions of wisdom are for men both intellectual and moral. True knowledge, i.e., knowledge of Truth, involves the perfection of the knower in both thought and deed" (5). How, though, do men become good so that they can then know what is true? In his incisive analysis of Hoopes's work, Rogers correctly notes that the concept of "right reason" developed along two different lines in the Christian world, in large measure because differing anthropologies led to different answers to this question (*Scripture in the Westminster Confession,* 84). While those who followed Aquinas emphasized the "essential goodness" of man and consequently conceived of "right reason" as a faculty that all possess, Augustine took the reality of original sin and the need for regenerating grace seriously and thus insisted that the regenerate alone can reason "rightly." For a more recent examination of this concept, see William J. Wainwright, *Reason and the Heart: A Prolegomenon to a Critique of Passional Reason* (Ithaca, N.Y., and London: Cornell University Press, 1995).

[84] Douglas Bush, *Paradise Lost in Our Time* (Ithaca, N.Y.: Cornell University Press, 1945), 37; cf. Hoopes, *Right Reason,* 3.

[85] Hoopes, *Right Reason,* 64; cf. Rogers, *Scripture in the Westminster Confession,* 83.

that there is a logical priority of the intellect in faith and thus were not "irrationalists" in any sense of the term, nevertheless they refused to give reason "a sphere of primary authority . . . in religious matters" because they recognized that the intellect and the will work together as a single substance in response to the governing inclination of the soul.[86] Indeed, they recognized that there is an intimate connection between the unitary operation of the soul and the quality of the reception of revealed truth, and as a consequence they insisted that the ability to apprehend revealed truth in something more than a merely speculative sense necessitates that the depravity "of both intellect and will" be taken away "by the power of God."[87]

For the followers of Augustine, therefore, "right reason" is not a faculty all human beings possess that forms the epistemological foundation for a natural theology and a naïve approach to evidentialist apologetics. Rather, it is an epistemological ability of the regenerated soul "which acknowledges the authority of God and which functions for moral, not [merely] speculative ends."[88] Whereas Rogers and McKim[89] would have us believe that Hodge's assimilation of the Scottish philosophy subverted his commitment to an Augustinian understanding of "right reason" and turned him into a scholastic rationalist who afforded reason "an independent sphere of operation prior to faith," in fact his understanding of "right reason" is remarkably similar to that of the Westminster Divines.[90] For not only did he recognize that reasoning itself is an inherently moral enterprise involving all the powers of the soul, but he also acknowledged that the extent to which truth is apprehended by the mind and then followed in life is ultimately determined by the moral character of the knowing agent. This suggests, in short, that "it [is] inappropriate to categorize Hodge as a doctrinaire rationalist or a curmudgeonly scholastic,"[91] for he stood with the Westminster Divines in the mainstream of an epistemological tradition that was, as Rogers himself insists, "quite clearly" opposed to the rationalism of the scholastic tradition.[92]

---

[86] Rogers, *Scripture in the Westminster Confession*, 230, 86, 85.
[87] Ibid., 232.
[88] Ibid., 231.
[89] Cf. Rogers and McKim, *Authority and Interpretation of the Bible*, 296.
[90] Rogers, *Scripture in the Westminster Confession*, 85.
[91] Stewart, review of *Philosophy of Charles Hodge*, 65.
[92] Rogers, *Scripture in the Westminster Confession*, 87 n. 226. For Rogers's full discussion of "right reason" and related matters, cf. 82-87, 222-253.

Postconservative Evangelicalism's Misunderstanding of the Princeton Mind

If we assume, for the purposes of this chapter, that Hodge's epistemological assumptions are representative of those of the best thinkers in the Princeton tradition, then we have grounds for concluding that postconservatism's repudiation of Old Princeton's "propositionalist understanding of the theological enterprise" is based upon at least two profound misunderstandings of the Princeton mind. The first has to do with the alleged rationalism of the Princeton theologians. Whereas postconservatives follow the consensus of critical opinion and thus presume that the theologians at Old Princeton Seminary were scholastic rationalists who were indifferent to the subjective and experiential components of religious epistemology, in fact the Princetonians were committed Augustinians who conceived of reason in a moral rather than a merely rational sense. They recognized, in other words, that the reception of revealed truth is an activity involving the "whole soul" rather than the rational faculty alone, and consequently they insisted, the allegations of Rogers and McKim notwithstanding,[93] that the regenerate alone could apprehend this truth in a "right" or saving sense. As Iain Murray has incisively argued:

> The *use* of the mind is not "rationalism"; it all depends on whether that use is right or wrong. Rationalism is a use of the mind which trusts in its own ability to arrive at truth about God *without* his aid and *apart* from revelation: it treats the mind as a source of knowledge rather than as a channel. The Enlightenment was a classic demonstration of innate human pride in the exaltation of the human intellect. To equate that spirit with the teaching of the Princeton men, who believed that it is the grace of God alone which sets men free to understand, is to stand truth on its head.[94]

The second misunderstanding follows from the first and has to do with the nature of Old Princeton's opposition to the rise of theological liberalism. While the Princeton theologians certainly were convinced that those who are "taught by God" articulate their thoughts about the things of God in an "orthodox" fashion,[95] nevertheless their opposition to the rise of theological

---

[93] Cf. Rogers and McKim, *Authority and Interpretation of the Bible*, 290; Rogers, "Van Til and Warfield on Scripture in the Westminster Confession," 154.

[94] Iain H. Murray, *Evangelicalism Divided: A Record of Crucial Change in the Years 1950 to 2000* (Edinburgh: Banner of Truth, 2000), 197.

[95] For example, see Charles Hodge, "The Indwelling of the Spirit," in *Princeton Sermons*, 77; cf. John 6:44-45.

liberalism was grounded in more than just a stubborn reluctance to allow "more light and truth to break forth from God's Word" (after all, even B. B. Warfield was a proponent of "progressive orthodoxy").[96] The Princetonians were opposed to the rise of theological liberalism, in short, not simply because liberals advanced interpretations of doctrine that differed from their own dogmatic assertions, but more specifically because liberals conceived of doctrines in an "anti-intellectual" or "feminized" sense.[97] Whereas the Princetonians conceived of doctrines as foundational summaries of biblical truth that must be believed in order for there to be faith, liberals conceived of doctrines as little more than expressions of an ineffable religious experience for a particular time and place. They considered doctrines to be true, in other words, not because they corresponded to real states of affairs in the external world, but rather because they captured the subjective experience of religion in the thought forms of a particular age.[98]

Although this pragmatic conception of truth certainly allowed for a broadening of theological boundaries along intra- and even intertextual lines, it needed to be opposed, the Princetonians reasoned, because it left fallen sinners without access to a source of salvation outside of their own (or their community's) experience. Indeed, it presumed an experiential orientation that emptied the Christian religion of enduring cognitive substance, and as a consequence it engendered a progressive inclination that confounded the stating of Christian belief "in terms of modern thought" with the stating of modern thought "in terms of Christian belief."[99] While the denominational heirs of classical theological liberalism have milked this progressive tendency

---

[96] John Robinson, quoted in Dorrien, *Remaking of Evangelical Theology*, 11. Theologians like Roger Olson employ this phrase to help them distinguish between evangelicals who are "reformists" and evangelicals who are "traditionalists." Whereas "reformists" are open to "new light," "traditionalists," apparently, are "unwilling" to modify their positions ("Future of Evangelical Theology," 42, 47). While this rather strained distinction certainly packs a rhetorical punch, it is grossly unfair to both past and present members of the "traditionalist" camp. Warfield, for example, believed in "progressive orthodoxy" (cf. Robert Swanton, "Warfield and Progressive Orthodoxy," *Reformed Theological Review* 23 [October 1964]: 76-77), and today traditionalist evangelicals like Ardel B. Caneday and Thomas R. Schreiner are challenging accepted understandings of perseverance and assurance in a constructive rather than a destructive fashion (cf. *The Race Set Before Us: A Biblical Theology of Perseverance and Assurance* [Downers Grove, Ill.: InterVarsity, 2001]). This suggests, among other things, that the categories of commentators like Olson have become sufficiently hardened to warrant immediate revision. For an interesting discussion of "hardening of the categories," which apparently is an affliction that cripples even the most irenic of evangelicals, see Olson, *Story of Christian Theology*, 554-569.

[97] Cf. Richard Hofstadter, *Anti-Intellectualism in American Life* (New York: Vintage, 1962, 1963), 55-141; Ann Douglas, *The Feminization of American Culture* (1977; reprint New York: Noonday, 1998), 3-13, 17-43, 121-164.

[98] See, for example, Shailer Mathews, *The Faith of Modernism* (New York: Macmillan, 1924), 100, 115, 119, 148, 174-175; and idem, *New Faith for Old* (New York: Macmillan, 1936), 225, 233, 237.

[99] B. B. Warfield, review of *Foundations: A Statement of Christian Belief in Terms of Modern Thought,* by Seven Oxford Men, in *Critical Reviews,* vol. 10, *The Works of Benjamin Breckinridge Warfield* (1932; reprint, Grand Rapids, Mich.: Baker, 1991), 322. On the definite meaning of the word "Christianity," cf. idem, "'Redeemer' and 'Redemption,'" in *Biblical Doctrines,* vol. 2, *The Works of Benjamin Breckinridge Warfield* (1929; reprint, Grand Rapids, Mich.: Baker, 1991), 396.

for practically all it is worth,[100] it is unfortunately enjoying something of a renaissance in certain quarters of the evangelical camp, albeit in a strangely nuanced form.[101] That this is the case, and that a new kind of fundamentalism is rising within the ranks of those who are searching for a "generous orthodoxy" with a large, forgiving center,[102] is manifest in the baldly imperialistic tendencies of postconservative evangelicals like Robert Webber.

III. PARADIGM THINKING AND THE POSTCONSERVATIVE EVANGELICAL

The Postconservative Project

According to Robert Webber, Professor of Ministry at Northern Seminary and a prominent leader in the postconservative evangelical movement, the thinking of the evangelical community has been shaped by the "paradigm" of the modern era for too long, and thus it is high time for evangelicals to "rethink" the faith for a postmodern age. His recent offering, *Ancient-Future Faith: Rethinking Evangelicalism for a Postmodern World,* is intended for precisely this purpose. Evangelicals will liberate themselves from their bondage to the rationalistic assumptions of Enlightenment thought and faithfully "re-present" the faith in our postmodern world, he suggests, neither by "preserving the Christian faith in its modern form," nor by running "headlong into the sweeping changes that accommodate Christianity to postmodern forms."[103] They will "re-present" the faith "in a fresh way," rather, by recovering the insights of an age very similar to our own, namely that of clas-

---

[100] Cf. Peter Jones, *Spirit Wars: Pagan Revival in Christian America* (Mukilteo, Wash.: WinePress; Escondido, Calif.: Main Entry Editions, 1997).

[101] Note the interesting remarks of B. A. Gerrish in "The New Evangelical Theology and the Old: An Opportunity for the Next Century?" available online at http://www.union-psce.edu/news/Publications/archive/aisit-gerrish.html. Commenting on postconservative evangelicalism in general and Grenz's attempt to conceive of theology as a second-order discipline in particular, Gerrish notes that,

> I couldn't agree more. But I can't help thinking that I've heard it before. Grenz does not seem to recognize, or perhaps he prefers not to say, that his theological program for the twenty-first century is pretty much the program that the supposed arch-liberal Friedrich Schleiermacher proposed for the nineteenth century. Differences there may be. But the threefold emphasis on experience, community, and context was precisely Schleiermacher's contribution to evangelical dogmatics. Successive waves of neoorthodox and postmodernist attacks on him have submerged his contribution beneath an ocean of misunderstandings. He never renounced his evangelical-pietistic experience: rather, his theology at its center was reflection upon this experience from within the believing community in its new situation. He was certain that his experience must point to something constant since the time of the apostles, yet always to be conveyed in language that is historically conditioned. No less a critic of his doctrines than Karl Barth correctly perceived in Schleiermacher's faith "a personal relationship with Jesus that may well be called 'love.'"

[102] For example, see Grenz, *Renewing the Center,* 325-351; Olson, "Future of Evangelical Theology," 42. For a brief explanation of how the word "fundamentalism" is being used in this chapter, please see note 13 above.

[103] Robert E. Webber, *Ancient-Future Faith: Rethinking Evangelicalism for a Postmodern World* (Grand Rapids, Mich.: Baker, 1999), 14.

sical Christianity (100–600 A.D.).[104] "The fundamental concern of this book," Webber writes,

> is to find points of contact between classical Christianity and postmodern thought. Classical Christianity was shaped in a pagan and relativistic society much like our own. Classical Christianity was not an accommodation to paganism but an alternative practice of life. Christians in a postmodern world will succeed, not by watering down the faith, but by being a countercultural community that invites people to be shaped by the story of Israel and Jesus.[105]

At first glance, the basic thrust of Webber's proposal will undoubtedly resonate with thoughtful members of the "evangelical establishment." After all, both Luther and Calvin were indebted to the insights of classical Christianity, and even B. B. Warfield, the "lion of strict Presbyterian orthodoxy,"[106] insisted that Christians must state their beliefs in terms of the thought of the age in which they live.[107] More critical readers will quickly recognize, however, that Webber's approach to the Christian faith is altogether different from "the Book-oriented approach" of Luther, Calvin, and Warfield.[108] Indeed, whereas evangelicals like Warfield emphasize "the foundational nature of Scripture" and consequently acknowledge that the Christian faith can be "rationally explained and defended," Webber insists that the authoritative nexus of both faith and truth is found in an inherently mysterious, "event-oriented perception of the world" that is handed down from age to age in "the community of God's presence," the church.[109] Webber therefore argues that the responsibility of the church in the postmodern world is not to recover an articulation of this perception that was "incarnated" in an earlier age.[110] It is rather to "construct a theology that will be consistent with historic Christianity yet relevant to our new time in culture."[111] What is needed, he contends, is a faithful application of the essence of the Christian faith "to a postmodern worldview."[112]

---

[104] Ibid., 16.

[105] Ibid., 7.

[106] George M. Marsden, *Fundamentalism and American Culture: The Shaping of Twentieth-Century Evangelicalism 1870–1975* (New York: Oxford University Press, 1980), 98.

[107] Cf. Warfield, review of *Foundations*, 320-334. "No one will doubt," he argued, "that Christians of to-day must state their Christian beliefs in terms of modern thought. Every age has a language of its own and can speak no other. Mischief comes only when, instead of stating Christian belief in terms of modern thought, an effort is made, rather, to state modern thought in terms of Christian belief" (322).

[108] Webber, *Ancient-Future Faith*, 45.

[109] Ibid., 45, 18, 78, 46.

[110] Ibid., 17.

[111] Ibid., 20-21.

[112] Ibid., 12; cf. idem, *Younger Evangelicals*, 14-17.

Paradigm Thinking and the Continuity of the Christian Tradition

At the heart of Webber's attempt "to interface historic Christian truths into the dawning of a new era" is his insistence that evangelicals will "face the changing cultural situation with integrity" only if they allow themselves to think paradigmatically.[113] According to Webber, there have been six discernible "paradigms of time" throughout the history of the church in which believers have struggled to articulate the essence of the faith in response to the prevailing cultural circumstances of the day.[114] While the circumstances have changed from age to age and the "incarnations" of the faith have thus varied according to "the specific cultural context in which [they were] expressed (e.g., medieval Roman versus sixteenth-century Reformation)," what has remained constant throughout the ages, Webber contends, is a "transcultural framework of faith . . . that has been blessed by sociocultural particularity in every period of church history."[115] Since the "multiplicities of faith expressions" reflect merely the "attempts within a particular cultural moment and geographical place to express the faith in a fresh way," those who would "incarnate the historic faith in the emerging culture" will do so only by recovering "the framework of faith that is common to the diversity."[116] It follows, therefore, that if we would faithfully "re-present" the faith in the postmodern context we must not "root" or "freeze" our understanding of the faith in a particular "incarnation" of the faith from the past (like that of the Reformation, for example).[117] Rather, we must "affirm the whole church in all its previous manifestations" by retrieving

> the universally accepted framework of faith that originated with the apostles, was developed by the Fathers, and has been handed down by the church in its liturgical and theological traditions. . . . Our calling is not to reinvent the Christian faith, but, in keeping with the past, to carry forward what the church has affirmed from its beginning. We change . . . "not to be different, but to remain the same."[118]

While there is little doubt that most conservative readers will be intrigued by Webber's call for theological reconstruction, they likely will wonder if the

---

[113] Webber, *Ancient-Future Faith*, 14, 17.
[114] Ibid., 13.
[115] Ibid., 17.
[116] Ibid., 16, 17.
[117] Ibid., 16.
[118] Ibid., 16, 17. On the process of "deconstruction and reconstruction" that accompanies the re-presentation of the faith in each new age, cf. Webber, *Younger Evangelicals*, 17.

call sounds plausible only because Webber has emptied religious language of real significance. After all, they might ask, is it not possible that one theological formulation differs from another because the framers of the two formulations were actually talking about different religious realities? In other words, if the words that are used in theological formulations are significant precisely because the framers presume that the words they use correspond to extra-linguistic realities, and if as a consequence the framers of those formulations are convinced of the extra-linguistic truthfulness of the particular "incarnation" they affirm, then can it really be true that "while we are all Christians, some of us are Roman Catholic Christians, Eastern Orthodox Christians, Reformation Christians, twentieth-century evangelical Christians, or some other form of modern or postmodern Christians"?[119]

It can and indeed it must be true, Webber assures us, if all genuine expressions of the faith in fact share a common core. What, then, might this unifying core be? The answer is found in the assumptions that inform "the hermeneutic of paradigm thinking."[120] In the first place, Webber insists that religious truth is found in subjective encounter with the classical origins of the Christian tradition. Following the postmodern theorist Hans-Georg Gadamer, Webber argues that it is possible for one paradigm of history to speak to another because it is possible for an individual living in one historical "horizon" to "fuse" with the "horizon" that is the source of the tradition.[121] In Webber's thinking, this "fusion" takes place in the life and worship of the church, the "body of Christ" that is the living sign of *Christus Victor,* "the community of people where the victory of Christ over evil becomes present in and to this world."[122]

In the second place, Webber contends that a "fusion of horizons" is possible in the community of faith because the truth-value of the religious utterances that sustain the community—be they the propositions of Scripture or

---

[119] Webber, *Ancient-Future Faith,* 17. Conservative readers will remain baffled by postconservative proposals as long as they fail to recognize that conservative and postconservative evangelicals have significant disagreements over theological method. Webber describes this disagreement as follows: "The method of the traditionalists is to treat theology as a science, subject, as all other sciences are, to the empirical method. Through an analysis of the data of revelation, one could be brought to propositional truth. Theology, the traditionalist says, is a system of objective truth understood by the mind." Postconservative evangelicals, on the other hand, see theology "as the way to understand the world. It is an understanding based on the biblical narrative. This is the approach to faith that has captured the postmodern mind. Postmoderns have abandoned the modern worldview in which the supremacy of interpretation is given to science. In this context younger evangelicals are calling us to see the world primarily through the Christian story. . . . Theology [they contend] is not a science but a reflection of God's community on the narrative of God's involvement in history as found in the story of Israel and Jesus" (idem, *Younger Evangelicals,* 91-92).
[120] Webber, *Ancient-Future Faith,* 16.
[121] Ibid., 24, 29; cf. Hans-Georg Gadamer, *Truth and Method* (London: Sheed & Ward, 1995).
[122] Webber, *Ancient-Future Faith,* 81, 77.

of historic confessions—is not found in a correspondence between the words themselves and the extra-linguistic realities to which they refer, but in the religious function those words perform. Following the "cultural-linguistic" approach of postliberal theologian George Lindbeck, Webber insists that the truth-value of religious utterances is "intratextual" rather than "extratextual."[123] That is to say, religious utterances are true because they form a perspective on life that is consistent with the perspective of a particular tradition, not because they correspond to "extratextual" reality as such.[124] Since the perception of the world that is characteristic of the Christian tradition was articulated by the apostles and summarized by the early church in the "rule of faith" (the classical summary of the apostolic interpretation of the Christ event that is embodied in the ecumenical creeds), it follows that the religious utterances of Christians from various "frame[s] of reference" are true to the extent that they form a "framework of thought" that is shaped by the central component of that "rule," namely the cosmic reality of *Christus Victor.*[125] The theme of *Christus Victor,* Webber insists, is "central to the classical Christian vision of reality. It does not stand alone, but is connected to all other aspects of the Christian faith as the central thread to the entire tapestry."[126]

When we consider Webber's call for unity within diversity in light of these hermeneutical assumptions, the justification for his reluctance to make one expression of the faith the "standard" by which all other expressions are measured suddenly comes into clearer focus.[127] The church is the community of faith in which the perception of the world that is grounded in the reality of *Christus Victor* and summarized in the "rule of faith" is "handed over" from one generation of believers to another in the life and worship of the body, the "fellowship in faith."[128] The task of the church in each successive age and in every sociocultural context, then, is not to explain and defend a specific incarnation of the faith (for the essence of faith is found in a perspective on life rather than in submission to propositions that correspond to objective reality as such). It is, rather, first to express the faith "within the context of his-

---

[123] Ibid. 30, 185; cf. idem, *Younger Evangelicals,* 74-75; George A. Lindbeck, *The Nature of Doctrine: Religion and Theology in a Postliberal Age* (Philadelphia: Westminster, 1984).

[124] Webber, *Ancient-Future Faith,* 30, 46, 182-185; cf. idem, *Younger Evangelicals,* 90-92. According to William Placher, "A good Lindbeckian, postliberal theologian will . . . operate less like a philosophically oriented apologist and more like a sensitive anthropologist, who tries to describe the language and practice of a tribe in terms of how they function in the life of that community and how they shape the way that community sees the world, rather than trying to defend these people's way of talking by the standards of some universal rationality or experience" (*Unapologetic Theology: A Christian Voice in a Pluralistic Conversation* [Louisville: Westminster John Knox, 1989], 163).

[125] Webber, *Ancient-Future Faith,* 180-186, 196.

[126] Ibid., 31.

[127] Ibid., 16.

[128] Ibid., 180-183, 79.

tory and culture" through "the critical use of human methods of thought," and then to beckon "seekers" into the ongoing fellowship of the community so that their perspective on life can be shaped by that which is shared by all genuine expressions of the faith, namely the perception of the world that is embodied in the Word, liturgy, and symbolism of the "people of the Event."[129] "The goal of the church," Webber contends,

> is to be a divine standard, a sign of God's incarnational presence and activity in history. In a postmodern world the most effective witness to a world of disconnected people is the church that forms community and embodies the reality of the new society. People in a postmodern world are not persuaded to faith by reason as much as they are moved to faith by participation in God's earthly community.[130]

Say What? The Imperialistic Nature of Neo-Fundamentalism

No matter what one's initial reaction to Webber's proposal might be, even the harshest critic must concede that the typical author would kill for the kinds of reviews *Ancient-Future Faith* has received. Clark Pinnock, for example, not only suggests that *Ancient-Future Faith* presents a faith that has "the power to speak to the postmodern world," but more significantly he praises Webber in much the same way that the editors of liberal newspapers praise staunchly conservative politicians for voting in the "correct" fashion on conspicuous social issues.[131] Just as editors cite those votes as evidence that the politician in question has "grown" while in office, so too Pinnock cites *Ancient-Future Faith* as evidence of "Webber's own experience of growth as a hearer of God's Word."[132]

Most conservative readers will likely wonder, however, just what exactly

---

[129] Ibid., 196, 163; Robert E. Webber, "Out with the Old," *Christianity Today* 34 (February 19, 1990): 17.
[130] Webber, *Ancient-Future Faith*, 72, 79. Postconservative evangelicals like Webber advocate an "embodied" or "incarnational" apologetic because they are persuaded that the believing community has the power not only "to communicate the reality of the gospel," but also "to lead people into conversion." The gospel, they contend, is a "story" that must be experienced; it is "not a noncontradictory, rationally defended, logically consistent fact [to be] apprehended by cognitive acquiescence." Since postconservative evangelicals are convinced that gospel truth is "embodied by individuals and by the community known as the church," they insist that this truth is "known" not when it is "proven," but when an individual "step[s] inside the community and into the stream of its interpretation and experience of reality." From this it follows that faith "is not born outside the church" in submission to propositions that are presumed to be objectively true. Rather, faith involves "participation in truth embodied by the community," and as such it is born "within the church as individuals see themselves and their world through the eyes of God's earthed community. . . . In sum the community embodies the Christian narrative, the unchurched 'step into' the narrative, the narrative grasps them even as they grasp it, and eventually the individual embodies the reality of the church's story as he chooses to live his life from the standpoint of the community of faith" (*Younger Evangelicals*, 95, 101, 220, 49, 101, 104, 101, 104).
[131] Webber, *Ancient-Future Faith*, back cover.
[132] Ibid.

it is that Webber has been hearing, for his proposal is marred by an ambivalence that undermines his attempt to move the evangelical camp out of the
modern era and into the postmodern paradigm, an ambivalence that I would
suggest is characteristic of the postconservative project. While Webber incisively critiques the deleterious influence that modern thought has had and
continues to have on certain habits of the evangelical mind, nevertheless his
own proposal is profoundly modern in three distinct yet interrelated senses.[133]
In the first place, it is based upon the assumption that Christianity is, as
J. Gresham Machen used to say when critiquing theological liberalism, "a life,
not a doctrine."[134] Postconservative evangelicals do not draw people into the
Kingdom of God by proclaiming propositions that articulate the objective
foundations of the Christian life; rather they draw people into the corporate
experience of the "fellowship in faith," and it is this experience that then
moves seekers to embrace the "framework of faith" in some mysterious fashion.[135] As Machen made clear in his classic work *Christianity and Liberalism,*
such an approach not only has it backwards, but more importantly it can survive only because its advocates tragically presume that fallen sinners need an
ineffable experience rather than a gospel that is proclaimed objectively.

If Webber's proposal is profoundly modern in one sense because it con-
founds the relationship between life and doctrine, it is so in another because it
presumes that the *sine qua non* of the Christian religion is subjective rather than
objective. This presumption, which is grounded in the modern era's relocation
of the divine-human nexus, is perhaps nowhere more clearly manifest than in
the "communal epistemology" that informs Webber's functional understanding of doctrine.[136] "Information," he contends, "is no longer something that can
be objectively known and verified through evidence and logic. Knowledge is
more subjective and experiential. Knowledge comes through participation in a
community and in an immersion with the symbols and the meaning of the community."[137] When the relationship between life and doctrine is considered in
light of this decidedly anti-intellectual understanding of religious epistemology,
it becomes immediately clear that religious life precedes doctrine in Webber's

---

[133] Thus, I am challenging Webber's contention that postconservative evangelicals "are *not of the
twentieth century and its mindset*" (*Younger Evangelicals,* 24).

[134] J. Gresham Machen, *Christianity and Liberalism* (1923; reprint, Grand Rapids, Mich.: Eerdmans,
1990), 19. See, for example, Webber, *Younger Evangelicals,* 102-105.

[135] Webber, *Ancient-Future Faith,* 77-83.

[136] Webber, *Younger Evangelicals,* 104. I recognize that Webber would reject the notion that his
subjectivism is grounded in the modern era's "retreat from the intellect into the heart" (cf. *Ancient-Future
Faith,* 121-125). It is not entirely clear how he can avoid this charge, however, given his emphasis on the
functional rather than the propositional significance of religious utterances in the corporate experience
of the Christian community.

[137] Webber, *Ancient-Future Faith,* 101.

thinking not because there is something substandard about doctrine itself, but rather because doctrines *qua* doctrines must be kept in their proper place. Doctrines are not important because they carry the "'cognitive and informational meaningfulness'" that must be appropriated in order for there to be faith.[138] Rather, they are the expressions of faith that sustain the religious life of the community and mediate the "framework of faith" to those who are drawn into the corporate experience of the "fellowship in faith." Doctrines, in short, are of secondary—not primary—significance, because they simply express the "framework of faith" for a particular time and place.[139]

Finally, Webber's proposal is profoundly modern because his functional understanding of truth reduces to pragmatism. Not only does he insist that Scripture must be read "theologically" rather than propositionally—i.e., we read the text not to discover the foundational meaning of the text but to ask how "this book, this passage, this verse has been used in the history of the church" to form the life of the people of God—but he also contends that doctrines are true to the extent that they form a "framework of thought" that is consistent with the perspective of the Christian tradition.[140] The truth-value of the Nicene Creed, for example, "is not to be found in words that correspond with an exact reality, but in words that truthfully signify the religious reality of the Trinity in the system of thought (in this case, Hellenistic) in which it is articulated."[141] But as F. LeRon Shults has incisively argued,

---

[138] Lindbeck, *Nature of Doctrine*, 16, quoted in Webber, *Ancient-Future Faith*, 19.

[139] In personal correspondence, Grenz suggests that it is inappropriate for me to argue that postconservatives like Webber are subjectivists. I am misrepresenting theologians like Webber, he insists, because I am "reading these folks through Enlightenment lenses" (Grenz to Helseth, November 21, 2001). While I do affirm with Stephen J. Nichols that "By basing truth in the interpretive community of the church and rejecting truth as grounded upon objectivity, one is left with a subjective faith and a subjective apologetic" ("Contemporary Apologetics and the Nature of Truth" [paper presented at the annual meeting of the Evangelical Theological Society, Orlando, November 1998]: 7), I have yet to be convinced that being critical of those who engage in an extended polemic against the concept of objective truth is necessarily evidence of indebtedness to Enlightenment categories of thought. Again, Nichols makes the crucial point: "While it is true that objectivity is a crucial part of the enlightenment, it is not true that the enlightenment is a crucial part of objectivity. In the enlightenment project, objectivity was predicated upon the autonomy of the individual. If, however, objectivity is predicated upon something different, can one affirm objectivity?" (ibid., 6). With Nichols and the Princetonians, I would argue that one can and indeed one must, since it is the objective content of faith that saves, not faith as a merely subjective phenomenon.

[140] Webber, *Ancient-Future Faith*, 19-20, 30, 189-190. Webber's understanding of the authority of Scripture is difficult to get a handle on. He insists that the text is inspired; yet he rejects *sola Scriptura*. He is less than enthused about the doctrine of inerrancy because it is grounded in "the notion of propositional truth." And he is convinced that "in the modern era biblical criticism has eroded the authority of Scripture." Such commitments, it seems, are difficult to square with what evangelicals have historically believed about Scripture. For a concise statement of how he uses the Bible in doing theology, see Robert E. Webber, "An Evangelical and Catholic Methodology," in *The Use of the Bible in Theology: Evangelical Options*, ed. Robert K. Johnston (Atlanta: John Knox, 1985), 150-158.

[141] Webber, *Ancient-Future Faith*, 30. Despite his contention that postconservative evangelicalism is altogether different from the pragmatic evangelicalism of the twentieth century (cf. *Younger Evangelicals*, 17-18, 54, 91-92), Webber's formulation of postconservatism reduces to pragmatism in at least two senses: Not only does his functional understanding of truth reduce to pragmatism—doctrines are true if they work, i.e., if they form what is thought to be a Christian perspective on life—but his version of

although the Nicene Divines certainly developed doctrines in order to shape the life of the Christian community, they did so "because of certain things they thought were ontologically true."[142] Surely, to miss this point is to gut the creed of its truth content, to consign the believer to "a theological *cul-de-sac* of the worst kind, mired in the circular reasoning of fideism,"[143] and to raise the specter of religious imperialism. In an age when all truth claims are reduced to the level of subjective preference, any claim to universal truthfulness that is not grounded in an objective state of affairs in the external world will smack of precisely that kind of religious chauvinism that committed postmodernists rightly despise. While Webber repeatedly asserts that the Christian narrative is universally true, he fails to recognize that such an assertion is baldly imperialistic when it is grounded in nothing more than the experiential "ethos" of the believing community.[144] Indeed, we could say that it is in the inherently chauvinistic nature of truth claims that presume a functional understanding of truth while simultaneously privileging the corporate experience of the Christian community that the fundamentalism of postconservative evangelicalism is to be found.[145]

IV. CONCLUSION

I have argued in this chapter that despite what the consensus of critical opinion would have us believe, the Princeton theologians ought not to be regarded as scholastic rationalists, because they conceived of reason in a moral rather than a merely rational sense. They recognized, in other words, that cognition involves the "whole soul" rather than the rational faculty alone, and consequently they insisted that the regenerate alone could apprehend revealed truth in a "right" or saving sense. I have also suggested that since postconservatism's repudiation of Old Princeton's "propositionalist understanding of the theological enterprise" presumes the consensus of critical opinion, this repudiation, in short, is based upon a caricature of Old Princeton rather than upon the views of the Princetonians themselves. This is unfortunate, not simply because it severs postconservative evangelicals from the epistemological

---

embodied apologetics does so as well. In short, it is difficult to imagine how inviting "seekers" to participate in the life of the believing community could take place in anything other than pragmatic terms when important questions about the extratextual truthfulness of Christianity are either begged or ignored at the start. Why, realistic "seekers" will likely ask, should we look for "authentic spirituality" (cf. ibid., 222) in the Christian community, and not in the Buddhist, Baha'i, or even homosexual communities, to name a few? The answer, it seems, demands something more than what is offered in an embodied approach.

[142] Shults, "Truth Happens?" 35.

[143] Ibid., 36.

[144] Cf. Webber, *Ancient-Future Faith,* 93-115; see note 141 above.

[145] For a brief explanation of how the word "fundamentalism" is being used in this chapter, please see note 13 above.

capital of Old Princeton's emphasis upon the unity of head and heart, but more significantly because it leaves them without the epistemological wherewithal to claim that the Christian worldview is universally true. Without the willingness to affirm that the regenerate are "taught by God," and without the eagerness to acknowledge that this teaching has reference to something more than merely subjective states of affairs, all claims to universal truthfulness—even those articulated by the most irenic among us—necessarily clank with the bigoted ring "of triumphalism, elitism, and separatism, which is the hallmark of fundamentalism."[146]

This, then, is what I take to be one of the more significant obstacles to the viability of postconservative evangelicalism's "narrativist-communitarian model" of theology. While postconservative evangelicals are convinced that the heart of Christian faith is found in an "identity-producing" experience that is facilitated by an "interpretive framework" that is shaped by an "identity-constituting narrative," they nonetheless acknowledge that different kinds of religious experiences are facilitated by different kinds of "interpretive frameworks."[147] But if all that sets one religious experience apart from another is the "interpretive framework" that facilitates the experience, on what basis can Christians claim that their experience is truer than another, when the truth-value of the religious utterances that shape their "interpretive framework"—including the utterances of Scripture and of historic confessions—is functional rather than propositional, "intratextual" rather than "extratextual"? Postconservatives might suggest that the universal truthfulness of the Christian narrative is ultimately found in "the explicative power of the Christian faith," and in "the value of the Christian worldview for illuminating human experience, as well as our human understanding of our world."[148] Yet how can such claims be anything more than blatantly chauvinistic when they are grounded in utterances that themselves can only be subjectively true? Although Grenz and Webber and their postconservative colleagues might imagine that the "explicative power" of the Christian faith surpasses that of other religious traditions, thinkers from other religious traditions—who are similarly convinced of the "explicative power" of their own "interpretive frameworks"—will certainly want to know who died and left

---

[146] Olson, "Future of Evangelical Theology," 47; cf. note 13 above. According to Nichols, "by rejecting the possibility of asserting objective truth, one necessarily comments against the objective reality of the historical event that forms the basis of the faith and against the objective truths recorded about that event. The result of rejecting objective truth is that one cannot escape subjectivity in apologetics. In an increasingly pluralistic society, evangelicalism has no right to assert claims to exclusivity given this framework, and such may not be the healthiest for evangelical apologetics in any case" ("Contemporary Apologetics and the Nature of Truth," 6).

[147] Grenz, *Renewing the Center*, 202-203.

[148] Ibid., 205.

the postconservatives in charge. A number of years ago, Millard Erickson zeroed in on this problem with characteristic clarity, and it is with his evaluation that I conclude this chapter:

> We now are aware of the claims of other religions, whose adherents are to be found even within what have previously been primarily Christian cultures. Many of them have the same sort of subjective certitude about the validity of their faith as do Christians. If indeed postconservative evangelicals hold that Christianity is the true religion, they must make some note of this phenomenon and offer a further reason for their conclusion. If not, this either looks like ethnocentrism or at least ignorance of the postmodern scene.[149]

---

[149] Millard J. Erickson, *The Evangelical Left: Encountering Postconservative Evangelical Theology* (Grand Rapids, Mich.: Baker, 1997), 84.

10

PIETISM AND THE HISTORY OF AMERICAN EVANGELICALISM

William G. Travis

IN THE FIRST CHAPTER OF *Renewing the Center,* Stanley Grenz summarizes his view of how evangelicalism has changed. Eighteenth-century evangelicals had an understanding of the gospel characterized by "convertive piety" and "experimental religion." While experimental religion is the outworking of one's faith in practice, convertive piety is "the vision of faith that sees a personal experience of regeneration through the new birth coupled with a transformed life, rather than adherence to creeds and participation in outward rites, as the essence of Christianity." By the mid-twentieth century, however, many evangelical theologians had augmented "the traditional interest in gospel proclamation with another, decidedly cognitive concern, namely, the desire to maintain correct doctrine."[1] Thus, to the material principle of the early evangelicals the more recent evangelicals added a formal principle,[2] correct doctrine, and these more recent advocates see the two principles as together constituting the genius of the movement or, in Grenz's view a worse case, the formal becoming the material. Grenz believes that the additional principle altered the historic meaning of evangelicalism, and his book, among other things, calls for a return to what he sees as the original understanding of the movement. This paper attempts to test the Grenz hypothesis: did evangelicalism begin with its material principle in the place of honor, and was it

---

[1] Stanley J. Grenz, *Renewing the Center: Evangelical Theology in a Post-Theological Era* (Grand Rapids, Mich.: Baker, 2000), 17, 53.

[2] A material principle is that of which something is made, its basic constituent; in Grenz's view, evangelicalism is made of "convertive piety" and "experimental religion." A formal principle is that which acts upon the material and produces changes in the "something," but without the loss of the material principle. Grenz asserts that the (later) addition of correct doctrine as a formal principle alters the understanding of the nature of evangelicalism, leading to a distorted picture of evangelicalism's beginnings and the course of its history. Contra Grenz, this chapter argues that both convertive piety and an emphasis on correct doctrine were constituent of evangelicalism from its beginnings.

the case that later evangelicals changed the movement by adding and overemphasizing the formal principle? An introduction details the Grenz view, after which we will look at the Pietism of the seventeenth and eighteenth centuries, followed by studies of Methodists, Lutherans, and other religious groups in the United States.

INTRODUCTION: GRENZ'S VIEW OF HISTORY

Evangelicalism started in the Protestant Reformation, particularly with Luther's emphasis on justification by faith, but especially in Calvin's separation of sanctification from justification. However, there is not a single line from the Reformation to later expressions of evangelicalism, for while "the theological trajectory that gave it birth may have begun in the Reformation, it underwent twists and turns, permutations and augmentation, during its journey from the sixteenth century to the present." The rise of Puritanism and Pietism in the seventeenth century and their confluence in the eighteenth century is the more immediate source of evangelicalism. These two movements—emphasizing a personal conversion experience, the life of sanctification, and assurance of one's election—constitute traditional evangelicalism, and what occurred to evangelicalism by the twentieth century was an aberration from the eighteenth-century beginnings. Those beginnings will fare much better in a postmodern, post-theological world than will the twentieth-century version.[3]

Though Puritanism "was without a doubt the single most powerful molder of the ethos and theology of the evangelical movement," evangelicalism drew equally from German Lutheran Pietism. These two "kindred spirits" saw themselves as completing the work of the Reformers, the Pietists for example arguing that the Lutheran reformation had been only partial. Philipp Jakob Spener (1635–1705), one of the founders of Pietism, was convinced along with his followers that, more than head knowledge and adherence to outward forms, the essence of Christianity "is a personal relationship with God expressed in a life that reflects God's will. And this idea, in turn, became the central hallmark of the Pietist movement." Thus, writes Grenz, "[w]hereas the major issue of the Reformation had been the origin of faith,

---

[3] Ibid., 33. Compare Douglas Jacobsen, a professor at Messiah College very much interested in creating a "new center" that will transcend the old "two-party system" of conservatives versus liberals, who argues that Pietism "refers to any form of Christian faith that values conversionistic faith and warmhearted spirituality more than it does doctrinal precision and/or ecclesiastical orderliness." Also, "[t]he Pietistic completion of the Reformation centered on the subjective side of faith—the lived experience of faith." Jacobsen hopes that Pietism can play an important role in revitalizing the ecumenical movement (Douglas Jacobsen, "Pietism and the Postmodern Context of Ecumenical Dialogue," *Ecumenical Trends* 29 [February 2000]: 1-10). The quotations are from page 1.

in Pietism the focus shifted to the outcome of faith, as Pietists elevated the new birth to center stage."[4]

A series of consequences followed from moving the new birth to center stage. One was a shift from the Reformers' emphasis on what God does *for* his people to an emphasis on what God does *within* his people. This led to a move in soteriology from justification as the foundational doctrine to regeneration as the foundational doctrine. In turn, two other consequences followed. "The older Protestant theology had generally spoken of salvation as an objective given. . . . The Pietists, in contrast, highlighted the subjective, the inner nature of salvation." And second, "the locus of true Christianity shifted from baptism to personal salvation." While some of this may have been subtle, the overall effect was an "unmistakable shift" which, when completed in the context of the eighteenth-century British and New England revivals, "marked the genesis of the evangelical movement with its focus on the gospel of the new birth."[5]

Armed with this basic interpretation—evangelicalism has roots in the Reformation, its immediate forebears are Puritanism and Pietism, and its advent is really only in the eighteenth century—in the next several chapters Grenz proceeds to describe what went wrong. In the nineteenth century the formal principle, especially scriptural authority, gradually replaced the material principle. Begun by the Princeton Theology, this replacement influenced the fundamentalist movement of the late-nineteenth and early-twentieth centuries, and its successor, the new evangelicalism that emerged in the middle of the twentieth century. Grenz writes from the late-twentieth century vantage point: "[u]nder the influence of this understanding of the movement's

---

[4] Grenz, *Renewing the Center*, 40, 42. Grenz's sometime coauthor Roger Olson, *The Story of Christian Theology: Twenty Centuries of Tradition and Reform* (Downers Grove, Ill.: InterVarsity Press, 1999), asserts that doctrine was integral to the thinking of Puritans, who were "basically Calvinistic in theology" (494), "thoroughly and persistently Calvinistic" (498), and who "proclaimed the absolute sovereignty of God and the total depravity of humanity" (498). In his section on Jonathan Edwards, a premier figure in the Great Awakening in America, Olson says Edwards's theology "was a hybrid of Calvinism and pietism in that it was not so different from classical Puritan thought, although the pietist emphasis on religious feelings is more pronounced in Edwards than in earlier Puritan divines" (505). The hybrid is shown in that the "three main consistent marks" (505) of Edwards's theology are his emphasis on the glory and freedom of God—"[n]o theologian in the history of Christianity held a higher or stronger view of God's majesty, sovereignty, glory and power than Jonathan Edwards" (506)—"the depravity and bondage of humans" (507), and "the affections as the 'anthropological center.' . . . the core of human personality out of which identity and actions flow" (508). The last mark certainly has affinity with the Pietist emphasis on "convertive piety" (indeed, Edwards strongly advocated "experimental religion"), but given these three marks, it is difficult to see how Edwards and his Puritan forebears can be understood as other than having a very strong interest in the formal principle of correct doctrine. Therefore, this paper will focus on Pietism in its Lutheran expression, and leave to one side what is at times called "Reformed Pietism."

[5] Grenz, *Renewing the Center*, 42, 43. "This vision of the faith that focuses on personal regeneration rather than on outward rituals as the key to a changed life has continued to dominate evangelical theology to the present" (44). Whatever the background and influences, Grenz sees the eighteenth century as "the advent of evangelicalism" proper (45).

formal principle, its material principle became not so much the gospel itself but what mid-century evangelical theologians saw as the basic doctrines of the Bible."[6] This was new, as Grenz sees it, for the older evangelicals "were generally in agreement that the Bible is inspired by God. Nevertheless, like their Pietist forebears, they were not particularly concerned to devise theories to explain the dynamics of inspiration. Further, evangelicals displayed a remarkable fluidity of opinion about the ins and outs of inspiration." Further, "the evangelicals who emerged from the awakenings exhibited little interest prior to the 1820s in elaborating precise theories about biblical infallibility or inerrancy."[7] But later in the nineteenth century, Scripture emerged as the central "fundamental," which "had the effect of transforming the ethos of the evangelical tradition of the purveyors of convertive piety from that of a gospel-focused endeavor that viewed the Bible as the vehicle of the Spirit's working to that of a Bible-focused task intent on maintaining the gospel of biblical orthodoxy."[8]

What happened to the subjective as primary and the doctrinal as secondary during this long period when the formal principle came to dominate? The older view did not die, but was preserved in various parts of the larger evangelical movement, particularly in those influenced by Pietism: John Wesley and the Wesleyans, the Methodists in general and the Holiness groups in particular, and perhaps the Pentecostals. An apt illustration of this is how Grenz views the relationship of current theologians Millard Erickson and Clark Pinnock to Pietism. Erickson, he says, "never lost sight of the gospel-centered and Pietist influenced nature of evangelicalism," and "retained enough of the Pietist heritage of the Swedish Baptists to maintain the practical aspect of theology." However, "in the waning years of the twentieth century, as Erickson picked up the mantle of [Carl F. H.] Henry, he

---

[6] Ibid., 54. Grenz is still emphasizing this contrast at the end of the book, where he advocates a "generous orthodoxy," which asserts that "even while the church is oriented toward doctrine, its focus must always remain the gospel. The great insight of the Pietists in the context of Lutheran Orthodoxy was that doctrine is not the be-all and end-all of the Christian faith" (343).

[7] Ibid., 65. In a 1998 article Grenz summarizes the relation between doctrine and life by asserting that the "language evangelicals use is, of course, theological. And the theological statements we use are crucial because they *facilitate* our experience; they even make this experience possible. But in the end, it is the shared encounter—more so than the theological deposit that *defines* and *nurtures* it, and therefore is *instrumental* to it—that forms the foundation of our common identity" ("An Agenda for Evangelical Theology in the Postmodern Context," *Didaskalia* 9 [Spring 1998]: 4, emphasis added). Four years later he used similar language: "right doctrine has *a role to play* in the transformation of heart and life. . . . [it] is important insofar as it *plays a role* in the transformation of heart and life"; therefore, "the truly evangelical spirit acknowledges that doctrinal formulae will always have *a type of provisionality* to them" (*"Die Begrenzte Gemeinschaft* ["The Boundaried People"] and the Character of Evangelical Theology," *Journal of the Evangelical Theological Society* 45 [June 2002]: 310, emphasis added).

[8] Grenz, *Renewing the Center,* 84. Just before this, Grenz captured the trajectory in a single sentence: "By perpetuating the fundamentalist struggle against liberalism as waged on the terms set out by the Princeton theology, the new evangelical theology oriented itself to questions of propositional truth, in contrast to the issue of one's relationship with God characteristic of classical evangelicalism" (ibid.).

seemed to be drifting to the right."[9] This rightward drift was the stress on doctrine as primary, on the scholastic as opposed to the experiential. By contrast, Clark Pinnock, rather than turning to Henry, rediscovered the "Pietist impulse," which has allowed him "to greet the postmodern emphasis on the particular and experiential, for he saw these developments as boding well for an 'evangelical pietism.' . . . And it is here above all that his contribution as a catalyst for a rebirth of centrist evangelical theology may be found."[10] Erickson, given his background, could have retained his pietism but chose not to; Pinnock the "scholastic," upon discovering pietism, made the crucial choice to embrace it.

Other writers offer support to this general picture. And some argue that the original evangelicalism not only did not die but remained alive and well during the era of aberration described by Grenz. For example, William J. Abraham argues that greater voice should be given to the Wesleyan ingredient in evangelicalism, agreeing with Grenz that the twentieth century saw a move away from the longer evangelical history.[11] Donald Dayton goes a step farther, contending that the Wesleyan view has been the predominant one over the history of American evangelicalism. Dayton asserts that while the "Reformed paradigm," with its strong emphasis on order and doctrinal clarity, was dominant among twentieth-century evangelicals, this was really a recent development, and the Wesleyan/Arminian view is actually the long-term understanding of evangelicalism. What Dayton has sometimes described as the "Pentecostal paradigm" means that rather than having a closed set of features, evangelicalism is an innovative, fluid, radical movement with much fuzzier edges than the Reformed view allows.[12] In one of his recent discussions he sees three paradigms for evangelicalism (in effect splitting the

---

[9] Ibid., 133.

[10] Ibid., 150. Grenz contends that "seeds of divergence lie deep within the heart of neo-evangelical theology. . . . This is exemplified by Millard Erickson's move from young innovator to establishment statesman and by Clark Pinnock's odyssey from young establishment apologist to theological pilgrim" (151).

[11] William J. Abraham, *The Coming Great Revival: Recovering the Full Evangelical Tradition* (San Francisco: Harper & Row, 1984), 11-26. For the longer view Abraham offers the Wesleyan version of the evangelical tradition as "a refreshing alternative to the standard models [Reformed] of the evangelical heritage currently available" (56). Citing several strands to the genius of Wesley, Abraham says that "Wesley's significance as a theologian rests fundamentally on his ability to hold together elements in the Christian tradition that generally are pulled apart and expressed in isolation." This means that "Wesley cannot be tamed by placing him in the categories of the fundamentalist paradigm" (57).

[12] Dayton's view can be found in several places: two chapters in a book he edited with Robert K. Johnston, *The Variety of American Evangelicalism* (Knoxville: University of Tennessee Press, 1991), "The Limits of American Evangelicalism: The Pentecostal Tradition" (36-56); and "Some Doubts About the Usefulness of the Category 'Evangelical'" (245-251); "'The Search for the Historical Evangelicalism': George Marsden's History of Fuller Seminary as a Case Study," *Christian Scholar's Review* 23 (September 1993): 12-33 (plus a rejoinder, 62-71); "Interview with Donald Dayton: Are Charismatic-Inclined Pietists the True Evangelicals? And Have the Reformed Tried to Highjack the Movement?" *Modern Reformation* 10 (March/April 2001): 40-49.

Reformed paradigm in two): the Lutheran/Reformation one emphasizing justification by faith and the other sixteenth-century *solas,* the pre-fundamentalist Wesleyan movement rooted in the eighteenth-century evangelical revival, and the post-fundamentalist neo-evangelicalism which emerged in the 1940s and 1950s. Of the three, "the most useful and historically appropriate way of using the word 'evangelical' is, I believe, according to the second or Wesleyan paradigm—what I would call classic evangelicalism." Evangelicalism is "basically Wesleyan even beyond the boundaries of Methodism as such."[13]

Whether Grenz would fully agree with this last contention, the issues before us are several in number: Is it the case that Pietism stressed the experiential as its material principle, and the doctrinal as at most only a formal principle? Is it the case that such a relationship characterized the eighteenth-century revivals, John Wesley and his American followers, and groups like American Lutherans and Pentecostals? Is it the case that the long dominance of the Reformed tradition reversed the relationship, and as a consequence encouraged the loss of the central meaning of evangelicalism? One of the primary questions in all these issues has to do with the nature and role of Pietism, the movement this chapter specifically addresses. Puritanism and other sources of evangelicalism will appear only here and there tangentially.[14]

CLASSICAL PIETISM

Dale Brown's *Understanding Pietism,* cited positively by Grenz and others, provides a helpful survey of early Pietism. Admitting that Pietism has had a number of interpretations and manifestations, and specific names such as Reformed Pietism, Radical Pietism, Moravianism, English Evangelicalism, Methodism, and the Great Awakening, Brown notes that his study "will primarily use the name Pietism in the more narrow sense and apply specific labels when referring to kindred movements." But even in the narrow sense there are multiple sources of Pietism. "The early Pietists espoused continuity with Luther and reform orthodoxy." But it is also the case that the "genesis

---

[13] Dayton, "Interview," 41. Dayton had earlier written "that the 'age of Methodism' in American life (usually the century from 1820 to World War I) is roughly equivalent to the 'age of Evangelicalism.' I would argue that what happens in Methodism is thus determinative for our interpretation of *American evangelicalism* as a whole" (Dayton, "'The Search for the Historical Evangelicalism,'" 14).

[14] A convenient catalogue of Puritan piety is Jerald C. Brauer, "Types of Puritan Piety," *Church History* 65 (March 1987): 39-58. Brauer cautions against making too close a connection between Puritanism and Pietism: "F. Ernest Stoeffler attempted to subsume English Puritanism under the term pietism by developing an indefensible distinction between so-called polemical English Puritans and pietistic Puritans" (40). What Brauer characterizes as "evangelical piety" among Puritans is closest to the thinking of the Continental Pietists, with of course the Reformed doctrinal base as a given. See note 3, above, for further explanation for not including Puritanism as a major component of this chapter.

of German Pietism owes much to the Reformed tradition, particularly to its Puritan strands." Two other sources are Anabaptism and mysticism, though the latter "has been overemphasized by some historians."[15]

And what of the doctrinal matters in Pietism? Pietists were reacting to a "dead" Lutheran Orthodoxy, which orthodoxy sprang in part from conflict in the sixteenth century with Calvinists and Jesuits, but it's also true that Luther's "insistence on correct doctrine was no doubt an impetus to the rise of Lutheran Orthodoxy." From a positive standpoint, "this movement toward Orthodoxy can be viewed as faith seeking understanding, the necessity for a young and growing Lutheranism to define itself amid political maneuverings and theological cleavages." Furthermore, even in the seventeenth century, "Orthodoxy retained a reform party and some who shared Luther's suspicion of philosophy." Therefore we need to keep in mind "that many of the caricatures and criticisms of Orthodoxy by Pietists were directed more against its extremes and degenerations than against its solid center and finest representatives." Negatively, the Pietists "claimed that correct doctrine did not seem to make a difference in the morality and lives of all those who possessed it." Did this lack of making a difference lead to making doctrine a secondary consideration? Apparently not, for "it is interesting that in later eighteenth- and nineteenth-century manifestations of conservative Protestantism, one often finds the merger of what had previously been the sharp opposing strands of Orthodoxy and Pietism." We can conclude from this that instead of seeing Pietism as a modification of Lutheran teaching, and a deemphasizing of doctrine, it may equally be seen as augmenting (or supplementing) doctrine.[16]

---

[15] Dale W. Brown, *Understanding Pietism*, rev. ed. (Nappanee, Ind.: Evangel, 1996), 15, 16. The literature on Lutheran Pietism is voluminous and conflicted. I have tried to avoid extremes in interpretation in the use of sources, and while using Brown for the general exposition, I cite other sources in the notes. Though both have been faulted in some regards by critics, a beginning for the study in English is two books by F. Ernest Stoeffler: *The Rise of Evangelical Pietism* (Leiden: E. J. Brill, 1971 [original edition, 1965]), centering on Reformed Pietism more than German Lutheran Pietism; and *German Pietism During the Eighteenth Century* (Leiden: E. J. Brill, 1973). Stoeffler summarizes the central features of Pietism by asserting that "[e]arly Pietism had its roots in the Protestant Reformation, adhered faithfully to its basic doctrinal norms, and tried to keep alive its spiritual dynamic," was "a major reform movement, the influence of which made itself felt in various phases of Protestantism during the seventeenth and eighteenth centuries" and beyond, and its "four characteristic emphases, the experiential, perfectionistic, biblical, and oppositive, have to a greater or lesser degree penetrated all Protestantism, and are still discernible elements in present-day American Christianity" (Stoeffler, *Rise of Evangelical Pietism*, 23). Taxonomies of Pietism abound, a useful one the fourfold division—*natura pietatis, collegia pietatis, praxis pietatis, reformation pietatis*—laid out in Egon Gerdes, "Theological Tenets of Pietism," *The Covenant Quarterly* 34 (February/May 1976): 25-60.

[16] Brown, *Understanding Pietism*, 19, 20. Brown notes that though "Spener coveted for the Lutherans the almost blameless lifestyle of nearby Mennonites, he disagreed in certain matters of doctrine" (18). In support of a doctrinal presence even later, Vernon P. Kleinig says that "[f]idelity to the Lutheran symbols was by no means as dead in the eighteenth century as the historical textbooks would lead us to believe" ("Confessional Lutheranism in Eighteenth Century Germany," *Concordia Theological Quarterly* 60 [January/April, 1996]: 97).

Pietists are noted, of course, for their ethical and practical concerns, but Brown also sees "underlying theological presuppositions. . . . Pietist mentors accepted Luther's order of salvation which began with his central theme of justification by grace through faith. They adopted Luther's critique of any attempt to work out our salvation apart from Christ. . . . This focus on practical Christianity may be indicative that Pietism fostered no theology of its own; however, the emphasis on practice, exegesis, and mystical appropriation of the grace of God often assumed and represented certain theological presuppositions."[17]

Having attempted in his first chapter to answer the general question, What is Pietism? Brown spends the major part of the book treating the two founders of Pietism, Spener and Francke, to discover "the theological presuppositions which undergirded their practical activities," and to "examine the validity of the charge of subjectivism in the major areas of ecclesiology, exegesis, ethics, experience, and eschatology." As for Spener, he "repeatedly professed to be a *rechtglaubig* ('orthodox') Lutheran in complete agreement with the teachings of the church and the Formula of Concord 'in all articles and points.'" Though accused of unorthodoxy, Francke on several occasions was cleared of the charge. Still, there were important differences between the Orthodox (also in historical studies called the Scholastic) Lutherans and the Pietist Lutherans, for despite the "protestations of true Lutheranism on both sides, a fundamental cleavage evolved between later Lutheran Orthodoxy and German Pietism."[18] But was the cleavage a matter of experience versus doctrine?

One of the claims made about Pietism is that it shifted the doctrine of

---

[17] Brown, *Understanding Pietism*, 21, 22.

[18] Ibid., 28, 29. The debate between Francke and Halle on the one hand and the Orthodox establishment on the other hand, at three points—1692, 1695–1700, and in the second and early third decades of the eighteenth century—led to conclusions that the Pietists were orthodox in belief (James O. Duke, "Pietism Versus Establishment," *The Covenant Quarterly* 36 [November 1978]: 3-16). Duke catalogues the Orthodox worries. On the question of faith and piety, "the Christian proclamation was at stake; [in Pietism] one no longer preached Jesus Christ, crucified and resurrected, now one preached one's personal experience of Jesus"—a potentially dangerous subjective element. On the issue of the Scriptures and piety, "must one be pious before reading the Scriptures in order to understand them or must one understand the Scriptures in order to become rightly pious?" On the church and ministry, symbolized in the conflict over the confessional, "[t]he Orthodox felt bound by conscience to grant absolution freely. By this means they witnessed to God's unconditional pardon. The Pietists felt bound by conscience to grant forgiveness cautiously. By this means they witnessed to God's uncompromising righteousness" (ibid., 13, 14, 15). Scott Kisker, "Radical Pietism and Early German Methodism," *Methodist History* 37 (April 1999): 175-188, supports this assessment of Francke and others as he draws a distinction between "church-related Pietism" and "radical Pietism." Citing Martin Schrag, Kisker says "[c]hurch-related Pietists, such as the Spener-Halle movement, worked within the framework of orthodox Protestant theology, and established churches" (175). For radical Pietism, Kisker quotes Chauncy David Ensign: "[t]hat branch of the pietistic movement in Germany, which emphasized separatistic, sectarian and mystical elements, particularly those originating in Boehmenism" (175). Jakob Boehm (1575–1624), a lay theologian, "was influential throughout the seventeenth century, especially in spiritualist and quietist circles" (175 n. 3).

justification by faith (with its juridical emphasis) from its central role in Luther and the Lutheran Orthodox to regeneration (a biological metaphor) as the center. This shift may be characteristic of some later manifestations of Pietism, but not so for Spener. "Spener felt that the Johannine and Pauline metaphor of regeneration represented a completion and an enhancement rather than a replacement of the equally biblical metaphor of justification." Though still early on in his book, Brown at this juncture gives a summary of what the book does: "Spener and his followers opened the door for many manifestations of Protestant individualism; nevertheless, they did attempt to maintain a balance between their understanding of God's objective activity in Word and Sacrament and their stress on the individual and corporate human appropriation of Word and Sacrament."[19]

The objective and the subjective elements noted in the previous quotation become a leitmotif in Brown's book and, by implication, the heart of the views of the founding Pietists. In understandings of the nature of the creeds and symbols, the nature of the church, the Bible, sanctification, the work of the Holy Spirit, and the nature of the world, there is a constant both/and quality among the early Pietists. In the midst of his chapter on "Doctrine and Life" Brown states the two sides: "the leaders of Pietism professed orthodoxy. They did not desire to disparage doctrine; they insisted that doctrine encompass life. Spener's concern was that the interests of pure doctrine and *Gottseligkeit* ["godliness"] be preserved equally and at the same time." Citing Max Gobel, Brown agrees that Spener was "as much the enemy of heresy as he was the enemy of ungodliness."[20]

A test case for the Pietists and their views on doctrine, specifically the doctrine of Scripture, is Johann Albrecht Bengel (1687–1752). Alan J. Thompson notes that Pietism in general, and often Bengel in particular, are seen by later

---

[19] Brown, *Understanding Pietism,* 30. "Rather than repudiating doctrine as ineffective for life, the Pietists felt that there should be a reformation of both doctrine and life. On many occasions Spener agreed with his orthodox colleagues concerning the necessity of fixed doctrinal forms and the insufficiency of the good life without correct belief" (31). Where he disagreed strongly with the Orthodox was on the question of the church's infallibility (ibid.). For an emphasis on reformation of life from the Orthodox side in the seventeenth century, see Craig J. Westendorf, "The Piety of the Orthodox in Seventeenth-Century Postille Literature," in *Lutheranism and Pietism: The Lutheran Historical Conference: Essays and Reports 1990,* ed. August R. Suelflow (Minneapolis: Augsburg Fortress, 1992). Postilles were collections of sermons given on the traditional pericopes of the church year.

[20] Brown, *Understanding Pietism,* 59. On doctrine, for example, "Spener and Francke held tenaciously to the dogmas of original sin and the human incapacity to do good" (60). Brown gives a general summary at the end of his book: "We have seen how they professed a mediating position between dogmatic rigidity and emotional warmth, faith and works, law and gospel, justification and sanctification, judgment and love of the world. They desired a corrective rather than a revolutionary movement. Reformation rather than separation constituted their ecclesiastical goal, though they often empathized with a Radical Pietist mood which considered the church to be Babel" (90). Roger Olson agrees about doctrine: "The classical Protestant Pietists such as Spener, Francke and Zinzendorf and their followers were conservative in theology" (*Story of Christian Theology,* 488).

writers as espousing "a 'person-oriented' view of inspiration that allowed for errors in the text; a 'limited' view of inerrancy that allowed for errors in Scripture with regard to history, geography, and chronology; [and] a reluctance to equate the word of God with Scripture." It follows from these notions that Pietists argued for partial inspiration, and they helped prepare the way for the rise of textual criticism.[21] Thompson's thorough study calls into question each of these assertions. In the lengthy preface to his work as well as in his detailed comments on selected biblical passages, Bengel "repeatedly draws attention to the truthfulness, perfection, purity, and unimpaired nature of the original manuscripts in part (words, syllables, and even letters) and in whole (including historical narrative), as the written word of God." Bengel "is one Pietist (and a significant one) who cannot be claimed as an ally in opposition to evangelical formulations of the doctrine of inerrancy of Scripture." Citing other studies as well as his own, Thompson concludes that the doctrine of inerrancy was not a novelty introduced by Reformed theologians in the nineteenth century; rather, "Bengel's belief as a Lutheran Pietist in the inerrancy of the 'original autographs' falls within a broad tradition that stretches throughout the history of the church."[22]

Brown's book recognizes important differences between the Pietists and the Orthodox in seventeenth- and eighteenth-century Germany, but without seeing the differences as experiential versus doctrinal. A quite different picture of Pietism, drawn against the background of the rise of the New Evangelicalism after World War II, emerges in a study done by C. John Weborg. "Pietism and evangelicalism are critiques—pietism of orthodoxy, whether Lutheran or Reformed; and evangelicalism of both fundamentalism and liberalism. Pietism has sought the life and liveliness of faith, evangelicalism more the truth of faith." Even though Weborg is referring to the "new evangelicalism" of recent decades, he is seeing Pietism as a contrasting movement different over time from evangelicalism, rather than saying that recent evangelicalism has lost some original Pietist influence. Part of the contrast is in ecclesiology, which "has not received its due in pietism studies." If it had, the charges of inwardness and subjectivity "would have been mitigated to some extent. I argue that pietism seeks a sociological apologetic for the gospel, where coherence is looked for between Scripture

---

[21] Alan J. Thompson, "The Pietist Critique of Inerrancy? J. A. Bengel's *Gnomon* as a Test Case," *Journal of the Evangelical Theological Society* 47 (March 2004): 76. My discussion here is based on the Thompson article, which cites a significant number of authors espousing the view described in the quotation above.

[22] Ibid., 87, 88. Thompson arrives at these conclusions after, among other matters, study of Bengel's hermeneutical method, rationale for textual criticism, analysis of specific texts, discussion of the historical portions of the Scripture, and harmonization of Scripture (passim).

and life."[23] More telling, "Pietism offers caution to the American revival tradition with which it is often identified." Pietists certainly had a strong belief in conversion, but not to the extent of making it "a discernible moment of decision." This may derive in part from the Lutheran doctrine of baptism, in part from "organic and biological language [which] tends more toward process than to decisive moments," and in part from what Weborg has developed in the article, a phenomenology of religion that did not specify the when, before, or after of conversion. "More interest was expressed in living faith and its fruit than in the nature and time of its beginning."[24] In Weborg's view, Pietism and evangelicalism are really separate movements, rather than the former being influential in creating the latter.

What we have in Brown and the other studies is a picture of Pietism that shows a shift in emphasis, and a theology that develops with it, but not a move away from doctrine nor even a move away from an interest in doctrine, including the doctrine of Scripture. For the Lutheran Pietists of the seventeenth and eighteenth centuries the various confessions are still in place. More radically in Weborg is the contention that Pietists may not have been interested in doctrine, but this lack of interest means they are not one of the constitutive foundations for evangelicalism. Egon Gerdes walks a middle way: for the Pietists, "the ordering of life is more fundamental than the ordering of doctrine."[25] But as we have seen, for the Pietists doctrine still needs to be "ordered."

JOHN WESLEY AND THE METHODISTS

Since it was John Wesley and the Methodists who were the major "carriers" of Pietism in America, we will look at them in some detail, then address several other groups more briefly. The Great Awakening in America was called the Evangelical Revival in England, and John Newton (1725–1807), the one-time slave trader who wrote "Amazing Grace," illustrates much of the British experience of early evangelicalism. "Newton and his contemporaries did not use the word 'evangelical' very often, but they used the word 'Gospel' (usually with capitalized initial) to the same effect as a ubiquitous prefix of

---

[23] C. John Weborg, "Pietism: Theology in Service of Living Toward God," in *The Variety of American Evangelicalism*, 161-183. The quotations are from 161, 164. Later, Weborg says, "[i]t may be the case that [the new] evangelicalism has more to do with classical pietism than pietism with evangelicalism" (174).
[24] Ibid., 178.
[25] Gerdes, "Theological Tenets," 37. An object lesson from the Orthodox point of view was the relatively rapid loss of orthodoxy at Halle. Founded in 1692 under Pietist influence, it "very early incorporated rationalism into its faculties and its theology, first mixing rationalism with Pietism, and then promoting rationalism itself, especially after 1740 when Christian Wolf returned to the faculty" (Robert F. Scholz, "Henry Melchior Muhlenberg's Relation to the Ongoing Pietist Tradition," in *Lutheranism and Pietism*, 50).

approval." So there were Gospel clergy, Gospel sermons, Gospel conversa-tion, and sinners rejoiced to see Gospel light. The central emphasis in the eigh-teenth century was upon conversion, and in Newton's *Authentic Narrative* we see "how an evangelical version of the self was shaped by the central theme of personal conversion." Though Newton was a Calvinist, he saw him-self as a "middleman" among the various groups in the Evangelical Revival, all of whom had "a common experience and understanding of the gospel [which] formed the basis for identifying those who were regarded as within or without the evangelical milieu (the 'Gospel world'), whether from the Established Church or Dissent."[26]

Party elements like periodicals came soon enough (the first one, *Gospel Magazine, or Spiritual Library, Designed to Promote Religion, Devotion, and Piety, from Evangelical Principles,* appeared in 1766, and embraced both Dissenters and Churchmen), but at the time "evangelical" was less a party word and more a theological term. Newton "chiefly emphasized human depravity, Christ's atonement, and sanctification by the Spirit and the Word. . . . John Wesley offered a similar reduced creed of essentials in 1764: original sin, justification by faith, and holiness. These were evangelical basics." Like other Church of England ministers Newton subscribed to the Thirty-nine Articles, but it was theology *and conversion* that made an evan-gelical. At times in his correspondence he inquired about those who were "awakened clergy," i.e., had had a conversion experience. How did Newton and others recognize those awakened clergy? It was "their common belief in a simple but supernatural gospel, their common experience of climactic con-version, and their common commitment to a style of preaching aimed at 'awakening' sinners in their need of the gospel." Their commonness did not prevent quite different theologies, of course; Hindmarsh has a convenient summary of four "[d]istinct theological positions maintained during the Evangelical Revival," ranging from Evangelical Arminianism to High Calvinism, which underscores the variety of evangelicals.[27]

Newton is important in demonstrating the common characteristics of persons in the Evangelical Revival, among them John Wesley, but of course Wesley was much more influential. Having noted above Wesley's reduced list

---

[26] D. Bruce Hindmarsh, *John Newton and the English Evangelical Tradition Between the Conversions of Wesley and Wilberforce* (Oxford: Clarendon, 1996), 1, 15, 115.

[27] Ibid., 116, 117-118, 124. Bebbington says that conversion was, in the eighteenth century, the most emphasized of the characteristics of evangelicalism. Hindmarsh agrees, noting that "in the first generations of the evangelical movement, the immediate experience of God's grace came first" (D. Bruce Hindmarsh, "'I Am a Sort of Middleman': The Politically Correct Evangelicalism of John Newton," in *Amazing Grace: Evangelicalism in Australia, Britain, Canada, and the United States,* ed. George A. Rawlyk and Mark A. Noll [Grand Rapids, Mich.: Baker, 1993], 17-18).

of creedal essentials, it is worth pointing out that this list did not constitute his whole creed. Thomas Oden contends that Wesley's Twenty-five Articles (based on the Church of England's Thirty-nine Articles) "are older than Wesleyan theology by two centuries," and "stand in the moderate center of the Protestant confessional tradition. . . . The *Articles* intend to preserve the unity of the body of Christ and guard against false, unscriptural teaching."[28] Oden quotes approvingly, "[t]he theology of American Methodism is essentially that of the Anglican Church in all things which according to that Church and the general consent of Christianity are necessary to theological orthodoxy or the doctrines of grace, unless the entire omission of the historically equivocal Seventeenth Article on 'Predestination and Election' be considered an exception."[29]

But what of Wesley's famous "catholic spirit" sermon, preached in 1750, at times summed up with his phrase "if your heart is as my heart, give me your hand"? Both Oden in a 1994 book and H. O. Thomas in an article published in the Fall 2001 issue of *Wesleyan Theological Journal* address the question. Wesley distinguished between essentials and opinions. Aware of criticism that Methodists were simply "enthusiasts," i.e., guilty of making opinions into essentials to the loss of the genuine essentials, Wesley assured a recipient of one of his letters in 1745 "that no singularities are more, or near so much, insisted on by me as the general, uncontroverted truths of Christianity."[30] This means that the "catholic spirit" is exercised in the context of the orthodox faith, for as Oden says, "Wesley distinctly rejects doc-

---

[28] Thomas C. Oden, *Doctrinal Standards in the Wesleyan Tradition* (Grand Rapids, Mich.: Francis Asbury Press, 1988), 99, 100, 106; Oden charts a comparison of the Thirty-Nine Articles, the Twenty-Five Articles and the Augsburg Confession (101-103). A recently published volume, *"Heart Religion" in the Methodist Tradition and Related Movements*, ed. Richard B. Steele (Lanham, Md.: Scarecrow, 2001) confirms Oden's emphasis. Steele says in the introduction, "we must underscore the fact that an authentically Wesleyan theology does not *reduce* Christian faith to religious emotion. On the contrary, it regards faith as 'a cord of three strands,' a dynamic complex of three distinct and equally necessary ways by which a Christian stands related to the living God. These we shall call 'right belief,' 'right conduct,' and 'right passion' [more technically, orthodoxy, orthopraxy, and orthopathy]." On the first, Wesley expected his followers "to regard the Christian Scripture as the preeminent source of God's self-revelation, and to accept the doctrines of orthodox Christianity, as summarized in the ecumenical creeds, as the hermeneutical norms for rightly understanding and applying the biblical message" (xxii; emphasis his). A differing view is Ernest F. Stoeffler, "Pietism, the Wesleys, and Methodist Beginnings in America," in the work he edits, *Continental Pietism and Early American Christianity* (Grand Rapids, Mich.: Eerdmans, 1976), who dismisses the importance of the Articles of Religion for American Methodists because the Articles "contain nothing specifically related to the religious dynamic of historic Methodism. They simply indicated to the fathers of the movement that Methodism is not severed from the stream of the historically continuous religious self-understanding of Christians" (197). By contrast, Wesley's *Standard Sermons* and his *Notes Upon the New Testament* are much more important, and Stoeffler attempts to make the case they are heavily influenced by Pietism (196-206).

[29] Abel Stevens, *History of the Methodist Episcopal Church in the United States of America*, 3 vols. (New York: Carlton & Porter, 1864–1867), 2:206, cited in Oden, *Doctrinal Standards in the Wesleyan Tradition*, 106.

[30] Cited in H. O. Thomas, Jr., "John Wesley: Conception of 'Connection' and Theological Pluralism," *Wesleyan Theological Journal* 36 (Fall 2001): 96.

trinal latitudinarianism and sets out [in the sermon] the doctrinal core assumed in the catholic spirit."[31] The doctrinal core includes God and his attributes, providence, Christ, justification by grace through faith, and the Holy Spirit and the Christian life. Where is the Bible in all this? It is the source of the doctrinal core.[32] Thomas summarizes for us: "[i]mplicit evangelical faith which already presupposed certain experiential and objective theological realities was the pre-understanding for Christian union of those with differing 'opinions.'"[33]

Thus, as innovative as Wesley may have been in some regards, the innovations did not include moving away from, nor muting, orthodox Christianity. In a book replete with all kinds of theological debate and discussion, Richard P. Heitzenrater says Wesley "was not hesitant to accept radical manifestations of the work of the Holy Spirit, but he was also cautious enough to measure such experiences by biblical norms to test their authenticity. Although he allowed for extraordinary gifts of the Spirit, Wesley was prone to emphasize the ordinary gifts—love, peace, joy. Although his aim was to reform and renew the Church, the limits of his reverence for ecclesial authority and order were determined as much by his understanding of the Early Church as by the rules of the Church of England."[34]

Not only that, it is also the case that Wesley was involved in a number of doctrinal disputes. Heavily influenced early on by the Moravians, Wesley nevertheless came to believe that their emphasis on "stillness" doctrine was wrong. Stillness meant that until someone had assurance of full faith the person ought to remain "still"—abstaining from the means of grace, such as the communion service, until the assurance came. Wesley argued for degrees of faith, and the use of the ordinances like baptism and communion to strengthen one's faith, even contending that communion was a "converting ordinance," not just a "confirming" ordinance. The conflict reached the point in 1740 where Wesley and the Moravians broke permanently over the issue.[35] Another major problem was the Whitefield-Wesley rupture over predestination, symptomatic of a larger Calvinist-Arminian dispute. Wesley's 1740 sermon on "Free Grace," followed by Whitefield's open letter on the subject

---

[31] Oden, *Doctrinal Standards*, 97.
[32] Thomas C. Oden, *John Wesley's Scriptural Christianity: A Plain Exposition of His Teaching on Christian Doctrine* (Grand Rapids, Mich.: Zondervan, 1994), 55-64; note the series of statements on page 56.
[33] Thomas, "Conception of 'Connection,'" 98.
[34] Richard P. Heitzenrater, *Wesley and the People Called Methodists* (Nashville: Abingdon, 1995), 319.
[35] See the account, among other places, in Warren Thomas Smith, "Eighteenth Century Encounters: Methodist-Moravian," *Methodist History* 24 (April 1986): 141-156. Though the break was made in 1740, recurring stillness problems "did not disappear. For years there were local outbreaks and periodic purgings" (Henry D. Rack, *Reasonable Enthusiast: John Wesley and the Rise of Methodism* [Nashville: Abingdon, 1993], 204).

early in 1741, brought the predestination issue to a head and produced a division at Wesley's Foundery Chapel. Though the two men did cooperate on later occasions on a personal level, they never reconciled on the issue, and their respective proponents formed sides in the revival. In later phases of the Calvinist controversy, at different times in the 1750s through the 1770s, the acrimony reached a high level on both sides. It seems fair to conclude that Wesley had a strong interest in doctrine, his "catholic spirit" modified by doctrinal issues.[36]

In a 1999 article on Wesley's relation to both Puritanism and Pietism, Scott Kisker asserts that "Wesley's heritage is not Puritanism [per se], but a type of experiential piety which found expression in certain wings of English Puritanism." Therefore it's a mistake to think that Wesley was theologically close to Puritan Calvinism. What he was close to were Puritans like Richard Baxter, who "[t]hough not ambivalent toward systematic theology, . . . felt no compulsion to tow the line on Reformed orthodoxy." Pietistic Puritans like Baxter are the ones to whom Wesley was drawn, and then only to their pietistic side. To show this, Kisker notes that of "the Puritan authors Wesley reprints, all with the exception of John Fox [*sic*] were active in the time that . . . pietistic Puritanism was coming to the fore." Absent a detailed study of the thirty authors Kisker lists, to draw this general connection is dubious at best.[37]

But, even granting Kisker's general point that Wesley was selective in his reprinting of works, surely the very act of selecting was based (at least in part) on theological considerations. And Kisker supports this inference in discussing some of Wesley's other theological concerns. Wesley tied together Pietist perfectionism, Puritan moralism, and the devotionalism of the mystics "within the structure and doctrine of the Church of England." In spite of Moravian influences Wesley "did not adopt a form of Lutheranism, nor did he adopt the evangelical Calvinism of the revivalists with whom he began outdoor preaching." He broke with the Moravians over the "[i]ssues of sanctification, and particularly of the role of works in salvation." "Despite shared history, contacts, and spiritual experiences, the conflict over doctrine between Whitefield and Wesley began early." Wesley's *Predestination Calmly Considered* (1752) "offers a very negative, and not necessarily 'calm,' view

---

[36] The Whitefield-Wesley split is recounted often; a handy summary of it is in Rack, *Reasonable Enthusiast,* 198-202. Rack also discusses the later Calvinist controversies (ibid., 450-461).

[37] Scott Kisker, "John Wesley's Puritan and Pietist Heritage Reexamined," *Wesleyan Theological Journal* 34 (Fall 1999): 266, 270, 270-271. Wesley was famous for reprinting the writings of others, implicitly approving the writings unless he stated demurrals about some points. An interesting study of Wesley reprinting, with demurrals, several works of a noteworthy Calvinist is Charles A. Rogers, "John Wesley and Jonathan Edwards," *Duke Divinity School Review* 31 (Winter 1966): 20-38.

of Calvinism." In all these matters it appears that Wesley too was "not ambivalent toward systematic theology."[38]

On the American scene, evangelicals made their presence felt up and down the colonial seaboard in the eighteenth century. Besides the obvious names, George Whitefield and Jonathan Edwards, many were active in the years during and following the Great Awakening, including Methodists. Already in North Carolina by the 1760s, says Richard Rankin, the new lights, as the evangelicals of the mid-eighteenth century were called, "anxiously sought a sensible experience of conversion, which they understood to be a spiritual rebirth that indicated that God had rescued them from sin and death." This shared experience became a social bond, enhanced by the belief that "endowed the convert with a new set of holy affections" with which to live. In contrast, nonevangelical Anglicans "understood religious affections to be a natural endowment that only needed to be cultivated within the church to come to fruition, not a supernatural quality that was transplanted at the moment of conversion as for evangelicals. . . . The power of evangelical preaching was the main attraction. Methodist ministers delivered sermons with authority and conviction because they knew what it meant to be 'born again.'"[39]

Dee E. Andrews says that until his death in 1770, Whitefield dominated the evangelical networks in America, "effectively excluding Wesleyan influence and preserving a distinctly Calvinist tone to the American revivals." But in the 1760s Methodists began arriving, and they soon were to change the tone. The dominant features of the American Methodists were "experimental" religion, revival as the primary means to produce the experimental religion, and "missionizing," i.e., preaching the gospel at every opportunity. Nor was doctrine absent: "Dwelling on the Christian doctrines of original sin, redemption through Christ's sacrifice and resurrection, free will, justification, and final judgment as well as the perfectionist emphasis on the Holy Spirit's transformation of the emancipated heart, Methodist preaching, like that of other evangelical movements, impressed its hearers as inspired oratory."[40]

---

[38] Kisker, "John Wesley's Puritan and Pietist Heritage Reexamined," 266, 275, 277. It is true that Wesley in one of his writings said only a "hair's breadth" separated him from Calvinism at some points, but the "some" turns out to be the matter of salvation by grace, and even that is modified by Wesley's view of free will (278).

[39] Richard Rankin, *Ambivalent Churchmen and Evangelical Churchwomen: The Religion of the Episcopal Elite in North Carolina, 1800–1860* (Columbia, S.C.: University of South Carolina Press, 1993), 3, 31.

[40] Dee E. Andrews, *The Methodists and Revolutionary America, 1760–1800: The Shaping of an Evangelical Culture* (Princeton, N.J.: Princeton University Press, 2000), 31, 78. She gives virtually the same list when commenting on an 1809 book by Methodist James Snowden: the Methodists were marked by "their straightforward doctrine, encompassing the basic Christian teachings (as seen through the prism of Wesleyan interpretation) of original sin, justification by faith, the free agency of the believer, the free grace of God, and the second conversion of holiness" (237).

Philip N. Mulder's very recent study of evangelicalism in the South among Baptists, Presbyterians, and Methodists shows this same theological concern, though from another angle. Mulder contends that the eighteenth-century awakenings produced a New Light religion, stressing conversion, and ecumenical in intent. But, in contrast to what most studies say, he believes that New Light religion was not the same as evangelicalism. His study of Baptists and Presbyterians shows "how they adapted the techniques of awakening for their own purposes, and it traces how Methodists, founded in the awakenings, fell into the same pattern in their pursuit of converts." The adaptation constitutes the creation of evangelicalism. The ecumenism ideal held until the Revolution, but once the common ecclesiastical enemy, the Church of England, was removed, the three denominations turned to inter-group competition. Denominational issues actually began in the eighteenth-century awakening for Baptists and Presbyterians, for they each developed pro- and anti-New Light factions. These internal separations were more or less healed in that era, but once the post-revolutionary period began, all three denominations set about distinguishing themselves from one another. "In their contemporary preoccupations with each other, they substituted the new term, 'evangelical,' as they transformed New Light concern for the universal into obsession with the particular." Clearly, we are looking here at both rituals and doctrine, the very things that Grenz says were so muted by the eighteenth- and early nineteenth-century evangelicals. Even the "comparatively ecumenical" Methodists (with no pre-awakenings history to cloud the ecumenical ideal) "would stumble in the post-Revolutionary era of evangelicals."[41]

While we can question whether Mulder is correct in saying that evangelicalism, rather than deriving from the awakenings, is a movement that made use of awakenings for denominational purposes, after reading his and Kisker's studies it is difficult to rule out concern for doctrine and rituals among the evangelical denominations. Contrary to Grenz and others, then, doctrinal matters are present from the beginning, even in what many say is among the most pietistic of the denominations, the Methodists.

When black Methodists chose to separate from white Methodists early in the nineteenth century, one of the matters they did not separate on was Methodist belief. Both the African Methodist Episcopal Church (AME), founded in 1816, and the African Methodist Episcopal Church, Zion

---

[41] Philip N. Mulder, *A Controversial Spirit: Evangelical Awakenings in the South* (New York: Oxford University Press, 2002), 5, 8, 9. By the time of the Second Awakening, "[c]ompetition and differentiation became the essential element of evangelical religion. . . . Earlier New Lights had been content to spread the gospel of active Christianity, but evangelicals had a more specific calling" (136). In Mulder's hands the New Light versus evangelicalism pattern prevails throughout American Christianity's history (170-171).

(AMEZ), founded in 1821, stayed with Methodist teaching. For the AMEZ, "Zion's founders adopted, with only minor modifications, the *Book of Discipline,* Twenty-Five Articles of Religion, and the ecclesiastical structure of the mother church." For the AME, "[t]he *Discipline,* Articles of Religion, and General Rules of the Methodist Episcopal Church were adopted as their own, except that the office of presiding elder was abolished."[42]

Moreover, doctrinal concerns were also evident in the Methodist-dominated holiness movement. Melvin Dieter, noted holiness historian, sees the holiness movement as "a unique and distinct composite of the development of American evangelicalism." In the pre-Civil War era holiness created "a new emphasis in American revivalism by applying the logic of revivalism to the special promotion of Wesleyan perfectionism." In the years after the Civil War, holiness became a permanent emphasis "in the thought and life of all of evangelical Protestantism around the world." Dieter subscribes to the notion that holiness had both a Puritan and a Pietist background, "the 'puritan' element generally used to denote the revivalists' concerns for morality, conduct, and the reform of the church and society according to the laws of God; 'pietist' is used to refer to their concern for individual Christian experience, centering in both conversion and sanctification—all under the direct and personal guidance and power of the Holy Spirit."[43]

How the holiness movement changed from an attempt at leavening all the churches, beginning with its "natural" home, the Methodist Episcopal Church (MEC), to a series of holiness associations related to holiness revivalists and eventually to the creation of a number of separate holiness denominations is a complex story.[44] But by the 1880s tensions between holiness advocates and their opponents within the MEC had reached an impasse. By the next decade the MEC had "moved beyond" Wesley's holiness teaching:

> Supported by a radical transition in the scholarship in its theological institutions in the last decade of the century, the [ME] church turned to the new and green pastures in more modern teachers and theologies. The legacy of entire sanctification, with whatever modifications may have been made to

---

[42] On the AMEZ, see Larry G. Murphy, J. Gordon Melton, and Gary L. Ward, eds., *Encyclopedia of African American Religions* (New York: Garland Publishing, 1993), 9. On the AME, see Emory Stevens Bucke, *History of American Methodism,* 3 vols. (New York: Abingdon, 1964), 1:606.

[43] Melvin Easterday Dieter, *The Holiness Revival of the Nineteenth Century,* 2nd ed. (Lanham, Md.: Scarecrow, 1996), 8, 9; the Puritan and Pietist quotation is on page 12 n. 25.

[44] And in regard to that natural home: "In 1876, American Methodism, in spite of being divided in its organizational structure, was predominantly of one voice in its theology. The evangelical Arminianism which it had received from John Wesley guided the main stream of Methodist preaching" (Gerald O. McCulloch, "The Changing Theological Emphases," in *History of American Methodism,* 2:593). McCulloch goes on to survey the changes in Methodist theology in the decades following the Civil War, culminating in two famous heresy trials shortly after 1900 (594-599).

it during the course of the American deeper life revival, was now being surrendered, in large part, to the holiness movement; it had become difficult
for the tradition to survive within its original Methodist Episcopal Church
and Methodist Episcopal Church South home.[45]

Beginning in 1880 several new Wesleyan holiness denominations were
formed, accompanied by the establishment of schools where holiness teaching could be freely stressed. Most of the new denominations retained an affinity with Methodism in articles of faith and in structure. And some holiness
organizations stayed in the ME church. The events are recounted by Timothy
L. Smith, a Church of the Nazarene historian, in a lengthy article in the three-
volume history of Methodism published in 1964. Smith blames the rift in part
on "a rural and more radical phase of the holiness revival" that appeared
after 1875, with independent holiness organizations, associations, and evangelists, which led to the option of "come-outism" in relation to the MEC.
This was aided by bishops who feared the separatist tendencies of the holiness movement, and rebuffed some of the holiness pleas for more emphasis
on Wesley's perfection doctrine. In turn, on the anti-holiness wing, two books
appeared, one in 1888 and the other in 1895, questioning the whole belief
about second blessing or perfection. This, compounded by a growing liberal
tendency in the denomination's schools, meant that "Methodist leaders in
both the North and the South witnessed a growing disruption of fellowship
in their communions which they seemed powerless to halt."[46] The holiness
groups broke from the parent bodies largely over doctrinal issues.

As we have seen, Grenz says that there was "little interest" in matters of
precision about biblical infallibility and inerrancy before 1820. A recent study
of Reformed thought shows the interest to be far more than "little." Ernest
Sandeen, in his *The Roots of Fundamentalism* (1970), had argued that
inerrancy was a late-nineteenth-century creation, particularly of two
Princeton Seminary professors, A. A. Hodge and B. B. Warfield. And since
inerrancy is a hallmark of fundamentalism, then fundamentalism is an aber-

---

[45] Dieter, *Holiness Revival*, 256.
[46] Timothy L. Smith, "Controversy and Disruption," in *History of American Methodism*, 2:618, 626;
Smith lists the schools (624-625). A recent summary of Nazarene belief is Wes Tracy and Stan Ingersol,
What Is a Nazarene? Understanding Our Place in the Religious Community (Kansas City, Mo.: Beacon
Hill, 1998): "Nazarene beliefs are founded first of all in the Bible and classic Christian doctrines. Our
Articles of Faith descend from the Thirty-nine Articles of Religion of the Church of England as amended
and abridged by John Wesley into the Twenty-five Articles of Methodism" (16). The Nazarene Articles
of Faith and statements on The Church (161-165) include reference to the "plenary inspiration of the
Holy Scriptures . . . inerrantly revealing the will of God concerning us in all things necessary to our
salvation" (161). The first of the Wesleyan spin-offs was the Church of God (Anderson, Indiana), dating
to 1880. Earlier separations had created the Wesleyan Methodists (1843; since 1968, the Wesleyan
Church) and the Free Methodists (1866); in both cases the holiness component was only a part of the
background to the divisions.

ration from Reformed thinking. But Ronald Satta's recent article disputes this view and shows clearly that inerrancy was a concept in place well before this time. Thus, despite Sandeen's (and others who follow the idea) notion that there is a split between the Princeton Theology and earlier Reformed thinking, such is not the case. For example, both Archibald Alexander and Charles Hodge, predecessors of Warfield and A. A. Hodge at Princeton, taught inerrancy. Also, "both the ancient and Reformation church traditions possessed a well-defined, carefully articulated and often passionately defended doctrine of biblical authority (which included inerrancy) centuries before the Princetonians promulgated it." This in turn suggests that "regarding the doctrine of biblical authority, Fundamentalism, rather than perverting mainstream Christian orthodoxy, actually extends it."[47]

And what was true of the Reformed was also true of the Methodists, even though some have argued that Methodists did not subscribe to inerrancy, that inerrancy was a peculiarly Reformed theology approach to the biblical text. A very recent paper by Daryl E. McCarthy looks at a number of nineteenth-century American Methodist theologians to test the validity of the assertion. He sees the beginning point of Methodist discussion on scriptural authority in the eighteenth century in the "unequivocal stand for the inspiration and inerrancy of Scripture by John Wesley, Adam Clarke, and Richard Watson—the triumvirate which formed the fountainhead of Wesleyanism."[48]

Proceeding from this base, McCarthy cites the writings of seven nineteenth-century Methodist theologians. Four of the seven—Samuel Wakefield, Thomas Ralston, Miner Raymond, and Randolph S. Foster—clearly defend the doctrine of inerrancy. Wakefield, whose *Complete System of Christian Theology* (1869) was the first major Wesleyan systematic theology to appear after the long domination of Watson's *Institutes,* set the tone: "Affirmation of divine inspiration of Scripture is based on the belief that by God's power the Scriptures were 'infallibly preserved from all error.'" Ralston's 1876 *Elements of Divinity,* Raymond's 1877 *Systematic Theology,* and Foster's 1889 *Evidences of Christianity* agree.[49]

---

[47] Ronald F. Satta, "Fundamentalism and Inerrancy: A Response to the Sandeen Challenge," *Evangelical Journal* 21 (Fall 2003): 66–80. The quotations are from page 80. Satta cites George Marsden's influential work as accepting the Sandeen thesis. On earlier inerrancy, see the comment by Roger Olson, *Story of Christian Theology:* "The Westminster Confession is thoroughly Calvinistic with a distinctly Puritan spin. It emphasizes the verbal inspiration and inerrancy of Scripture" (497).

[48] Daryl E. McCarthy, "Inerrancy in American Methodism During the Nineteenth Century," unpublished paper read at the annual meeting of the Evangelical Theological Society, Atlanta, November 2003.

[49] Ibid. McCarthy quotes Ralston on verbal inspiration: "The very *words,* as well as the *thoughts* [emphasis his] were inspired by the Spirit; [t]he Bible is the 'Word of God.' What the Bible says, God says, what the Bible declares to be true is true" (3). Raymond wrote similarly, the Bible "is pure from any admixture of error and is an authoritative rule of faith and practice . . . what it says, God says" (4).

Daniel D. Whedon's *Statements: Theological and Critical* (1887) marks the first move away from the high view of Scripture, but it was not a large move. He distinguished between "matters of faith and practice" and "secular or historical fact." But even here he argued that while a biblical writer might be discovered in a mistake in the latter, and we are still waiting for such an occurrence to be proved, the authority of the text still stands over us. Thus he "wants to maintain the actual inerrancy of Scripture, while granting the theoretical possibility of errancy without disturbing Scripture's infallibility." So Whedon left unresolved the matter of what to do with "an errant revelation from an unerring God of truth."[50] McCarthy says that John Miley's *Systematic Theology* (1894) is the transition, writing that he "advocated a looser, more dynamic theory of inspiration" and, significantly, "was careful *not* to affirm any type of inerrancy."[51] The full change comes with Milton S. Terry who, in the course of several publications between 1883 and 1907, gradually moved from denying that there were errors in the biblical text to accepting that view. In *Biblical Dogmatics* (1907) Terry arrives at his final judgments: we should "oppose and drive away, so far as we are able, the dogma of verbal inerrancy of the records. . . . the dogma of verbal inerrancy is inconsistent with existing facts, extravagant in its assumptions, and mischievous in its tendency to provoke continual controversy in the church . . . and is a positive hindrance to the rational study of the Bible." We should reject the idea that the Bible *is* the Word of God, which statement is true "only in a loose and inaccurate way of speaking," as a synecdoche.[52]

The change in views on inerrancy described in McCarthy's paper took place in the context of the increasing biblical and theological controversies in Methodism as the denomination, both North and South, moved toward liberalism. "But the drift was irreversible. In the first twenty years of the new century, official Methodism moved away from many traditional Wesleyan doctrines. The Bible came to be understood merely as *Heilsgeschichte*. Affirmation of biblical inerrancy was not only inessential; it was positively harmful." Wesleyanism began with inerrancy in the eighteenth century, and most Wesleyans maintained it in the nineteenth century. It is simply not the case, as some contemporary Wesleyan scholars maintain, that inerrancy was a Reformed theological belief and "has no part in authentic Wesleyan-

---

And Foster: "We must claim for it, therefore, that it is true in its original deliverances, its recitation of facts, and its historical statements from beginning to end; and true in its doctrines and ethics assumed, implied, and enunciated on a fair principle of interpretation" (6).

[50] Ibid., 5.

[51] Ibid., 7, emphasis his.

[52] Ibid., 10, 11.

Arminianism. We have seen that the historical evidence clearly refutes such an allegation. It is in the best of Wesleyan tradition that Wesleyans and Methodists today affirm alongside their Calvinist, Reformed, Pentecostal, Baptist, and Anabaptist brethren, 'The Bible is the inerrant and infallible Word of God.'"[53]

OTHER GROUPS

Most Lutherans who came to America brought Pietism with them. To get at a part of that experience, we will concentrate on two "moments" in American Lutheran history, one in the eighteenth century and the other in the nineteenth. Henry Melchior Muhlenberg (1711–1787), often seen as the patriarch of American Lutheranism, arrived in Pennsylvania in 1745, bringing with him a particular expression of Lutheranism, one that mediated between Orthodoxy and Pietism.[54] "It was this synthesis that Muhlenberg brought to the American colonies, where it served effectively to differentiate the church of the Augsburg Confession from other emerging Christian denominations and where it was applied for the 'cure of souls' within his congregations." The symbols of Lutheranism—the Augsburg Confession, the Formula of Concord, the Smalkald Articles and the Small Catechism—and the "focusing his understanding of Christian piety on Luther's understanding of Baptism as a daily dying and renewal" form the context for his Pietism. When parishioners inquired about the "'exercises of piety,' Muhlenberg urged on them daily reading in the Bible, the Small Catechism and Arndt's *True Christianity.*" The experience element in the Christian life was focused on the "Pauline dynamics of law and Gospel, sin and repentance, flesh and Spirit, the two kinds of righteousness, rebirth through water and the Spirit in the new life of Holy Baptism." Thus, Muhlenberg was "a self-consciously confessional theologian, trained in the dogmatics of Orthodoxy, who deliberately affirmed a moderate Pietism in the service of an inclusive Lutheranism that

---

[53] Ibid., 12, 13.

[54] Robert F. Scholz, "Muhlenberg's Relation," distinguishes among five expressions of Pietism—Spenerian, Wurttemberg, Radical, Halle, Moravianism—and shows that there are common elements among them: "Although many motifs and emphases can be found within these several forms of Pietism one stands out first and foremost—repentance. The concern for genuine repentance that Luther introduced with his attack on penance and the Roman Catholic penitential system in the 95 Theses. . . . Other characteristics common to all the above-mentioned forms of Pietism are *praxis pietas,* personal spiritual awakening, study and use of scripture, revitalization of congregational life, a tendency to democratize life and an ethical concern" (44, 45). Scholz places Muhlenberg in the Spenerian category, "a form of moderate Lutheranism with Orthodox and Pietist elements that eschewed radical Pietism and its separatist conventicles but had room for nonseparating *collegia pietas.* Its Pietism was distinct from Halle Pietism, being traceable to Arndt and Spener, yet open to Halle's considerable influence" (46). For a contrary, and minority, view that contends Muhlenberg did not mediate a position between Orthodoxy and Pietism, see Paul P. Kuenning, *The Rise and Fall of American Lutheran Pietism: The Rejection of an Activist Heritage* (Macon, Ga.: Mercer University Press, 1988), 33-46.

he believed embodied the outlook of Luther and the Lutheran Reformation." The combination of Orthodoxy and Pietism was used "to lay the foundations of Lutheranism in North America."[55]

Muhlenberg's synthesis was not to hold, however. His encounters with more rigidly Orthodox and more rigidly Pietist opponents had diminished by the 1750s, to be replaced with concern over the rise of rationalism, and its potential for a marriage not between Orthodoxy and Pietism but between rationalism and Pietism. After his death, "the confessional stance of the Pennsylvania and New York ministeriums collapsed . . . between 1790 and 1815." As a result, "Pietism in America rapidly lost its confessional and doctrinal content. The theory that informed *praxis pietatis* was now largely a minimalistic, scripturally based, protestantized theology (sometimes with a rationalist overlay) that in its emphasis on sin and salvation focused on the atonement."[56]

In the mid-nineteenth century the contest between Lutheran Orthodoxy and Pietism reemerged, in the form of a debate between Samuel Simon Schmucker of Gettysburg Seminary and Charles Porterfield Krauth of the seminary in Philadelphia over the question of theological authority.[57] Both Schmucker and Krauth, at their respective schools, took oaths of office (each of the men being the author of the oaths). The oaths were similar in many regards, but a major difference was that the word "fundamental" appears in the Gettysburg statement as a qualifier to the full subscription to the confessions, while there is no qualifier in the Philadelphia document. This difference is reflected in how the two teachers approach the biblical texts. On evidences, especially for the Bible's claims, "Schmucker is confident of the rationality of the biblical claim, available to all open and willing to see it. Krauth places his confidence of verification of that claim ultimately in the person come to faith." On the use of the Bible, both men taught their students a proof-text method, but Krauth asked the students to look also for the "system" in the Bible expressed by Lutherans in the confessions. Therefore, though "the Bible

---

[55] Scholz, "Muhlenberg's Relation," 47, 48, 54. Scholz's final words show the combination:

> Orthodoxy supplied a scholastic analysis of the order of salvation; Pietism promoted a hermeneutic for the scriptural interpretation of faith as repentance-centered, focused simultaneously in both justification and sanctification. Muhlenberg's difficulty with Orthodoxy was the rigid separation of justification and sanctification . . . which compartmentalized religious experience; his rule shift to bring the two into proximity was, from the perspective of his practical theology, a pastoral necessity for which he found precedence in Luther (66 n. 66).

Johann Arndt's *True Christianity* (1606) is viewed by a number of scholars as presaging Pietism, and Arndt is seen as the "father" of Pietism; Scholz calls him "pre-pietistic" (42).

[56] Ibid., 51. This loss of interest in, and to some extent opposition to, the confessions is shown in a study by James Lawton Haney, "John George Schmucker and the Roots of His Spirituality," in *Lutheranism and Pietism*, 67-95. J. G. Schmucker (1771–1854) is the father of Samuel Simon Schmucker.

[57] This summary of the debate follows Verlyn O. Smith, "Theological Authority in S. S. Schmucker and C. Porterfield Krauth," in *Lutheranism and Pietism*, 99-118.

is of central and supreme authority for both, that authority is not threatened by confessional subscription for Krauth the way it was for Schmucker."[58] Krauth summarizes his position: "The pure creeds are simply the testimony of the true Church to the doctrines she holds; but as it is the truth they confess, she, of necessity, regards those who reject the truth confessed in the creed, as rejecting the truth set forth in the Word."[59]

Schmucker saw himself as heir to the Pietist tradition, "a faithfully Lutheran tradition. When attacked by the rising confessionalist party, he interpreted the attack as directed against this whole tradition and defended himself by showing adherence to it."[60] But his publication of the *Definite Synodical Platform* of 1855 as the basis for the various Lutheran synods in the General Synod, with its announced "rescension" of the Augsburg Confession, was more than the confessionalists could take. Twelve years later the General Synod Lutherans divided over the *Platform*, a breach not healed until fifty years after that. American Lutherans had a variety of attitudes about and kinds of Pietism, and they configured them differently in relation to the confessions. It seems clear that a single approach—that all Pietists were "open" on the confessions, and all Orthodox were "closed" to Pietism—does not sufficiently allow for the variety of views in the seventeenth through the nineteenth centuries.

The turn of the century in 1900 saw the rise of Pentecostalism, a movement viewed by some as in the Pietist tradition, not so much in the formal sense of direct links to seventeenth-century Pietists as in approach, emphasizing experience over doctrine. An excellent recent study is *Heaven Below: Pentecostals and American Culture* (2001), by Grant Wacker, an evangelical historian with sympathy for the movement.[61] Wacker, who calls the Pentecostals "radical evangelicals," says four streams converged to create the movement. First, that which "emphasized heartfelt salvation through faith in Jesus Christ," a notion dating back to the Great Awakening. "Late-

---

[58] Ibid., 107.

[59] Cited in ibid., 107, 107-108. Strikingly, Smith contends that Schmucker's thinking is more in line with the Enlightenment-rationalism stress on empiricism, and Krauth closer to the idealism of the nineteenth century, almost the reverse of what one would expect philosophically of the two men (110-113).

[60] Ibid., 114.

[61] Grant Wacker, *Heaven Below: Pentecostals and American Culture* (Cambridge, Mass.: Harvard University Press, 2001). Raised in a Pentecostal family, now a member of an evangelical but not charismatic United Methodist Church congregation, Wacker says, "in many ways my heart never left home. Pentecostals continue to be my people. I embrace many of their values" (x). It perhaps goes without saying that Wacker is looking at classic Pentecostalism, but there was a use of the term by some in the late nineteenth century which did not connote speaking in tongues. "None of the groups which became a part of the Church of the Nazarene accepted glossolalia as a genuine spiritual gift, and the adjective 'Pentecostal' in the name of the denomination became so confusing that it was officially dropped by the General Assembly in 1919" (W. T. Purkiser, *Called unto Holiness: Volume 2: The Second Twenty-Five Years, 1933–58* [Kansas City, Mo.: Nazarene Publishing House, 1983], 24).

nineteenth-century evangelicals perpetuated both the ideology and the experience of the new birth with little change. Like their forebears, they made it the nonnegotiable marker that divided Christians from non-Christians." The second stream, Holy Spirit baptism, flowed from three tributaries: Wesley's notion of entire sanctification, the Oberlin perfectionism that appeared prior to the Civil War, and the Keswick movement, dating from 1875—each stressed a postconversion experience, though the Wesleyan doctrine seemed more to emphasize purity and the other two power. Added to this was the emphasis on divine healing that can be traced to mid-nineteenth century proponents in Switzerland, Germany, and Britain who contended that healing was in the atonement. Finally, dispensational premillennialism's emphasis on the imminent return of Christ was the fourth stream. To these streams was added speaking in tongues as an evidence that one had been baptized by the Holy Spirit, the idea particularly developed by Charles Parham as a necessary component in one's spiritual development: conversion, sanctification, tongues.[62]

In the three main theological subgroups in Pentecostalism—Wesleyan trinitarians, Reformed trinitarians, Oneness believers—"virtually all converts would have said that legitimate authority rested finally in the Bible, in the doctrines the Bible contained, and in the Holy Spirit's direct communication of biblical and doctrinal truths. The key point here is that all three sources of authority—Bible, doctrine, and Holy Spirit—served as interlocking components in a single mechanism not subject to historical change." As the "first and final authority" Pentecostals had "an abiding conviction that the Bible had been preserved from errors of any sort—historical, scientific, or theological." Even though the earliest statements of faith used phrases like "all sufficient rule for faith and practice," did this mean, asks Wacker, "that early pentecostals harbored doubts about the Bible's plenary accuracy? Or did it mean that they presupposed it so completely it never occurred to them to raise the question? The evidence, taken in context, strongly suggests the latter explanation." Their approach to understanding the Bible was "[r]igorous literalism—hard and unforgiving—[which] served as an ethic for daily life." Though the Pentecostals did not do much work on systematic theology until the 1950s and later, partly because of the lack of seminary training and because of a lack of emphasis on writing theology, "the simple reason was the supposition that the Bible's words explained themselves."

---

[62] Wacker, *Heaven Below,* 2; the streams are briefly described, pages 2 and 3; on Parham, see page 5. On healing, see Donald Dayton, "The Rise of the Evangelical Healing Movement in Nineteenth-Century America," *Pneuma* 4 (Spring 1982): 1-18.

Nor has this stopped, says Wacker in his epilogue: "Biblical inerrancy and wooden literalism hovered as close to the ground at century's end as they did at the beginning."[63]

As to doctrine, Wacker speaks for the Pentecostal view, saying that "the Bible's teachings should be articulated carefully and defended vigorously. True Christianity began not in the froth of exuberant emotion but in the bedrock of correct thinking." And just how fluid were the Pentecostals? "The evidence for pentecostals' determination to exact goose-step conformity in matters of doctrine is so voluminous it is hard to understand how the contrary notion ever arose." That some of the doctrinal debates centered on relatively smaller issues cannot be doubted, but that doctrine was centrally important cannot be denied. At times, this meant turning on other apostolics (as early Pentecostals sometimes called themselves), or other evangelicals, certainly on the liberalism of mainline Protestantism, on Roman Catholics, and on new religious movements like Christian Science and Mormonism. There were lots of foes to deal with.[64] Pentecostals eagerly sought the experiences of the spiritual gifts, but they did so with doctrine intact.

Where does fundamentalism stand in the mix of evangelicalism? In Joel Carpenter's view, fundamentalism is one more "era" in evangelicalism's history. There was the Methodist era in the first half of the nineteenth century, the holiness era in the latter half, then the fundamentalist era—soon, he believes, to be supplanted by the Pentecostal-charismatic movement creating its own era. Of course during each of the "eras" the name given to the era does not capture all that was going on. To take one example, the Methodist era was not exclusively Methodist in nature; in a parallel way, the fundamentalist era was not exclusively fundamentalist. Carpenter points out that Nazarenes and other holiness groups, Missouri Synod Lutherans, and Pentecostals, all of whom subscribed to the fundamentals of the faith (and some were also strict separationists), had disagreements with fundamentalists, even when fundamentalism "dominated":

> So it went with other groups of evangelical or conservative Protestants who were by their own recognition and affiliation something other than fundamentalist. These many nuances of difference and a relative lack of fel-

---

[63] Wacker, *Heaven Below*, 70, 73, 74, 76, 266.

[64] Ibid., 76, 77; the debates are described on pages 178-184. The Pentecostal denominations had their own statements of faith; e.g., the Assemblies of God (AG), provoked in part by the trinitarian controversy, arrived at its "Statement of Fundamental Truths" in 1916, reproduced in William Menzies, *Anointed to Serve: The Story of the Assemblies of God* (Springfield, Mo.: Gospel Publishing House, 1971), 385-390. If anything, doctrinally, "the AG has become more precise since [its founding in] 1914," says noted AG historian Edith Blumhofer, "Assemblies of God," in *Dictionary of Christianity in America*, ed. Daniel G. Reid et al. (Downers Grove, Ill.: InterVarsity Press, 1990), 87.

lowship (or even contact, in some cases) characterized the American evangelical mosaic of the 1930s and 1940s. Nevertheless, fundamentalism was probably the most broadly influential American evangelical movement in the second third of the twentieth century; its ideas, outlook, and religious "goods and services" penetrated virtually all of the other movements and traditions.[65]

Thus, rather than viewing fundamentalism as an aberration, it can just as well be seen as a subset of the larger movement called evangelicalism, one more example of the rise and fall pattern that "adds another kind of thematic unity to the history of modern evangelicalism. The story adheres not only because there have been some central or 'classic' touchstones of belief and outlook, or because of the continuing dynamic interplay with the evolution of modern society, but also because of this recurring [rise and fall] motif." Switching metaphors, Carpenter says evangelicalism is more like a kaleidoscope than a mosaic, which means that no one paradigmatic viewpoint "can make sense of the whole career of modern evangelicalism."[66]

And, lest we forget, fundamentalism had its own healthy share of concern about what some see as quintessential Pietist interests: sanctification and the development of the Christian life. The Keswick movement is the chief example here. With antecedents in evangelicalism prior to and after the Civil War, Keswick formally began with meetings held in Keswick, England in 1875. Stopping short of the Wesleyan view of "entire sanctification," and the eradication of the propensity to sin, the Keswickians emphasized the overcoming and victorious Christian life: sin cannot be eradicated, but it can be more than suppressed; it can be counteracted. In the 1880s and 1890s this view came to prevail among many non-Wesleyans in the fundamentalist

---

[65] Joel A. Carpenter, *Revive Us Again: The Reawakening of American Fundamentalism* (New York: Oxford University Press, 1997), 237, 9; elsewhere Carpenter says the fundamentalist era is the second quarter of the twentieth century, then almost immediately states it was most influential from the 1920s to the 1960s (237).

[66] Ibid., 238. That fundamentalism was not an aberration is confirmed by Kirsopp Lake in *Religion of Yesterday and Tomorrow* (Boston: Houghton Mifflin, 1925): "It is a mistake, often made by educated men who happen to have but little knowledge of historical theology, to suppose Fundamentalism is a new and strange form of thought. It is nothing of the kind: it is the partial and uneducated survival of a theology that was once universally held by all Christians. How many were there, for instance, in the Christian Churches, in the eighteenth century, who doubted the infallible inspiration of all Scripture? A few, perhaps, but very few. No, the Fundamentalist may be wrong; I think that he is. But it is we who have departed from the tradition, not he" (cited in N. M. de S. Cameron, "The Logic of Infallibility: An Evangelical Doctrine at Issue," *Scottish Bulletin of Evangelical Theology* I [1983]: 39-43, at page 40); see also John Fea: "While there is a tendency to treat fundamentalists as extremists or ecclesiastical outcasts, for the most part they make up a unique part of the American evangelical tradition and should be understood in that light" ("Understanding the Changing Façade of Twentieth-Century American Protestant Fundamentalism: Toward a Historical Definition," *Trinity Journal* 15 [NS] [1994]: 199; Fea has a helpful analysis of the extensive historical literature on fundamentalism in his "American Fundamentalism and Neo-Evangelicalism: A Bibliographic Survey," *Evangelical Journal* 11 [Spring 1993]: 21-30).

movement.[67] By the 1920s "Keswick holiness teaching was thoroughly integrated into the fundamentalist network of Bible schools, summer conferences, and faith missions." Its tie-in with missions was particularly powerful, for "[n]ot only did the 'surrendered life' ethos permeate the independent faith missions . . . but the very act of fully surrendering one's will and all claims to one's life seemed to fundamentalists to point to the mission field." Beyond that, a generation of people were influenced by the devotional writings of widely read authors who "conveyed visions of love, truth, beauty, and holiness with considerable literary artistry."[68] Fundamentalism, too, had its warm piety side.

CONCLUSIONS

First, rooted in the Reformation, Pietism was a movement to "complete the Reformation" by emphasizing the importance of sanctification in the life of believers. A conversion experience, followed by "experimental religion," were its hallmarks, but not to the diminishing of an interest in doctrine.

Second, "Pietism" is a term that covers multiple expressions, from close-to-orthodoxy groups to more free-wheeling groups less interested in doctrine. For the seventeenth and eighteenth centuries, it is safe to say that Spener, Francke, and those immediately influenced by them saw orthodox doctrine as a given; they were not just "oriented toward" doctrine; doctrine was foundational.

Third, on the American scene in particular, most Methodists, most Pentecostals, and some Lutherans married Pietist influences with interest in doctrinal orthodoxy. The view that a formal principle, correct doctrine, was added by nineteenth- and twentieth-century evangelicals to augment and even fundamentally alter the material principle, convertive piety, cannot be sustained. Both principles were there from the beginning.

Fourth, specifically on the Scriptures, it seems clear that belief in an inerrant Bible was not a teaching that began only in the nineteenth century. Such a belief is fundamental for J. A. Bengel, the most noteworthy Pietist Bible

---

[67] A standard description of the Keswick movement, emphasizing the Keswick method, is Steven Barabas, *So Great Salvation: The History and Message of Keswick Convention* (Los Angeles: Revell, 1952). George F. Marsden, *Fundamentalism and American Culture: The Shaping of Twentieth-Century Evangelicalism: 1870–1925* (New York: Oxford University Press, 1980) situates Keswick among the evangelical spirituality systems (72-80), and describes the debates about the Keswick approach (94-101). Among Pentecostals, some groups were Wesleyan, others were Keswickian.

[68] Carpenter, *Revive Us Again,* 81, 82, 85. Even the Princeton Theology was not without its piety. See W. Andrew Hoffecker, *Piety and the Princeton Theologians: Archibald Alexander, Charles Hodge, and Benjamin Warfield* (Phillipsburg, N.J.: Presbyterian & Reformed, 1981). On Hodge, consult the carefully nuanced Mark A. Noll, "Charles Hodge as an Expositor of the Spiritual Life," in *Charles Hodge Revisited: A Critical Appraisal of His Life and Work,* ed. John W. Stewart and James H. Moorhead (Grand Rapids, Mich.: Eerdmans, 2002), 181-216.

scholar of the eighteenth century; was present in the beginnings of the Wesleyan movement; was prevalent among Methodists for most of the nineteenth century; was integral to the holiness movement and its denominational spin-offs; and was a given among the majority of Pentecostals.

Overall, the views of Grenz and those who agree with him on both the nature and role of Pietism in the evangelical movement need significant revision. In terms of the history component, "renewing the center" needs serious rethinking.

11

DEFINING EVANGELICALISM

Chad Owen Brand

IN THE LAST COUPLE OF decades a cottage industry has sprung up among social scientists. The new discipline centers around how to define evangelicals and evangelicalism. James Davison Hunter was one of the first sociologists to give sustained attention to the evangelical movement, in the early 1980s, but since that time scholars have flooded the bookshelves and magazine racks of libraries with so many studies that it would involve another cottage industry just to read them all.[1] Alongside the sociological studies, historians of the church have attempted to position the evangelical movement within the stream of Christian heritage, particularly within the flow of Anglo-American church history. "Evangelical" historians have been the ones most interested in pursuing these studies, for obvious reasons. In 1982 Wheaton College established the Institute for the Study of American Evangelicals. Two years later the Institute's first book, *Evangelicalism in Modern America,* attempted to position the movement with respect to fundamentalism, as well as to earlier revivalism, the sort that is connected to the awakenings in America and Britain in the eighteenth and nineteenth centuries.[2] Evangelical theologians have also taken a stab at defining the movement, both as a matter of course in articulating their ideology as over against liberalism and/or fundamentalism, and in self-conscious reflections on the various issues that supposedly *define* evangelicalism. An example of the former would be such diverse works as Carl

---

[1] James Davison Hunter, *American Evangelicalism: Conservative Religion and the Quandary of Modernity* (New Brunswick, N.J.: Rutgers University Press, 1983). Hunter followed this volume with a second book four years later: idem, *Evangelicalism: The Coming Generation* (Chicago: University of Chicago Press, 1987). Other important studies include John C. Green, James L. Guth, Corwin E. Smidt, and Lyman A. Kellstedt, *Religion and the Culture Wars: Dispatches from the Front* (Lanham, Md.: Rowman & Littlefield, 1996); Christian Smith, *Christian America? What Evangelicals Really Want* (Berkeley: University of California Press, 2000); and James M. Penning and Corwin E. Smidt, *Evangelicalism: The Next Generation* (Grand Rapids, Mich.: Baker, 2002).

[2] George M. Marsden, ed., *Evangelicalism in Modern America* (Grand Rapids, Mich.: Eerdmans, 1984).

Henry's *Uneasy Conscience,* a book that sets evangelicalism over against some of its fundamentalist predecessors, and the various systematic theology texts that have been produced by self-professed evangelical theologians in the last half-century.[3] Evangelical works that are self-conscious reflections on the nature of evangelical theology include both monographs[4] and symposia.[5]

There is a tendency among some recent analysts (and some not-so-recent) to question whether evangelicalism can be defined, or even whether there *is* such a thing at all. Donald Dayton argued that evangelicalism was prominent in America up to the period of Reconstruction after the Civil War, but that it slowly evaporated after that due to the rise of premillennialism, the Princeton theology, and the fundamentalist movement, and that it has yet to stage a comeback.[6] His position is somewhat novel, but it shares with others the fact that evangelicalism is a phenomenon that dates back at least to the evangelical revivals. Donald Bloesch raised the question of the identity of the evangelicals. Are they the New Pietists, the Pentecostals, the evangelists, the "Young Evangelicals," the theologians of the visible evangelical academies?[7] David Wells noted that defining evangelicalism is difficult because its center has become elusive and hard to describe.[8] He goes on to contend that evangelicals since World War II have seen themselves in three different ways: confessional, transconfessional, and charismatic.[9] He then develops that typology and offers the conclusion that as long as we affirm the diversity of these three traditions it is still possible to speak intelligibly of "evangelicalism." More recently D. G. Hart has offered the opinion that there really is no such thing as evangelicalism. "Evangelicalism needs to be relinquished as a religious identity because it does not exist."[10] Hart's point is that evangelicalism was always

---

[3] Carl F. H. Henry, *The Uneasy Conscience of Modern Fundamentalism* (Grand Rapids, Mich.: Eerdmans, 1947); see also the systematic theologies by Wayne Grudem, Millard Erickson, J. Oliver Buswell, James Leo Garrett.

[4] Millard Erickson, *The New Evangelical Theology* (Westwood, N.J.: Revell, 1968); and David F. Wells, *God in the Wasteland: The Reality of Truth in a World of Fading Dreams* (Grand Rapids, Mich.: Eerdmans, 1994).

[5] See, for instance, David F. Wells and John D. Woodbridge, eds., *The Evangelicals: What They Believe, Who They Are, Where They Are Changing* (Nashville: Abingdon, 1975); Kenneth Kantzer, ed., *Evangelical Roots: A Tribute to Wilbur Smith* (Nashville: Thomas Nelson, 1978); and Robert Webber and Donald Bloesch, eds., *The Orthodox Evangelicals: Who They Are and What They Are Saying* (Nashville: Thomas Nelson, 1978).

[6] Donald W. Dayton, *Discovering an Evangelical Heritage* (New York: Harper & Row, 1976), 121-135.

[7] Donald G. Bloesch, *The Future of Evangelical Christianity: A Call for Unity amid Diversity* (New York: Doubleday, 1983), 8-22.

[8] David Wells, "On Being Evangelical: Some Theological Differences and Similarities," in *Evangelicalism: Comparative Studies of Popular Protestantism in North America, the British Isles, and Beyond, 1700–1990,* ed. Mark A. Noll, David W. Bebbington, and George A. Rawlyk (Oxford: Oxford University Press, 1994), 389.

[9] Ibid., 391.

[10] D. G. Hart, *Deconstructing Evangelicalism: Conservative Protestantism in the Age of Billy Graham* (Grand Rapids, Mich.: Baker, 2004), 16.

something chimerical, and that in recent years the unraveling of coalitions in the "movement" simply makes clear that there was no such thing in the first place. He suggests a return to confessional identity and the abandonment of the notion of a transconfessional evangelical movement.[11] While I am sympathetic to Hart's concerns about "unraveling," I am still persuaded that Wells is correct in his typology of distinctions and that the term "evangelical" is still of use in describing the broad coalition of conservative Christianity today.

THE ROOTS OF EVANGELICALISM

I am a Baptist. There is an old saying in the Baptist tradition that if you ask any two Baptists the same question you are liable to get three different answers. Likewise, when one asks about the roots of evangelicalism, one is likely to get different responses depending on whether the respondent is Methodist or Presbyterian, Pentecostal or Holiness. Our approach here will be to make the list of contributors to evangelicalism as broad as is feasible without simply listing a catch-all of every Protestant from A.D. 1600 onward. That is one of the difficulties in finding the genuine roots of the evangelical movement. There is another difficulty as well. Without a working definition of "evangelicalism," how will we know just who are its forebears? The reader who has scanned over the outline of this chapter will have noted that we do not get around to defining evangelical theology per se until after we explore its roots. This is something like putting the historical cart before the ideological horse. How do you match the cart to the horse without first examining the animal? Since I believe it is important to get the historical survey down as a prelude to discussing theology, we will have to begin with an assumed and abbreviated definition of what evangelical theology is, and then we can refine it in the next section of this essay. By "evangelicalism" I am referring to a movement within generally North American and British circles that emphasizes the classic Protestant doctrines of the authority and reliability of Scripture, the triune God, and the historical second coming of Christ, and which promotes the need for fervent evangelism, a conversion experience, and a life of discipleship before God.

So, just what are the proximate roots of the evangelical movement? Out of what soil did it spring? Can we have any sense of confidence that our answers to this question are historically plausible?

---

[11] Ibid., 32.

Eighteenth-Century Awakenings

The evangelical revival that sprouted up around the ministries of John Wesley and George Whitefield in England was nothing if not unexpected. That such a revival would begin in the Arminian Church of England rather than among the Calvinist dissenters made it even more of a wonder, since these dissenters had long spoken of the need for such a renewal.[12] The common threads that held together personalities (and theologies) as disparate as those of Wesley and Whitefield are significant for our study. One of the key factors that led to the revival was the threat of rationalism, seen by the participants in the revival as the enemy of revelation.[13] In part this was an infidel rationalism, but Wesley was also the foe of the kind of Christian rationalism that substituted general revelation for the dogmas of Scripture.[14] In the years after the failure of Cromwell's attempt to reform the Church of England through the influence of Independent Calvinistic Puritans, a resurgent "liberalism" flooded the higher universities in England. These theologians were united in their opposition to the sort of Calvinism represented by John Owen, Thomas Goodwin, and even John Milton. Earlier Anglican Arminians, such as John Goodwin and Richard Hooker, were orthodox, but even they found some consolation in the rising Socinianism, since the new rationalists agreed with their anti-Calvinist stance. John Goodwin refused to condemn the Socinians as heretics, though he found Calvinist doctrine "ever and anon gravellish in my mouth and corroding and fretting to my bowels."[15] The move toward Socinianism took root in the work of John Bidle, John Knowles, and Henry Hedworth, and by the early eighteenth century luminaries such as John Locke and Isaac Newton would openly espouse not simply Socinianism but Unitarianism.[16] As Unitarianism turned to deism, even the young John Wesley would be nearly caught in its snare. At Oxford one of his peers almost convinced Wesley to follow the new path, and in 1738 during a spiritual crisis he agonized over whether the Bible was "a cunningly devised fable."[17]

The revival was an antidote, or, better, an apologetic in defense of scriptural Christianity over against all of that. "The world in which the Wesleyans

---

[12] John Walsh, "'Methodism' and the Origins of English-Speaking Evangelicalism," in *Evangelicalism: Comparative Studies of Popular Protestantism in North America, the British Isles, and Beyond, 1700–1990,* 22.

[13] Ibid., 23.

[14] I am focusing more on Wesley than on Edwards or Whitefield in this section since Wesley is sometimes co-opted by postconservatives as their ally over against the more Calvinistic strain in the revival.

[15] John Goodwin, *Redemption Redeemed,* quoted in H. John McLachlan, *Socinianism in Seventeenth-Century England* (Oxford: Oxford University Press, 1951), 52.

[16] Ibid., 163-339.

[17] Vivian H. H. Green, *The Young Mr. Wesley* (London: Arnold, 1961), 147-148.

flourished believed that [deist] criticism of Christianity was being refuted by a visible display of divine power in everyday life."[18] In addition, Wesley stood squarely in the tradition that affirmed the trustworthiness of the Bible. For Wesley, the Bible was "the only standard of truth, and the only model of pure religion."[19] Wesley further held that the Bible was free from all error. "Nay, if there be any mistakes in the Bible, there may as well be a thousand. If there be one falsehood in that book, it did not come from the God of truth."[20] He also maintained that every part of Scripture came from God. "Every part thereof is worthy of God; and all together are one entire body, wherein is no defect or excess."[21] Further, the Bible alone was the source for theological construction. Wesley referred to himself as a "man of one book."[22] Though the Wesleyan tradition would develop a system of theological formulation known as the Wesleyan Quadrilateral, for Wesley, Scripture was the source for theology, and all else was subordinate.[23]

A second factor that explains the rise of the revivals was the spiritual and moral malaise in church and society of that day, both in England and in the American colonies. In England drunkenness was epidemic. One house in four in London was a gin house. The sign that hung over one such house said, "Drunk, one shilling. Dead drunk, two shillings. Free straw."[24] There were over 160 crimes for which a person could be hanged, including pickpocketing more than five shillings or stealing a loaf of bread from a baker. Since poverty was extreme, lots of bread-thieves were hanged, including not a few under the age of twelve. Life was, truly, "nasty, brutish, and short." Anglican priests were often paid less than fifty pounds a year salary (nowhere near subsistence), while high-ranking bishops often earned salaries of seven thousand pounds or more.[25] This resulted in pastors neglecting their churches in order to make money to raise their families.

The situation was similar in America. The once-vibrant Puritan Congregationalists of New England had slipped into a cycle of legalism to

---

[18] John Kent, *Wesley and the Wesleyans: Religion in Eighteenth-Century Britain* (Cambridge: Cambridge University Press, 2002), 49.

[19] John Wesley, *A Plain Account of Christian Perfection,* vol. 11 in *The Works of John Wesley* (Grand Rapids, Mich.: Zondervan, 1959), 367.

[20] John Wesley, *The Journal of the Rev. John Wesley, A. M.,* ed. Nehemiah Curnock, 7 vols. (London: Epworth Press, 1909), 6:117.

[21] John Wesley, "Preface" to his *Explanatory Notes upon the New Testament,* quoted in Wilbur T. Dayton, "Infallibility, Wesley, and British Wesleyanism," in *Inerrancy and the Church,* ed. John Hannah (Chicago: Moody Press, 1984), 229.

[22] R. P. Heitzenrater, *John Wesley, His Own Biographer,* vol. 1 of *The Elusive Mr. Wesley* (Nashville: Abingdon, 1984), 149.

[23] Dayton, "Infallibility, Wesley, and British Wesleyanism," 236-246.

[24] Earle E. Cairns, *An Endless Line of Splendor* (Wheaton, Ill.: Tyndale, 1986), 52.

[25] Of the 10,000 parishes in England, 6,000 paid less than fifty shillings a year (ibid., 53).

such a degree that the patriarch, Increase Mather, penned a critique in 1702, *The Glory Departing from New England*. Jonathan Edwards would discover after taking the pulpit in Northampton from his deceased grandfather that he had many "Mr. And Mrs. Goodman's" in his church, but few "Mr. And Mrs. Gospel's."[26] The situation on the American frontier was even worse. One Anglican survey of frontier life in the mid-1700s indicated that over 90 percent of young women were pregnant on their wedding day.[27] Alcoholism was rife; life on the frontier was brutal. Whether we are talking about the situation in the cultured eastern cities or on the uncouth frontier, there was a decided need for spiritual renewal.

Such renewal did not seem likely to break forth from the prevailing Protestant establishments in either England or the colonies. The Anglican colonies were in a spiritual malaise and New England was, as Increase Mather noted, at a low spiritual ebb. The fact that First Church in Boston was pastored by the Arminian Charles Chauncy, whatever one's opinion on Arminianism, is an indication of the shift that had taken place since staunch Calvinists John Cotton and Richard Mather had arrived in Massachusetts nearly a century earlier. "By 1750 Boston was a vastly different place than it had been in 1640. Theologically, no one was in charge."[28] The awakening that took place under Jonathan Edwards in the Connecticut River valley in 1734–1737 centered around a return to preaching on justification by grace through faith as over against the moralistic preaching that had arisen in the context of emphasizing the corporate covenant of the New England settlers.[29] Much the same can be said of the preaching of Whitefield, especially in his first tour in the colonies, 1739–1741.

For Jonathan Edwards and George Whitefield the source of theology is divine revelation, and the purpose of preaching that revelation is the glorification of God and the salvation of sinners. Edwards's view of Scripture is clearly seen in his opposition to the rationalistic spirit that came with the rising anti-Calvinist trend in the middle of the eighteenth century. Edwards opposed both the theological aberrations of the rationalists and their doubts about the authority of Scripture.[30] For him, theology was to be constructed on Scripture and Scripture alone.[31] Edwards argued for a unity between

---

[26] Iain Murray, *Jonathan Edwards: A New Biography* (Edinburgh: Banner of Truth, 1987), 97-112.
[27] For the preceding statistics, see Cairns, *An Endless Line of Splendor*, 39-41, 52-55.
[28] George M. Marsden, *Jonathan Edwards: A Life* (New Haven, Conn.: Yale University Press, 2003), 436.
[29] Marsden, *Jonathan Edwards*, 150-169; Allen Carden, *Puritan Christianity in America: Religion and Life in Seventeenth-Century Massachusetts* (Grand Rapids, Mich.: Baker, 1990), 33-46, 71-98.
[30] Marsden, *Jonathan Edwards*, 430-436.
[31] Peter Gay, "The Obsolete Puritanism of Jonathan Edwards," in *Jonathan Edwards and the Enlightenment*, ed. John Opie (Lexington, Mass.: D. C. Heath, 1969), 101-106.

Spirit and Word in the construction of theology, but never of Spirit over or against the Word.[32]

Liberalism and the Conservative Response

The new rationalism that followed on the heels of the Reformation and that is best seen in figures such as Faustus Socinus and Michael Servetus settled quickly, as we have seen, into the intellectual centers of England. This deism served as a challenge to the Church of England and called forth, as we have also seen, a response on the part of the evangelicals. But this rationalistic spirit, with its opposition to that which could not be established by reason itself, could only assault the faith with doubts about its truth claims in nontestable areas. That was nothing new. The arrival of liberalism constituted a much greater threat than that. Liberalism actually transformed the nature and the foundations of the faith into something entirely new.[33] Such a transformation could never have come about without a revolution in the arena of epistemology. That assistance was provided by Immanuel Kant.

Kant's goal was to subject all knowledge claims to critique. "Our age is the authentic age of criticism, to which everything must submit."[34] The Prussian philosopher argued that humans can only know that arena of reality that they have been hardwired to know. That arena of reality is the phenomenal world around us. Further, they do not even know those things in themselves, but instead know them only as they are capable of knowing them, according to the human categories of cognition.[35] Two entailments from this reasoning are important to our present concern. First, this means that anything that is outside the phenomenal realm can never be an object of knowledge.[36] No one can *know* God, for instance, nor can anyone *know truth,* if such claims to truth concern that which is beyond the phenomenal realm. If that is so, then the claims of the biblical writers that they have received revealed truths from God can no longer be accepted at face value. "Truth" itself must now be reinterpreted. The second entailment is that since even in the phenomenal realm we cannot know the thing in itself (the *Ding an Sich*), we do not even have certain or true knowledge of the phenomenal world. We

---

[32] Stephen J. Stein, "The Spirit and the Word: Jonathan Edwards and Scriptural Exegesis," in *Jonathan Edwards and the American Experience,* ed. Nathan O. Hatch and Harry S. Stout (Oxford: Oxford University Press, 1988), 127-128.

[33] J. Gresham Machen, *Christianity and Liberalism* (Grand Rapids, Mich.: Eerdmans, 1957).

[34] Immanuel Kant, *Critique of Pure Reason,* trans. Norman Kemp Smith (London: Macmillan, 1933), 9.

[35] Jeffery Hopper, *Understanding Modern Theology I: Cultural Revolutions and New Worlds* (Philadelphia: Fortress, 1987), 46-54.

[36] Claude Welch, *Protestant Thought in the Nineteenth Century: Volume I, 1799–1870* (New Haven, Conn.: Yale University Press, 1972), 45.

only know the world as we are constructed to know it. This is Kant's so-called Copernican Revolution in epistemology. The world "out there" does not correspond to my ability mentally to perceive it; rather I perceive what it is I am capable of perceiving. That is all. The world does not correspond to my cognition, but instead my mind parses the world as it is able to do so.

This Kantian revolution in epistemology set the stage for a plethora of liberal theologies that would come to dominate first Continental, then British and American academic theology well into the twentieth century. Kant's approach allowed theologians to reject claims to divine revelation on the part of biblical authors and yet still maintain that the Bible is a special book for faith. It gave them what they considered to be sound epistemological grounding for rejecting as factual many of the historical accounts presented in Scripture, even those regarding the uniqueness of Jesus while still considering themselves to be Christian believers.[37] It also enabled them to question or even to repudiate doctrines long considered to be at the heart of orthodoxy, such as the Trinity and the deity of Christ, without ceasing to be theologians in the Christian tradition. Socinian rationalism and deism had been little more than harbingers of the flood of reconstruction that now swept through traditional Christian orthodox theology.

British scholars responded primarily to the liberal criticism concerning the New Testament. F. C. Baur had alleged that the New Testament portrayal of an essentially united church in the first century was fraudulent, and that instead there were two major factions, factions that were virtually at war with each other over the true meaning of Christianity. In the face of the threat from Gnosticism at the end of the second century, however, the two factions decided to patch up their differences and join together to battle a new enemy.[38] Several new documents were written that showed the early Christians as unified (e.g., Acts, 2 Peter, the Pastoral Epistles) in order to convince friend and foe alike that "traditional Christians" had more in common with each other than they did with the Gnostics.[39] Baur's thesis thus constituted a revisioning of the history of early Christianity and the rejecting of the authenticity of a number of New Testament documents. Cambridge scholar

---

[37] Wilhelm Herrmann, writing in the early twentieth century from the liberal position on Scripture, argued that religious assurance could not be found in the Bible, but only in experience. Since the Bible had to be subjected to the canons of historical analysis, it could not be trusted as the foundation for faith (Wilhelm Herrmann, *The Communion of the Christian with God,* ed. Robert Voelkel, trans. J. Sandys Stanton [Philadelphia: Fortress, 1971], 74-79).

[38] Horton Harris, *The Tübingen School: A Historical Investigation of the School of F. C. Baur* (Oxford: Oxford University Press, 1975), 181-182.

[39] Peter C. Hodgson, *The Formation of Historical Theology: A Study of Ferdinand Christian Baur,* Makers of the Modern Theological Mind, ed. Jaroslav Pelikan (New York: Harper & Row, 1966), 221-236.

J. B. Lightfoot subjected this allegation to a withering criticism, demonstrating linguistically, and to the satisfaction of virtually the entire academy, that Luke—Acts was a first century document, and so could not be used to support Baur's radical claims.[40] Lightfoot had done a great service in using scholarship to support traditional claims about the Bible's trustworthiness, but he was not an inerrantist, and his defense of Scripture did not extend to some of the allegations against the historicity of the Hebrew Scriptures being made at the same time.[41] That task would fall mainly to American scholars.

Princeton Seminary provided much of the intellectual power in defending a traditional reading of the historicity of Scripture against its critics as well as in calling to task the new theologies associated with Schleiermacher, Hegel, Ritschl, and others who were redefining the Christian faith. What were the Princetonians' ideas about preaching for conversion and about revivals and religious experience in general? In some circles these men are viewed as academic theologians for whom the work of the Spirit is irrelevant or secondary. At times their own language about revivals might be taken as proof that they would not have supported the advocates of the Great Awakening. Samuel Miller, writing in 1833, offered this assessment of revivals: "I will not say that such revivals are never connected with sound conversions; but I will be bold to repeat, that the religion which they are *fitted to cherish,* is altogether a different one from that of the Gospel."[42] One must understand that Miller intended these words not for revivals as a whole, but for Finney's New Measures. The Princetonians were in favor of the work of Whitefield and Edwards in the Great Awakening. They placed a large emphasis on the place of religious experience and the work of the Holy Spirit in the life of believers, and so showed themselves to be the heirs of Reformed piety in general, especially as mediated through the Puritans and the Calvinists of the Awakening.[43] Ashbel Green, a member of the board of directors and a founder of the Seminary, addressed the students in May 1831 and enjoined, "We hope that there is no student in this seminary who is not a cordial friend to such a display of divine grace, as is commonly called a *revival of reli-*

---

[40] Lightfoot accomplished this in part through a critical analysis of the Letters of Ignatius (J. B. Lightfoot, *The Apostolic Fathers,* part 2, vol. 1 [London: Macmillan, 1889]). He also critiqued a book by J. A. Cassels which had created quite a stir in alleging that the Gospels were not trustworthy. Again, by careful scholarship Lightfoot showed that Cassels's arguments were spurious. As a result of Lightfoot's response, publishers were forced to dump large amounts of Cassels's book into the remainder market (Stephen Neill, *Interpretation of the New Testament, 1861–1961* [Oxford: Oxford University Press, 1964], 37).

[41] Mark A. Noll, *Between Faith and Criticism: Evangelicals, Scholarship, and the Bible in America* (San Francisco: Harper & Row, 1986), 71.

[42] Quoted in David B. Calhoun, *Princeton Seminary: Faith and Learning, 1812–1868* (Edinburgh: Banner of Truth, 1994), 228, emphasis his.

[43] Andrew Hoffecker, *Piety and the Princeton Theologians: Archibald Alexander, Charles Hodge, and Benjamin Warfield* (Phillipsburg, N.J.: Presbyterian & Reformed, 1981).

gion."[44] Princeton was founded on the conviction that piety of the heart and solid learning go hand-in-hand, and that students ought to cultivate a missionary spirit as well as a "wholehearted support of revivals."[45] That does not mean that the campus of Princeton exhibited a continuous spirit of revivalistic "enthusiasm," or that there was a common consensus on the theology of religious experience.[46] It does mean that there was a fundamental similarity between Princeton and the Evangelical Awakenings of the previous century both in commitment to defending the faith against biblical criticism and in its emphasis on evangelism and godly living.

The 1920s turned out to be a truly "roaring" decade in the battle between conservatives and liberals in several major American denominations, especially the Northern Baptist Convention and the (northern) Presbyterian Church in the U.S.A.[47] Conservatives launched campaigns to rescue these denominations from the influence of encroaching modernism. Northern Baptists had already been at war over liberalism—in 1913 conservatives in that denomination had founded Northern Baptist Seminary in Chicago to counter the influence of the University of Chicago Divinity School, the Northern Baptist school where liberal Shailer Mathews was an influential professor.[48]

The key years for both denominations were 1922 through 1925. At the 1924 General Assembly of the Presbyterian Church, Clarence Macartney was elected as moderator by a narrow margin over Charles Erdman. Both men were conservatives, but Erdman was more tolerant of diversity. It seemed, then, that the Assembly was siding with the conservatives. Macartney and the conservatives did not, however, challenge the Assembly to deal with several major issues that had been raised by the liberals. "This failure would later come back to haunt the fundamentalist forces."[49] The next year Erdman was elected, in part because many in the church perceived him to be a voice of

---

[44] Calhoun, *Princeton Seminary,* 187.

[45] Ibid., 188.

[46] Mark A. Noll, "The Princeton Theology," in *Reformed Theology in America: A History of Its Modern Development,* ed. David F. Wells (Grand Rapids, Mich.: Baker, 1997), 24.

[47] On the Northern Baptists, see, for instance, William Vance Trollinger, *God's Empire: William Bell Riley and Midwestern Fundamentalism* (Madison: University of Wisconsin Press, 1990). On the Presbyterian crisis, see especially Bradley J. Longfield, *The Presbyterian Controversy: Fundamentalists, Modernists, and Moderates* (Oxford: Oxford University Press, 1991).

[48] In 1924 Mathews wrote the book, *The Faith of Modernism* (New York: Macmillan, 1924). This would become liberalism's most widely read book in that decade (T. P. Weber, "Shailer Mathews," in *Dictionary of Christianity in America,* ed. Daniel G. Reid, Robert D, Linder, Bruce L. Shelley, Harry S. Stout [Downers Grove, Ill.: InterVarsity Press, 1990], 717).

[49] Longfield, *Presbyterian Controversy,* 125. Longfield's statement relates specifically to the failure to address the Auburn Affirmation, a statement of protest from key liberal leaders; but the Assembly also did not call for a vote to censure Harry Emerson Fosdick, though many conservative leaders had called for such a move.

moderation between the warring factions of liberals and conservatives. J. Gresham Machen was seen increasingly as representing a serious problem in the church—a threat to its unity—while Erdman represented the best hope to hold the denomination together.[50] At issue was the ordination of Henry P. Van Dusen by the New York presbytery. Van Dusen did not believe in the virginal conception of Christ. Liberals threatened to secede if the ordination was withdrawn. It was not. It seemed clear that the liberals and moderates in the denomination had won the day.[51]

Shailer Mathews and Harry Emerson Fosdick were at the heart of the Northern Baptist controversy. Mathews argued that at its heart, Christianity was not about doctrine, but life. "It is a moral and spiritual movement, born of the experiences of God known through Jesus Christ as Savior."[52] Mathews argued that because "modernists" placed their emphasis on Jesus Christ as a revelation of a "Savior God," they were, therefore, evangelicals.[53] Yet, he denied the historical nature of the miracles of Elijah and Elisha, the accounts of providence in Joshua, and the monotheistic nature of Moses' religion.[54] Fosdick, like Mathews, questioned the miracle accounts in Scripture and denied that they ought to be taken as literal fact.[55] In addition, he argued that "the incarnation in Christ is the prophecy and hope of God's indwelling in every one of us."[56] Other theologians teaching in the seminaries, such as William Newton Clarke, had also adopted the modernist conclusions.[57] Throughout the twenties there had been concerns about the orthodoxy of some Northern Baptist missionaries. In 1922 William Bell Riley moved that the denomination adopt the New Hampshire Confession of Faith, as heretofore Northern Baptists had no official confession. Cornelius Woelfkin, representing the liberals in the convention, offered a counter-motion, that "the New Testament is an all-sufficient ground for faith and practice."[58] Woelfkin's motion passed.

In both denominations the conservatives failed to win the day. This resulted in several denominational splits, with two new Presbyterian denom-

---

[50] D. G. Hart, *Defending the Faith: J. Gresham Machen and the Crisis of Conservative Protestantism in Modern America* (Baltimore: Johns Hopkins University Press, 1994), 117. See also Ned B. Stonehouse, *J. Gresham Machen: A Biographical Memoir* (Grand Rapids, Mich.: Eerdmans, 1954), 364-381.

[51] Longfield, *Presbyterian Controversy,* 147-153.

[52] Mathews, *Faith of Modernism,* 12.

[53] Ibid., 9.

[54] Ibid., 51.

[55] Harry Emerson Fosdick, *The Modern Use of the Bible* (New York: Harper & Row, 1924), 22-30.

[56] Ibid., 270-272.

[57] L. Russ Bush and Tom J. Nettles, *Baptists and the Bible* (Nashville: Broadman & Holman, 1999), 300-305.

[58] Trollinger, *God's Empire,* 55-56.

inations forming (the Orthodox Presbyterian Church and the Bible
Presbyterian Church), and, over the next two decades, two new Baptist
denominations (General Association of Regular Baptists and Conservative
Baptist Association). Many conservative Presbyterians saw their last hope for
victory sliding away when the General Assembly of the Presbyterian Church
in 1927 addressed the issue of reorganizing Princeton Seminary. Two years
later the Assembly voted to do just that. This reorganization meant that the
traditional Presbyterian theology of Hodge, Machen, and Warfield would
soon become a thing of the past in that institution.[59]

The American South had little sympathy for liberalism in the late-1800s.
Alexander Winchell was expelled from the Southern Methodist church in
1878 for teaching higher-critical views at Vanderbilt.[60] Crawford Toy was
fired by the president of The Southern Baptist Theological Seminary in
Louisville the next year for advocating Darwinism and the Kuenen-
Wellhausen theory of Pentateuchal criticism.[61] Southern scholars had been
raising the battle cry for some time before the beginning of the twentieth century that a religious and culture war was in the offing.[62] When the battles
were raging over modernism in northern denominations in the 1920s, for the
most part southern churches and institutions were not affected.[63] It is important to note, however, that southern rejection of liberalism differed in some
ways from the same rejection found in northern circles. Southerners had a
tendency to be more conservative than those in the north, as a matter of
course.[64] One of the major differences between southern conservatives and
those in the North in the early twentieth century was that the Southerners
were not prone to be premillennial, and the ones who were generally were
not dispensational.[65] The major exceptions would be the more visible and
often the more controversial figures, such as J. Frank Norris of Texas. Within
a generation the South would be rocked by encroaching modernism, and the
southern churches would offer the same set of responses as had been seen in

[59] David B. Calhoun, *Princeton Seminary: The Majestic Testimony, 1869–1929* (Edinburgh: Banner of Truth Trust, 1996), 378-398.
[60] See the discussion of these issues in Donald G. Mathews, *Religion in the Old South* (Chicago: University of Chicago Press, 1977).
[61] William A. Mueller, *A History of Southern Baptist Theological Seminary* (Nashville: Broadman, 1959), 137.
[62] Josiah Strong, *Our Country: Its Possible Future and Its Present Crisis* (New York: Baker & Taylor, 1885).
[63] This is not universally the case. Some Southerners, such as Wake Forest University's president, William Louis Poteat, were agitating for liberal theological and social ideals in the 1920s (Randall L. Hall, *William Louis Poteat: A Leader in the Progressive-Era South* [Lexington: University of Kentucky Press, 2000]).
[64] Ted Ownby, *Subduing Satan: Recreation and Manhood in the Rural South* (Chapel Hill: University of North Carolina Press, 1990), chapter 1.
[65] William R. Glass, *Strangers in Zion: Fundamentalists in the South, 1900–1950* (Macon, Ga.: Mercer University Press, 2001), 45.

the North. Some would capitulate, but others, such as the Southern Baptist Convention (SBC), would slowly gear up for a significant response to the liberal threat. Successively in 1958, 1963, 1971, and 1979 conservatives responded to the moderates by firing professors, offering resolutions, and finally by electing a series of conservative presidents that enabled the SBC to restore evangelical voices to its faculties and agencies.[66] For Southern Baptist conservatives, the issues were theological and pragmatic—inerrancy and evangelism. They had learned from observing the Northern Baptist Convention that moderates and liberals would often use the cry of "evangelism and missions" to distract attention from the theological conflict over modernism.[67] But they had also learned that those things can become a smokescreen, and that eventually, when one capitulates on the authority of Scripture, most of the evangelism and missions is dramatically affected as well.[68]

Fundamentalism was more than just a battle over theological orthodoxy. In its thought patterns it was anti-modernist and willing to fight over the matter. But at its heart it was evangelistic, revivalistic, and committed to a strong notion of Christian sanctification. This commitment to a warm-hearted faith as well as a hard-headed orthodoxy can be seen in such figures as R. A. Torrey and Lewis Sperry Chafer. Torrey was "one of the principal architects of fundamentalist thought."[69] Torrey contributed to many works that were theological in nature, but he is probably best known for volumes he wrote on evangelism and Christian devotion. Torrey was always ready to combat liberalism (and Pentecostalism), but often spoke of the need for a work of the Holy Spirit in the life of believers.[70]

Chafer was a Congregationalist pastor when he met C. I. Scofield in 1901. Scofield encouraged him to become an effective preacher and defender of God's Word.[71] In 1924 Chafer founded Dallas Theological Seminary, with an emphasis on "defending the fundamentals through expository preaching of the Bible."[72] Chafer was convinced that both the Bible colleges and the seminaries of his time were failures. The Bible colleges had the "right spirit, but did not have the rigorous curriculum necessary for training a new gener-

---

[66] For details see Jerry Sutton, *The Baptist Reformation: The Conservative Resurgence in the Southern Baptist Convention* (Nashville: Broadman & Holman, 2000).

[67] Trollinger, *God's Empire*, 133-150.

[68] Paul Pressler, *A Hill on Which to Die* (Nashville: Broadman & Holman, 1999), 149-160.

[69] George M. Marsden, *Fundamentalism and American Culture: The Shaping of Twentieth-Century Evangelicalism, 1870–1925* (Oxford: Oxford University Press, 1980), 47.

[70] Ibid., 48.

[71] John A. Witmer, "'What Hath God Wrought'—Fifty Years of Dallas Theological Seminary; Part I: God's Man and His Dream," *Bibliotheca Sacra* 130 (October 1973): 292-295.

[72] Glass, *Strangers in Zion*, 110-111.

ation of pastors capable of teaching the Bible with authority."[73] Most of the seminaries, on the other hand, produced little more than a "floodtide of educated unbelief."[74] Chafer's goal was to produce evangelistic, church-building expositors who would preach the Bible with authority because they believed it implicitly. Along with this Chafer was firmly committed to helping his students develop their spiritual lives. One of his most endearing books promoted a Keswick approach to spirituality, an approach that has been shared by a number of other dispensationalist fundamentalists, such as Robertson McQuilkin, R. A. Torrey, and C. I. Scofield.[75]

Fundamentalism was and is a complex phenomenon. There is no way to gather all of its elements into a simple and uniform model. But the majority of fundamentalists have been committed to at least the three values of defending orthodoxy, spreading the gospel through passionate preaching, and emphasizing the importance of the godly life.

From Fundamentalism to Evangelicalism

The Scopes trial of 1925 brought a significant amount of public opprobrium to the fundamentalist cause. Some of this criticism was well-deserved, since William Jennings Bryan used the trial as a means for grandstanding for his causes. But the liberal bias of media moguls such as H. L. Mencken painted the fundamentalists in Dayton, Tennessee, as nothing more than ignorant hacks. Such an assessment says perhaps as much about Mencken as it does about the people of Dayton.[76] Regardless, after that event the "strength of the movement in the centers of national life waned precipitously."[77] But that is not to say that the movement itself weakened or fell into disarray. Though *Christian Century* did write fundamentalism's obituary in 1925, the story of the movement's demise was premature.[78] What actually did happen was that the leaders of the movement accepted their rejection, and saw in it a parallel with the way in which Christ accepted his. Fundamentalism turned more inward, more in the direction of separation from all compromisers, and focused on building the infrastructure of the movement itself. In a sense, the years 1925 to 1950 witnessed the largest growth of fundamentalism, especially in regard to its institutions.[79]

---

[73] Ibid., 111.

[74] Letter from Chafer to James Bowron, quoted in Glass, *Strangers in Zion,* 111.

[75] Lewis Sperry Chafer, *He That Is Spiritual* (Grand Rapids, Mich.: Zondervan, 1952).

[76] Marsden, *Fundamentalism and American Culture,* 184-188.

[77] Ibid., 185.

[78] "Vanishing Fundamentalism," *Christian Century* 24 (June 1926): 799.

[79] Joel A. Carpenter, *Revive Us Again: The Reawakening of American Fundamentalism* (Oxford: Oxford University Press, 1997), 13-32.

This period also witnessed the rise of a new direction. There were many who were sympathetic with the theology of the "fundamentals," but who were dissatisfied with much of the spirit of fundamentalism, especially what they perceived to be its isolationism, its exclusive commitment to a dispensational system of theology, and its lack of commitment to social concerns.[80] Carl F. H. Henry, along with Harold John Ockenga, Bernard Ramm, Wilbur Smith, and others, had been seeking to encourage non-separationist conservatives to develop ways to impact their churches and to work together to further conservative scholarship. Henry's book *The Uneasy Conscience of Modern Fundamentalism* called evangelicals to work out a comprehensive worldview that would do more than simply emphasize personal piety and evangelism.[81] The year 1943 witnessed the creation of the National Association of Evangelicals. This gave these "questioning conservatives" a forum for cooperation.[82] *Christianity Today* was founded in 1956 as a journal of conservative theological thought, with Henry as founding editor.

The new evangelicalism was clear in its commitment to the "fundamentals" that had been adopted in 1910 by the Presbyterian General Assembly, though it may not have listed the issues in quite the same order and might not have considered all of them as under the same level of assault as they had been early in the century. Harold John Ockenga affirmed, "Doctrinally, the fundamentalists are right, and I wish always to be classified as one."[83] These heirs of fundamentalism were unambiguous in their affirmation of the full reliability of the Bible and of its role as the sole "norming norm" for Christian theology. This belief in a fully trustworthy Bible "represents a basic unifying factor throughout the whole of contemporary evangelicalism."[84]

EVANGELICAL IDENTITY: ARE POSTCONSERVATIVES FAITHFUL TO THE TRADITION?

Evangelicals have not always walked lock-step. They have disagreed on matters such as free will versus sovereignty in salvation and exclusivism versus inclusivism, and on matters of ecclesiology and eschatology. Some have had a greater social conscience than others. Some have been more passionate

---

[80] Daniel B. Stevick, *Beyond Fundamentalism* (Richmond: John Knox Press, 1964), 28.
[81] Henry, *Uneasy Conscience of Modern Fundamentalism*, chapters 1–2.
[82] Bruce Shelley, "Evangelicalism," in *Dictionary of Christianity in America*, 416.
[83] Harold John Ockenga, "From Fundamentalism, Through New Evangelicalism, to Evangelicalism," in *Evangelical Roots: A Tribute to Wilbur Smith*, 40.
[84] Kenneth Kantzer, "Unity and Diversity in Evangelical Faith," in *The Evangelicals: What They Believe, Who They Are, Where They Are Changing*, 73.

about evangelism and missions, some less passionate, though part of the definition of "evangelical" is a commitment to the "evangel." Until the middle of the twentieth century, though, "evangelicals" have been committed to certain core beliefs, such as the sole sufficiency of Scripture as the source of our theological knowledge, the complete and utter reliability of God's Word, and the nature of theology as a study of what God has said to us. In the current discussion, though, some who call themselves "evangelicals" have questioned those core beliefs. In this section we will examine some of these statements and ask some pertinent questions about the views of these thinkers.

The Sources for Theology

Evangelicals have historically contended that the source for theological construction is the Bible. They have recognized the importance of tradition but do not see it as the source for theological construction. Similarly, contemporary culture is not a source for theology but is the context in which theological constructions are offered. Theology is to be "expositional" in that it "expounds the abiding truth of God's Word in Holy Scripture and then relates it to the contemporary situation."[85] The source, though, is the Word of God.

Some thinkers in the postconservative camp offer a different perspective. Stanley Grenz proposes three norms or sources for theology: "Our task moves from the biblical message, through the theological heritage of the church, to the thought forms and issues of the cultural context in which we live."[86] For Grenz, the community produced the Bible, and now, with the community in a different cultural context, the culture of this time plays a role in the sources of truth. The difficulty, of course, is that culture is constantly shifting and is generally in rebellion against God. Finding those elements within any prevailing culture that might be deemed as authoritative is, therefore, an ambiguous task at best, a fruitless one more likely.

Nancey Murphy offers an even more sophisticated approach to the question of the sources for theology. Since she rejects any form of foundationalism, including what she calls "biblical foundationalism," and opts rather for a Quinean understanding of knowledge as a "web," for her there are a variety of sources that stand alongside the Bible in the task of theological construction. Murphy addresses the question of the nature of the human person and the problem of the "soul," for instance. Murphy rejects the notion of the

---

[85] Donald G. Bloesch, *God the Almighty* (Downers Grove, Ill.: InterVarsity Press, 1995), 28.
[86] Stanley J. Grenz, *Revisioning Evangelical Theology: A Fresh Agenda for the Twentieth Century* (Downers Grove, Ill.: InterVarsity Press, 1993), 18.

soul as a substance separate from the body.[87] She notes, correctly, that in Scripture, "soul" is not spoken of in terms consistent with Platonism. Rather, the biblical terms *nephesh* and *psyche* have a range of meanings that sometimes includes the physical body itself, and at other times includes states of emotional euphoria or distress.[88] She concludes from her brief excursion into the biblical doctrine of the soul that the New Testament does not present a clear picture, and that the reader will "end up frustrated and confused."[89] She concludes, though, that two possible solutions arise out of the biblical data. Christians can be faithful to Scripture while holding either to holistic dualism or to nonreductive physicalism. These are the two centrist positions, with eternal, metaphysical dualism (Plato) at the one extreme and reductive physicalism (committed naturalists) at the other.[90]

Since the biblical material is inconsistent and confusing, how might one make a decision between these two apparently viable options? Murphy appeals to modern examinations in the field of neuroscience and to models of psychology that are compatible with those new studies. While most Christian theologians have held to a form of holistic dualism or substance dualism, Murphy believes this is no longer defensible: "I argue that what neuroscience shows is that such an organism [the human person] is indeed capable of all those higher human capacities that have been attributed to the soul."[91] Further, "Our brain, with its large neo-cortex, is what enables us to recognize God's holiness, to recognize a still small voice as the word of God."[92] The "soul," traditionally understood, is nothing more than the material substance of the human person.[93]

For Murphy, studies in neuroscience, philosophical speculation, new directions in human cultural convictions, and Christian tradition all share an equal role with Scripture in the process of theological formulation. The

---

[87] She is not alone in this. A fairly large group of theistic philosophers now advocate a complementarian approach to the relationship between religion and the sciences. "There is a strong prima facie case for re-examining the claimed cognitive content of Christian theology in the light of the new knowledge derivable from the sciences. . . . If such an exercise is not continually undertaken, theology will operate in a cultural ghetto" (Arthur R. Peacocke, *Theology for a Scientific Age* [Minneapolis: Fortress, 1993], 6, 7). Murphy regularly cites the work of Peacocke as being consistent with her own, and is engaged in a large project on such issues in collaboration with Peacocke.

[88] Nancey Murphy, *Reconciling Theology and Science: A Radical Reformation Perspective* (Kitchener, Ontario: Pandora, 1997), 56-58.

[89] Ibid., 57.

[90] Ibid., 58-59.

[91] Ibid., 59.

[92] Ibid.

[93] Grenz moves in a similar direction in his employment of information from the social sciences as a source for anthropological understanding in the first volume of his new systematic theology (Stanley J. Grenz, *The Social God and the Relational Self: A Trinitarian Theology of the Imago Dei*, The Matrix of Christian Theology [Louisville: Westminster John Knox Press, 2001], 58-97).

Quinean web is very democratic. But of course this is contrary both to the Bible's own approach to knowledge and the approach of generations of evangelical theology. The human sciences may be used to provide a context in which discussions are held, but they ought never to be used to solve an "ambiguity" in Scripture or to provide the answer to a question raised by an interpretation of a biblical text. One thinks here of Origen appealing to the Platonic doctrine of the preexistence of the soul to solve the "problem" of the statement in Scripture, "Jacob I have loved, Esau I have hated."[94] These "solutions" create more problems than they solve.

The Full Reliability of Scripture

In a recent essay, Grenz argues that two approaches to the role of Scripture have prevailed among evangelicals since the Reformation. On the one hand, some in the tradition of Turretin have held that the Bible is "source of correct doctrine."[95] Others, characterized more by Pietism and Puritanism, see the Bible as a "source of spiritual sustenance."[96] By the end of the article, Grenz identifies himself as one who wishes to bridge this gap. It seems to me that this typology is overly simplistic. Most of the people to whom he appeals as being polarized (Wayne Grudem, Charles Hodge, and Francis Schaeffer, for example) would consider themselves as being examples of a balance between these two principles. Grudem's commitment to charismatic renewal and Schaeffer's passion for evangelism would certainly seem to stand as witness of their balanced perspectives. On the other hand, it is interesting that Grenz never identifies the potential for imbalance in the other direction—those who focused on "spiritual sustenance" to the exclusion of correct doctrine. Nor did he note that it was the Pietist tradition that produced a Schleiermacher—as one who sought spiritual sustenance but eschewed correct doctrine.

Of even more concern is the approach taken to biblical authority and reliability by Nancey Murphy. Murphy is opposed to all types of "foundationalism" in theological construction. Her concern is certainly understandable when the culprits are Cartesian or positivist forms of foundationalism. One has to wonder, though, when she turns her criticism against those she calls "biblical foundationalists," such as Donald Bloesch.

---

[94] I am of the opinion that the Bible does offer a consistent and understandable theology of "soul." See Chad Brand and Fred Smith, "Soul," in *Holman Illustrated Dictionary of the Bible*, ed. Chad Brand, Charles Draper, and Archie England (Nashville: Broadman & Holman, 2003), 1522-1523.

[95] Stanley J. Grenz, "Nurturing the Soul, Informing the Mind: The Genesis of the Evangelical Scripture Principle," in *Evangelicals and Scripture: Tradition, Authority, and Hermeneutics*, ed. Vincent E. Bacote et al. (Downers Grove, Ill.: InterVarsity Press, 2004), 23.

[96] Ibid.

Bloesch is a "biblical foundationalist," according to Murphy, and "explicitly"[97] so, since he even employs the designation "foundations" as the title for his new seven-volume project in systematic theology.[98] Further, while Bloesch does not consider biblical words as the ground for erecting a theological edifice, he does distinguish between historical events and their "revelational meaning," so apparently resorting to the fact-value distinction; and, more significantly, he believes the authority of the Bible is unquestionable:

> So we see here a softening of the original foundationalist demand for *universally* accessible truth based on *indubitable* foundations. Yet despite the hesitancy regarding inerrancy (and the absolute certitude such a doctrine provides), it is still the case that the authority of Scripture [for Bloesch] is *unchallengeable*. There is no other norm by which it can be called into question, not religious experience, church teaching, or culture.[99]

Bloesch fails the test of being a postmodern theologian since he maintains a commitment to biblical factuality and inerrancy, even though his is a guarded and highly qualified affirmation of inerrancy.[100] It seems quite clear from these statements that Murphy is unwilling to grant the words of the Bible the status of final and reliable authority in matters of faith and practice, as we have already seen in the discussion of sources for theology. This is even more clearly the case when one considers that Murphy's criticism is leveled against Donald Bloesch, a theologian whom no one would consider to be on the far "right" of the evangelical tradition.

Murphy extends her application of "foundationalist" to the hermeneutics of Alister McGrath. McGrath, in her opinion, is a "narrative foundationalist, rather than a scriptural foundationalist."[101] He "gives biblical revelation an unchallenged role in theology,"[102] by arguing that the Bible is

---

[97] Nancey Murphy, *Anglo-American Postmodernity* (Boulder, Colo.: Westview, 1997), 92.

[98] Nancey Murphy, *Beyond Liberalism and Fundamentalism* (Valley Forge, Pa.: Trinity, 1996), 17.

[99] Murphy, *Anglo-American Postmodernity*, 93, italics in original. Virtually the same statement can be found in Murphy, *Beyond Liberalism and Fundamentalism*, 17-18.

[100] While Scripture is "without error in its matter, i. e., in its basic teaching and witness, . . . this does not imply perfect factual accuracy in all details" (Donald Bloesch, *Evangelical Renaissance* [Grand Rapids, Mich.: Eerdmans, 1973], 56). He further resists defending a "naive biblical literalism" in which the "credibility of the Bible rests upon the edibility of Jonah" (Bloesch, *Future of Evangelical Christianity*, 119). In the volume on Scripture in his new work on systematic theology, Bloesch articulates a position he calls "derivative inerrancy": "I see the truth of the Bible lying in the revealed mystery of God's self-condescension in Jesus Christ, and by the inspiring work of the Spirit this truth is reflected in every part of the Bible" (Bloesch, *Holy Scripture*, Christian Foundations [Downers Grove, Ill.: InterVarsity Press, 1994], 307 n. 21). He rejects as rationalistic the type of inerrancy found in writers such as Henry, Schaeffer, Warfield, and especially Lindsell.

[101] Murphy, *Beyond Liberalism and Fundamentalism*, 19.

[102] Ibid., 18.

"the ultimate source of Christian theology."[103] McGrath goes on to affirm that Scripture serves this role in its historical witness to Israel and Christ.[104] Further, he notes, "The narrative of Jesus Christ, mediated through Scripture and eucharistic celebration, is presented, proclaimed, *and accepted* as the foundational and controlling narrative of the community of faith."[105] Murphy comments on McGrath,

> Doctrine provides a conceptual structure by which scriptural narrative is interpreted. McGrath recognizes that doctrinal formulations can lead us to reread the narrative in a different light, and so there is a sense of two-way interchange between the foundation and the superstructure. Thus we can see that McGrath is chafing against the foundationalist model, even while he uses especially vivid foundationalist imagery in describing the relation between the scriptural narrative and the doctrinal superstructure.[106]

Murphy seems convinced that moving from narrative to conceptual formulation is itself a foundationalist and hence an Enlightenment move.

In Murphy's view, "liberals" and "fundamentalists" must start over if they are to engage in relevant theological discourse. There are at least three components to this new strategy. First, theologians must employ new reading strategies with regard to the biblical text. They ought to take the Bible literally, "so long as they begin with the Sermon on the Mount,"[107] and so long as they utilize a narrative hermeneutic, even in the didactic texts.[108] Second, they must abandon the attempt to justify Scripture as being authoritative "since to do so is what it means to be a Christian theologian."[109] Instead they ought to take note of David Kelsey's claim that the statement "Christian Scripture is authoritative for Christian theology" is analytic.[110] That is, theologians already treat Scripture as the context for their web of reality. There is no need to articulate a theory for just how Scripture functions. That would, in fact, be counterproductive, for the root of the lib-

---

[103] Alister E. McGrath, *Christian Theology: An Introduction* (Oxford: Basil Blackwell, 1994), 119, quoted in Murphy, *Beyond Liberalism and Fundamentalism*, 19. (This is a reference to the first edition of this work by McGrath.)

[104] McGrath, *Christian Theology*, 119.

[105] Alister E. McGrath, *The Genesis of Doctrine: A Study in the Foundations of Doctrinal Criticism* (Oxford: Basil Blackwell, 1990), 55.

[106] Murphy, *Beyond Liberalism and Fundamentalism*, 19. She is especially concerned about this passage in McGrath's *Genesis of Doctrine*: "The transition from a narrative to a conceptual framework of thinking would have potentially destructive effects for Christian theology if the narrative concerning Jesus of Nazareth, having been allowed to generate a specific framework of conceptualities, were forgotten" (McGrath, *Genesis of Doctrine*, 64).

[107] Murphy, *Reconciling Theology and Science*, xi.

[108] Murphy, *Beyond Liberalism and Fundamentalism*, 105; idem, *Anglo-American Postmodernity*, 122.

[109] Murphy, *Beyond Liberalism and Fundamentalism*, 104.

[110] Murphy, *Anglo-American Postmodernity*, 120.

eral/fundamentalist debate lies in the failure of foundationalists to find a "single set of indubitable foundations."[111] Third, theologians must recognize that traditions always begin with some finite starting point. "A tradition is a historically extended, socially embodied argument about how best to interpret and apply the formative texts."[112] This means that all systems are socially constructed, and, while Murphy does not wish to be aligned with the radical postmodernists, she urges at least a mild sort of deconstructionism of the inherited traditions so that theologians can clear the ground and move forward with the new project.[113]

What is the basis for the hermeneutical move that claims that all theological reflection should begin with the Sermon on the Mount? Ritschl, of course, held a similar view. Is this the recrudescence of classical liberalism? In addition, why must one utilize a narrative hermeneutic in interpreting didactic texts? Is Murphy concerned to battle the specter of grounding of the Christian faith in an alien philosophical system, or is she opposed to the obvious teachings found in some of the apostolic writings? One wishes to give the benefit of the doubt, but this reconstruction is so radical that it is difficult to do so.

The Nature of the Theological Task

Evangelicals have generally seen the task of theology first of all as an examination of what God has said to us in Holy Scripture, since Scripture is the norming norm for all theological endeavor. This means that, while theological construction is certainly a human act, it begins with something that does not have a human origin, Scripture, and allows that divine Word to make its impact on the heart and mind as a preliminary act to any kind of theologizing. Grenz, on the other hand, writes that the "central task" of evangelical theology is "the intellectual reflection on the faith we share as the believing community within a specific cultural context."[114] For him, theology is essentially an act of the community in reflecting on itself and its beliefs in the light of Scripture. "Theology systematizes, explores and orders the community symbols and concepts into a unified whole."[115] This is partly because Grenz believes that the *imago dei* lies specifically in the "relationality of persons in

---

[111] Murphy, "Textual Relativism, Philosophy of Language, and the Baptist Vision," in Stanley Hauerwas, Nancey Murphy, and Mark Nation, *Theology Without Foundations: Religious Practice and the Future of Theological Truth* (Nashville: Abingdon, 1994), 268.

[112] Murphy, *Beyond Liberalism and Fundamentalism*, 103.

[113] Murphy, "Textual Relativism," 254.

[114] Grenz, *Revisioning Evangelical Theology*, 18.

[115] Ibid., 78.

community."[116] This relationality is part of the matrix out of which theological construction is done, and stands alongside biblical exegesis as one component of the theological task. "Our cherished theological commitments, in turn, are important insofar as they serve and facilitate this shared life-orientation."[117] Rather than beginning, then, with God and the text of Scripture, the community begins with itself, and one aspect of the task of exegesis is the exegesis of the believing community.

Part of the difficulty here may lie in Grenz's understanding of Scripture: "Scripture is the foundational record of how the ancient faith community responded in the context of a trajectory of historical situations to the awareness that God has acted to constitute this people as a covenant community."[118] This is surely an inadequate understanding of the nature of Scripture. Certainly Scripture contains a record (or "records") of God's dealings with humanity. But Scripture is not ultimately about us, but about God and his redemptive work to rescue human beings from their lost condition. One of the major differences between conservatives and postconservatives lies in this very point of controversy—what exactly is the Bible all about?

Communitarianism is also at the heart of John Franke's essay on *sola Scriptura*.[119] Franke traces the development of the concept of the authority of tradition from the time of Basil through the Reformation, noting Heiko Oberman's helpful distinction between "Tradition I," which notes the development of church tradition but grants it no self-supporting authority, and "Tradition II," which sees tradition as an authority alongside the Bible.[120] Franke argues that the Reformers saw the Bible as authoritative since it was produced by the Spirit of God as he moved upon prophets and apostles. These persons, though, were part of a community formed by the Spirit even before the production of such texts: "The same Spirit whose work accounts for the formation of the Christian community also guides that community in the production and authorization of biblical texts."[121] Therefore, the Bible is "the product of the community of faith that produced it."[122] These documents, then, "represent the self-understanding of the community in which they were developed."[123] This leads Franke to deny to either Scripture or tradition the

---

[116] Grenz, *Social God and the Relational Self,* 305.
[117] Grenz, *Revisioning Evangelical Theology,* 35.
[118] Ibid., 77.
[119] John R. Franke, "Scripture, Tradition, and Authority: Reconstructing the Evangelical Conception of Sola Scriptura," in *Evangelicals and Scripture,* 192-210.
[120] Ibid., 195. See Heiko Oberman, *The Harvest of Medieval Theology: Gabriel Biel and Late Medieval Nominalism,* rev. ed. (Grand Rapids, Mich.: Eerdmans, 1967).
[121] Franke, "Scripture, Tradition, and Authority," 202.
[122] Ibid.
[123] Ibid., 202-203.

ability to enable us to construct theological assertions in any non-inferential or incorrigible fashion, and to assert that "nonfoundational understanding of Scripture and tradition locates ultimate authority only in the action of the triune God."[124] He further notes that the Spirit has guided the church through the centuries in eschewing theological nonsense and in developing a great tradition of orthodoxy, and that this must be seen as a component of the work of the Spirit's guiding the church into truth along with the gift of the text of Scripture itself. Then, after noting that "all theological formulations are culturally embedded,"[125] Franke proposes that the task confronting us today is something like a Shakespearean play in five acts, of which only four have survived, with the task of reconstructing the fifth act lying in the hands of highly trained and sensitive Shakespearean actors.[126]

Franke is correct that tradition is a valuable asset in the hands of the theologian, and that we ought not to see ourselves as insulated from the context of what has gone on before in theological construction. The great councils, the debates over soteriology and ecclesiology in the Reformation, and the recent rash of pneumatological work that has come in the aftermath of Pentecostal/Charismatic renewal all contribute to our understanding of the Christian faith. But the notion that the Bible is essentially the self-understanding of the community of faith is a purely reductionistic notion. Locating authority in the "triune God" over against Scripture simply makes a distinction that the Bible itself does not make. The New Testament writers and teachers, when appealing to the Old Testament text to establish a point, can say either "God says" or "the Scripture says" with no sense of the need to offer Franke's distinction. Further, the notion that Scripture does not allow us to make non-inferential theological statements is simply absurd. "Jesus died for our sins according to the Scriptures" is a non-inferential theological asseveration in anyone's book. While we would agree with Franke that the Spirit has guided the church through dangerous waters, in the sense of Tradition I, that tradition is always subject to and under the authority of the text of the Bible, and not in dialectical relationship with it. Finally, the notion that the Bible is like a play missing the final act, one which we must write, is both a bad analogy and a dangerous one. In all of Franke's essay on how the Spirit is guiding the church into new understandings, he never offers any warnings about the limits of such "guidance." By Franke's standards, one could argue that the Spirit is now guiding the church into an acceptance of

---

[124] Ibid., 205.
[125] Ibid., 206.
[126] Ibid., 209.

homosexuality, an argument that has been made by defenders of the gay lifestyle. Perhaps in a later essay he will set some limitations on what he thinks this "trajectory" might entail.

THE FUTURE OF EVANGELICALISM

In this essay I have attempted to lay out a minimalist perspective on what it means to be an evangelical in the North American tradition. I have focused on three issues: a commitment to biblical reliability that results in a stand for Scripture against the prevailing trends of assault; an emphasis on evangelism and the need for a conversion experience; and the importance of the life of discipleship. Virtually all evangelicals in the great awakenings held these views, as did the champions of orthodoxy in combat with liberalism, the fundamentalists of the early twentieth century, and the neo-evangelicals. I have also pointed out that the entailment of this has been a commitment to the reliability of Scripture, a commitment to the Bible as the source of theological construction, and the nature of the theological task being one of reflecting first on Scripture as the grounds for both theology and life. More could certainly be said, but at the very least this has been the evangelical heritage.

My concern is that the postconservative movement is mobilizing against these convictions. In the interest of defending relational theology, the postconservatives are turning a blind eye to the need to uphold the authority and reliability of Scripture. In the interest of anti-foundationalism they are employing a democratic set of ideologies and methodologies for doing theological construction, methodologies that place Scripture only on the level of equal partner. In the interest of contextualizing Scripture and emphasizing the importance of tradition, they are in danger of seeking the "Spirit's guidance" in an uncontrolled epistemological environment. While the postconservatives have offered some helpful insights, there must be some kind of reining in of the speculation. My concern is that some postconservatives are motivated by a sort of theological seeker-sensitivity that compels them to a sort of theological worldliness that is antithetical to Scripture and the faith once delivered to the saints. I hope I am wrong.

PART FIVE

POST-POSTMODERNISM

12

A REQUIEM FOR POSTMODERNISM— WHITHER NOW?[1]

James Parker III

THE CERTAIN DEMISE OF THE POSTMODERN

Postmodernism is highly overrated.[2] While one theologian after another is rushing to turn out books and articles about some aspect or implication concerning the end of modernism or about the implications of postmodernism, it can be plausibly argued that postmodernism is overrated and that it will come to a certain (and perhaps soon) demise—or at least will be relegated to the realm of the curious but passé.

First of all, modernism (which holds that reason is autonomous and that only scientific truth is normative and universal, and which propounds a progressive optimism and proud confidence in technological fixes), while not the only worldview, is still alive and well at the educational- and cultural-shaping institutions of Western Europe and North America. I spoke recently with two Ph.D. students at two different major Ivy League research universities in North America, and they both said that while one did certainly find postmodern thought on the campuses (particularly in English and related departments), the intellectual culture of the university was still predominantly

---

[1] This chapter is an updated, expanded version of James Parker III, "A Requiem for Postmodernism— Whither Now?" *Southern Baptist Journal of Theology* 5, no. 2 (Summer 2001): 50-61. Used with permission. I want to acknowledge that this revision was aided by the careful insights of Sloan Lee, a friend and recent Ph.D. in philosophy.

[2] Many challenge the legitimacy of the term "postmodern" and assert that in reality it should be called "ultra-modern" since postmodernism is in many ways the logical extension of modernism, or as Anthony Gideens calls it, the "radicalizing of modernity" (*The Consequences of Modernity* [Stanford, Calif.: Stanford University Press, 1990], 52). Paul Vitz calls it "morbid" modernism because "postmodernism . . . is the dissolving of modern certainties using modern logic itself" (Paul Vitz, "The Future of the University: From Post-modern to Transmodern," in *Rethinking the Future of the University*, ed. David Lyle Jeffrey and Dominic Manganiello [Ottawa: University of Ottawa Press, 1998], 106).

modern.[3] They frankly said that they basically ignored postmodernism.[4] One has only to skim the university press catalogues to find out that modernism is alive and well. Ironically Foucault, Derrida, and other French postmodernist thinkers have been passé in France for a good while, substituted by a generation of younger scholars one can only call "neoconservatives" (who will be discussed further below).

Second, the simple reason why postmodernism's days are numbered is that it commits epistemological suicide. Postmodernism makes the assertion that truth is merely a social construct—or as one postmodernist puts it, truth is whatever your colleagues let you say.[5] If that is the case, then postmodern thought is also just another social construct and has neither universal nor normative force. Therefore, there is no reason that one should be compelled to let it be a normative criterion to shape and determine one's beliefs. Moreover, if one takes the postmodernists' idea of the hermeneutics of suspicion seriously, then there is every reason to believe that their whole academic exercise is simply a thinly veiled disguise to get political power over anyone who holds a view different than their own.[6] Since postmodernists have shown their hand, one can easily avoid being taken in by their verbal con game. Most simply stated, postmodernism is guilty of being self-referentially absurd. When postmodernists give up the idea of objective truth, there is no reason whatsoever to take what they say as true—particularly since they have conceded up front that nothing is genuinely true.

There have been several excellent critiques of postmodern thought from evangelical Christians on grounds that are philosophically solid.[7] While this chapter will not add to those critiques, it commends those who have resisted reshaping theology to conform to an outside influence that is ultimately hos-

---

[3] The politicization of the university with homosexual, feminist, and politically correct agendas has undermined the scholarly credibility of many academic disciplines. See Dinesh D'Souza's *Illiberal Education: The Politics of Race and Sex on Campus* (New York: Free Press, 1991).

[4] One was a political philosophy major at Princeton University and the other in the humanities at Yale—one can find few if any postmodernists in the science departments, at least when they are applying the precepts to their own academic discipline.

[5] Richard Rorty, *Contingency, Irony and Solidarity* (Cambridge: Cambridge University Press, 1989), 6-7.

[6] M. Foucault, "Nietzsche, Genealogy, and History," in *Language, Counter-Memory, and Practice: Selected Essays and Interviews,* trans. Donald F. Bouchard and Sherry Simon (Ithaca, N.Y.: Cornell University Press, 1977), 162.

[7] For a sampling, see the following: Millard J. Erickson, *Postmodernizing the Faith: Evangelical Responses to the Challenge of Postmodernism* (Grand Rapids, Mich.: Baker, 1998); idem, *Truth or Consequences: The Promise and Perils of Postmodernism* (Downers Grove, Ill.: InterVarsity Press, 2001); Roger Lundin, *The Culture of Interpretation: The Christian Faith and the Postmodern World* (Grand Rapids, Mich.: Eerdmans, 1993); Douglas Groothuis, *Truth Decay: Defending Christianity Against the Challenges of Postmodernism* (Downers Grove, Ill.: InterVarsity Press, 2000); D. A. Carson, *The Gagging of God: Christianity Confronts Pluralism* (Grand Rapids, Mich.: Zondervan, 1996); Peter Hicks, *Evangelicals and Truth: A Creative Proposal for a Postmodern Age* (Leicester, England: InterVarsity Press, 1998); Dennis McCallum, ed., *The Death of Truth* (Minneapolis: Bethany, 1996); and D. A. Carson, ed., *Telling the Truth: Evangelizing Postmoderns* (Grand Rapids, Mich.: Zondervan, 2000).

tile to the very possibility of doing any genuine theology. The study of historical theology is often a study of how theology has been shaped and conformed to alien ideologies and philosophies that have had the effect of neutering the basic content of historic orthodox Christian theology. Rather than conforming to these external demands, it is sometimes appropriate for Christian thought to challenge and contest philosophical systems that are internally confused or hostile to Christian theism. Process theology is a perfect example of a philosophy to which theology has been conformed. Here is a philosophy that rarely lives in philosophy departments, except as a relic in the history of philosophy division, since its credibility as a philosophical system has been fundamentally rejected.[8] Yet it lives on as a parasite in theology departments. The same may well be the destiny for postmodern thought.

Solid work has demonstrated the deficiency of the thought of those evangelicals who are all too ready to reshape doctrine and their agenda to conform to some of the major tenets of postmodernism.[9] The fundamental error of such scholars is in making the false assumption that the evangelical scholarly approaches they criticize have conceded too much to modernism. The great irony is that Carl F. H. Henry is often singled out as the most egregious example of an evangelical whose system is determined and undermined by modernism. Henry, in his six-volume work, *God, Revelation and Authority,* distinguishes himself as a severe critic of the Enlightenment's view of the sufficiency of autonomous human reason unaided by revelation, has fundamentally decried the naïveté of secular humanism's progressive optimism, and would categorically deny that science is the savior.[10] He also knows that human reason and the laws of logic were not an invention of the Enlightenment. When one reads certain writers on postmodernism (including some evangelicals), one would get the impression (if one did not know better) that reason, along with its dependence on the reality of objective truth and its recognition of the legitimacy of a rational defense of the faith, is the illegitimate offspring of the Enlightenment. Several have even suggested the abandonment of apologetics and the project of natural theology. While most evangelicals enamored with postmodernism say that they do not want to give up Christianity's truth claims (or as the postmodernist would say, "Christianity's metanarrative"), most of them also think that a rational defense of the faith is not a legitimate enterprise that deserves serious atten-

---

[8] For a critique of process thought, see Royce Gordon Gruenler, *The Inexhaustible God: Biblical Faith and the Challenge of Process Theism* (Grand Rapids, Mich.: Baker, 1983).

[9] For critiques of these evangelicals, see especially Erickson's and Groothuis's works cited above.

[10] Carl F. H. Henry, *God, Revelation and Authority,* 6 vols. (1976–1983; reprint, Wheaton, Ill.: Crossway, 1999).

tion and effort. What the church needs, it is said, is not apologetics or the rational defense of the faith, but a loving and caring Christian community (for that is a postmodern priority).[11] No doubt it is of the highest priority for the church to be a caring and loving body—but this is not postmodern (since postmodernism, via Foucault, appears to replace truth with the mere struggle for power); this is simply biblical. Moreover, one cannot avoid the following critical question: How do we adjudicate between conflicting truth claims, religious or otherwise? Moonies or Mormons may have communities as caring as those of Christians. Then what? Like it or not, if one is going to make a truth claim for the Christian faith, reason and the testing of truth claims will play a significant role in the process.

WHITHER SHALL WE GO?

Since both modernism and postmodernism have been dealt with elsewhere in this volume, the question we shall examine is not from whence the culture has come or where it is (premodern, modern, postmodern), but whither shall it go? Paul Vitz has suggested that it is time for conferences to be given titles like "The Death of Postmodernism." He sees indicators on the horizon of a new transition in culture that he calls the "coming transmodern period." By transmodern, he means "something that transforms modernism, something that transcends it and moves beyond it. In doing this, it certainly does not reject all things modern, and thus it is far from a reactionary vision of the future."[12] Transmodernism would indeed constitute a rejection of both the overreaching claims of modernism and the nihilistic absurdity of postmodernism, while benefiting from the positive contributions of both. Is there evi-

---

[11] For example see the following: Robert Webber, *Ancient-Future Faith: Rethinking Evangelicalism for a Postmodern World* (Grand Rapids, Mich.: Baker, 1999); and the essays in chapters 7 and 8 in Timothy R. Phillips and Dennis L. Okholm, eds., *Christian Apologetics in the Postmodern World* (Downers Grove, Ill.: InterVarsity Press: 1995). Ironically, the publishers are probably producing more works on apologetics than ever before, and evangelical schools are teaching more apologetics than before. Also, churches specializing in reaching "postmoderns" often make great use of apologetics. Two examples of popular apologetics picked up by Harper Collins Publishers are Lee Strobel's *The Case for Christ* (Zondervan/Harper Collins, 1998) and Jeffrey L. Sheler's *Is The Bible True? How Modern Debates and Discoveries Affirm the Essence of the Scriptures* (Zondervan/Harper Collins, 1999). Strobel was formerly a teaching pastor at Willow Creek Community Church (Chicago), known for reaching the secular culture. He is now on staff at Saddleback Valley Community Church in Southern California, holding a similar position to the one held at Willow Creek.

[12] Vitz, "Future of the University," 13. In an attempt to provide minimal formulation of Vitz's notion of the transmodern, one might say that the transmodern (a) rejects skepticism and subjectivism by affirming the possibility of attaining genuine knowledge—that is, it affirms that there are non-subjective facts that can be known; (b) takes the deliverances of empirical science seriously—at least when those deliverances are not viewed as the only source of interpersonal knowledge; (c) affirms the centrality of value, along with moral and theological knowledge, in rationally shaping and directing human experience; and (d) recognizes that the mere application of technology will neither rid the human heart of wretchedness or cruelty nor endow life with significance or nobility. Whether or not the transmodern will turn out to be something new—or simply a retooling of the premodern—isn't entirely clear.

dence for "the birth of this new ideal of hope, of wisdom, of virtue and the good, of beauty and harmony, . . . the resurrection of classicism and other pre-modern concepts in the different arts and the intellectual life itself"?[13]

Indicators of the quiet dawning of this new vision are discernible from several segments of our culture, including music, architecture, the visual arts, poetry, literature, and the core of intellectual tradition, including philosophy and moral theory. While it is too soon to identify a movement (even as it is difficult to identify a postmodern movement), there are common characteristics and a shared vision that appears to be emerging at varied, unexpected, and non-coordinated places.

The Transmodern in Music?

In music, an alternative to John Cage's music of irrationality and chance is appearing: a music that is informed from beyond modernistic naturalism or postmodern irrationalism. Consider two composers. American composer Terry Riley was called the greatest composer pianist since Prokofiev in his reviews at the Sergei Kuryokin Festival in St. Petersburg.[14] John Adams's works have been performed by major European orchestras and virtually every major orchestra in the United States.[15] Both are minimalists with an Eastern spiritual bent. In addition to these two, there is a virtual wave of non-pop musicians who are influenced by explicit classical Trinitarian theism. This is a sign of a change in the wind. My purpose here is not to suggest that all of these developments move in the direction of truth, but rather that this is one aspect of the emerging cultural evidence that postmodernism is not the only game in town.

When a classical album rises to number six on the British charts right behind Paul McCartney (Gramophone's "Best-selling CD in 1993"), prompts a review by *Rolling Stone* magazine, and is introduced into mainstream retailers like Sound Warehouse so that the CD is found on the checkout counter in Muleshoe, Texas, even the most casual cultural observer begins to notice that there's a disturbance in the cultural environment. Such was the case at the 1992 release of Catholic and Polish composer Henryk Gorecki's *Third Symphony*. Gorecki has been associated with the avant-garde wing of contemporary classical music. The *Third Symphony* was composed in 1976 with the title *Symphony of Sorrowful Songs*.

Gorecki grew up in the Polish town of Katowice, an unknown town

---

[13] Ibid., 116.

[14] Available online at http://www.terryriley.com/biography.htm.

[15] Available online at http://www.schirmer.com/composers/adams_bio.html.

except for its neighbor—Oswiecim, called "Auschwitz" in German. The texts of the three movements that drive the symphony are (1) a lamentation of fifteenth-century monks; (2) a prayer by a teenager imprisoned by the Gestapo written on a wall where she tries to find the good out of her dire circumstances; and (3) the demanding question of a mother who asks, "Why did you kill my son?" While the work is appropriately viewed as sorrowful, it nevertheless clings to vestiges of hope in the face of despair. Gorecki sees his art as a form of prayer and he has continued to produce significant works "carrying forth the musical, emotional and spiritual concerns with which he has been preoccupied from the beginning."[16]

Many people all over the world were introduced to the works of John Tavener when his composition was featured at the funeral of Diana, Princess of Wales. Tavener joined the Russian Orthodox communion in 1977, and his spiritual concerns have been prominent in his numerous works since then. The desire that shapes his work is to "create an icon in sound."[17] His *Fall and Resurrection*, which premiered in January 2000 in London at St. Paul's, was wildly popular. In the same year he was knighted for his "Services to Music."

Arvo Pärt is an Estonian who has incorporated Russian Orthodox spirituality into his minimalist compositions.[18] It has been said, "by means of almost purely tonal structure, frequently broken triads and scales, Pärt creates an inner balance of form and harmony, which can be understood in terms of his deep religious faith and inclination to mysticism."[19]

Acclaimed as "the foremost composer of the Nineties," Scottish composer James MacMillan's "music is notable for its extraordinary directness, energy and emotional power. Strongly held religious beliefs (which in his own words he calls a 'spiritual anchor') and political beliefs coupled with community concerns inform both the spirit and subject matter of his music."[20] MacMillan's setting of the *Magnificat* has been performed at Wells Cathedral (and BBC's *Radio Three Evensong*), and he collaborated on the extended song-cycle *Parthenogenesis* (or Virgin Birth), featured in the first BBC Philharmonic's mini-series, *MacMillan in Manchester*. The story of the Virgin

[16] James Harley and Maja Trochimczyk, "Henryk Mikolaj Górecki"; available online at http://www.usc.edu/dept/polish%5Fmusic/composer/gorecki.html. For an extensive list of works, discography, and bibliography, see the following: http://www.usc.edu/dept/polish_music/VEPM/gorecki/gortitle.html.

[17] G. Schirmer Promotion Department, "John Tavener"; available online at http://www.schirmer.com/composers/tavener/bio.html.

[18] Paul Hillier, *Arvo Pärt: Oxford Studies of Composers* (Oxford: Oxford University Press, 1997).

[19] Trey Clegg, "Arvo Pärt"; available online at http://www.musiclog.com/part_periods.asp.

[20] Patrick 2000, "The Company of Heaven"; available online at http://www.peelcom.com/partick2000/pages/cohmusic.html.

Birth as a theatrical production in the West End of London sends a significant cultural signal.

Major shifts come rarely in any discipline, whether in science or music.
Yet pop musical prognosticators have said that there is a new rock group on
the horizon that will redefine rock music in much the same way that the
Beatles did. Simon Raymonde was so impressed with the group Lift to
Experience (from Denton, Texas), that he exclaimed that they represented
"the future of music" (presumably rock music).[21] After hearing the group perform at the famed South by Southwest musical showcase in Austin, Texas,
Raymonde and his musical partner Robin Guthrie, from the Cocteau Twins,
signed the unknown Texas band to the Bella Union label of London that very
night. One critic said, "they use dynamics and instrumentation to surround
you and draw you into the mood they create. One of the ways that mood is
created is through emotion-filled lyrics that are full of gospel and cultural references."[22] The members of Lift to Experience learned church hymns and
gospel songs from the cradle in central Texas, and those roots are evident in
their music and ethos. While contemporary Christian music has no doubt
served the Christian subculture, it has always lacked a distinct identity as a
musical discipline and has failed to affect the musical culture at large.
Contemporary Christian bands are often (though not always) poor imitations
of bands found in the mainstream music industry. Lift to Experience appears
to be an exception to this, being a strikingly original musical endeavor shaped
and influenced by Trinitarian theistic belief.

The lyrics are some of the few in popular music that have a mature
understanding of Christianity and a genuine, heartfelt sense of longing for the
divine, quoting scriptural concepts and phrases while leaving out Christianese
clichés. This is pioneering, cutting-edge music that would not appeal to most
CCM devotees. This is what music is supposed to do—touch the heart in the
deepest, softest place and enrich the life of the listener.

The Transmodern in Visual Arts?

In the world of the visual arts, publications like *Image* and the *American Arts
Quarterly* have provided a forum for this new wave. *Image,* in particular,
intentionally explores the relationship between the Judeo-Christian faith and
the various arts. In nominating *Image* for its twelfth-annual Alternative Press
Awards, the *Utne Reader* said, "taking to task the representation of spirituality and religion in the arts, this quarterly journal digs into the depths of a

---

[21] Wade Chamberlain, "Lift to Experience"; available online at http://fakejazz.com/reviews/lift.shtml.
[22] Ibid.

taboo subject: what it means to be a spiritual being in the modern world."[23] One artist featured, for example, is Mary McCleary, whose work represents a "fullness of vision. . . . It is a particular and peculiar kind of fullness, one that is engorged with the fecundity of earth and the senses, and yet simultaneously inhabited by a silent and spiritual presence hovering—both immanent and transcendent—amidst all that is sensuous and of the earth."[24]

Transmodern art is not breaking onto the scene without controversy. An intense debate went on at the Norwegian Academy of the Arts and in the newspapers of Norway in the mid-1990s over the issue of whether the Academy should offer classes in traditional figurative painting—seen by many as a reactionary reversion to classical education and a rejection of modernistic experimentation—and whether Odd Nerdrum, one of Norway's best-known artists, should teach these classes. In the end, he withdrew his candidacy, but classical figurative painting was restored to the curriculum at the Academy.[25]

Bruno Civitico, an Italian contemporary classical painter who now resides in Charleston, South Carolina, specializes in the idealized female form. While he is not seen as a reactionary "resistant anti-modernist," "classicism in the hands of Civitico is a traditional linguistic structure that is used to suggest a very contemporary story."[26] Sculptor Frederick Hart, who has been called America's greatest living representational artist, has challenged the accepted "wisdom" in the contemporary art world. Running against the current, he affirms that the chief criteria of his artwork is beauty and substance. "My work," he says, "isn't art for art's sake, it's about life. I have no patience with obscure or unintelligible art—I want to be understood."[27] J. Carter Brown, Chairman Emeritus of the National Art Gallery, Washington, D.C., was quoted in the *New York Times* as saying, "in the contemporary spectrum Hart represents one end of it in comparison to contemporary sculptors who are working in total abstraction

---

[23] Cited online at http://www.imagejournal.org.

[24] Wayne L. Roosa, "A Fullness of Vision: Mary McCleary's Collages," *Image* 23 (Summer 1999): 32.

[25] For a sample of Nerdrum's works, see http://www.nerdrum.com. For a discussion of the issue from the Academy director's perspective (where he conceded that such classical training was making a comeback in Europe) see http://www.norway.origo.no/culture/embla/art/pettersson.html. For a very interesting and intriguing discussion of attempts to "change the guard" of the New York art establishment (complete with protests) see "Adieu to the Avant-Garde: As the Artistic Regime Shifts, Realism, Rhyme, and Representation Make a Comeback" by Kanchan Limaye in *Reason Online,* at http://www.reason.com/9707/fe.limaye.html.

[26] Mary Gilkerson, "Bruno Civitico's Exploration of the Female Figure"; available online at http://www.free-times.com/reviews/art_reviews/civitico.html. Other artists to be considered in this wave would be James Aponovich's landscapes and still-life works and the works of John Stuart Ingle, Martha Mayer Erlebacher, and Audrey Flack. As evidence of a growing interest in this traditional approach to art pedagogy, the New York Academy of Art: Graduate School of Figurative Art in New York City attracts people from around the world to come and study traditional approaches to painting, figure drawing, anatomy, art history, and sculpture. Ironically one of the founders of the institution in 1982 was Andy Warhol because he felt that his artistic preparation was lacking due to the absence of this kind of curriculum.

[27] Cited at http://www.frederickhart.com/hexton.html.

or dissolving the medium into mutations. In his chosen end of it, he was as good as they get, a superb craftsman, a deeply spiritual person who was concerned with spiritual values."[28] His distinct contribution is summarized as follows: "In a century marked by nihilism, abstraction, and deconstruction, Hart exemplifies a returning tide to aesthetic and moral agendas embodied in the great ages of art in the past."[29] A circle of artists and other people of letters (self-named "Centerists") have gathered around Hart to perpetuate this vision with meetings and continued discussions.

The Transmodern in Architecture, Poetry, and Cinema?

Notice should also be made in the field of architecture. Leon Krier is probably most popularly known as the planner of Poundbury, a planned British town in Dorset (created under the sponsorship of the Prince of Wales). Similar New Urbanism ideas lie behind such communities as Seaside in Florida (the setting for *The Truman Show*). Krier's goal is for architecture to help us understand our place in history and the world. This "humane classicism," or "modernity of traditional architecture," has been opposed by others in the discipline, and he has been predictably called "reactionary." In *Architecture: Choice or Fate,* Krier argues that those architects are responsible for producing their own obsolescence: "As long as artists arbitrarily assume the right to decide what is or is not art it is logical that the public will just as arbitrarily feel that they have the right to reject it."[30]

As Dean of the School of Architecture at Notre Dame University, Thomas Gordon Smith leads a revival of classicism—but with tradition continued in innovative and creative ways.[31] Architects like Smith are not just reactionary. Rather, they affirm that the past must be consulted for models of form and beauty.

The poet Dick Allen says, "we've gone on too long about how poetry should 'show, rather than tell,' when actually many—perhaps even most of our finest poems tell, make a judgment, are even didactic."[32] Allen believes that poetry should play a role in changing people's lives, and hence it has a teaching role. The recovery of narrative and formalism is seen in Allen as well as in poets like Jack Butler, Lewis Steele, Paul Lake, and Fred Feirstein, while the

---

28 Cited at http://www.frederickhart.com. See this site for a fair sampling of his works and bibliography.
29 James F. Cooper, "Frederick Hart: Rebel with a Cause"; available online at http://www.worldandi.com/public/ 1992/ april/ar10.cfm.
30 Cited at http://www.salon.com/books/sneaks/1998/10/29sneaks.html.
31 Thomas Gordon Smith, *Classical Architecture: Rule and Invention* (Layton, Utah: G. M. Smith, 1988) presents the case for the revival of classical forms and precepts.
32 Cited at http://www.csf.edu/countermeasures/colloquium7-4.html.

modern- and postmodern-dominated university has been passed by. In reviewing Feirstein's *Ending the Twentieth Century,* Arthur Mortensen says that "we are reminded of what we nearly lost in the long academic obsession with confessional poetry. We nearly lost what we find in Feirstein's narratives: character; coherent story; historical context; location; and all those details of life external to the author's private thoughts that make poetry worth reading, nearly sacrificed on the altars of Modernism and post-Modernism, whose high priests presumed the telling of stories outside one's self to be not possible."[33]

Ian Hamilton Finlay, known as "Scotland's leading concrete poet," draws on classical traditions while presenting his poetry almost entirely through visual art—"an art which led naturally to the arrangement of words on stone, wood, and other materials . . . (which) led naturally to the art of incorporating concrete poetry with garden design."[34] In Englishman Roger Wagner's art, one finds several strands of artistic tradition merging: biblical themes and the pastoral English landscape, as well as the Renaissance. Wagner's work is fundamentally rooted in the belief that God's love brings hope in the face of evil and despair. Through his landscapes and still-life paintings, American David Ligare affirms that "painting is not only about what is, but what must be done . . . about goodness and morality . . . and a renewed sense of humanist values and social responsibility."[35] Art historian Charles Jencks says that Ligare "adopts unadulterated traditional conventions, but puts them to non-ideological use."[36]

---

[33] Arthur Mortensen, at http://home.earthlink.net/~arthur505/rev996.html. Mortensen continues:
  Jump outside of poetry for a moment and imagine *Paths of Glory,* Stanley Kubrick's picture of the First World War. Take away the portraits of corrupt general officers, of the four young men condemned to die, of the colonel caught in the middle of a conspiracy. Take away the precisely observed life and death of trench warfare. Take away the enlisted men's club where Dietrich sang. Take away the refined insulation of the officers' club. What's left? Of course nothing is left. Yet for a long time after the Second World War, particularly since the late 1960's, critics and poets alike in America have debunked what is interesting in narratives, rationalizing that by saying that the story-teller's choices are only personal or political preferences, thus giving the lie to the narrator's claim to be able to tell a story outside of his or her own prejudices. What bunk! Of course authors pick according to their preferences; so do all human beings. Where there is a conjunction of an author's preferences with those of other people, an author gets an audience, and, if that conjunction lasts or reoccurs later on, the author will come back into fashion. So what? This is news? Frederick Feirstein has wondered about that kind of intellectual sleight-of-hand for decades, written essays about it, demonstrated on behalf of different directions he felt were right, but his most significant action was to be one of the founders of the Expansive poetry movement, which for the last 20 years has been the most exciting source of poetry in America. For, in joining that cause, Feirstein bucked theory and went to work as a poet. The results, both here, and in his other books, are strong stories, vivid characters, and unforgettable locations, all conveyed with a poetic art as good as anyone in his generation.
[34] For a discussion of the history and development of concrete poetry, see http://www.greenfairy.com/dissertation.intro.html.
[35] See http://www.hackettfreedmangallery.com/hfg/html/contemp-html/ligare_html/ligare_main.html for some of his paintings.
[36] Charles Jencks, *Post-Modernism: The New Classicism in Art and Architecture* (New York: Rizzoli International Publications, 1987), 37.

When one looks at popular cinema, one undoubtedly finds the standard fare of narcissistic hedonism and indulgent physical conflict that one has come to expect from this particular venue. However, when one takes a closer look at the nature of film, one recognizes that this medium is also well-suited to express the transmodern. After drawing parallels between the sufferings of Job and the protagonist of Clint Eastwood's film *Unforgiven* (1992), one author says, "Movies such as *Unforgiven* may offer the most compelling places today to raise questions of religion and value."[37] Following the thought of Gerardus van der Leeuw, another writer affirms that, "It is not necessary to equate the essence of [cinematic] art with the essence of religion," but, he continues, "we can observe . . . an essential unity between art and religion, for holiness and beauty appear in the same guise."[38] Without too much effort, one can find outstanding films that could arguably be said to exemplify a transmodern approach. Directors such as Andrei Tarkovsky and M. Night Shyamalan come to mind.

Tarkovsky's vision has been called "devoutly God-centered," and the same author indicates that Tarkovsky himself endorses the view that legitimate knowledge must be based on morality.[39] Such an affirmation coincides with the Platonic (and Augustinian) thesis of a connection between knowledge and virtue. Whether or not Tarkovsky is drawing on the resources of Plato or Augustine, such an endorsement, from the director of *Solaris* (1972), seems to constitute a decisive rejection of the postmodern denial of genuine knowledge and also a rejection of the modernist move to relegate value to the realm of the subjective.

Consider Shyamalan's film *Signs* (2002). Here, without trivializing the horrors that smash down upon one's life and without offering explanation for the brutality of suffering, Shyamalan embeds this horror and suffering within the context of an almost invisible and unfolding providence. No one particular thing can be singled out as *the sign* of providence. Rather, all the lines on the cinematic page simply converge and coalesce. One comes away from the film with an unmistakable sense of order—even though all the particulars seem to manifest the chaos of pain, grief, and waste. In other words, there is no particular thread that can be pointed to as a providential sign—the signs of providence emerge from the story's tapestry as a whole.

---

[37] Sara Anson Vaux, *Finding Meaning at the Movies* (Nashville: Abingdon, 1999), 20.
[38] Robert K. Johnston, *Reel Spirituality: Theology and Film in Dialogue* (Grand Rapids, Mich.: Eerdmans, 2000), 56.
[39] Vaux, *Finding Meaning at the Movies*, 72.

The Transmodern in Ethics and Social-Political Philosophy?

If the gurus of postmodernism such as Foucault and Derrida are passé in their own homeland, what thinkers are beginning to shape philosophical thought in France today? One can find students reading such radical statements as the following from Philipps Beneton:

> Tolerance is an ambiguous word greatly valued by the zeitgeist. Who dares declare himself against tolerance? There would be nothing left to say, however, if the contemporary idea of tolerance was not fundamentally distorted. Properly understood, tolerance implies respect for people but not agreement with their error or fault. Thus ideas do not have to be "tolerant"—it is enough if they are correct. Real tolerance, in other words, is not incompatible with either firm convictions or the desire to persuade others. Tolerance simply rejects force and intimidation toward those who think differently. But today tolerance generally signifies something else—initially it tends to be equated with relativism and then it is identified with new norms of human life and thought. Put differently, tolerance now speaks a double language: The Reduction of Truth to Opinion.[40]

Beneton challenges this reduction. This challenge is reflected in the work of French political philosopher Pierre Manent. He argues that contemporary Western liberal democracies find themselves in a situation where political life does not serve any higher purposes. He traces this idea back to Machiavelli, who desired to separate politics from any idea of a cosmological moral order. Manent says the West has found itself in a situation where it has rejected the laws of God and nature in its quest for autonomy. The acquisition of this autonomy has come at a great loss: the meaning of humanity. Since everyone is autonomous and there are no objective common virtues, a common language for moral discourse has evaporated. The solution to this dilemma is to address the root causes by drawing upon the resources of both the classical and Christian traditions.[41]

We now turn to North American philosophy. Recent decades have shown a massive resurgence in the traditional philosophical disciplines from Christian theists. In recent years, books and articles written for the philosophical community from a Christian theistic perspective have flooded the

---

[40] Cited at http://www.catholic.net/RCC/Periodicals/Crisis/Apr96/beneton.html. See how this plays out in the area of human rights in Philipps Beneton, "The Languages of the Rights of Man," *First Things* 37 (November 1993): 9-12.

[41] Pierre Manent, *An Intellectual History of Liberalism* (Princeton, N.J.: Princeton University Press, 1996); and idem, *The City of Man* (Princeton, N.J.: Princeton University Press, 1998).

press. The journal *Faith and Philosophy*, the journal of the Society of Christian Philosophers, has provided institutional support for influencing the discipline strategically.[42] Noticeable is its influence and direction in moral and political philosophy. Natural law theory has its ablest defender in John Finnis of Notre Dame.[43] Robert George, of Princeton University, also a leading authority on natural law, defends objective truth, traditional marriage, and the sanctity of human life.[44] In a public debate, George won an amazing concession from a leading postmodernist, Stanley Fish, when Fish, who denies the existence of universal truths, admitted that important moral issues can be debated even when people proceed from very different starting points.[45]

Western tradition from Aristotle to Aquinas has affirmed that moral law was innate. While modern philosophy (1) fundamentally rejects the notion of innate moral knowledge since man is reduced to mere ideological reflexes (as in Marxism), or (2) affirms a distinction between *fact* and *value* (as some philosophers of an empiricist bent attempt to maintain), or (3) posits moral statements as social constructs or fictions (as found in the postmodernism of Richard Rorty or Michel Foucault), other thinkers are now pointing forward by looking backwards.[46]

Alasdair MacIntyre leads the renewal of interest in the concept of virtue.[47] MacIntyre argues that the language of moral discourse has been ripped from its historical context. So, while we have words like "good" and "moral," true moral reasoning has been undermined. Leaving Marxism behind, MacIntyre draws upon the resources of both theology and the Aristotelian tradition. Martha Nussbaum, Bernard Williams, and Iris

---

[42] In the United States names such as Alvin Plantinga, George Mavrodes, Nicholas Wolterstorff, William P. Alston, Robert Adams, Robert Audi, Eleonore Stump, Peter van Inwagen and many others too numerous to name have made historic theism a force to be reckoned with in the philosophical world.

[43] John Finnis, *Aquinas: Moral, Political and Legal Theory* (Oxford: Oxford University Press, 1998); and idem, *Moral Absolutes: Tradition, Revision and Truth* (Washington, D.C.: Catholic University of America Press, 1991).

[44] Robert George, *Making Men Moral: Civil Liberties and Public Morality* (Oxford: Oxford University Press, 1995) deals with public policy, while his authority on natural law was established with *In Defense of Natural Law* (Oxford: Oxford University Press, 1999).

[45] Robert George had critiqued Fish's liberal views on abortion and particularly the issue of whether the right to life of a fetus was a purely "religious" issue. Fish held that it was, until he was convinced by George's arguments and proceeded to publicly repudiate his former pro-choice views at the American Political Science Association. See the story online at http://www.boundless.org/1999/departments/isms/a0000029.html.

[46] In *Contingency, Irony, and Solidarity,* Rorty says that there is no normative and universal answer to the question, "why not be cruel?" Of course, if morality is a fiction, then he is right. Ironically Rorty and Foucault make all kinds of moral judgments, but since the basis for those judgments has evaporated, the result is incoherence.

[47] See especially Alasdair MacIntyre, *After Virtue: A Study in Moral Theory* (Notre Dame, Ind.: University of Notre Dame Press, 1984); and idem, *Whose Justice? Which Rationality?* (Notre Dame, Ind.: University of Notre Dame Press, 1989). For a helpful overview, see Edward T. Oakes, "The Achievement of Alasdair MacIntyre," *First Things* 65 (August/September 1996): 22-26.

Murdoch (both in her technical philosophy as well as in her literary output) have led the attack against such contemporary cultural assumptions as Kant's identification of morality with duty and Hume's erroneous distinction between facts and values.[48] In this same tradition Philippa Foot argues that virtue is necessary for happiness.[49] As a theologian, Stanley Hauerwas seeks to build up moral discourse within the Christian community and wants to see virtue as a fundamental component of the Christian life.[50]

In his book *The Moral Sense,* James Q. Wilson argues against Thomas Hobbes (as well as against the majority of contemporary philosophical theories of human behavior), that people have an innate moral sense that is rooted in our biological makeup, while simultaneously being influenced by the environment and the socialization process. He argues that the cultural relativists focus too much on difference and not enough on cross-cultural similarities like fairness, self-control, and duty.[51]

CONCLUSION

A new transmodern vision seems to be emerging from diverse disciplines.[52] This vision is neither uniform nor monolithic—nor is it necessarily theistic. But what it has in common is the rejection of the philosophical naturalists' or materialists' claims of modernism (viz., autonomous reason and unjustified progressive optimism) and the rejection of the fundamental assertions of postmodernism (viz., that truth is a community fiction, morals are social constructs, and tradition and classical influence are undesirable and illegitimate). Transmodernists affirm objective and normative truth without capitulating to a naturalistic scientism, and they affirm true moral values and virtues. They hold out beauty, harmony, and wisdom as real possible

---

[48] For a summary of Murdoch's thought, life, and complete bibliography, see http://kirjasto.sci.fi/imurdoch.htm and http://murdoch.shape9.nl. On the theological importance of Murdoch's writings see Alan Jacobs, "Go(o)d in Iris Murdoch," *First Things* 50 (February 1995): 32-36. For a bibliography of Nussbaum's works, see: http://sun3.lib.uci.edu/indiv/scctr/philosophy/nussbaum.html.

[49] For example, see Philippa Foot, *Virtues and Vices—And Other Essays in Moral Philosophy* (Oxford: Clarendon, 2002).

[50] Stanley Hauerwas, *Christians Among the Virtues* (Notre Dame, Ind.: University of Notre Dame Press, 1997); idem, *Wilderness Wanderings: Probing Twentieth Century Theology and Philosophy* (New York: Westview, 1997); and idem, *Sanctifying Them for the Truth: Holiness Exemplified* (Nashville: Abingdon, 1998) are three of his recent works that build his virtue-based Christian ethic.

[51] James Q. Wilson, *The Moral Sense* (New York: Free Press, 1995). A writer having a significant influence in the area of modern identity-formation is Canadian Charles Taylor in his works *Sources of the Self: The Making of Modern Identity* (Cambridge, Mass.: Harvard University Press, 1989) and *The Ethics of Authenticity* (Cambridge, Mass.: Harvard University Press, 1992). He deals foundationally with the formation of human identity. He affirms the inherent cultural worth in "The Politics of Recognition," in *Multiculturalism,* ed. Amy Gutmann (Princeton, N.J.: Princeton University Press, 1994).

[52] It could be noted that in the culture at large over one million copies of one Spanish Benedictine album have been sold, over two million hardcover copies of William Bennett's *The Book of Virtues,* as well as several million copies of John Paul II's *Threshold of Hope* (1994), where he articulates what could be called a transmodern vision.

entities. Cynicism based on modernistic naturalism and postmodern fictions are replaced by hope—a hope that is based on the very nature of things. While one might hesitate to predict the future of this movement (if indeed it can be called a movement), developments on the horizon appear to indicate that a significant (or even monumental) cultural shift is in the offing. Time will tell.

13

ON FLYING IN THEOLOGICAL FOG

Millard J. Erickson

EVERY PILOT LOVES FLYING IN CAVU conditions—ceiling and visibility unlimited. Ground reference points can be clearly seen and identified. The horizon is easily discerned, enabling the pilot to maintain straight and level flight. Obstacles and other aircraft can be recognized. It is not difficult to keep one's bearings.

Unfortunately, such meteorological conditions do not always prevail. When visibility is less than three miles and the cloud layer is less than 1,000 feet above ground level, it is not legal to operate an aircraft VFR—under visual flight rules, and usually well before such limits are reached, the pilot will become uncomfortable flying VFR. The pilot who is instrument rated and current, however, may file an IFR flight plan, and operate under instrument flight rules, but the mode of operation is quite different than VFR. Now one cannot tell from looking outside the cockpit whether the plane is climbing or diving, or turning right or left. The pilot cannot determine his location by identifying landmarks.

In this situation, one's visceral feelings can be quite misleading. What apparently happened to John F. Kennedy, Jr. on the evening of July 16, 1999, was that, not being instrument rated, he continued into instrument meteorological conditions and became disoriented. He probably literally did not know which way was up, and not having the presence of mind to turn on the autopilot, crashed, taking his life and that of his wife and sister-in-law. Feelings are notoriously unreliable. One need not be a pilot to discover this. Certain travel movies in panoramic theaters create the definite impression that one is moving down a river or through a canyon, but one's seat never moves. Without a fixed reference point, such as looking out a window of the theater, if there is one, one cannot tell that he is not actually moving.

One lesson every flight instructor pounds into the student is, "Trust your instruments; don't trust your feelings." In the early days of aviation, before reliable flight instruments were developed, the average life expectancy of an air mail pilot was rather short. Of the first 40 pilots hired to fly the mail, 31 were killed.[1] Today, however, reliable instruments take the place of visual reference points. A gyroscopically operated artificial horizon tells the pilot whether the plane is turning or climbing or diving. The altimeter, airspeed indicator, and vertical airspeed indicator also tell him whether the plane is maintaining altitude. The turn coordinator tells him whether the plane is turning, and if so, whether the turn is coordinated, or the plane is either slipping (inward) or skidding (outward).

This aeronautical analogy may help us understand the present situation in theology. When I was in graduate school, the cultural and intellectual visibility was high. Theologies were clearly identified and classified. Cultural trends were fairly evident, and in general, fairly uniform within a given culture. Great schools of thought existed, not only in theology but also in other disciplines. It was relatively easy to tell where one was on the ideological map. The categories were quite firm and fixed. My doctoral mentor was a conservative neo-orthodox, and I was an evangelical. Each of us knew what he was and what the other was.

Things have changed, however. One development is the fragmentation of theories, and of the communities of their adherents. There really are no great systems, nor great leaders who symbolize them. Part of this is the aversion of our time to all-inclusive theories, or as postmodernists call them, "metanarratives." In addition, categories and terms have become quite elastic. I term one aspect of this, "category slide." A person who once was considered neo-orthodox may now be termed evangelical and someone who formerly was clearly identified as an evangelical may now be branded a fundamentalist, without the actual views of the persons involved having changed in any significant way. My mentor noted this stretch of terms when he said of what he called the new conservatives, "To both the fundamentalist and the nonconservative, it often seems that the new conservative is trying to say, 'The Bible is inerrant, but of course this does not mean that it is without errors.'"[2] One of my graduate philosophy professors often spoke of the "infinite coefficient of elasticity of words": their ability to be stretched and stretched so that they covered almost anything, but without breaking. I have noticed the length to which "evangelical" has been stretched. I once heard a discussion

---

[1] *Instrument Commercial Manual* (Englewood, Colo.: Jeppesen-Sanderson, 1999), chapter 1, 8.
[2] William Hordern, *New Directions in Theology Today*, vol. I, *Introduction* (Philadelphia: Westminster, 1966), 83.

of evangelicalism at a meeting of the American Theological Society, in which one scholar wanted to be known as a "liberal evangelical," and another, a self-identified process theologian, called himself an "evangelical liberal." These represented the limits of elasticity of the word in my experience, until I saw an article by Martin Miller of the *Los Angeles Times* entitled, "Evangelical Atheists Need to Learn Civility."[3]

All of these factors, and a number of others, are contributing to the present low level of visibility in theological discussions. Are there some steps we may take to enable us to navigate more surely in the present and in the coming period? I believe we are beginning to emerge from some of the obscuration resulting from postmodernism. In the theology that will follow this period, I believe there are several characteristics that will enable us to find the landmarks.

This volume was conceived as a help to us in finding our way out of this low visibility. In the pages that follow, I hope to draw together the insights of the preceding essays and sketch the contours of the type of theology that I believe evangelicalism will need to follow in the years that lie ahead. I want to emphasize the word "sketch," for that is all this proposal should be considered to be, not some final and detailed program.[4] There are, however, several characteristics that seem to be emerging. I have used the term "post-postmodern theology," not because I think it is a good term, but to highlight the fact that postmodernism is also beginning to be transcended. Some of these suggestions involve a return to values and ideas from an earlier period, although they will not simply be a repetition of that earlier form.

GLOBAL

Theology, including evangelical theology, during the past several centuries, has been largely formulated and propounded in Europe and North America. Consequently, it has reflected the culture of those parts of the world. When evangelical scholars discuss evangelical theology, usually they actually mean North American evangelical theology. More recently, the momentum and even the numerical strength of Christianity have been shifting southward and

---

[3] Martin Miller, "Evangelical Atheists Need to Learn Civility," *Star Tribune* (Minneapolis), July 4, 2002, A21.

[4] For a discussion of the different senses of ideological mapping, see my *Truth or Consequences: The Promise and Perils of Postmodernism* (Downers Grove, Ill.: InterVarsity Press, 2001), 13-14. Failure to appreciate these nuances leads Grenz to suggest that I have identified the evangelical left as "a self-conscious definable group" (*Renewing the Center: Evangelical Theology in a Post-Theological Era* [Grand Rapids, Mich.: Baker, 2002], 176). Similarly, the subtlety is not noticed by John Stackhouse, who finds me to divide the spectrum into "two discrete halves" ("The Perils of Right and Left," *Christianity Today* 42 [August 10, 1998]: 59).

eastward, toward Latin America, Africa, and Asia. Thus Philip Jenkins points out that of the 2 billion Christians in the world, while 560 million of these are found in Europe, Latin America is already at 480 million, Africa has 360 million, 313 million Christians are in Asia, while only 260 million are in North America. Extrapolating from these figures, he projects that by 2050, only about one fifth of the Christians in the world will be non-Hispanic whites.[5] Conversions are actually taking place much more rapidly in these Third World countries, so that the percentage of Christians in Europe and North America will probably be much smaller.

What is striking about this figure is the relative neglect of these other segments of Christendom by establishment scholars, including evangelicals. Not only ecclesiastically but theologically, the influence of the Third World believers will increase. It is important in this connection to note the nature of this growing Third World Christianity. In Jenkins's words, "At present, the most immediately apparent difference between the older and newer churches is that Southern Christians are far more conservative in terms of both beliefs and moral teaching. . . . Southern Christians retain a very strong supernatural orientation, and are by and large far more interested in personal salvation than in radical politics."[6] He believes that this very conservatism may account for the neglect of this Third World Christianity by North Americans and Europeans: "Western experts rarely find the ideological tone of the new churches much to their taste."[7]

What the empirical study of Christianity in the world reveals can also be supported anecdotally. As long ago as 1994, when I taught a course on contemporary issues in the doctrine of salvation in São Paulo, Brazil, I felt that I should say something about liberation theology. The students, however, insisted that they had already heard too much about that movement, and that liberation theology was already passé in Brazil. I have since experienced similar reactions in such places as Zimbabwe, India, and even Japan. Many of these Christians not only are not attuned to postmodernism, but in some cases their people have not even entered the modern age. Not only must indigenous theologies be developed that relate to the unique needs and problems of the Third World, but the theology of European and North American Christians needs to interact with these Third World theologies.

Commendably, this was a part of the announced agenda of postconservative evangelicalism. In his defining article, Roger Olson listed as one of the

---

[5] Philip Jenkins, *The Next Christendom: The Coming of Global Christianity* (New York: Oxford University Press, 2002), 2-3.
[6] Ibid., 7.
[7] Ibid.

defining characteristics of the movement a desire to free theology from its domination by white males and Eurocentrism.[8] Unfortunately, however, this concern has not thus far found fruition in postconservatism. With a few exceptions, most notably William Dyrness, himself a white male American, the theology seems to build almost exclusively on traditional theologians. Olson himself, in his major work *The Story of Christian Theology*, gives just four of 613 pages to all forms of liberation theology, examining only James Cone, Gustavo Gutierrez, and Rosemary Ruether.[9] In just one paragraph, he suggests that perhaps the needed reformation of theology may come from the Two-thirds World.[10] His almost total neglect of theologies that are not Euro-American apparently stems from a belief that theology from alternative cultures is future. Consequently, he said in an interview with the publisher, "Twenty years from now when I write the expanded and revised version of the book, it will probably have another chapter entitled something like 'How Non-Western Christian Thinkers Breathed New Life into the Story.'"[11] The volume on twentieth-century theology that he and Stanley Grenz coauthored has a chapter on liberation theologies but otherwise suffers from a similar blind spot.[12] Grenz's major theology textbook, which presumably gives flesh to the outline he sketched in *Revisioning Evangelical Theology*, shows a similarly heavy emphasis on European and North American theologians. An examination of its name index reveals 16 references to Calvin, 18 to Luther, 16 to Barth, 10 to Schleiermacher, 5 to Tillich, 18 to Pannenberg, even 16 to Erickson, but only one to Ruether, one to McFague, one to Cone, one to Soelle. The index has no reference to Guttierez, Boff, Pobee, Koyama, Kitamora, or any other theologian who is not a white European or American male (with the possible exception of Africans like Augustine). In his more recent work, *Renewing the Center*, Grenz does quote Indian theologian Ken Gnanakan a few times, but this is only in connection with the discussion of the religions, not his substantive doctrines.

John Stackhouse has acknowledged this problem. Commenting on the participants in the conference that led to the publication of *Evangelical Futures*, he writes, "It is obvious, however, that these essays are not all that

---

[8] Roger E. Olson, "Postconservative Evangelicals Greet the Postmodern Age," *Christian Century* 112 (May 3, 1995): 480-481.

[9] Roger E. Olson, *The Story of Christian Theology: Twenty Centuries of Tradition and Reform* (Downers Grove, Ill.: InterVarsity Press, 1999), 602-606.

[10] Ibid., 612.

[11] "Heroes, Villains, Tragedy, Redemption: Roger Olson Tells the Story," *Academic Alert* 8.2 (Spring 1999): 5.

[12] Stanley J. Grenz and Roger E. Olson, *Twentieth-Century Theology: God and the World in a Transitional Age* (Downers Grove, Ill.: InterVarsity Press, 1992),

diverse. They reflect the fact that the contributors do not vary much in age (all between forty and fifty-five years old, with Jim Packer the venerable exception) . . . and in race (all white). All of us, furthermore, are male." He then offers an explanation: "For this unhappy narrowness of field we can only plead in defense that the state of evangelical theology is itself dominated by such demographics. In putting together both the conference and resulting volume, we did try to include a greater variety of participants, and failed. We promise, however, that our future conferences and volumes will succeed better in this important respect."[13] The explanation in terms of the demographics of theology reflects this restriction of evangelicalism to Euro-Americanism. No effort was made to invite such Japanese evangelicals as Susumu Uda and Yoshimi Ito, for example. Similarly, Olson's 2003 article shows the same narrow focus, so that when he discusses the northern and southern versions of evangelicalism, it is in terms of the northern and southern United States,[14] rather than the larger categories that Jenkins employs. Somehow the agenda Olson spelled out has not yet been translated into reality.[15]

The future evangelical theology will broaden itself to include the voices of these Two-thirds World and female theologians. This will be done, not condescendingly, but out of a conviction that these theologians have something important to say. Already the center of balance evangelistically has shifted from Europe and North America, and the center is shifting theologically. Increasingly, I try to spend as much time listening as I can, in places like Sofia, St. Petersburg, Rio de Janeiro, Manila, Buenos Aires, Nagoya, Bangalore, Hong Kong, and Harare. On two recent occasions (Havana, 2000; and Rio de Janeiro, 2003), I have listened quietly as Latin American theologians taught European theologians where the center of gravity of that international theological discussion group was.

OBJECTIVE

One important feature of the theology we are proposing will be that it returns to an emphasis on objectivity, but not the type of relatively naïve objectivity that modernism thought it had attained. There are several aspects to this.

Correspondence theory of truth. For much of its history, philosophy and theology held to a correspondence view of truth, that is, the view that truth

---

[13] John Stackhouse, *Evangelical Futures: A Conversation on Theological Method* (Grand Rapids, Mich.: Baker, 2003), 10.
[14] Roger Olson, "Tensions in Evangelical Theology," *Dialog: A Journal of Theology,* 42 (Spring 2003): 77.
[15] An examination of the list of signers of the manifesto, "The Word Made Fresh," reveals a paucity of those who are not male Euro-Americans.

is the agreement of language or ideas to reality. For this, postmodernism has substituted either a coherence or a pragmatic theory. One who has most vigorously contested the correspondence view is Richard Rorty. He has rejected the "mirror" theory of truth—the idea that there are real essences existing independently, to which then our ideas and words must accord. In rejecting the more objective epistemology, however, he claims not to be substituting some more adequate epistemology. Rather, we are simply to try ideas and theories out and see how they work out.[16]

In his earlier writing, Grenz insisted that a correspondence view of truth must be retained:

> Concerning one important aspect of the postmodern agenda, such fears [by Christians] are well founded. Postmodernism has tossed aside objective truth, at least as it has classically been understood. . . . This rejection of the correspondence theory not only leads to a skepticism that undercuts the concept of objective truth in general; it also undermines Christian claims that our doctrinal formulations state objective truth.[17]

More recently, however, this concern does not seem prominent in his thought. Although neither he nor John Franke overtly reject the correspondence view, it is so closely allied with foundationalism that their rejection of the latter seems to entail the negation of the former as well. This is implied by several statements. "Like the move to coherence or pragmatism, adopting the image of 'language games' entailed abandoning the correspondence theory of truth."[18] Of Pannenberg, whose theology they suggest is a helpful model for a nonfoundationlist theological method, they say, "Perhaps no theologian has exemplified more clearly the application to theology of the noncorrespondence epistemological theories of the modern coherentists and pragmatists than Wolfhart Pannenberg."[19] That the correspondence view is part of a package is stated as, "Foundationalism, allied as it was with metaphysical realism and the correspondence view of truth, was undeniably the epistemological king of the Enlightenment era."[20] Despite an apparent hesitancy to renounce the correspondence view, these postconservative evangelicals seem by implication to have moved beyond it.

The theology we envision for the future will cling resolutely to the cor-

---

[16] Richard Rorty, *Contingency, Irony, and Solidarity* (Cambridge: Cambridge University Press, 1989), 9.
[17] Stanley J. Grenz, *A Primer on Postmodernism* (Grand Rapids, Mich.: Eerdmans, 1996), 163.
[18] Stanley J. Grenz and John R. Franke, *Beyond Foundationalism: Shaping Theology in a Postmodern Context* (Louisville: Westminster John Knox, 2001), 42.
[19] Ibid., 43.
[20] Grenz, *Renewing the Center*, 190; cf. 169, 194, 198.

respondence view, together with metaphysical realism. A close reading of Scripture will reveal that it presupposes throughout what might be considered an uncritical correspondence view. The world exists independently of our perception of it, deriving its ultimate reality from God. Although our perception may be far from identical with that reality as it is, the goal is to bring our beliefs into a conformity with that reality. Douglas Groothuis, in his chapter in this volume as well as in other writings, has expounded and argued for such a view.

Neo-foundational. One consistent theme in postconservative theological literature is the rejection of foundationalism. Whether it uses the terminology "nonfoundational" or "postfoundational," the conclusion is the same: foundationalism, of whatever variety, is obsolete and untenable. Grenz and Franke, for example, speak of "the *demise* of foundationalism" (emphasis added).[21]

When we say that our new theology must be neo-foundational, we do not mean that a foundationalism will arise that is invulnerable to the objections the postconservatives and others have raised against it. Actually, such a foundationalism is already alive and well. In fact, it was already extant when most of these criticisms were leveled at foundationalism! A rather large number of foundationalisms have arisen since about 1975 that differ in significant ways from the older, conventional types of foundationalism. In a significant definitive article, Timm Triplett wrote, "It is not clear that the standard arguments against foundationalism will work against these newer, more modest theories. Indeed, these theories were by and large designed with the purpose of overcoming standard objections."[22] Among these newer varieties of foundationalism are those advanced by William Alston and Robert Audi.[23]

What is striking about reading the nonfoundational and postfoundational literature is the virtually total absence of any reference to the works of Alston, Audi, or the article by Triplett. The entire book *Beyond Foundationalism,* by Grenz and Franke, does not contain a single mention of this literature, nor does Grenz's chapter in *Evangelical Futures.* There is an acknowledgment of such a soft or modest foundationalism, but that is in terms of persons like Thomas Reid, based largely on secondary works such

---

[21] Grenz and Franke, *Beyond Foundationalism,* 23.

[22] Timm Triplett, "Recent Work on Foundationalism," *American Philosophical Quarterly* 27 (April 1990): 93.

[23] E. g., Robert Audi, *The Structure of Justification* (Cambridge; New York: Cambridge University Press, 1993); idem, *A Contemporary Introduction to the Theory of Knowledge* (London, New York: Routledge, 1998); William Alston, "Two Types of Foundationalism," *Journal of Philosophy* 73 (1976): 165-185.

as that of Jay Wood, and shows no familiarity with recent primary litera-ture.[24] The same is true of the writings of LeRon Shults.[25] His mentor, Wentzel van Huyssteen, refers only to Nancey Murphy's reference to Alston, and does not mention Audi.[26] Murphy's reference to Alston is only in terms of his chap-ter "Christian Experience and Christian Belief."[27] Referring to Stout, Murphy speaks of "the modern period's foundationalism—that is, the concern with the reconstruction of knowledge on self-evident foundations (whether intu-itionist or empirical)."[28] Her *Anglo-American Postmodernism* displays a sim-ilar silence. One of the distinguishing features of postmodernism that Murphy and her husband, the late James McClendon, cited in their definitional arti-cle was that it was outside a line that represented a continuum between foun-dational certainty and skepticism.[29] The work of Audi or the article by Triplett are not mentioned by any of these authors. The most one can find is an occasional reference to the modest type of foundationalism found in Reformed epistemologists like Plantinga and Wolterstorff. It is apparent that the postconservative non-/post-foundationalism is seriously out of touch with recent developments in foundationalism. No rebuttal of nonfoundationalism or postfoundationalism need be written. As we pointed out earlier, it has already been written.

Future evangelical theology will be based on a foundationalism of this latter type, a foundationalism that regards some conceptions and proposi-tions as basic, from which other propositions derive their validity, but with-out claiming indubitability as did classical foundationalism. A number of these are viable candidates for our time, including the version set forth by J. P. Moreland and Garrett DeWeese in their chapter in this volume.

While postconservatives have offered either a coherentist or a pragma-tist view of truth, it should be noted that foundationalism does not necessarily exclude these as secondary criteria of truth. In fact, certain varieties of foun-dationalism and coherentism have a considerable amount of commonality.[30]

---

[24] Grenz and Franke, *Beyond Foundationalism*, 32.

[25] E. g., F. LeRon Shults, *The Postfoundationalist Task of Theology: Wolfhart Pannenberg and the New Theological Rationality* (Grand Rapids, Mich.: Eerdmans, 1999); idem, *Reforming Theological Anthropology: After the Philosophical Turn to Relationality* (Grand Rapids, Mich.: Eerdmans, 2003).

[26] J. Wentzel van Huyssteen, *Essays in Postfoundationalist Theology* (Grand Rapids, Mich.: Eerdmans, 1997), 50, 85; cf. idem, *Theology and the Justification of Faith: Constructing Theories in Systematic Theology* (Grand Rapids, Mich.: Eerdmans, 1989).

[27] Nancey C. Murphy, *Theology in the Age of Scientific Reasoning* (Ithaca, N.Y.: Cornell University Press), 159-163.

[28] Ibid., 3.

[29] Nancey Murphy and James William McClendon, Jr., "Distinguishing Modern and Postmodern Theologies," *Modern Theology* 5 (April 1989): 193.

[30] Audi, *Structure of Justification*, 138.

The postconservatives, however, in their coherence construction, clearly do not avail themselves of the values of foundationalism.

Post-newhistoricist. One feature of postmodernism that has received relatively little treatment is what is known as the New Historicism. This is related to the events of history in a fashion roughly parallel to the relationship of reader-response criticism to the text of the Bible or other literary works. It is especially distinguished by what William Dean has referred to as "creative imagination." In an aptly named book he writes:

> Furthermore, while the old historicism emphasizes that imagination replicates in history certain universal realities, the new historicism argues that imagination constructs history—sometimes rather freely, and always with the contribution of the interpreter and its community. In short, with the old historicism, the imagination is mimetic; its purpose is to reproduce in history something extrahistorical. With the new historicism, the imagination is interpretive; its purpose is to communicate with past historical particulars—not merely to reproduce but to interact, to initiate, to create, as one does in a conversation.[31]

The new historicism to which Dean refers is also a new historiography or way of writing history, involving the "creative imagination." For our purposes, the historiography is more interesting than the actual history written.

Those familiar with Richard Rorty's neopragmatism will notice the parallel between what Dean here calls the mimetic role of the imagination and what Rorty refers to in philosophy as the mirror theory of reality. Rorty rejects the approach of Philosophy, which attempts to determine what is really True and Good, rather advocating that we disregard such questions and try an idea to see how it works out. Accordingly, instead of refuting a competing idea, he recommends that "anything could be made to look good or bad, important or unimportant, useful or useless, by being re-described."[32] Jacques Derrida prefers the ambiguity and supplementarity of writing over speech: "the meaning of meaning (in the general sense of meaning and not in the sense of signalization) is infinite implication, the indefinite referral of signifier to signified."[33] This creative activity is also found in Foucault's concept of fictioning history, where the aim is not necessarily exact reproduction of the past, but rather, "the possibility exists for fiction to function in truth, for a fictional

---

[31] William Dean, *History Making History: The New Historicism in American Religious Thought* (Albany, N.Y.: State University of New York Press, 1988), 3-4.
[32] Rorty, *Contingency, Irony, and Solidarity,* 7.
[33] Ibid., 25.

discourse to induce effects of truth, and for bringing it about that a true discourse engenders, or 'fabricates' something that does not yet exist, that is, 'fictions' it."[34] Stanley Fish insists that there is no intrinsic meaning in words themselves, but that the meaning is supplied by the interpretive community.[35] He also emphasizes the advantage gained by stipulating the meaning of terms: "Getting hold of the concept of merit and stamping it with your own brand is a good strategy."[36]

This is the approach that writes history backward. The history is written, not by attempting to determine and record what actually happened, but by ascribing to the past, events and actions that justify one's present position. In his essay in this volume, D. A. Carson suggests that the historical judgments in Grenz's *Renewing the Center* are "tendentious." Elsewhere I have suggested that some of what Grenz sketches in that volume is not only historically inaccurate at a number of points, but also highly imaginative in its interpretations.[37] For example, he greatly exaggerates my stature within evangelical theology, and imagines a shift of my loyalties from Bernard Ramm to Carl Henry. Apart from the fact that I have never accepted uncritically any theologian's view, he really offers no evidence for this contention, and totally omits any mention of Edward J. Carnell, the new evangelical who in many ways had the greatest influence on me. He also speaks of a rift in the personal relationship between Clark Pinnock and me, which neither of us recognizes. Grenz's sometime colleague, Roger Olson, also makes the interesting observation that "Henry and Carnell were both presidents of Fuller Seminary,"[38] a piece of information that must have surprised Henry.

The old historicism attempted to practice rationality: carefully attempting to determine the historical facts and then drawing conclusions from it. The new historicism, on the other hand, practices rationalization: asserting a conclusion, and then justifying it by creating historical data to fit it, or simply letting them stand on the basis of unsubstantiated assertions.

Recent events in the field of journalism suggest that our society still strongly disapproves of the type of writing that creates accounts and presents

---

[34] Michel Foucault, "The History of Sexuality," in *Power/Knowledge*, ed. Colin Gordon (New York: Pantheon, 1980), 193.

[35] Stanley Fish, *Is There a Text in this Class? The Authority of Interpretive Communities* (Cambridge, Mass.: Harvard University Press, 1980).

[36] Stanley Fish, *There's No Such Thing as Free Speech, and It's a Good Thing, Too* (New York: Oxford University Press, 1994), 6.

[37] Millard J. Erickson, "Evangelical Postmodernism and the New Historiography," in *The Cosmic Battle for Planet Earth: Essays in Honor of Norman R. Gulley*, ed. Ronald A. G. du Preez (Berrien Springs, Mich.: Old Testament Department of Seventh-day Adventist Theological Seminary, 2003).

[38] Olson, "Tensions in Evangelical Theology," 78.

them as if they were accounts of what actually occurred. The Jayson Blair affair at the *New York Times* produced quite a shock to the journalistic world. He was forced to resign after it became clear that he had fabricated at least parts of several stories he wrote. For example, Tandy Sloan, a minister whose son died in Iraq, said that he had not met or spoken to Blair, although Blair quoted him and described him at a church service. Sloan said, "The article he wrote was totally erroneous. He hadn't talked to me. He fabricated the whole story, is basically what he did."[39] Several other persons gave similar reports. Blair had to resign, and two high-ranking editors at the *Times* subsequently resigned.[40] More recently, Jack Kelley of *USA Today* was found to have fabricated stories he had written.[41] The reaction to these cases of postmodern journalism indicates that our society is still strongly committed to a correspondence theory of truth.

The theology we are developing and advocating here will take historical research very seriously. Rather than starting with a preconception of what is right and then selecting, manipulating, or even creating data to support that historically, we will want to be as objective and careful as possible. There is a practice that in some disciplines is referred to as "data mining"—careful screening of data so that what supports one's thesis is retained and contradictory data is discarded, the way slag is discarded by those who mine for precious metals.

It will be important, not only in historical but in other areas of scholarship to be impartial. By this I do not mean being neutral. Because these two terms are sometimes confused, let me draw a distinction. Impartiality means being open-minded, not prejudging issues, treating all viewpoints fairly and examining all of the evidence. Neutrality means not taking a stand, not declaring a conclusion. Judges, referees, and umpires are expected to be impartial; that is, they treat both sides or both teams equally and fairly. They are not to be neutral, however. They must rule on motions made by the two parties in a legal case, and must call fouls on a team or player who violates the rules. Evenhandedness in the administration of the law or rules constitutes to impartiality whereas neutrality would mean not applying those regulations at all.

One major thrust of postmodernism in its deconstructive form has been the insistence that scholarship is not impartial. Foucault went to great lengths to argue that rather than the traditional formula that knowledge is power, the

[39] Howard Kurtz, "More Reporting by Times Writer Called Suspect," *Washington Post* (May 8, 2001), C01.
[40] Michael Powell, "Two Top N.Y. Times Editors Quit," *Washington Post* (June 6, 2003), A01.
[41] Blake Morrison, "Ex-USA Today Reporter Faked Major Stories," *USA Today* (March 19-21, 2004), 1A.

reverse is true: power is knowledge.[42] Those who have the power determine what is the truth and control what is learned. This is not a bad thing, in the judgment of postmodernists, and they have themselves seized the initiative in the matter. So, for example, as we noted earlier, Stanley Fish proposed that it was a good thing to seize an idea and stamp it with one's own brand.

What the objectivity we propose will require is looking at all the evidence, not simply what supports one position. In practice, never does all of the evidence fall on just one side of an issue. It will be necessary to acknowledge this diversity, and not try to explain away the minority evidence, but come down on the side of the greater preponderance of evidence, all the while continuing to hold it in tension with the opposing evidence.

One of postmodernism's helpful contributions has been its emphasis that none of us is truly and fully objective. We are all affected by our situation in life, by the social and cultural conditioning that has helped make us the type of persons we now are. This insight is not unique to postmodernism, since careful scholars had noticed this previously, but the postmodernists have emphasized it most forcefully. We cannot simply proceed naïvely, assuming that our understanding and our interpretation of matters is just how things are. Unfortunately, some scholars have been unable to distinguish between how it appears to them, and how things really are.

To say that all ideologies are to some extent conditioned and thus not merely completely objective is to tell only half of the story, however. The question then is what we are to do about this. Shall we simply acknowledge the partial nature of all views? In practice, most persons who do this emphasize the effect of conditioning upon the views of others, but are more reluctant to discuss what effect this might have on their own views. The type of theology we are proposing here will not simply accept its own conditionedness. It will endeavor to find ways to limit and reduce that subjectivity. There are several means of doing this. One is to interact with those of a differing persuasion. Cross-cultural dialogue, as I suggested earlier, is an especially important vehicle for such reduction. Beyond that, it will be necessary to make certain compensations for the fact that evidence for views that one favors will naturally tend to appear more persuasive to oneself.[43]

Part of this objectivity means that our theology will choose its language very carefully. One of the aims of postmodernism is to win persons to adopt one's view, and this may be done by rhetorical rather than logical means, or as Stanley Fish says, by the use of "persuasion" rather than "demonstra-

---

[42] Michel Foucault, *Discipline and Punish: The Birth of the Prison* (New York: Vantage, 1979), 133.
[43] I have developed this methodology at greater length in *Truth or Consequences,* 241-242.

tion."[44] Richard Rorty's terminology is "solidarity," the obtaining of a wider agreement, rather than "objectivity," the establishing of relationship between a belief and something outside the community.[45] We have noted how each attempts to accomplish this end by trying to seize the terminological high ground—giving terms one's own brand. Another is by the way in which an idea is described. Rorty says, "anything could be made to look good or bad, important or unimportant, useful or useless, by being re-described."[46]

Does postconservative theology ever follow the postmodern rhetoric in this matter? Note the way Grenz describes James Davison Hunter's writing: "Perhaps a more dramatic casting of this quasi-Manichean outlook in conflictual, even apocalyptic terms"; "As unfortunate, potentially devastating, and perilously self-fulfilling as this kind of language can be, and as 'un-Christian' as the combative spirit and uncharitable name-calling that often emerges from its use can become, for the purposes of this volume another, more directly theological danger is even more pressing."[47] By contrast, he speaks of Gerald T. Sheppard's conclusion as "poignant."[48] This type of descriptive language is illustrative, but not unique. Terminology like "fear," "consternation," "strong consternation," "peril," etc., is not helpful.[49] Olson also utilizes emotive language: "A chill has fallen over evangelical theological creativity"; "The specter of inquisition hangs over contemporary theological productivity"; "In 1998 I participated reluctantly in a heresy trial of a colleague."[50]

What is happening here is that evaluation is being slipped into what ostensibly is description or analysis. The terminology is not merely neutrally descriptive, it clearly is rhetorical, intended to create a bias in favor of one view and against another. This is acceptable and even commendable procedure among postmodernists. In the new period into which we are moving, this type of language will need to be replaced by more neutrally descriptive language.

Several essays in this volume have observed that the assertions of the postconservatives are rather poorly supported by argument. Under founda-

---

[44] Stanley Fish, *Is There a Text in This Class?* 365.
[45] Richard Rorty, "Solidarity or Objectivity?" in *Objectivity, Relativism, and Truth* (Cambridge: Cambridge University Press, 1991), 22-23.
[46] Rorty, *Contingency, Irony, and Solidarity*, 7; cf. 44.
[47] Grenz, *Renewing the Center*, 329, 330.
[48] Ibid., 330.
[49] Ibid., 130, 132, 137. Some of this language may be unintentional, reflecting Grenz's apparent penchant for clichés. For example, in *Renewing the Center*, he uses the language and imagery of being "catapulted into the limelight" regarding four different theologians, and in six separate cases speaks of someone's "mantel descending upon" another.
[50] Olson, "Tensions in Evangelical Theology," 83.

tionalism, there was a definite method for ordering arguments in relation to conclusions. Unanimously, the postconservatives have rejected that form of justification. Unfortunately, however, they do not seem to have sufficiently substantiated their own conclusions by an alternative method. Although not really classified as a postconservative, Wentzel van Huyssteen is clearly a post-foundationalist and has influenced some of the postconservatives, especially Shults. He most clearly illustrates this shortcoming. He frequently makes statements such as "I am fully convinced that,"[51] "it now becomes clear that,"[52] "indisputable interrelatedness,"[53] and "in conclusion,"[54] when insufficient support has been offered for the conclusion advanced. It may be that this problem is a result of rejection of any sort of foundationalism.

Unfortunately, this practice is also present in a considerable amount of the postconservative writings, as documented elsewhere. Simply asserting that something is so, or dismissing an alternative view by labeling it as modern, rationalistic, or scholastic, is not making a sufficient case for one's view, in any period of time. For a postmodernist, this may be considered sufficient. In the coming period, it will not be.

PRACTICAL AND ACCESSIBLE

One special feature of the new conservative theology we are describing is that it will not be simply an ivory-tower theology, worked out by academic theologians, in abstraction from lay Christians and the practice of ministry.

One of the interesting things about the theologies of the twentieth century is that some of the most influential of them were the outgrowth of actual ministry situations, rather than merely the product of abstract theologizing. Karl Barth's theology, for example, came out of the frustration of attempting to preach to the people in his small mountain parish the type of liberal message he had learned in his theological studies. This type of message did not satisfy or help his hearers. Almost in desperation, he tried something rather radical for that time—he attempted to preach the Bible to them—and found that his people responded. His message was speaking to them where they were. Similarly, Paul Tillich's ground-of-being theology emerged from his ministry as a military chaplain on the Eastern front during the First World War, where, in the midst of death all around him, he "peered into the abyss of non-being." Reinhold Niebuhr's doctrine of humanity was formed during

---

[51] Van Huyssteen, *Theology and the Justification of Faith*, 155. The point we are making here is especially striking in view of the book title.

[52] Ibid., 163.

[53] Ibid., 125.

[54] Ibid., 161.

a thirteen-year pastorate among auto workers in Detroit. While Jürgen Moltmann's theology of hope did not stem directly from ministry as such, it did come to fruition out of his experience of imprisonment. Langdon Gilkey's prison experience, described by him in *Shantung Compound,* constituted what was actually a rediscovery, empirically, of the doctrine of original sin.[55] Gustavo Gutierrez's liberation theology grew out of his ministry to poor parishioners. When one reads these theologies, whether one agrees with them or not, one finds a ring of realism that is clear and virtually unmistakable, and which marks them off from some other more abstract theologies.

Years ago, Helmut Thielicke wrote a small volume, *A Little Exercise for Young Theologians.* It was a series of brief instructions to his theological students, which were very practical pieces of advice, designed to help bridge the gap between the theological classroom and hallways and the life of the ordinary Christian. One particularly striking chapter deals with the "instinct of the children of God," their ability to sense what is true and good in theology, whether they have extensive theological sophistication or not.[56] There has sometimes been a sort of imperialism about professionally produced theology. This perhaps came most strongly to the fore in the modern period, when theology was thought of as a type of science, which only the initiated could understand fully, and certainly only such persons could construct theology. Particularly under the influence of critical studies, the Bible became practically inaccessible to the laity. If not versed in the intricacies of critical methodology, one could not discover the true message of the Scripture. The clergy, and especially theology professors, became a type of new priesthood, whose work was simply to be accepted by the laity.

Unfortunately, this aspect of modernism continued on into the postmodern period. While there is a popular postmodern culture, the theoretical postmodern philosophy that has been written is directed to a highly sophisticated audience, sometimes referred to as the "cultural elite." This has also been true of a considerable amount of postmodern theology. So, for example, Peter Hodgson wrote, in a review of Mark C. Taylor's *Erring:*

> Taylor's god, it appears to me, is for those who don't need a real God—a God who saves from sin and death and the oppressive powers—because they already have all that life can offer; this is a god for those who have the leisure and economic resources to engage in an endless play of words, to

---

[55] Langdon Gilkey, *Shantung Compound: The Story of Men and Women Under Pressure* (New York: Harper & Row, 1966).
[56] Helmut Thielicke, *A Little Exercise for Young Theologians* (Grand Rapids, Mich.: Eerdmans, 1962), 25-26. In addition to his faculty position at the University of Hamburg, Thielicke preached regularly at St. Michael's Church, Hamburg.

spend themselves unreservedly in the carnival of life, to engage in solipsistic play primarily to avoid boredom and attain a certain aesthetic and erotic pleasure. Taylor's god is a god for the children of privilege, not the children of poverty; a god for the oppressors, not the oppressed (although of course he wants to do away with all the structures of domination); a god for the pleasant lawns of ivied colleges, not for the weeds and mud of the basic ecclesial communities; a god for the upwardly mobile, not for the underside of history.[57]

The theology of the postconservatives cannot be simply described in this fashion. And yet there are some elements of similarity in this rather academic, middle-class, Western theology. Properly, theology is not something simply for discussion. It must be related to life, for the gospel is very much concerned with humans and their predicament. Just as Jesus did not come as a member of the religious elite or an official rabbi but as an ordinary person, and a poor person at that, so theology for our time will need to be similarly incarnated. Of course, it will be written primarily by trained theologians, who have the specialized knowledge and methodology to work with the types of materials that go into theology. Just as psychiatry is done and psychiatric theory developed by those trained in psychiatry, rather than by the patients, so technical theology cannot ordinarily be done well by those lacking special educational training and experience. Yet, just as psychiatric theory can only be validated by success in its application to those in need of such treatment, so part of the validation of theology depends upon its utility in the lives, not just of theologians, but of ordinary Christians.

For many years theological schools have required practical ministry experience of students for the ministerial degree (the M.Div. or its equivalent). Successful accomplishment of this requirement was regarded as just as important as knowledge of formal theological disciplines. It seems to me that a similar type of ministry competency should be expected of those who attempt to prepare these future ministers for their calling. Beyond that, some sort of ongoing practical contact with the life and ministry of the church should be expected, just as other professions require continuing education. For those who would teach need to be models of the application of what they are teaching to those to whom their students will minister.

This means that the theology being developed in the coming era will need to be subjected to the experience of Christians who are not themselves professional theologians. If it is truly to be a theology for the whole church, it

---

[57] Peter C. Hodgson, review of *Erring* by Mark C. Taylor, *Religious Studies Review* 12, no. 3-4 (July/October 1986): 257-258.

might be helpful to remember that professional theologians constitute a small fraction of one percent of all Christians, in the American church scene. If theology is to be more than just a theology for professional theologians, it will need to be formulated with laypersons in mind. In many cases, theology professors live rather sheltered lives. Like Hodgson's comment, the theology of post-postmodernism will be a holoecclesiastical theology, not simply a theology for the elite.

In part this involves the language of theology being translated into common language accessible to all persons, not merely members of the guild. Every discipline has its jargon, and that language is essential for the accurate analysis and formation of the issues and answers. When that theory needs to be understood by those to whom it is applied by practitioners, however, it is essential that the terminology be clarified and contextualized. One of the most valuable contributions of analytic philosophy has stemmed from the fact that it is language analysis. Instructors repeatedly pressed the question, "What do you really mean?" If one cannot take the high-sounding terminology and reexpress the concepts into categories for which the ordinary person has some analogical experiences, there is reason to question whether there is real meaning behind the jargon. Like the emperor's new clothes, someone needs to ask whether there really are clothes or not.

POSTCOMMUNAL

One of the strongly emphasized words in postmodernism and in postmodern theology is "community." There is a reason for its prominent place. When postmodernism rejected the idea that truth and meaning simply exist independently of the knower, and substituted the idea that all knowers are conditioned by their background, culture, setting, and many other factors, it faced a potentially very serious problem. In theory, every person's truth might be different from that of every other person, resulting in subjectivism. The check upon such subjectivism was to be found in the community, which establishes the norms of truth within its own bounds.

Postconservative evangelical theology has similarly laid heavy emphasis on the role of community. Indeed, Grenz makes this the very locus of theology. Rather than the traditional definition of theology as the systematic compilation of the doctrinal teachings of Scripture, he defines it as "the believing community's reflection on its faith."[58] Thus, the guarantee of belief's objectivity is the normative role of communal belief.

---

[58] Grenz, *Revisioning Evangelical Theology*, 81, 85, 87, 88-89.

There is a genuine benefit to community, of which the theology we are proposing will take advantage. Paul's writings make clear that the church is a body, and that, on the one hand, no one has every spiritual gift necessary for the Christian life, and no one gift is possessed by every Christian (1 Cor. 12:4-31). Thus, each member of the body needs every other member, and none is to be more highly regarded than any other. The value of the group in correcting the eccentricities of individuals is also illustrated in Scripture, for example, Paul correcting Peter (Gal. 2:11-14).

Yet having said this, it has become apparent that communities carry certain liabilities. One of the places where this can be seen is in the subdiscipline of economics called behavioral economics. This gives us insight into the effect of group psychology upon individuals. History is strewn with examples of manias or bubbles of various types. Whether the tulip bulb craze in seventeenth-century Holland, the South Sea craze, the Mississippi scheme, or the investments in canals, plank roads, or the stock market bubbles of the 1920s and the 90s, the lessons are instructive. As group enthusiasm increases, individuals get swept up into it, and their usual cautions melt away. Because prices are rising and increasing numbers of persons are purchasing the particular investment, the bandwagon effect is marked. Investment prices become disconnected from the customary measures of investment value. The community provides the validation of the individual's action. Unfortunately, however, reality eventually sets in, and the result is a disastrous "crash."[59]

The same principle could be illustrated in politics. Especially under the influence of a charismatic leader, individuals' usual reserve and judgment become nullified. Persons do things as part of the group that they would not do as individuals. A very dramatic example is Germany during the 1930s. The Nazi leadership made a strong effort to emphasize the group, the nation, and the importance of commitment to it. Individuals confessed that they did things that they never thought they would do. As a documentary on the History Channel put it, "the group was everything; the individual was nothing."

This principle also applies to theology. A certain amount of enthusiasm is generated by what appears to be a new and creative view. Here it should be noted that evangelical theologians function under a certain liability. If one propounds that Jesus was only a man until the Council of Nicea elevated him to deity in 325, that he was married to Mary Magdalene, with whom he fathered children, that will certainly arouse interest, for it is novel. The evangelical who limits himself to the teachings of the canonical books will be

---

[59] A large number of works document this history of economics. For a brief and accessible version, see John Kenneth Galbraith, *A Short History of Financial Euphoria* (New York: Penguin, 1993).

much more restricted in what he can advance. In an age that tends to be bored with the old and familiar, there is a natural attraction to the novel. Witness the popularity of the book, *The Da Vinci Code*. The problem lies in the tendency to get caught up in the swell of enthusiasm and support.

The importance of being contrarian is most evident at this point. Contrarianism is not a matter of being negative, cynical, or disagreeable. It is rather a matter of being skeptical, of thinking critically. It is the practice of asking of any proposed idea, no matter how popular and how many adherents it has, "But is it true?" In the case of theologies, it is especially an endeavor to make certain that one's theology is not simply being fitted to the culture of the day. Here postconservative theology has been rightly concerned about those cases where evangelical theology too closely aligned itself with the modernist philosophy prevalent at the time. The theology we are advocating will be similarly concerned about its relationship to postmodernism. Unless we are prepared to contend that postmodernism is the final and conclusive view, we will want to maintain a certain arms-length distance from it.

Just as financial bubbles end badly, so do theologies based on popular enthusiasm or affinity for popular culture. Classical liberalism, for example, when the culture turned against it, was largely unable to adapt, and faded in its popularity and influence. The danger with postconservative evangelicalism is that it will be unable to adapt to the changing situation as postmodernism begins to decline. There are increasing indications that the high point of postmodernism has indeed been passed.[60] Of course, the danger for this new theology is that it will also wed itself to the spirit of the age, and consequently be compromised.

The aim is to be thoroughly familiar with the culture into which one wishes to speak the Christian message, and to contextualize the message in such a way as to be better understood. Earlier theologians and apologists spoke of finding a "point of contact" for the message. An analogy would be the task of a missionary. The missionary, to be effective, must learn the language and culture of those to whom she would minister. She must understand the concepts with which they function, to try to find a basis for bridging the gap between their thinking and the Christian gospel. Every mission executive, however, knows the danger of the missionary "going native"—not merely understanding and relating to the natives, but actually becoming one of them, perhaps being converted, rather than attempting to convert. The same could be said for the evangelical theologian and apologist. The goal is to understand

---

[60] At the time of this writing, the popularity of *The Purpose-Driven Life* and the movie *The Passion of the Christ* are recent indications of the increasing trend away from postmodernism.

the culture, in this case, postmodernism, so that one may somehow communicate to its members, but without becoming a postmodernist in the process. Of course, just as the missionary must be certain that it is a genuine Christian worldview to which she is attempting to convert people, and not simply Western culture, so must the theologian be careful that it is essentially biblical Christianity, not simply modernism, postmodernism, or some other particularized thinking, that is the backbone of the theology.

Speaking the language of the time suggests that different models of communication may be helpful. If the model of modernity was the article and the lecture, which Alasdair MacIntyre suggests was a spoken article,[61] then something different may be appropriate in the postmodern period and the time that follows. It is surprising to me to see how much postconservative theology follows the traditional form of propositions and outline, rather than by a narrative or other postmodern technique.[62] I term this "paradoxical postmodernism." I recall a postmodern evangelical flatly dismissing the idea of the use of sound bites in contemporary sermons.[63]

METANARRATIVAL

One of the most characteristic themes of postmodernism has been its aversion to metanarratives, or inclusive theories. For a number of reasons, these are regarded as either impossible, undesirable, or both. At best, we can hope to construct petit narratives, local theories or stories.

Postconservative evangelicalism has sought to resist this dimension of postmodernism. Early in his writing, Grenz said of the postmodern hostility to metanarratives, "To put this in another way, we might say that because of our faith in Christ, we cannot totally affirm the central tenet of postmodernism as defined by Lyotard—the rejection of the metanarrative. . . . Contrary to the implications of Lyotard's thesis, we firmly believe that the local narratives of the many human communities do fit together into a single grand narrative, the story of humankind. There *is* a single metanarrative encompassing all peoples and all times."[64]

This concern is commendable, and we support it. The story of Scripture can hardly be read at anything resembling face value without catching its uni-

---

[61] Alasdair MacIntyre, *Three Rival Versions of Moral Inquiry: Encyclopedia, Genealogy, and Tradition* (Notre Dame, Ind.: University of Notre Dame Press, 1990), 32-33.

[62] An exception is Brian McLaren's *A New Kind of Christian: A Tale of Two Friends on a Spiritual Journey* (San Francisco: Jossey-Bass, 2001).

[63] As examples of attempts to do theology in a postmodern idiom, see the final chapters in my *Postmodernizing the Faith* (Grand Rapids, Mich.: Baker, 1998) and *The Postmodern World* (Wheaton, Ill.: Crossway, 2002).

[64] Grenz, *Primer on Postmodernism*, 164.

versal tone. Jehovah is depicted in the opening chapters of Genesis as the creator of all that is. The human race has descended from one pair, Adam and Eve. No other gods are tolerated, for the simple reason that Jehovah is the only genuine deity. Jesus alone is the savior of all people. All will appear before God in the final judgment.

In our empirically pluralistic world, however, this position of the exclusiveness and universality of the biblical message is becoming more difficult to maintain. Many religions exist, and each has adherents who are devout, sincere, and ethical. To suggest that one of these should be given a privileged position is to incur the labels of "intolerance" and "arrogance" by postmodernists. Yet to accept a type of pluralism, in which each religion is true for those who follow it, is to deny the very nature of Christianity, as it has traditionally been understood. It is apparent that such a claim of universality cannot simply be asserted dogmatically for the Christian story. It will need to be substantiated.

What is the effect of postconservative theology on such a claim? In *Renewing the Center*, Grenz considers the question of the relationship of evangelical theology to the religions. He cannot attempt to resolve the question by appeal to the obsolete approach of foundationalism, with its reliance upon certain indubitable starting points. Instead, he turns to the concept of community, for which he believes there is a universal quest. In effect, Christianity is to be considered the preferred religion because it does a better job than does any other religion of producing this community. He says:

> Evangelicals firmly believe that the Christian vision sets forth more completely the nature of community that all human religious traditions seek to foster. Christians humbly conclude that no other religious vision encapsulates the final purpose of God as they have come to understand it. Other religious visions cannot provide community in its ultimate sense, because they do not embody the highest understanding of who God actually is.[65]

Note the nature of the argument here. It is basically pragmatic, which is what one would expect from a postmodern approach. As such, however, it still leaves unanswered the question, "But is it true?" Beyond that, however, the assertion seems to be, "Evangelicals believe that Christianity best embodies the idea of God as Christians believe him to be." The transition from

---

[65] Grenz, *Renewing the Center*, 281-282.

"what Christians believe about God" to "who God actually is" is made without argument. This seems at best to be a circular argument. As I have shared this rationale with Christians in pluralistic cultures, they are not at all impressed with the value of such an assertion in their context.

It may be that this is an inherent weakness in postconservative theology. My doctoral mentor used to say that neo-orthodoxy had never produced an outstanding evangelist. Billy Graham could say, "The Bible says," but that form of unqualified authoritative statement did not consort with neo-orthodoxy's view of Scripture. Quite possibly, a similar problem attaches to postconservative theology.

In politics it is customary to utilize rhetoric, simply repeating an assertion, without support, until it comes to be believed. The presentation of the gospel deserves a more rational argument. Although Grenz actually espouses a form of foundationalism, based on the community, this hardly seems to justify an exclusiveness or a metanarrative for Christianity. A case along the lines of that advocated in this volume by Groothuis or by Moreland and DeWeese is called for.

DIALOGICAL

The evangelical theology we are contemplating here must be dialogical. By that I mean that it interacts with differing theologies, considering thoughtfully their claims, and advancing its own with cogent argumentation.

This does not mean that theology must be polemical, in the worst sense of that word. It is not improper to differentiate one's view from others, or to offer reasoned critiques of those others. One sometimes gets the impression from postconservative evangelicals that differentiation is wrong. Grenz's strong statement about Hunter's espousal of the "two-party system" is an example of this. Similarly, John Stackhouse takes both Roger Olson and Millard Erickson to task for perpetuating this two-party system.[66] What is ironic, however, is that the postconservatives, by their suggestion that the older evangelical approach must be transcended, and by their rather stern rejection of such, are the ones who have set the terms of the debate. Paradoxically, it seems legitimate and even desirable for a postconservative to distinguish himself from a conservative, but not vice versa. Apparently, conservative evangelicals are not to draw a distinction between themselves and postconservatives, but a reciprocal action is legitimate. This, again, is

---

[66] Stackhouse, "Perils of Right and Left," 59.

standard postmodern procedure. Yet on virtually any kind of usable logic, if A is not-B, then B is also not-A.[67]

It does appear that a two-party schematism is inadequate, although not for the reason that Stackhouse thinks. It might be helpful to classify theologies along two continua: the degree of traditionalism (conservatism) and of innovation (liberalism) of the doctrinal position, and the degree of traditionalism and innovation of the form in which those doctrines are expressed. Although all labels are somewhat arbitrary, I'll illustrate with a matrix with two continua and four quadrants, as shown in fig. 13.1.[68]

On such a model, it is possible to maintain the traditional doctrinal positions and express them in the traditional form. Those who minister in this way would be conservative in both respects. They would not necessarily attempt to contextualize the message to make it understandable in different cultures and different times. These are what I have described as "non-dialogical," or "transplanters," or what David Clark has recently termed, "transporters,"[69] those who simply take a message from one "culture" and "transport" it to another without providing for adaptation. They conform to the originating culture. Examples of this can be found in surprising places. One noted American pastor and specialist in church growth is known for giving the message an accent familiar to the culture in which it is being ministered. He was invited to Germany to lecture on church growth and used his familiar example of the baseball diamond, in which one must first get to first base, then to second, then to third base, and finally, home. My friend who lived in Germany at the time remarked to me, however, "Germans don't play baseball!" It was the equivalent of an Englishman speaking to an American audience and using an illustration drawn from the sport of cricket.

The "transformers" are those who do not merely modify the form of expression but also the content of the doctrine, generally because they do not believe there is a permanent doctrinal content. Those who revise the doctrinal content but express it in traditional fashion would be "deformers."

On this model, the theology we hope to develop will be situated somewhere in the upper right quadrant, holding firmly to the doctrines clearly taught in Scripture, but finding creative and effective ways of expressing

---

[67] Postmodernists and postconservatives may assert that this assumes modernistic rules. That is not the point, however. Rather, what we are insisting is that whatever rules are followed should apply to all parties, all players of the game.

[68] Individual persons or ministries will not fit neatly into just one quadrant, but will only tend toward one corner of the chart, to a greater or lesser degree. Every distribution of a population of instances over a continuum has a median and varying deviations of those instances from the mean and median.

[69] David K. Clark, *To Know and Love God: Method for Theology,* Foundations of Evangelical Theology, ed. John S. Feinberg (Wheaton, Ill.: Crossway, 2003), 53.

them. In our judgment, postconservative theology is somewhat to the left of center, with different contributors to this volume differing in their judgment of just how far. What is of some concern to me, however, as indicated in the discussion of globalism and language, is that postconservatism appears quite traditional in its formulation and communication.

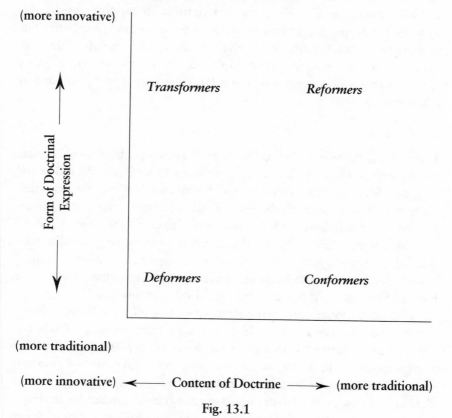

(more innovative)

Transformers　　　　**Reformers**

Form of Doctrinal Expression

Deformers　　　　**Conformers**

(more traditional)

(more innovative) ◄——— **Content of Doctrine** ———► (more traditional)

Fig. 13.1

It is extremely important that the discussion be carried on in the proper spirit, however. Much has been written about irenicism in theology. At times, however, this seems to be the designation of a particular position, rather than of the fashion in which that theology is enunciated. On this basis, Grenz classifies Ramm, Pinnock, and Sanders as more irenic, and Henry, Erickson, and Grudem as less so. Note, however, the kind of language that Pinnock and Sanders have used in the openness debate, as contrasted with some of their debate partners.[70] Recall the language Grenz used in describing the work of

---

[70] These can be found at www.etsjets.org. Click "2003 Membership Challenge on Open Theism," then "Dr. Pinnock's Response," and "Dr. Sanders's Response" (to "Dr. Nicole's Extended Charges").

Hunter. Note, also, the language used by one of these self-styled irenic evangelicals: "triumphal entry of fundamentalist leader Jerry Falwell into the SBC," "fundamentalist take over of the SBC," "demagoguery," "hyper-conservative, control-oriented take over," "take over of the denomination," "SBC fundamentalist take over," "tactics of demagoguery," "spirit of fear and strife that comes disguised as passion for truth." Some postconservatives consider it improper to refer to someone as being on the evangelical left, while they freely use such terms as "fundamentalists" and "neo-fundamentalists."[71] Civility and irenicism are not identified with a particular position; they involve acting with respect and using language that is not pejorative or inflammatory.

FUTURISTIC

Theology for the next period of history must not simply be content to relate to the then-current scene. It must be attempting to anticipate the future and preparing for it, so that its answers will not be merely to the questions that are then past. In economics, there are leading indicators, concurrent indicators, and lagging indicators. Wise persons seek to discern the leading indicators and govern their action by those, rather than by lagging indicators. Similarly, in religion and theology there are anticipations of what is coming, and we should try to discern those. I have suggested a number of these that I see, and the list could be expanded considerably at this time.[72]

One of the criticisms of postconservative evangelicalism in this volume is that it is too focused on the present, or in some cases, on the past, which it thinks to be the present. It also sometimes looks at the present and describes it as the future.[73] The future cannot be known with great exactness or extensiveness, but more can be seen by looking at the horizon than at our immediate circumstances. As one driving instructor regularly asked his students, "Can you see the next traffic light? How far away is it? What color is it? What are you going to do about it?"

Futurism is not an exact science, and probably does not deserve to be termed a science at all. There are, however, several principles that help us discern possible future directions: early "straws in the wind," increasing in number; a trend that has built to such an extreme that a reaction is likely; trends in other disciplines and areas of culture.[74] For too long theology in general

---

[71] Olson, "Tensions in Evangelical Theology," 78.

[72] Erickson, *Truth or Consequences,* chapter 16; *Postmodern World,* chapter 5.

[73] Thus the paradoxically named *Evangelical Futures,* some chapters of which are seriously dated.

[74] I have dealt with some of these criteria at greater length in *Where Is Theology Going?* (Grand Rapids, Mich.: Baker, 1994), 18-28.

and evangelical theology in particular has been slow to recognize changes and adjust to them. Our aim is not to tie ourselves too closely to any given cultural situation, but to be prepared to contextualize the message in such a way as to make it more easily understood by our contemporaries. The exact course of evangelical doctrinal formulation is unknown, but we have suggested in this chapter some instruments that will help us plot the course.

Scripture Index

PERSON INDEX

SUBJECT INDEX

Accommodation, 26, 33, 158-159, 183, 217, 218, 232, 240, 241

Anti-foundationalism (see "Postfoundationalism")

Apologetics, 21, 22, 28, 34, 45n, 61, 68, 71, 77, 164, 176, 188, 200, 200n, 203-204, 211, 211n, 215, 217, 218, 218n, 230, 231, 237, 244n, 245n, 247, 248n, 249n, 255n, 260, 284, 309, 310n, 342

Arminianism, 228n, 230n, 255, 262, 264, 268n, 272, 284, 286

Assumption (see "Presupposition")

Augustinianism, 229, 230, 235-237, 238, 317

Authority of Scripture (see also "Methodology," "Sola Scriptura," and "Theology, extrabiblical sources for"), 25, 27, 28, 30, 34, 44, 48, 50, 61, 63, 69, 105, 106, 107, 109, 110, 120, 123, 138, 139, 152, 152n, 157, 158, 162, 167, 168, 171, 171n, 174n, 177, 177n, 183n, 185, 185n, 186, 189, 193, 194, 223, 224, 224n, 226, 229, 241, 247n, 253, 254, 260, 263n, 264, 265, 268, 268n, 269, 269n, 270n, 271, 271n, 272, 274, 275, 276, 277n, 278, 283, 285, 286, 287, 288, 289, 293, 295, 296, 298, 299, 299n, 300, 302, 303, 304, 345

Bebbingtonian quadrilateral, 19, 200

Buddhism, 72, 128, 258n

Calvinism, 43, 228n, 236, 253n, 259, 262, 264, 265, 265n, 266, 266n, 270n, 272, 284, 286, 289

Coherence theory of truth (see also "Kantian Thought" and "Pragmatism"), 26, 27, 35, 36, 53, 73, 74, 79, 81, 86, 145, 148, 150, 168, 169, 174, 187, 201, 201n, 202, 260, 300, 329, 331, 332

Community, 19, 21, 23, 24, 25, 26, 30, 35, 36, 37, 39, 40, 41, 48, 50, 51, 52, 53, 54, 81, 94, 101, 115, 116, 118, 119, 119n, 120, 122, 123, 124, 125, 126, 128, 129, 130, 131, 132, 140, 143, 144, 147, 148, 148n, 149, 150, 151, 153, 154, 157, 163, 173, 175, 176, 178, 180, 181, 181n, 182, 188, 189, 191, 192, 193, 201, 202, 202n, 203, 204, 204n, 206, 208, 209, 209n, 210, 212, 212n, 213, 216, 217, 218, 219, 225, 226, 240n, 241, 243, 243n, 244, 244n, 245, 245n, 246, 246n, 247, 247n, 248, 248n, 249, 296, 301, 302, 310, 324, 332, 333, 336, 340, 341, 344, 345

Constructivism, 19, 38, 45, 71, 79, 126, 152n, 154, 166, 167, 175, 206, 210, 211

Correspondence theory of truth (see also "Metanarrative"), 19n, 20, 27, 30, 60, 61, 66, 67, 68, 69, 70, 73n, 74, 75, 76, 77, 79, 83, 84, 85, 85n, 88, 112, 115, 117, 122, 125,